UNDER THE BLACK FLAG

Blackbeard the Pirate

UNDER THE BLACK FLAG

Exploits of the Most Notorious Pirates

DON C. SEITZ

DOVER PUBLICATIONS, INC.
Mineola, New York

Bibliographical Note

This Dover edition, first published in 2002, is an unabridged republica-
tion of the work originally published in 1925 by The Dial Press, New
York.

Library of Congress Cataloging-in-Publication Data

Seitz, Don Carlos, 1862–1935.
   Under the black flag : exploits of the most notorious pirates / Don C.
Seitz.—Dover ed.
      p. cm.
   Originally published: New York : L. MacVeagh, The Dial Press, 1925.
   ISBN 0-486-42131-7 (pbk.)
      1. Pirates. I. Title.

G535 .S4 2002
364.16'4—dc21

                                                          2001052698

Manufactured in the United States of America
Dover Publications, Inc., 31 East 2nd Street, Mineola, N.Y. 11501

FOREWORD

That a Respectable Person should take an interest in the Doings of Robbers and Villains may seem Reprehensible to those who mistake Prudishness for Morals. To such I make no excuse, but proceed regardless of their Opinions to the narration of this History, heedless of consequences, but well knowing that many Gentlemen accounted Worthy profited by these Transactions.

D. C. S.

CONTENTS

CONTENTS

UNDER THE BLACK FLAG

INTRODUCTION

OF PIRACY IN GENERAL

"Who are ye, and whence do ye come?"
"Gentlemen of fortune, from the Sea."

Pirates' Hail.

PIRACY is the second oldest profession in the world. It began when men learned to truss two logs together and other men swam out to waylay them, as they sought to use the waters to lighten the burden of a load. It grew when the logs were hollowed into canoes, it expanded with the builded boat and the billowing sail, and lived until Steam, the Monster, hunted it into the last corner of the China and Malay Seas. We have the authority of Macaulay's *Lays of Ancient Rome* that the Iberian shore was haunted by freebooters, as when the valiant Horatius at the far end of the bridge over the Tiber struck down Lausulus, with the exclamation:

> "Lie there," he cried, "fell pirate!
> No more aghast and pale,
> From Ostia's walls the crowd shall mark
> The track of thy destroying bark;
> No more Campania's hinds shall fly
> To woods and caverns when they spy
> Thy thrice-accursed sail."

The first record of piratical organization occurs in Thucydides, who notes that with the development of commerce the Greeks were compelled to defend themselves against pirates, "commanded by powerful chiefs, who took this means of increasing their wealth and providing for their poorer followers." These would "fall upon the unwalled and straggling towns, or rather villages, which they plundered, and maintained themselves by the plunder of them; for, as yet, such an occupation was held to be honorable and not disgraceful." Because of this peril, towns, both on the mainland and the islands, were built distant from the sea as a measure of protection. The islanders, says the historian, "were even more addicted to piracy than the inhabitants of the mainland," they being mostly Carian or Phœnician adventurers. It

[3]

was left for Minos, King of Crete, to suppress these sea robbers. He created a navy, colonized the island with orderly settlers and maintained an established order that lasted until the period of the Trojan War.

Plutarch gives us a later allusion to the industry. During the civil wars in Rome, the republic lost its command of the sea and there sprang up along the Cilician coast bands of robbers, who made use of sail and oar galleys in plundering the traffic of the Mediterranean between Greece, Rome, and Egypt. Sylla, who saw "many a Marius in that dissolute youth," demanded that Julius Cæsar, then but little more than eighteen, put away his wife Cornelia, daughter of Cinna, the tyrant's predecessor in the rule of Rome. This Cæsar refusing, Sylla compelled him to take refuge in exile, first in the country of the Sabines, where he was captured by Roman soldiers and escaped by bribing Cornelius, their captain, with two talents. He now made for Bithynia, where, after a short stay with King Nicomedes, he sought to return home by ship. What befell is thus related by Plutarch: "In his passage back he was taken near the Island Pharmacusa by some of the pirates, who, at that time, with large fleets of ships and innumerable smaller vessels infested the seas everywhere. When these men first demanded of him twenty talents for his ransom, he laughed at them for not understanding the value of their prisoner and voluntarily engaged to give them fifty. He presently dispatched those about him to several places to raise the money, till at last he was left among a set of the most bloodthirsty people in the world, the Cilicians, with only one friend and two attendants. Yet he made so little of them that when he had a mind to sleep he would send to them and order them to make no noise. For thirty-eight days, with all the freedom in the world, he amused himself with joining in their exercises and games, as if they had been not his keepers but his friends. He wrote verses and speeches and made them his auditors, and those who did not admire them, he called to their faces, illiterate and barbarous, and would often in raillery threaten to hang them. They were greatly taken with this and attributed his free talking to a kind of simplicity and boyish playfulness. As soon as his ransom was come from Miletus, he paid it and was discharged and proceeded at once to man some ships at Miletus, and went in pursuit of the pirates, whom he surprised with their ships still stationed at the island, and took most of them. Their money he made his prize and the men he secured in prison at Pergamus and made application to

Junius, who was then Governor of Asia, to whose office it belonged as Prætor to determine their punishment. Junius, having his eye upon the money, for the sum was considerable, said he would think at his leisure what to do with the prisoners, upon which Cæsar took his leave of him and went off to Pergamus, where he ordered the pirates to be brought forth and crucified: the punishment he had often threatened them with while he was in their lands, and they little dreamed he was in earnest."

To these gentlemen is due the distinction of inventing that chaste method of Happy Despatch called walking the plank, for it was their habit when taking a prisoner to ask him if he were a Roman. Upon the victim's making a proud reply in the affirmative, they would bow low and tender their most humble services. Then, when the Roman was gulled into the belief that he had awed them to his own security, they would politely request him to mount upon the ship's ladder and step to liberty—in the sea!

During the troubled period of Rome they grew in numbers and wealth; their galleys were gorgeously ornate, with gilded prows, oars plated with silver, and wearing purple sails. Nor did they stop at the sea, but plundered villas along the shore, carrying off high-born ladies for ransom and laughing at the power of Rome. Two prætors, Sextullus and Bellinus, passing from the capital to their provinces were taken captive, and no limit seemed set upon the piratical audacity. At last Pompey the Great, effecting order, raised a force of sufficient strength to deal with the situation and brought it to an end.

Wealth having an invariable tendency to coagulate, its redistribution has always been one of the problems of mankind, those who earn being constantly exposed to the exactions of those who desire to make their fortunes without honest exertion. This prevails in modern times despite what is called the Progress of Civilization: the hives are always being emptied while the bees continue their industry.

Of course we must look to China as the oldest of nations for systematic effort in plundering commerce, which has kept pace since the beginning with the teachings of Confucius, but with that history we can have only passing concern. Chinese pirates within the last century have maintained large fleets, held ports, and even now furtively operate. It is with the story of the Western world we have mainly to do in this chronicle, and for a starting point the Scandinavian peninsula. That singular semi-arctic region, whose sagas shed historical light on Norway, Sweden, and Denmark, was the birthplace of what can be called the modern history of adventure. For twelve centuries the Northmen and their descendants have been masters of the sea. Lawfully or unlawfully as the case might be, theirs was the dominion. It is more than a thousand years since Eric the Red found Iceland and steered his shield-decked ship to the shores of Vineland, while others of his kind:

> " . . . sailed on the sunland waters
> And under the Southern skies
> And stared at the puny princes
> With their blue, victorious eyes."

The watch towers still stand along the Calabrian coast, from which the Iberians gazed anxiously across the Mediterranean to note the coming of the Vikings. They made the British, the Normans, the Dutch, and the Germans of Hamburg, Bremen, and Dantzic, the famous free cities of the North Sea. Their blood is our blood, much mingled it may be, but with a similar fluid, that of the adventurous of all the world.

The strivings of the sea kings form a literature in itself, too copious to be followed here. The tincture they poured into British veins expelled the Cæsars from England after five hundred years of occupation and, retempered with that of the Normans under William the Conqueror, gave the impulse that leads to the unfolding of our tale.

It would seem a reasonable conjecture that Life found its commencement in the tropics where living conditions were easy and, developing, moved northward, seizing the fibers of plants and the skins of animals to clothe itself against weather and cold, but waxing stronger and more aggressive as it approached the pole. The output of energy from Scandinavia is marvellous, far excelling in its conquering results the favored regions of the sun, the English amalgamation being the most potent of all.

In the century of struggle that began with the abdication of Charles the Fifth, when Holland at last wrested itself free from the rule of Spain, there sprang up along the Friesland coast a great company of "sea-beggars," or privateersmen, hiding among the creeks and shoals that make the Dutch coast a labyrinth through which pursuit was next to impossible. These men sustained the Dutch cause to such purpose that for a time they formed its sole hope. Their relief of Leyden was a turning point in the tide of success. That these did not

[6]

take all their toll from Spain was hardly considered moral obliquity. Contemporaneously, the good Queen Elizabeth, flirting with Philip II, and making and breaking promises to the Prince of Orange, permitted what was a sort of glorified piracy. Without the excuse of war, Drake, Hawkins, Frobisher, Cavendish, and their kind, in trifling barks essayed such voyages as to write their names large upon the book of fame. In their eager search for treasure they became great explorers. Drake belted the world. The others amplified geography close to its modern limits. But gold was the stimulant, especially Spanish gold. The destruction of the Armada and the death of Elizabeth brought a respite for Spain. Under King James, outside of Sir Walter Raleigh's luckless search for the riches of El Dorado, English energy satisfied itself with the first effort to lodge upon the North American continent in Virginia, soon to be extended by the descent of the Puritans on New England.

The adventurers invaded the Eastern seas at an early date, and prominent among them was Thomas Jones, afterwards famous as the commander of the *Mayflower*, which brought the Pilgrims to Plymouth. Like Captain William Kidd nearly a century later, he was sent to the Indies in 1617, by Sir Robert Rich, afterwards Earl of Warwick, in the ship *Lion*, ostensibly to hunt pirates and relieve them of their spoil, which, as Sir Thomas Roe, ambassador of that day at the Court of the Great Mogul, remarked, was "a common pretense for becoming a pirate." He was caught by Captain Martin Pring, acting for the Honorable East India Company, while in pursuit of the ship of the Queen Mother of the Great Mogul. Overhauled, he showed fight and, as a result, Pring fired upon the *Lion* until she burst into flame and was burned. Some of the crew perished in the blaze, and Jones, with the survivors, was taken prisoner to London. He was never tried, however, the presumption being that his noble backer's influence saved him from that ignominy.

When Charles the First lost his crown and his head, the fleeing cavaliers and the second Charles found refuge in Holland, and here that robust genius, Prince Rupert of the Rhine, became a "Beggar of the Sea." He kept the cause of the Restoration alive and fed his indigent Prince with the proceeds of pillage upon the waters, venturing into the West Indies and at one time commanding a fleet of seven sail. His practices were no better than those of a plain pirate, as he sailed under no flag and with no proper commission, not even that of a letter of marque, but gave his high purpose to restore injured royalty as the justification for his irregularities.

For companion in his ventures Rupert had his brother Maurice. Their fleet was caught in a West India hurricane off the Virgin Islands in 1654 and all but one ship, the *Swallow*, were lost with many lives, including that of the gallant Maurice. The crippled *Swallow* crept back to France, reaching harbor at Dunkirk in 1655, far spent, and never again put to sea.

There now developed an organized series of forays against the riches of Spain, long neglected through the civil war period and up to the time of the Restoration. The taking of Jamaica by Cromwell's forces in 1648, headed by General Venables and William Penn's father, the Admiral Sir William, established a base for action too accessible to be neglected, and here rose the power of the Buccaneers. Their beginning was not in Jamaica, however, but in Hispaniola, still under nominal Spanish rule. Here on the broad savannas roamed great herds of wild hogs and cattle, the killing and curing of which became a profitable and easily undertaken industry, taken up by wanderers from all the world, but mainly English, French, and Dutch. Harrassed at times by the Spanish governors, these wanderers found a place of refuge on the little island of Tortuga, separated by a narrow strait from Santo Domingo, where they lodged with impunity and, starting with shallops, began to waylay commerce. Pierre le Grand, a Frenchman, was a notable leader, but one Mansvelt, a Hollander, got together a fleet and fell hard upon the Spanish Main. He had among his numbers Henry Morgan, a Welshman, who may be said to have raised freebooting to the dignity of a profession. He had, however, a warrant for his acts, ending in royal favor and great fame. He is too great company to be put with scurvy villains and so has no place in this chronicle. We have to deal with gallows birds, of which he was none! The sun of the buccaneers sank in 1680, when Morgan was knighted and made Vice-Governor of Jamaica, though it survived for four years in the South Seas, and then began the rise of the numerous English pirates whose story is here told. The scattering of the buccaneers which followed the establishment of peace with Spain, the death of Charles the Second, the expulsion of King James the Second and the accession of the Prince of Orange to the English throne, left many adventurers without a field. They had jingled unearned "pieces of eight" too long to abandon lightly their pursuit.

INTRODUCTION

Spain not being easy prey, plain piracy now became the rule. The Portuguese and Dutch had enjoyed a monopoly of the trade with the luxurious East, and England now turned seriously toward the sunrise in search of profits. The Honorable East India Company, feebly established in 1600, began to show its strength, founding the fort on the Hugli in 1675 that became Calcutta and the source of English power in Hindustan. The French effected a lodgment at Pondicherry a decade before. In their first essays the English were weakest and at the most disadvantage until the pirates came in to adjust the balance, setting up shop on Madagascar and assailing all comers with much impartiality, though wary of the well-armed ships of "Company John."

Spoil was plentiful, but much of it had to be carried far to market and this, of all places, was New York, lately wrested from the Dutch. Here the leading merchants favored the "Red Sea trade," which was nothing more or less than the receiving of stolen goods. In 1692, Colonel Benjamin Fletcher, a soldier of fortune who had served King William well, became Governor of New York. His pockets yearned after the manner of viceroys, and he took care to fill them by all accounts, though strenuously defending the virtue of his methods. During his reign the new "trade" weighted the wharves of New York and filled its warehouses. He was credited with giving commissions to some pirates and winking at the acts of others, until his course became so scandalous that he was removed and replaced by Richard Coote, Earl of Bellomont, though to make the mockery complete the latter had already become a partner with Captain Kidd, who still holds the highest and least deserved repute as a pirate.

Bellomont found New York a very prosperous seat of corruption, due to the "trade," and began at once to check it by refusing clearings and treating the cargoes with suspicion. The rules of his customs department became so stringent that "commerce" abandoned New York, and its merchants lodged grave charges against the Governor with the Lords of Trade as one who was ruining the community. Names ever since prominent in the history of the city are appended to the petition. The pirates and their mercantile associates retained the best legal talent in the city. Bellomont was sorely harrassed and died without solving his numerous problems, of which the Kidd scandal was not the least. He proclaimed that beside the "ring" in New York, the East End of Long Island, where now sleep the sober villages of

Sag Harbor, Greenport, and the Hamptons, was a "Nest of Pirates" while the Governor of Connecticut, a scion of John Winthrop gave their agents open shelter, and the deputy governor of Pennsylvania was in close relationship with the rogues, so much so that his own daughter married one of Every's men. But let the details come in their proper place in the narrative.

Following the decadence of the Madagascar and Red Sea trade, the outlaws were active along the Gold Coast, the West Indies, and the entire reach of North America from the Gulf of Mexico to Newfoundland, with the Bahamas as a rendezvous, whose low-lying, far-scattered islands formed ideal nesting places for pirates, commanding as they did Cuba, the Gulf of Mexico, and the North American coast. They infested these lonely coral keys, and even stole a name that belonged to Christopher Columbus. The great voyager called the spot where he first saw the feeble flicker of light that denoted the presence of land, a petty coral bank in the Bahamas, "San Salvador," as saved indeed he was in his mighty hopes. This became instead Cat Island and then Watling's, after John Watling, a tough old buccaneer. He was killed while marauding in 1681, but has for a monument the island where Columbus set his mark.

In 1717 the conditions at New Providence became so scandalous that Woodes Rogers, of Bristol, an experienced privateer and navigator, was sent to the island to straighten it out by a combination of force and clemency royally decreed by George the First. This was effective for a period, but the "trade" survived until 1724, when it was pretty well wiped out. There was then a pause in pirating for near a hundred years, when it broke out again among the Cuban keys and the remote islands of the Gulf of Mexico, enduring with greater or less activity until 1831, when the robbery of the Brig *Mexican* of Salem ended the history of lawless adventure upon the Western Atlantic.

The Malay pirates and those in the China seas endured the longest, even into our time, and from Charles the Fifth's day down to Commodore Preble there existed an authorized system of piracy maintained by the bashaws of Tunis, Tripoli, and Algiers, known as the Barbary States, and the Sultan of Morocco, who backed the rovers of Sallee. This is apart from the present volume. Their power was broken by the United States in 1804 and extinguished by England in 1816.

In all that follows it will be perceived that the palm goes to England. As my learned friend, Alleyne Ireland, observes with exact pertinency:

INTRODUCTION

"The English are a wonderful people. You may not like them, but you must admire them, and they are on earth to stay and acquire. The last dollar (meaning our American symbol) will be found in the British Museum."

Perforce I believe this to be true. The obolus is there, the Widow's Mite, the sesterce, and what not coins from the mints of Pharaoh and Agamemnon to the cowries of King Coffee!

I

OF THOMAS POUND

IN the confusion caused by the English Revolution of 1688, New England underwent a brief spasm between the expulsion of James II and the acknowledgment of William of Orange. Edmund Andros, the Royal Governor, was absent at Pemaquid on an expedition against the Indians of Maine, when news reached him on January 10, 1689, of the move against the King, and from that point he issued a warning proclamation against the usurper. He returned in March and on April 4th, John Winslow, reaching Boston from Nevis, brought a copy of King William's acclaim of sovereignty, which he printed and circulated, though prohibited by Andros, who caused him to be lodged in jail for two weeks. The town responded, however, and, rising on April 18th, deposed Andros and confined him, taking beside Joseph Dudley, president of the Council, and Captain George, of the Frigate *Rose,* then in harbor.

The warship's lieutenant, David Condon, a Jacobite, prepared to open on the city, despite his captain's predicament as prisoner, but the rebels, taking the fort, trained all the guns on the *Rose,* so that Condon submitted to having her stripped of sails by the aroused citizens and his crew took oath of allegiance to William, the authority of James then disappearing from New England.

Employed by Andros in some of his undertakings had been Thomas Pound, an intelligent mariner and pilot of excellent character, who seized upon the moment to become a pirate. There is no outward excuse for his conduct, beyond the surmise of John Henry Edmonds, his biographer, that the move was made so that Boston would restore the *Rose* her sailing gear, to send her to sea after the outlaws and thus make her free to carry Andros to France and King James. Pirates and privateers became numerous at the moment off the coast, so much so that a petition was circulated by the merchants praying that the *Rose* might be released and sent after them. This was taken under advisement, pending the furnishing by Captain George of proper security.

[13]

On July 4th a committee reported Captain George to be a Catholic and under suspicion of being "disaffected" to their new majesties, and the frigate was held. Andros escaped from confinement on August 3rd and, though recaptured at Newport on the 5th, in support of Mr. Edmunds's theory, on the night of the 8th, Thomas Pound, Thomas Hawkins, Thomas Johnston, Eleazer Buck, John Siccadan, Richard Griffen a Boston gunsmith, and Benjamin Blake a young boy, went down the harbor in a "Bermuda-fashioned" sloop, being one of the strong, light, cedar-frame craft built at that Colony, and were joined at Lovell's Island in the dawn by Daniel Lander, Samuel Watts, William Warren, William Dun, and Henry Dipper. Arms were carried and the open appearance of going a-pirating was made to the crew of a Hull sloop, which they met off Brewster and from which they got some mackerel and water. Isaac Prince, captain of the Hull sloop, at once made known their actions in Boston.

Three hours after parting with Prince, Pound and his companions stopped the *Mary*, a fisherman of Salem, Captain Helen Chard, holding the crew prisoners. Darby, one of the number, volunteered and a Frenchman was pressed to act as interpreter. The rest were transferred to the Bermuda boat while the pirates retained their vessel, promising to return it when they had found a better one. To Chard they announced that on gaining forty more men and a proper ship they would go to "plague the French." Chard reported to the authorities at Salem, who at once sent a vessel armed by local volunteers in search of the rovers, but with no result. The pirates sailed on to Casco Bay, where they were joined by seven deserters from the garrison at Fort Loyal, at Falmouth, now Portland. These recalcitrant warriors were Corporal John Hill, John Lord, John Watkins, William Bennett, William Neff, James Dannell, and Richard Phipps, possibly one of the twenty brothers of the famous Sir William.

John Darby coaxed the Falmouth physician on board to see the captain, pretending he was Chard; the real motive was to secure a surgeon, but the bait was declined. Captain Sylvanus Davis of Fort Loyal tried to retrieve his deserters and the belongings they had taken with them, but had no success, the pirates getting safely out of harbor and sailing for Cape Cod. Here under Race Point, on August 16th, they captured the sloop *Goodspeed*, of Piscataqua, John Smart, Master, lumber laden, and exchanged her for the *Mary*, giving him a message to Boston "that they knew where the Government sloop lay ready, but if she came out after them and came up with them she should find hot work for they would die every man before they would be taken." In reply to the challenge the authorities sent out the armed sloop *Resolution* under command of Joseph Thaxter, with forty men, instructed "strenuously to Endeavour the suppressing and seizing of all Pirates especially on Thomas Hawkins, Pound, and others confederated with them," at the same time to be "very careful to avoid the shedding of blood unless you be necessitated by resistance and opposition made against you." Thaxter did not find Pound, who had fitted himself snugly into Homes's Hole in Vineyard Sound, where he took on August 27th a Newburyport brigantine, the *Merrimack*, John Kent, captain.

She supplied them with flour, sugar, and like essentials, including rum, tobacco, and three guns, and was then released. Going thence, the *Mary* was blown to the Virginia coast, where they put into York River for eight days until the gale went down. The warship on the station was on careen for cleaning and her tender, a ketch, had been sunk. John Giddings and Edward Broome joined them here. A negro slave was carried off.

Returning now to New England, at Tarpaulin Cove, on the southeast side of Naushon Island, Vineyard Sound, a Salem ship, of which William Lord was master, was found too large to tackle, so submerging their character, they bought an anchor of Lord in exchange for sugar and sold him the kidnapped darkey for £12. Captain Alsop's ketch had a narrow escape from capture. Pound chased her into Vineyard Harbor and attempted to cut her out but was prevented by the inhabitants. They now returned to Cape Cod, where Thomas Hawkins deserted. A Pennsylvania sloop was halted but, having no pork on board, was permitted to pass. October 1st better fortune was had at Homes's Hole, where Captain John Picket's sloop, the *Brothers Adventure*, from New London, yielded abundant provisions. Thus provided for, the company went again to Tarpaulin Cove, intending to sail thence for Curaçao.

This voyage was destined never to occur. The authorities at Boston being well-apprised, had on September 20th commissioned Captain Samuel Pease, in the sloop *Mary*, of which Pound had once been commander in the service of Governor Andros, with Benjamin Gallop as lieutenant, to proceed in search of the pirates. She was well armed and carried twenty men. His instructions were to search out and surprise Pound and company, but to prevent the shedding of blood as far as possible. This laudable desire could not be fulfilled because, as it appears from the event, the pirates had made no idle resolutions not to be taken. Pease coming to Wood's Hole on October 4th and learning of Pound's presence at Tarpaulin Cove, at once went thither and found his quarry. He sent a shot across the *Mary's* bow, at which she hoisted a red flag to her peak. Coming near, Pease fired a musket athwart and summoned the pirates to surrender in the King's name.

Pound, standing on his quarter deck, flourishing a naked sword, called them dogs and invited them to board and he would there do the "striking," at the same time opening fire. A fierce contest followed. A powder explosion on the sloop did some damage and disabled two men, at which accident the pirates hastened their fire. Pound soon fell wounded and Pease offered quarter, which was refused. As the fight went on several of the sloop's men fell, and Captain Pease was so severely hurt that he went below, leaving Gallop in charge. He at once boarded the pirate. The unwounded on her fought bravely, but were too few to resist long; during the conflict four were killed, and twelve being wounded, only two were unscathed and the fight was over. The prize and the wounded were taken into Pocasset, where after some delay doctors came from Newport to care for the injured. Captain Pease died from his wounds on Saturday, October 12th.

The vessels arrived at Boston on October 18th, where a new jail with walls four feet thick welcomed the prisoners. The assets of the company approached £2,209. 4s. 6d, out of which Lieutenant Gallop had his medical and other charges amounting to £35-99. The Salem owners of the *Mary* declined to redeem her, so she was condemned and sold. Dr. Elisha Cooke, of Newport, received £21-10 for patching up the pirates. The deserter, Thomas Hawkins, had a rough experience among the fishermen at Nauset. He was put under arrest and conveyed to Boston by Jacobus Loper, a Portuguese fisherman, and lodged in the new jail, bedecked incidentally with shackles and chains. On January 9, 1690, the Grand Jury brought in indictments for piracy and murder. Ten were found guilty and held for sentence of death. Four, Pound, Hawkins, Johnston, and Buck were doomed to die on Monday, July 27th, but powerful influences were at work and Johnston, a friendless privateersman, alone was swung off. Credit for saving Pound was accorded "Mr. Epaphus Shrimpton and Sundry Women of Quality." Finally fines and imprisonment, or its favorite substitute, servitude in Virginia, were accepted as sufficient justice to all save Pound.

OF THOMAS POUND

The *Rose* sailed for Portsmouth, New Hampshire, on April 20, 1690, under command of the liberated Captain George. Hawkins, who had escaped with a fine, went along; Pound was carried in custody to be dealt with abroad, the fine hands of his friends again showing. She delayed a month at Portsmouth and then sailed on May 19th for England, conveying some ships laden with masts. Five days out she encountered a French warship off Cape Sable and a two-hour battle followed, which ended in a draw. George was killed in a duel with the French captain, and Thomas Hawkins lost his life in the affray. It was left for Pound to deliver a succinct account of the affairs to his friend, Sir Edmund Andros, on reaching Falmouth, England, July 8, 1690. His suspended sentence speedily disappeared and his first activity as a free man seems to have been to publish an excellent map of the New England coast from Cape Cod to Cape Sable, valuable to navigators, from surveys made by himself. The map was dedicated to Charles Gerard, Earl of Macclesfield. This patron seems to have secured him an appointment as captain in the British navy. He took command of an ex-pirate vessel, the *Sallee Rose*, taken from the Moors and put into royal service on August 5, 1691. Pound served in the *Sallee Rose* in Channel service until February 2, 1695, when he was given the *Dover Prize* and sent to the Irish station, and thence to Virginia, April 17, 1691, where Andros had become Governor, remaining until March 22, 1698, when he was ordered home. He soon retired from the navy and lived as a private gentleman at Islesworth in Middlesex, until his death in 1703.

If only an amateur, Pound certainly showed great possibilities, worthy of being predecessor of the long line of law breakers who were to follow him, in this the first venture of record after the subsidence of the Buccaneers.

II

OF CAPTAIN MISSON

C APTAIN MISSON, in whom piracy from Madagascar and, therefore, the profession in its modern state had its earliest exemplar, was one of the forbears of the French Revolution. He was one hundred years in advance of his time, for his career was based upon an initial desire to better adjust the affairs of mankind, which ended, as is quite usual in the more liberal adjustment of his own. The younger son of a good but too numerous family in Provence, which because of its size was unable to provide properly for all its members, Misson when of age joined his kinsman, Captain Fourbin, of the frigate *Victoire* as a gentleman-volunteer, boarding her at Marseilles. He had received an excellent education and had been destined for the army, which was not to his taste, his roving disposition responding better to the call of the sea.

The *Victoire* proceeded at once on a cruise in the Mediterranean, during which Misson studied the art of seamanship with the utmost zeal, soon becoming accomplished in all matters pertaining to the management of a ship.

Putting in at Naples, Misson there met in the person of a priest to whom he went at confessional, a man who was destined to influence the rest of his life. This confessor, named Caraccioli, being disgruntled with the doctrines of the Church, was easily persuaded to throw off his cassock and follow his new friend on board the *Victoire*, from which time they became inseparable. The ship had left Naples and the pair joined her at Leghorn. Again putting to sea, after a week's cruising the *Victoire* encountered two Sallee rovers, one of twenty and the other of twenty-four guns, whom she immediately engaged. The *Victoire*, though pierced for forty guns, had but thirty at the ports. A Spanish renegade commanded the larger of the rovers, called the *Lion* and he fought with the utmost gallantry, making repeated attempts to board the *Victoire*, but her guns were served with such accuracy that he was badly hulled and compelled to careen his vessel to lift the shot-

[18]

holes above water. In shifting weight to ensure this a mistake of balance was made, and the *Lion* completely capsized. Her consort now sought to escape, but this Captain Fourbin would not permit, and at length laid alongside to board. Misson and his friend were the first to leap over the bulwarks, but the party were beaten back by the Moors. The priest was wounded and carried below. Misson and the crew repeated the effort to board, when a desperate conflict occurred, both sides losing heavily. Misson, seeing a Moslem leap down the main hatch bearing a lighted match, concluded his purpose was to blow up the ship and followed him, reaching the magazine just in time to cut down the man as he was about to light the powder. When more men came from the *Victoire* the Moors ran to shelter and, quarter being promised, surrendered themselves without further resistance. Fifteen Christians who were found in slavery on board were freed, and the prizes and prisoners were taken into Leghorn and sold. The *Victoire* lost thirty-five men, mainly in the hand fighting, for the gun-fire of the rovers was directed at the rigging, their policy being to disable and board.

After a month's respite at Marseilles the *Victoire* was ordered to Rochelle to escort a merchant fleet to Martinique. Since the convoy was not ready, Misson and his companion volunteered for a cruise in the English channel on the *Triumphe*, Captain Le Blanc, where, between Guernsey and Start Point, they came upon the British ship *Mayflower*, Captain Balladine, of eighteen guns, carrying a valuable cargo from Jamaica. Balladine defended himself until the *Mayflower* was in a sinking condition, so the French got only such cash as was on board for their pains. Le Blanc would not permit the defenders to be deprived of their personal belongings, shutting off the murmurs of the crew by reminding them they were servants of the Grand Monarch,—not pirates.

Running up to Beechey Head, a British fifty-gun ship gave them chase, but the *Triumphe* being the better sailor evaded her and, doubling Land's End, ran up Bristol Channel to Nash Point, taking a small ship from Barbadoes, and chasing another which was lost in the night. A British ship beat them into Milford Haven. It now being wise to return, the *Triumphe* put into Brest where the Barbadoes ship was held and Captain Balladine released, Le Blanc giving him forty Louis for his sustenance. Returning to Rochelle, the pair rejoined the *Victoire*, which in another month sailed for the West Indies with her convoy. After she had delivered the ships safely at Martinique and Guadeloupe,

[19]

the *Victoire* went cruising after the British, with whom the Grand Monarch was at war, and met the *Winchelsea*, of forty guns, Captain Jones. The vessels engaged, and the first broadside from the *Winchelsea* killed Captain Fourbin and his three lieutenants, leaving only the master alive of her officers. He would have surrendered but Misson assumed command and, with Caraccioli for lieutenant, defended the ship with such vigor and kept up so determined a fire that for three hours the issue was in doubt. Then some sparks reached the magazine of the *Winchelsea* and she blew up. Her fate long remained one of the mysteries of the sea, for her head drifted ashore at Antigua some time later at the end of a great storm and it was assumed that she must have gone down in the gale, the *Victoire* never reporting to France for reasons that follow.

After the tragic end of the conflict, Caraccioli saluted Misson as captain and observed that it was a good time to assert the principles of common right often discussed between them. If they put in at Martinique the best Misson could hope for was a lieutenant's commission, whereas if they kept the ship he could go as far as he pleased as a free citizen of the world. His arguments persuaded Misson to call the crew to the mast and sound their opinions. Those who wished to follow he would welcome and treat as brothers; those who did not would be safely set ashore. One and all cried, "Vive le Capitain Misson," and at once embraced the New Freedom. Misson was confirmed as captain and Caraccioli as lieutenant and the places of the other officers were filled from the crew. A vote was now taken as to the next course, and it was decided to try the Spanish West Indies. Some were for hoisting the black flag at once, but Caraccioli demurred: saying that they were not pirates but liberty lovers, fighting for equal rights against all nations subject to the tyranny of government, and bespoke a white flag as the more fitting emblem. It was therefore adopted with the motto "A Deo a Libertate" added.

The ship's money was put in a chest to be used as common property, but upon Misson's proposing to add the late captain's plate the crew declared it must remain part of the cabin furnishings. Clothes were now distributed to all in need and the Republic of the Sea was in full operation. Misson in his address bespoke them to put aside all piques and grudges and to live in strict harmony among themselves; that a misplaced society would adjudge them still as pirates. Self-preservation, therefore, and not a cruel disposition compelled him to

[20]

declare war on all nations who should close their ports to him. "I do now," he said "declare such war, and, at the same time recommend to you my comrades a humane and generous behavior toward your prisoners, which will appear by so much more the effects of a noble soul, as we are satisfied we should not meet the same treatment should our ill fortune, or more properly, our disunion, or want of courage give us up to their mercy."

A muster showed two hundred fit for duty and thirty-five sick and wounded. While they were cruising in the Windward Channel a becalmed Boston sloop gave them a supply of rum and sugar. The captain, Thomas Butler, owned he had never been treated more civilly, regarding the *Victoire* still as a French ship of war. A few days passed without incident, when the ship's company were surprised to have a sloop stand boldly for them. She was made out to be a Jamaica privateer, which after a good look at them payed off rapidly to windward. One of the crew who was familiar with privateer tactics averred she would return near midnight and attempt to board. Watch was therefore kept and the surmise proved true. The privateer laid along the bowsprit over which her men came one by one, to be nabbed and throttled ere they reached the deck, without noise and with such small clash of arms that but one Frenchman was wounded and none of the privateersmen killed or injured. In this way the majority of the sloop's men were secured and those of the *Victoire* invaded the privateer, which made an effort to cut loose and escape—but too late. She was easily taken. In the morning Misson greeted the captain of the prize graciously. His name was Henry Ramsey and this was his first venture. The privateer carried no cargo. She was deprived of nothing but ammunition and, being put on parole for six months, was allowed to depart after detention for a few days.

The *Victoire* sailed to Carthagena and Porto Bello on the Spanish Main, meeting on the way two Dutch traders with letters of marque, one of twenty, the other twenty-four guns. Misson engaged the pair. Both were too well-manned to permit boarding and were accordingly hammered with cannon for six hours, when Misson, losing patience ran alongside the larger and pouring in a broadside sent her to the bottom, with the loss of all on board. He then turned to the other, which called for quarter which was granted. The *Victoire* lost thirteen killed and six out of her nine wounded died. The Dutchman had a rich cargo of fine goods, gold and silver lace, brocades, etcetera. It was now decided

[21]

to put into Carthagena and sell the prize as that of a French warship, Misson using the name of Fourbin to avoid suspicion. Reaching that port, Caraccioli went ashore in the barge, using the name of D'Aubigny, the dead lieutenant whose place he filled, bearing a letter to the Governor signed Fourbin, explaining his captures and the near expiration of his time limit, with the wish that merchants might be sent aboard to purchase the wares. Don Joseph de la Zerda, the Governor, was most graciously pleased to accede to the request and not only provided for the traders but received the prisoners and made a gift of fresh provisions to the French captain, who in return presented his excellency with a fine piece of brocade. The goods brought 50,000 pieces of eight. These transactions being performed in one day, the *Victoire* left the next morning. Word of her doings reaching Jamaica through some babblings of the liberated privateersmen, Admiral Wagner sent the *Kingston* in search of her and, hearing later quite incorrectly that she had been joined by a twelve-gun consort, ordered the *Severn* out to co-operate. The two met in the dark, each taking the other for the *Victoire,* and were near coming to an engagement when luckily they discovered their identity.

When the *Victoire* left Carthagena, Governor de la Zerda in the innocence of his heart wrote "Captain Fourbin" that the galleon *St. Joseph,* then lying at Porto Bello, would sail for Havana in eight or ten days and hoped the *Victoire* would guard her off the coast, as she had on board silver and gold bars to the value of 800,000 pieces of eight. The liberators received this intelligence with proper joy, Mission replying gravely that he felt he could safely stretch his instructions for a few days and would await the *St. Joseph* off Cape Gratias a Dios, at the same time advising the Governor of signals he would set for the galleon's recognition. Don de la Zerda was much gratified and forwarded instructions to the *St. Joseph* to accept the convoy, but, fortunately for her and his own repute for sagacity, she had sailed two days before his express reached Porto Bello and the *Victoire* was so advised by the boat which bore the message while waiting in the offing. It was decided to pursue, but the galleon was speedy enough to distance her and never came in sight.

A London ship bound for Jamaica now made up for a little of the lost *St. Joseph,* yielding 4,000 pieces of eight and some rum and sugar. On board were twelve French prisoners bound for an English war prison, who were only too delighted to join the Republic of the Sea.

They were Bordeaux seamen, of the crew of the *Pontchartrain,* which had been recently taken by the *Mermaid.* Misson still kept his pose as a Frenchman and let the ship go, which rather roused suspicion as to his true character. As the *St. Joseph* was surely safe at Havana by now, the *Victoire* sought a secluded spot on the north of Cuba to careen and clean, after which it was voted to make for the Guinea coast. Here the *Nieuwstadt,* of Amsterdam, Captain Blaes, eighteen guns, was made prize. She was kept as a consort, after giving up £2,000 in gold dust and seventeen slaves, part of a cargo Blaes had begun to accumulate. The slaves were added to the crew and clothed in the Dutchmen's spare garments, Misson making an address denouncing slavery, holding that men who sold others like beasts proved their religion to be no more than a grimace, as no man had power over the liberty of another. The ship being still very foul and some of her sheathing wormy, she was run into the river Lagoa, cleaned and repaired.

Decorum and man-of-war discipline had so far prevailed upon the ship despite its republican quality, but the Dutch prisoners began to set a bad example in the way of profanity and drunkenness. Using their captain as interpreter, Misson told these men that before their coming on board his ears had not been offended by bad language, which administered neither to profit or pleasure, and if the practice did not cease it would lead to severe punishment, nor would he be more tolerant of drinking. The next example would be brought to the gratings to be there well whipped and pickled. It will thus be seen that Misson tried to be a truly moral pirate. Good behavior followed upon his talk.

Off Angola a second Dutch merchant was taken with a very satisfactory cargo. She was emptied and sunk. Since she had much cloth on board, the crew were comfortably reclothed from the spoil. There now being ninety prisoners, too many for comfort, they were sent away in the prize which had been acting as consort, "not a little surprised at the Regularity, Tranquillity, and Humanity which they found among these new-fashioned pirates with whom eleven chose to stay, including two sail-makers, one carpenter and an armourer."

In Saldanha Bay, ten leagues north of the Cape, where it was planned to recuperate, an English ship appeared which made a stout fight but was beaten with the loss of her captain and fourteen men, the French losing twelve. She produced £60,000 in coin beside some bales of broadcloth. Misson buried the slain captain with all the honors of war and had a stone-cutter in the company erect a proper memorial

inscribed: "Ici gist un brave Anglois." Thirty of the captured crew
who desired to join were accepted under the condition that they must
not expect to indulge in a dissolute and immoral life. Their ship was
made consort, with Caraccioli as captain, and all the English, save the
officers, decided to remain with "the Republic."

They now encompassed the Cape of Good Hope and rescued the crew
of a sinking English East Indiaman, who were landed at Johanna, an
island in the Comoro group between Madagascar and the east coast of
Africa, which became well-known in pirate annals. Misson was
warmly welcomed and proceeded to make his headquarters on shore,
promising the Queen to aid her against her royal rival, the King of
Mohilla. Ten of the men left the ship to settle down on the island,
but thirty of the rescued English joined. Misson soon got deep in the
graces of her dusky Majesty and married her sister, while Caraccioli
took a niece for wife. The King of Mohilla now made a descent with
his army and was badly beaten by Misson and his men, supplemented
by native auxiliaries. More than one hundred prisoners were taken.
To save these from massacre Misson received them on his ships and
sent them to Mohilla as a peace offering to His Majesty. The proffer
of good-will was rudely rejected and Misson accordingly determined
to administer a severe lesson, descending on Mohilla with a heavy force,
setting the King's town in flames and doing much damage. This
brought an embassy from Mohilla to sue for peace. It was promised
if the King of Mohilla would send two of his children and ten nobles
as hostages. The terms were accepted and Misson, with only Caraccioli
and a boat's crew in attendance, went to Mohilla to dine with the King
in token of amity. Returning to their boat they were assailed from
ambush, both captains wounded by arrows, and four of their men
killed. The ships sent strong parties to the rescue, killing a number
of the natives and rescuing their surviving friends, though three more
were killed in the encounter, and of eight wounded two afterwards died.

Fearing the just reprisal now his due, the King of Mohilla sent two
men off in a canoe, bound as prisoners, representing them to be the
authors of the treason and so delivering them up to justice. This ar-
tifice was soon clear and the Johanna people urged the taking of the
canoemen and the prisoners on general principles, but Misson would
not consent to this barbarity and was for sending the captives on shore,
when they begged him not to, assuring him that the wily king had
made them victims, because they had argued against his treachery.

OF CAPTAIN MISSON

Misson and Caraccioli lay ill six weeks with their wounds. The Mohillians fled to the interior and so baffled vengeance.

When Misson recovered, a cruise was resolved upon, the prize, now named the *Bijoux*, keeping company with the *Victoire*. Ten days later, leaving Johanna, they assailed a sixty-gun Portuguese ship which yielded only after a long combat which cost the company thirty men and the Portuguese sixty. Twenty of Misson's killed were his English volunteers. Caraccioli lost his right leg in the affray. The prize yielded £25,000 in gold dust. It may be remarked that the Johanna wives of the two captains kept them company during the cruise and stood bravely by in the fighting. Caraccioli was kept out of the adventuring for two months, but Misson, adding ten guns from the Portuguese to the *Victoire's* thirty and filling the gaps in her crew from the *Bijoux*, went out again, exploring the Madagascar coast until he found a bay ten leagues north of Diego Suarez that promised good shelter. As the prospect was pleasant it was resolved to establish here the shore quarters of "the Republic," erect a town, build docks, and "have a place they might call their own."

They now set busily at work felling trees, clearing ground, and preparing habitations. Returning to Johanna, Misson notified the Queen of his purpose to found the settlement, and this was regarded with dismay by her councillors, who dreaded the coming of a new power so near by, which might in the end threaten their own existence. After much debate it was agreed to furnish men to aid Misson in building his town, with the understanding that all were to be returned in four moons and an alliance made against Mohilla. When Caraccioli had recovered he went on board the Portuguese ship with a detail of the natives, forty of the company, and fifteen Portuguese prisoners and proceeded to the colony. Misson gave his dominion the name of Libertatia and called his people Liberi, which was to cover all races who came under his flag. A fort was built and armed with forty cannon from the Portuguese ship, which was dismantled and laid up. The hunters met a native in the distant forest and, bringing him to town, Misson caused him to be treated with great consideration and sent home with a present of scarlet cloth and an axe to propitiate his people, though none of these were near the settlement. Later they followed him to his village and when the people returned the visit they were equally well treated and rewarded with gifts.

When the town was well under way Misson, leaving Caraccioli in

[25]

UNDER THE BLACK FLAG

charge, went upon another cruise, this time toward Zanzibar, and encountered a Portuguese ship of fifty guns, with three hundred in her crew—nearly twice his own number. A desperate battle followed with the issue long in doubt. At last Misson lodged a boarding-party and the Portuguese captain was killed, whereupon his ship surrendered. The prize was very valuable, having £200,000 in gold on board, but cost the lives of fifty-six of Misson's men.

Coming off the Madagascar coast, Misson fell in with the pirate sloop commanded by Thomas Tew and his subsequent adventures are detailed in the account of that individual, which follows.

III

OF THOMAS TEW

TO Thomas Tew, a Rhode Islander, apparently belongs the credit of steering the rich "Madagascar trade" to the warehouses of New York. He was familiar with the merchants trading out of the city and with the merchant mariners of the Providence plantations. He first appeared in Bermuda, where he found Governor Ritchie fitting out two sloops to proceed to the mouth of the River Gambia on the west coast of Africa, ostensibly to attack and despoil the stations of the French traders established at Goree in opposition to the English Royal African Company. The command of one of these was given him; the other to George Drew. They were to consult with the Royal Company's agent at Cape Coast Castle and proceed under his directions. Thus properly commissioned the two vessels departed in company, but were soon separated by a violent storm and never rejoined.

Tew, indeed, made no effort to find his consort, but resolved upon a bolder course than plundering shopkeepers. Calling his crew together, he bespoke them to this purport:

"That they were not ignorant of the Design with which the Governor fitted them out; the taking and destroying the French factory; that he, indeed, readily agreed to take a Commission to this end, tho' contrary to his Judgment, because it was being employ'd; but that he thought it a very injudicious Expedition, which did they succeed in, would be of no Use to the Publick, and only advantage a private Company of Men, from whom they could expect no Reward of their Bravery; that he could see nothing but Danger in the Undertaking, without the least Prospect of a Booty; that he could not suppose any Man fond of fighting, for fighting-sake; and few ventured their lives, but with some View either of particular Interest or publick Good; but here was not the least Appearance of either. Wherefore, he was of Opinion, that they should turn their Thoughts on what might better their Circumstances; and if they were so inclined, he would undertake to shape a Course which should lead them to Ease and Plenty, in which they might pass the rest of their Days. That one bold Push would do their Business, and they might return home, not only without Danger, but even with Repuration."

The crew made a ready response to the suggestion, crying out heartily and as of one voice: "A gold chain or a wooden leg! We'll stand by you."

They then proceeded to organize on a piratical basis, choosing a quartermaster to represent themselves in all matters of general concern, without whose behest the captain was powerless to proceed against the wishes of his men. Tew now shaped his course around the Cape of Good Hope, and by way of Mozambique to the Straits of Bab-el-Mandeb, where he lay with an eye out for the Mogul's ships trading with Arabia. One of these soon appeared, "a tall vessel" bound from the Indies to Arabia, the first of a squadron of six, which this one was equipped to guard, carrying beside her seamen three hundred soldiers. Her caliber was easily gauged in men and guns, but Tew with equal wisdom estimated that they "wanted two things necessary, skill and courage" and, exhorting his crew to this end, boarded and carried the Mogul craft without the loss of a man, the Hindus "taking more care to run and hide from danger" than in the defence of their goods. So rich was her cargo in jewels and rare wares that the crew divided the equivalent of £3,000 per man. Much that was bulky went into the sea. The powder was transferred and such of the guns as gave Tew more teeth.

Tew now wished to waylay the five other ships belonging to their captive's convoy, but in this he was opposed by the quartermaster speaking for the crew, who had now been long at sea and desired a frolic ashore. It was voted then to head for Madagascar. On arriving here, the quartermaster, who, with others, evidently had misgivings as to the stability of their occupation, proposed to part company and establish a settlement, finding the island "productive of all the Necessaries of Life, that the Air was wholesome, the Soil Fruitful, and the Sea abounding with Fish." Twenty-three of the men joined in this counsel. They were accorded their share of the spoil of the Mogul's ship and landed, with the plan of establishing a settlement among the natives, while Tew and the remainder proposed to return home.

At this juncture they spied the *Victoire* and her prize (as noted in the sketch of Captain Misson) and not knowing for the moment that these belonged to the profession, made for them with the idea of in-

[28]

creasing their opulence. Tew introduced himself to the newcomers by firing a gun to the windward and running up the black flag. The stranger fired a gun to the leeward and, sending a boat to Tew's ship, soon made clear that they were kindred souls. The lieutenant in charge of the boat invited him to visit Misson. To this Tew replied that he could not go unless by consent of his crew. Misson now came within hail and renewed the invitation, suggesting that his lieutenant remain hostage, "if they were the least jealous of him," adding that he was strong enough to have his way without stratagem. The company then agreed to Tew's visiting Misson, and to show their full confidence did not detain the officer. Tew was "handsomely regaled" on the *Victoire* and agreed with Misson to visit his settlement. They were properly surprised on arriving at Misson's town to see the extent of his defenses and saluted the fort with nine guns, which were returned by the shore batteries. All the prisoners were allowed to come on deck for the first time and view the wonders of Libertatia.

The settlers were overjoyed at Misson's appearance with his prize, but soon lost some of their cheer in the news of what she had cost Mission and his companions. Tew, however, was welcomed as making up for some of the loss. The disposition of the large number of prisoners became a problem. By agreement among them, they were separated by nationalities and set to work improving the settlement and building a dock. Some who would not labor were put within bounds. The pirates also cleared ground and planted vegetables and grain. All was now going comfortably, but the *Bijoux*, of Misson's fleet, was held to guard the dock builders and the Frenchmen, becoming restless, wished to make another cruise. Not having enough men to watch the captives and make the voyage, he proposed loading a ship with them and sending them away. This Tew opposed, fearing it would spread information that might bring a force against the colony. A council was called in which Misson's will prevailed. He accordingly brought the prisoners together and told them he well knew the risk he was running in turning them loose, as he was certain to be attacked as soon as his retreat was known; that he could put them all to death if he willed and so silence their tongues, but would only ask of them a parole that none should serve against him, trusting in his strength and that of his Malagasy allies to beat off any attack. The prisoners highly applauded his magnanimity and, the ship being provisioned for Zanzibar, one hundred and thirty-seven took their departure on her.

UNDER THE BLACK FLAG

A company of Malagasy coming in with slaves taken in native warfare, Misson bought and fed them and "by all possible demonstrations" made it clear that he was opposed to slavery. The Johanna men were now sent away to the number of one hundred on the *Bijoux*, which returned with ten of Misson's men, who had been left at Johanna and then made several voyages to return the rest of the captives. This being attended to, the *Bijoux* was turned over to Tew for a cruise to the Guinea coast.

The crew included two hundred hands, of whom thirty-seven were blacks, forty Portuguese, thirty English, and the balance French. North of the Cape of Good Hope, Tew took a Dutch East India galley of eighteen guns, after a slight encounter, losing but one man. Off Angola he captured an English slaver with 240 victims of the trade, many of whom were known to the negro members of his crew. There was great rejoicing when Tew caused their shackles to be broken and "made them free men and sharers of his fortune." Tew, it may be added parenthetically, "abhorred slavery."

The Dutchman yielded a great quantity of English crowns. Tew, now well satisfied with his cruise, returned to Madagascar, pausing only to land the Hollanders at Saldanha Bay, thirty miles to the north of Good Hope. The spoil was placed in the common treasury at Libertatia and the freed negroes added to the population, where, working in common, they proved "sensible of their happiness" in falling into Tew's hands and were "diligent and faithful."

Misson now built a couple of small sloops, mounting them with eight guns each from Tew's Dutch prize. They proved to be "not only shapely vessels, but excellent sailors."

Misson really had it in his heart to found a lawful dominion, and the sloops were sent out with surveying parties to map the coast and discover its resources, the schooner-master going along to make the records. The Angola captives were taken along in some number, being anxious to learn the French language and to become sailors. One sloop was called the *Childhood*, the other the *Liberty*. The two returned to Libertatia with charts and much information. The blacks having now been trained to sea work, Misson fitted two ships with five hundred men, giving command of one to Tew and set out for Arabia Felix, where they soon met one of the Mogul's ships filled with pilgrims for Mecca, making in all, with the crew, 1,600 souls. Though carrying 110 guns the Mogul's vessel made but a poor defense and was easily taken, her crew firing one volley of small arms at random and abandoning the decks. Misson and Tew lost not a man. It was resolved to put all the males and married women ashore and carry the single females with the ship to Libertatia. There were about one hundred girls thus torn from their families, amid much lamentation. Misson was moved to spare them, but was overruled by the crew. The ship was nearly lost on the return voyage, running into a series of severe gales. Once at Libertatia she proved a very rich prize, but, being little better than a huge ark, was taken apart for her timbers and metal, while the guns were used to man additional batteries.

The dock in the meantime had been completed and it was now decided to rebuild the *Victoire*, which was accordingly done. When ready for sea, and victualed for a voyage to Guinea for more black settlers, at almost the moment set for her departure one of the sloops which had been on a short trip came in with the report that five "tall ships" had chased her into the bay and the master judged them to be Portuguese, each of fifty guns. The alarms were sounded and the batteries manned, while one hundred of the freed negroes, who had been formed into a battalion and drilled by Misson stood to their arms, as did the less disciplined whites. Misson took over their direction while Tew commanded all the whites.

The Portuguese came bravely in and were met with a storm of heavy shot from the batteries, which brought one to the careen, but all made the inner port, where two were soon sunk by the fire and many men were drowned. They had very wisely selected the turn of the tide for the time of this attack, and accordingly the three survivors drifted out with its help from under the efficient guns of the fort. Misson now manned his ships and the sloops and pursued. There ensued one of the fiercest sea fights in history. The sloops twice boarded two of the Portuguese but were repelled and the latter made sail for the open sea, abandoning the third to the *Victoire* and *Bijoux*, which soon took her, although the Portuguese fought until their deck ran with blood. The captain at last called for quarter, which was given. Plenty of powder and shot were found on board, which replenished the arsenal at Libertatia. Two of the paroled Portuguese who had been freed were discovered and very properly hanged, after the Portuguese chaplain had confessed and absolved them, the officers of the warship conceding that the punishment was just. The latter were well treated by Tew and Misson and much complimented upon

[31]

UNDER THE BLACK FLAG

their gallantry. The two survivors of the fight got back at last to
Lisbon with a tremendous story of their adventure, which found its
way to London, with the credit given to Henry Every as "the pirate
king" of Madagascar, operating a navy of thirty-two sail.

There was some murmuring over the executions, hanging not being
popular, as many of the company now and then felt a clutch at the
throat. To allay this Caraccioli made an address in justification,
pointing out the broken promise and rough return made for their
kindness by guiding in the fleet. Tew sided with Misson in this
matter, though at first inclined to mercy, but yielded when "thoroughly
informed of the blackness of their ingratitude."

Some of the Englishmen under Tew and Misson's Frenchmen now
developed friction, which Tew suggested be fought out by the disputants. This Caraccioli thought would be bad for public policy
and asked the two captains to endeavor to bring their men to a
better understanding. To this end a meeting was called of the
"colonists" at which a form of government was proposed, it being
pointed out that where there were no protective laws the weakest
must always suffer at the hands of the strong and general confusion
result. It was decided to separate into companies of ten, each one of
whom should select a representative to aid in framing the necessary
laws. All treasure and cattle were to be equally divided and such
land as any man might inclose by his labor would become his own.
Before the assembly could meet, it was decided to build a state house
and this was accordingly done, all hands sharing in the labor. When
completed the assembly met and Caraccioli, presiding, made a very
handsome speech, outlining the objects of the session, the chief of
which was to elect a conservator to serve three years. Misson was
the unanimous choice. It was then agreed that the delegates of the tens
should meet annually, or as much oftener as exigencies might require
in the judgment of the Conservator and his council, nothing of moment
to be done without the consent of the estate as thus organized. Ten
days were spent in framing laws before the session adjourned. The
laws were duly printed, there being a press and type in the colony.
Tew was appointed Admiral, and Caraccioli Secretary of State, in
which capacity he selected a council from among the ablest of the
colonists. The treasure was equally divided and each began enclosing
land for his own support. Tew, as Admiral, urged the building of an
arsenal and the augmenting of the fleet, but this was rejected as

tending to draw too many from the tilling of the soil and it was thought better to postpone such measures until their numbers were greater.

Tew then proposed to invite the former members of his crew who had formed a settlement with the quartermaster to join the colony, but this the council opposed, holding that their desertion of Tew in the beginning was a mark of mutinous temper that might breed trouble should they come with the Libertatians. Notice was given, however, that any who chose to join would be welcomed if they gave a parole of honor to behave.

Tew asked permission to make a cruise in search of recruits, as these were most needed for the prosperity of the settlement, and promised to look in on his own men. The *Victoire*, therefore, sailed in a few days with three hundred in her crew. Agreeable to promise he called on the quartermaster, who received him politely but could see no advantage in joining Misson's colony, as they were now free and independent and in the enjoyment of all things needed; it would be madness to submit to any governor, who, however mild his rule, still exerted some power. The quartermaster said he was governor himself for three months at a time, but could rule only in small disputes, where he tried to be just. Each quarter a new governor was to be chosen by lot from among those who had not yet served; thus every one in time would have enjoyed supreme command, which prevented all canvassing and politics, leaving as it did no opening for parties or divisions.

"However," observed the quartermaster sagely, "if you will go to Europe or America and show the advantages that may accrue to the English by fixing a colony here, out of the love we bear the country, and to wile away the odious appellation of Pirates, with pleasure we'll submit to lawful government; but 'tis ridiculous to think we will become subjects to greater rogues than ourselves; and that you may know what to say to this Head (Misson), if you think it expedient to follow my advice take with you some few thoughts which I have couch'd in writing and which I will fetch you."

The document in question proved to be a very intelligent description of the advantage of Madagascar as a place of settlement, as to climate, production, and opportunities. It urged the establishment of a lawful colony as a curb on pirates and as a "great convenience" for the East India ships, and was a very sensible paper.

Tew visited the quartermaster again in the evening and while they were supping a sudden storm arose, so violent that he could not return to his ship and before it subsided the *Victoire* was torn from her anchorage and wrecked upon the rocky coast, where the crew perished to a man. Tew now remained with the quartermaster, pondering on ways to return to Libertatia. At the end of three months a ship appeared in view which he took for the *Bijoux*, but she did not respond to signals. A month later two sloops came in, which turned out to be those built by Misson, who was on board one of them. Tew was rejoiced to see him, but soon found he bore news as bad as that he had received. The natives had made a descent upon Libertatia in dead of night and murdered most of the colonists. Caraccioli had been killed while making a brave defense, and Misson, feeling all was lost, had saved such jewels and gold as he could seize and with forty-five men succeeded in reaching the sloops and getting away. The *Bijoux* was absent on a cruise and this with the number gone with Tew had so weakened the colony that its destruction was easy.

Misson was much cast down, as all his plans for a new state had fallen ill. The quartermaster urged that they return to America and secure a commission for legally founding a colony, but Misson had abandoned all ambition in that line. He offered to divide his treasure and to give one of his sloops to Tew. Four of the quartermaster's men elected to go with their late captain and thirty of those who had come with Misson. They waited a week for the *Bijoux*, but as she did not appear, Misson divided his treasure and the two sloops sailed in company for the Guinea coast, hoping to find the ship. Both were overtaken off Cape Infantes by a violent storm, in which Misson's sloop foundered within musket shot of his consort, which could give him no aid. Tew now continued to Rhode Island, where his men dispersed and he made a satisfactory accounting to his Bermuda backers.

On his return to Rhode Island, Tew made no secret of his adventures, nor of the opportunities in the Red Sea trade. He found plenty of worthy people ready to back him, but had too much respect for his neck to risk it without some sort of sanction. Failing to secure a commission from Governor John Easton and learning of Governor Fletcher's hospitable nature, he visited New York and was speedily deep in the latter's acquaintance, so much so that it bred scandal, for he went so far as to grant a commission to Tew to operate a sloop by the amiable name of *Amity*. It was signed at Fort William

Henry, where the governor was paying an official visit on November 2, 1694, and countersigned by Daniel Honan, his secretary, who seems to have been a handy man in such transactions. Tew gave a bond of £3,000, endorsed by Edward Coats, another Red Sea trader, the captain of the ship *Jacob*, and the handy Honan. On June 13, 1695, Peter de La Noy, former Mayor of the city, after accusing Fletcher of being in league with Indian swindling traders, ventured this further charge:

"I had almost forgot another useful piece of policy he has to get money. We have a parcell of pirates in these parts, which people call the Red Sea men, who often get great booties of Arabian gold. His excellency gives all due encouragement to these men, because they make all due acknowledgment to him; one Coats, a captain of this honorable order presented his Excellency with his ship, which his Excellency sold for £800 and every one of the crew made him a suitable present of Arabian gold for his protection; one Captain Tew who is gone to the Red Sea upon the same errand, was before his departure highly carressed by his Excellency, in his coach and six horses, and presented with a gold watch to engage him to make New York his port at his return. Tew retaliated the kindness with a present of jewels, but I can't learn how much further the bargain proceeded; time must show that."

The Lords of Trade were but mildly moved by this complaint. They did, however, among other things, write to Fletcher under date of February 6. 1696: "Further complaints have been made to His Majesty from other colonies and especially from Jamaica, that the great temptation to Piracy by the entertainment given to Pirates in several places has been another means of seducing their inhabitants from them. And his Majesty, being highly sensible how such practices tend to the dishonor of the English name and nation, has therefore ordered us strictly to require the respective Governors of all this Plantations to take due care for the future, that no Pirates or sea Robbers be anywhere sheltered or entertained under the severest penalties. We are obliged in giving you to recommend it so much particularly to your care, by reason that in the information lately given upon the Tryal of several of Every's crew, your government is named as a place of protection for such villains and your favor in particular to Captain Tew is given as an instance of it."

Whatever was brought out at the trial of Every's men does not appear in the printed report, but Fletcher's relations with Tew continued to plague him.   Answering the Lords of Trade, June 22nd, he averred: "Captain Tew brought no ship to this Port; he came here as a stranger, and came to my table as other strangers do, when they come into the Province; he told me he had a sloop of force, well Manned and not only promised but entered into bond to make war upon the French in the mouth of Canada River, whereupon I gave him a commission and instructions according."

Fletcher was relieved of his governorship by Richard Coote, Earl of Bellomont, on the second of April, 1698.   His earliest efforts were to inquire into the Red Sea trade concerning which he reported to the Lords of Trade on May 8, 1698: "I find that those Pirates that have given the greatest disturbance in the East Indies and the Red Sea, have been either fitted from New York or Rhode Island, and manned from New York.   The ships commanded by Mason, Tew, Glover and Hore had their commissions from the governor of New York.   The three last from Fletcher."   He observed further: "It is likewise evident that Tew, Glover and Hore had commissions granted them by Governor Fletcher when none of them had any ship or vessel in Colonel Fletcher's government, yet they had commissions and were permitted to raise men in New York and the design public of their being bound for the Red Sea.   And Captain Tew, that had been before a most notorious Pirate (complained of by the East India Company), on his return from the Indies with great riches, made a visit to New York, where (although a man of most mean and infamous character) he was received and carressed by Col. Fletcher, dined and supped often with him and appeared publicly in his coach with him, and they exchanged presents, as gold watches, etc., with one another. All this is known to most of the city."

On October 16, 1696 the Lords of Trade made a detailed report on affairs in New York to the Lords and Justices, in which Tew's relations with Fletcher came under further review.   By this it appears, before coming to New York, in 1694, "the said Tew being in Rhode Island did offer unto John Easton, then Governor of that Colony, £500 for a commission, which was refused, though it is certain others there have been very guilty of that fault.   And Governor Fletcher's commission to Tew, being dated in November the same year, makes it highly probable it was not granted for nothing."

Fletcher, returning to London, made answer to the various charges under date of December 24, 1698. Of the Tew relationship he had this to say in a letter to the Lords of Trade: "As for my intimacy and kindness with Captain Tew and the great presents from him, which is objected, this is the truth and the whole truth of that poor affair. This Tew appeared to me not only a man of courage and activity, but of the greatest sense and remembrance of what he had seen, of any seaman I had met. He was also what they call a very pleasant man; so that at some times when the labors of my day were over it was some divertisement as well as information to me to hear him talk. I wished in my mind to make him a sober man, and in particular to reclaim him from a vile habit of swearing. I gave him a boot to that purpose; and to gain more upon him, I gave him a gun of some value. In return thereof he made me also a present, which was a curiosity and in value not much; and this is the sum of all the kindness I am charged with; for as to the coming sometimes to my table, which I think was such as became my character, and hospitable to all, I hope that will not stick upon me, if your Lordships but inquire what others have done and still continue to do that kind."

Tew's end is but vaguely recorded. "The History of the Pirates" says that on his last voyage to the Red Sea, presumably in the interest of his New York backers, he attacked one of the Mogul's ships, and "in the Engagement, a shot carried away the Rim of Tew's belly, who held his Bowels in his hands some small Space, when he dropped. It struck such a terror in his men that they suffered themselves to be taken without resistance."

The name prevailed on Long Island into the Revolution. There is record of a "James Tew" being taken from a privateer and held prisoner in England at Forton in 1778.

IV

OF HENRY EVERY

HENRY EVERY was the next personage to win distinction in the Indian Seas. The uncertainties about him are considerable, even as to his name. In the indictment of six of his followers who were tried at the Old Bailey on October 19, 1696, under a bill in which their captain shared, he is described as "Henry Every (alias Bridgman) not yet taken"—nor indeed was he ever. So far as traceable it is known that Every, more often described as "John Avery," was a mariner of Plymouth in Devon, that home-port of so many who have risen upon the sea, and Bridgman his real name. According to Captain Charles Johnson, his first biographer: "He made a great noise in the World, as *Meriveis* does now"— meaning 1723. Who or what "Meriveis" was in George the First's day, is not clear, but he or it must have been prodigiously noisy to have equaled the acclaim about Every. Not only were his deeds a stimulus to many, high and low, to leave honest ways and take to piracy or dealing in its by-products, but chapbooks were written and a play, "The Successful Pyrate," graced the boards of Drury Lane, and was issued in octavo by Bernard Lintot in 1713. Mr. Charles Johnson is called the author, not he of "The History of the Pirates," which followed, but another Charles Johnson, a dramatist of note. As late as 1720, nearly a quarter of a century after he had vanished from view, Defoe worked off one of his sham histories in "The King of the Pirates. Being an Account of the Famous Enterprises of Captain Avery, the Mock King of Madagascar," which purported to give an account of "His Rambles and Piracies" in "Two Letters from Himself, one written during his stay in Madagascar and one since his escape from thence." Unfortunately this volume is belied in the report of the trial of his companions and by other records. Defoe also built up his "Life, Adventures, and Piracies of the Famous Captain Singleton" on Every's career. It was also published in 1720, three years before Captain Johnson completed his history.

[38]

Every, like his father, who was reported to have been a captain in Cromwell's navy under Robert Blake, had led an active life on board ship from his youth up, serving in the Royal Navy on the *Resolution* and the *Edgar*. He also made several voyages to the West Indies as a merchant captain, but began his exploits as a rogue from an employment designed to catch the dishonest. He had advanced himself to an officer's rank from that of seaman and in 1693 was engaged as first mate on a London barque called the *Charles the Second*, Captain Charles Gibson, which together with a consort, the *James*, Captain Humphreys, had been leased by Sir James Houblon to the Spanish Government. It was the purpose of the latter to load both ships with goods and passengers for New Spain, and then employ them as *guarda costas* to stop the smuggling trade between the French islands of Martinique and Guadeloupe and the ports along the Spanish Main, a flourishing commerce which cost the state much revenue.

The two vessels proceeded to Corunna, or "the Groin," as it was termed in sea parlance, early in 1694, and lay there for three months awaiting passengers, cargo, and orders from the authorities, none of which came. Nor did the crews receive their pay, and having been in all eight months on board, were restless and discontented. The idleness and liquor had a bad effect on all, including the captain, who was on shore or ill in his cabin most of the time, leaving Every the intimate dealings with the crew. The stories were drifting in of pirate play in Madagascar, and Every began to plot with the crew to take the sloop and make a venture. Finding many willing hands, he extended his treason to the *James*, where sixteen men were found ready to take the risk. Arrangements were made therefore to seize the *Charles the Second*. The men from the *James* were given a hail, "Is the drunken boatswain on board?" when they were ready to embark, which was the signal for Every to act. On the 30th of May, 1694, they manned the longboat and pulled to the *Charles the Second*, on approaching which they made the agreed inquiry. Every welcomed them, and as they were boarding Captain Humphreys called out to say that his men were deserting. Every replied coolly that he knew that well enough and began preparations to make sail. The commotion of their coming brought David Creagh, the second officer, to the deck, from which he was promptly escorted back to his cabin. Captain Gibson, who was ill in his berth, was now made aware of the purpose and told he could remain and be captain if he cared to go along. He declined the offer and with others who were loyal was sent ashore. Every justified himself on parting with the remark: "I am a man of fortune and must seek my fortune." Gibson expressed his regret that so rash a step should be taken and his sorrow that he, who had always treated them well, should be so served. This had no effect and, as he left, the side anchors were raised and the vessel set in motion. As she began to move Captain Humphreys fired several guns from the *James,* but without effect. The captain of a well-armed ship from Holland in the harbor was offered a liberal reward if he would head off the runaways, but preferred, Dutch fashion, to mind his own business. The exit was therefore safely made. Every was well provided for. The ship was a stout vessel carrying forty guns, with fuses and ammunition, and besides had 15 tons of food on board.

The *Charles the Second* then steered for the Cape Verde group, going first to Boa Vista, where some salt was taken on and then to the Isle of May. Going in under English colors, they captured three unsuspecting British ships and robbed them of provisions and valuables. The pirates carried the Portuguese governor on board the *Charles the Second* and held him hostage while they did as they pleased in the harbor. They next made the Guinea Coast, where the negroes coming on board with gold dust to trade were seized and shackled in the hold, their gold being taken from them. The Isle of Princes was the next objective, where they made themselves agreeable to the Portuguese by a present of seven of their captive negroes and replenished their own treasury by plundering two Danish ships carrying forty pounds of gold dust and considerable merchandise. On Every's offering to return one of the ships to her master he declined, saying she was insured and he did not want her back. The vessel was then burned and the other was kept for a while as a consort. Touching next at Fernando Po they here cleaned the ship without molestation and went on to Cape Lopez, and thence to Anamabu. This was their last stop, for they now rounded the Cape of Good Hope and made the northwest end of Madagascar. Once at Madagascar Every took on water, and bought from the natives cattle which were slaughtered and salted for stores. They then sailed for Johanna, where their presence was made known at Bombay, in May, 1695. Three of the East India Company's ships had endeavored to take him, but were eluded, a report to the company reading:

"Your Honor's ships going into that island gave him chase but he was too nimble for them by much, having taken down a great deal of his upper works and made her exceeding snugg, which advantage having been added to her well sailing before, causes her to sail so hard now, that she fears not who follow her. This ship will undoubtedly (go) into the Red Sea, which will procure infinite clamours at Surat."

This report was made to Sir James Gayer, Governor at Bombay. With it came a letter from Every, left by him at Johanna as notice to his pursuers or any others who might choose to come after him. It was dated "February ye 28th 1695/4," and read:

"To all English commanders lett this Satisfye that I was Riding here att this Instant in ye ship fancy man of Warr formerly the Charles of ye Spanish Expedition who departed from Croniae (Corunna) ye 7th of May 94: Being and am now in A Ship of 46 guns 150 Men & bound to Seek our fortunes I have never as Yett Wronged any English or Dutch nor never Intend whilst I am Commander. Wherefore as I commonly speake wth all ships I Desire who ever Comes to ye perusal of this to take this signall that if you or aney whome you may informe are desirous to know w^t wee are att a Distance then make you Antient Vp in a Bale or Bundle and hoyst him att ye Mizon Pekk ye Mizon Being furled I shall answer wth ye same & Never Molest you: for my men are hungry stout and Resolute: should they Exceed my Desire I cannott help my selfe.

"As yett
An Englishman's friend.
Henry Every.

"Here is 160 french armed men now att Mohilla who waits for opportunity of getting aney ship, take Care of you selves."

The Frenchman of whom Every so thoughtfully gave warning were ashore from a grounded ship, news of which reaching three Indiamen putting in for water at Johanna, they proceeded to Mohilla, plundered and burned the stranded vessel and took six of the Frenchmen prisoners to Bombay. Every now became active. While at Johanna he took a native ship, rice laden, and after looting the cargo sunk the vessel. Departing, they cruised for a time near the line, but without result. Running short of water and supplies, they returned to Johanna and landed several of their sick on shore. On the second day, several sail of large East Indiamen hoving in sight, they made a hasty departure,

[41]

leaving the sick behind. The wind blowing off they went to Comoro and on the cruise took and sunk a small French vessel, returning once more to Johanna and taking on their sick. Going again to a place in Madagascar called Meat, they burned the town because the natives refused their trade. It was now decided to cruise off the Arabian Coast and look for some of the Mocha fleet about due. In this pursuit the pirates fell in with five English ships, bound on the same errand. Three of these, commanded by Captains Wake, Farrell, and May, were from New York. While lying in wait the entire Mocha fleet passed them in the night. A native ship caught in the morning told them what they had missed. In doubt whether or not to follow, a council was held which voted to pursue. One straggler was overtaken, which yielded between £30,000 and £40,000.

Sailing on until about ten leagues off Surat, they encountered a ship with towering masts, and so large that she was at first taken for a Dutch East Indiaman, whom it might not be wise to tackle, but she soon showed the Mogul's flag and proved to be the *Gunj Suwaie* or "Exceeding Treasure" bound from Surat with a number of rich Moslems en route for Mecca and bearing beside the Mogul's daughter and her suite. The *Gunj Suwaie* carried eighty guns and a crew of four hundred men armed with matchlocks, and was proceeding without convoy. She far outmatched the *Fancy*, but Every attacked with vigor. In replying a gun burst on the *Gunj Suwaie*, killing four men and spreading panic throughout the ship. Her captain Ibrahim Khan failed to make a stand when the pirates boarded, running below in terror. As they were far outnumbered, the rogues could have been beaten with ease, but no defense was made, and she was soon a prize.

It was upon this capture that the London romancers built their legends. The spoil was given as amounting to £4,000,000 and Every was credited with wedding the Princess and founding an empire in Madagascar. As a matter of fact the ship yielded 100,000 gold sequins each worth $2.25 and £100,000 in pieces of eight, with considerable jewelry. The Princess was not harmed, though the same cannot be said of her women, several of whom threw themselves in the sea; others ended their degradation with daggers. After a week's orgy the *Gunj Suwaie* was released to drift back to Surat, but the news of the outrage so inflamed the great Mogul that he threatened severe reprisals upon the English merchants and factors in his domain. He ordered his army to Bombay and put the sixty-four English in Surat

[42]

OF HENRY EVERY

and Broach in prison, where they were held for nearly a year clamped in irons. The company included Annesley, local president for the corporation, representing the Mogul at Bombay. Itimad Khan was reasonable and did nothing inimical there, being willing to believe Sir John Gayer's plea that Every's rogues were not all English who, in proof that other rascals abounded, gave him the six Frenchmen taken at Mohilla.

Every, in the interval, rounded the point of Bengal, landing at Rachapore, where he took on water and provisions, incidentally taking the *Rampura*, a Cambay trader, with a cargo of 1,700,000 rupees. By now the neighborhood was getting warm so he departed for Mauritius after a pause at Degorees, dividing the spoil on the way, the amount running from £1000 down to £500 per man. At Mauritius twenty-five Frenchmen and fourteen Danes were put ashore, besides a few of the English who did not wish to risk their necks further. It was determined to make for America, which was speedily done, stopping only at the Island of Ascension. There was doubt as to the safest procedure. Some were for going to New England and scattering. They knew, of course, that the "trade" was well regarded in New York, but because of their irregular departure from "the Groin" they were troubled with doubts. It was accordingly determined to put in at New Providence in the Bahamas and feel out the situation.

They reached the island without incident, arriving at a fortunate moment for themselves. Jones, the governor sent out by the Lords Proprietors, had goaded his subjects into revolt and was on the eve of losing his government when the pirates appeared in the offing. When Every sent a letter promising on behalf of the ship twenty pieces of eight and two of gold from each man and twice as much from the captain, for a permit to come in, the Governor responded with instant assent. He soon made an alliance with Every for the support of his forty guns and one hundred and twenty men against his rebellious subjects. The Governor's power was restored and he remained in control as long as the ship stayed. Every sailed after a time, evidently in the thought of reaching the mainland and scattering his crew, but, some doubts recurring, again returned to the island. He was just in time to rescue Jones once more. It was now difficult to keep on with the ship unless he resumed pirating, which the majority opposed. Every therefore decided to sell the vessel, representing her as a privateer whose fortune had not turned out well and whose owners asked

[43]

to dispose of her to the best advantage. A customer was soon found and the ship sold. Every then bought a sloop, changed his name back to Bridgman and, with such of the crew as did not care to remain in the Bahamas, made a coasting voyage along the American shore, landing a few here and there without arousing suspicion, coming last to Boston, according to Johnson's history

The latter tells a tale about landing at a North of Ireland port and dispersing, some going to Dublin, where eighteen are recorded as receiving pardons, the others vanishing save the luckless six who were somehow caught, possibly through a reward of £500 offered by the Government and one of 4,000 rupees by the Company. These were Joseph Dawson, Edward Forseith, William May, William Bishop, James Lewis, and John Sparkes. It is quite evident from the tone of the indictment that the zealous prosecution of these men was the outcome of Company John's promises to the Great Mogul. It observes: "Their last piracy was this in the Indies, the greatest in itself and like to be the most pernicious in its consequences, especially as to trade, considering the power of the Great Mogul and the natural inclination of the Indians to revenge." Curiously the men were acquitted on their first trial, October 19, 1696, by a sympathetic jury "contrary to the expectation of the Court" and were reindicted and put again in jeopardy on October 31st. This time the "expectation" of the Court was better realized. The six were found guilty and hanged at Execution Dock, London, on November 25, 1696.

Johnson says Every in his home-coming placed some jewels and gold with several merchants of Bristol to dispose of under secret promise and to return him cash; that he got but little and lived in poverty at Biddeford "without making any figure." Needing money, he went in person to Bristol, but met with a "shocking repulse," being threatened with exposure, which caused him to go over to Ireland, whence he sent another appeal, without effect. Being reduced to beggary, he resolved to return and face them. Taking passage to Plymouth on a trader, he walked thence to Biddeford, where he was taken ill and died, "not being worth as much as would buy him a coffin."

All this appears apocryphal, for there is no evidence at the trial of the six of any such home-coming. William May, testifying in his own defense, said he returned from Virginia in the first ship after reaching there from New Providence, landing at Bristol, where he lay sick five days, after which he took passage on the coach for London and was taken three miles from Bath by the king's messenger, having been betrayed by one in whom he had confided. It seems incredible that if Every had reached England in the manner described by Johnson he could have escaped detection, with all the hue and cry about his riches and his name. It would seem much more probable that he remained well-submerged in the colonies, or left the world after the manner of his kind. A reward of £100 placed upon his head was raised to £500, with no takers.

The scattering of Every's men caused much mention of him in the colonial records. Edward Randolph, who had been sent to America by King William as Surveyor-General to attend to the better administration of justice and affairs, writing to the Lords of Trade, April 26, 1698, observes: "Colonel Nicholson hearing of some of Every's men were in Philadelphia forthwith sent the Lords Justices Proclamation (for apprehending them) to Mr. Markham (the Deputy Governor), who instead of securing supported and encouraged them; two of the chief (Clinton and Lassell) were carried to Carolina from Philadelphia, by one Medlicott, another of Every's men and surgeon of his ship; another of them (one Clause, a cooper) lives now in Philadelphia. I have seen him almost every day on the streets, and James Brown, also one of the company is married to Mr. Markham's daughter." Plainly being a pirate was no bar to social position. Was Philadelphia even then "corrupt and contented?"

On July 6, 1698, the Governor-General, Richard Coote, Earl of Bellomont, wrote from New York to the Lords of the Admiralty: "I have seized two supposed Pirates of Every's crew, but having no directions to send them to England, and not having evidence to convict them here, I have been forced to admit one of them to bail, and the other is still confined, not having yet procured bail, which I could not deny them, being only on suspicion."

A letter from the Lords of Trade, dated June 9, 1698, to Bellomont advised him that Every's name had been joined with that of William Kidd as a person to be exempted from pardon, "which we suppose hath been or accordingly will be done."

These dates, so long after the London executions indicate therefore that "Every, alias Bridgman" had well vanished from the ken of man.

In the presentation of "The Successful Pyrate" at Drury Lane, in Queen Anne's time, Barton Booth, the first of that famous name to make his place as a tragedian on the boards, played Arviragus, King

UNDER THE BLACK FLAG

of Madagascar. Laurence, the pirate port, becomes Laurentia. "Arviragus" is portrayed as a hero of the Dutch War, cashiered for caning a fellow officer who refused to fight a duel with him—a "Briton" now a "Prince," whose country, "his friend, and his mistress" all "us'd him with the utmost ingratitude."

The "Prince" orders a division of the spoil, to each particular head, five thousand dollars, to be paid

> ". . . without delay or fee:
> Your Life fhall anfwer for a Doit detain'd
> From any private Man—
> I'll have no Greafie Drones of Civil Power,
> Fat with the Spoils of Widows, and of Orphans,
> Spunge like, to fuck the Blood of the poor Soldiers."

He adds:

> "Have they not rang'd the Globe to ferve my Caufe;
> With me they made a Circle round this World,
> Difclaim'd Relation, Country, Friendfhip, Fame,
> They toil'd, they bled, they burnt, they froze, they ftarv'd,
> Each Element, and all Mankind their Foe,
> Familiar to their Eyes faw horrid Death,
> In every Climate, and in every Shape,
> When, in this Ifle, our fhatter'd Barks found Reft,
> With Univerfal Voice they call'd me King.
> And when th' Oppreffor laughs, when Right and Wrong
> Intangled lye in Law; while Wealth is Judge,
> When Merit begs defpis'd; while Juftice fleeps,
> Or winks for Bribes, unpunifh'd, may I fall,
> Like fome o'erweening Tyrant, who believes
> Himfelf a Law, and Governs by his Luft."

The distribution of the dollars is followed by the drawing of lots for wives, which produces some natural complications, especially when one of the alloted ladies recognizes a former husband among the participants in the lottery. In this old play also appears a bit of philosophy usually attributed to the French, when Piracquo, whose vengeful pursuit of Arviragus is the motif of the play remarks:

"I can't forgive him because I have wrong'd him."

The recovery of a long-lost son closes the play, with Arviragus announcing the fact that his name was originally "Averio."

The Epilogue, spoken by Mr. Norris, observes in part:

> "The Poet stands, indicted, for that he
> Combin'd with a grand Thief, one Avery,
> Illegally feducing Half a Crown
> From ev'ry Lover of a Play in Town."

[46]

V

OF JOHN BOWEN

JOHN BOWEN was one of the early group who followed Misson to Madagascar. His career as a pirate is much intermingled with that of several other captains notable in this history, and like theirs came to him mainly by chance. While serving as a petty officer on an English ship in 1700, it was his fortune to be taken off the coast of Guinea by a French pirate, who had several English captains and minor officers on board, held from captures because of their ability. Soon after the brigantine *Marygold*, of Barbadoes, Thomas White, master, was added to the spoil. The *Marygold* being the better vessel, the pirates transferred themselves, their belongings, and the other captives to her, and, retaining White and his crew, burned their own craft.

The French company was quite without the usual grace of that nation and for amusement would at times stand an English prisoner against a cask and shoot at him as a target. A number were killed in this cold-blooded fashion. White, though not used as a mark, chanced to offend one of the rascals, who planned to kill him in the night, but of this he was warned by a friendly hand, who placed him between himself and the hull while sleeping so that the would-be assassin was thwarted in his design.

Leaving the Guinea coast the pirate doubled the Cape of Good Hope with the intent of reaching Madagascar, but had the fortune to be wrecked near Elesa on the south end of the great island. White and Bowen, with several other English merchant captains and seamen who were detained on board, had the address to seize the longboat and make their way safely ashore, paddling some fifteen leagues to St. Augustine. Here the King gave them a kindly welcome and they remained for a year and a half, subsisting on His Majesty's bounty. A pirate ship commanded by William Read came in, on which the King requested them to depart, or to transfer themselves by land to some other part of the island. This course being impossible, they went on board the pirate. Read had but forty men in his company and

[47]

was cruising along the coast looking for men. He was glad, therefore, to receive Bowen and his companions and would have also taken on some of the French but for the story of their barbarities to their prisoners. These, however, met with their deserts for misusing the natives. Half of them were killed and the others sent into slavery among the Malagasy.

Having now sixty men, Read cruised into the Persian Gulf where he took a native grab and, disgusted to find nothing but bales of cloth, threw them into the sea, though he learned later that one of these contained a hidden store of coin. Read fell ill, died, and was succeeded by one James. Escorting the grab, the company made the island of Mayotta. As the brigantine was in ill repair, her spars were taken out and the grab remodeled into a passable vessel. She also had the luck to secure here a twelve-oared boat that belonged to the *Ruby*, a wrecked East Indiaman. The grab and her company remained at Mayotta, where food was plenty and cheap during the next six months while the monsoon blew.

On the subsidence of this wind they returned to Madagascar, where as they approached the east end they encountered a small French sloop, also "from the sea," with which they made a joint partnership. She had long been a contraband trader, running slaves and pirate goods into Mauritius, incidentally taking on slaves, and returning with wines and brandy for the rovers, and was captured by her new holders, who had boarded her under pretense of buying supplies. George Booth was her present commander. Fourgette, the captain of the former trader, was also a pirate by turns, and had fought well to save his ship. He was put ashore with his papers and sufficient arms and ammunition to furnish security and supplies. The crew of the *Dolphin*, a wrecked pirate, were found here and taken along, swelling the company to eighty.

With this force they sailed to St. Mary's and there found a New York trader, which had been commanded by Captain Mosson, one of the people favored by Governor Fletcher, lying empty off the beach. She had been cut out and her crew captured by the natives at the instance of Otto Van Tuyl, another New Yorker who had come thither with the traders and set himself up with a native wife and a black following. He was later to pay for this exploit.

The adventurers took water casks and other essentials from this ship and proceeded to Methelage. Here they anchored in the river, cleaned and repaired their ships, and were about to start on a voyage to waylay the Mocha fleet of the great Mogul when they were surprised to see a large vessel standing in. She had the look of a man-o-war capable of carrying fifty guns, as indeed she had been in the French service. They therefore sent out boats to question the oncomer, but on the ship firing a gun fled to the shore, at which the crews of the grab and the brigantine became panicstricken and ran them for the beach. The grab struck a mangrove snag and sank. The brigantine made an easy grounding, so that she was later got off, when it was found their flight had been for nothing, the ship which caused the alarm being the *Speaker*, a slaver hunting for a cargo and not the least warlike in intent. Her captain was a young man, who felt much elated at having so easily driven two vessels ashore, though at the moment ignorant of their character, having an equal right to think that two merchantmen might have fled, taking him for a pirate. The captain celebrated his success by shooting several round of shot into the hulls of the stranded vessels and then sent a few to the land. This annoyed the native population, who informed the King with the result that, when the captain announced his desire to trade, his ebon Majesty would permit no trafficking.

The pirates then cleverly planned his undoing, perceiving that the *Speaker* was just the craft for them, and persuaded the King into believing that the firing on the land was all a mistake, growing out of the English method of salutation, the shot having been left in the guns by a careless gunner. The King thus appeased, the captain was influenced to send his purser ashore to proceed to the capital with presents for the potentate, consisting of some finely inlaid firearms. No sooner did the purser land than he was put under arrest by Tom Collins, a Welshman who pretended he was to be held in satisfaction for the two "merchantmen" whom his vessel had forced ashore. The poor purser denied he was at fault and placed the blame where it truly belonged, on the head of the rash young captain, but promised his aid in securing satisfaction. They accordingly allowed him to proceed to the King's town, agreeable to the understanding they had brought about. The King responded with gifts of cattle and rice and the slaver opened a market, at which the pirates were able to sound out the crew and to calculate the strength of the vessel, finding that they would have to deal with no more than forty hands. Good watch was kept and the guns were always loaded, but Hugh Man, one of the crew, agreed for £100 to wet the priming and so render the cannon harmless.

The captain of the *Speaker* was now lured ashore and treated with much consideration, being forgiven, apparently for his rudeness in chasing them into the mangroves. He was invited to a barbecue—the eating of an ox roasted whole in the ground—and after enjoying the novel and substantial meal he was told by John Bowen that he was a prisoner. Upon demanding the reason for his captivity he was informed very coolly that the company desired a ship and that his was suitable for their purposes, besides taking amends for the harm he had wrought them by forcing their vessels ashore and pounding them with round shot. His crew had been well filled with roast beef and punch and showed small concern when informed that they, too, were under duress, some answering: "Zounds! We don't trouble our heads what we are. Let's have another bowl of punch."

At eight o'clock the company manned the twelve-oared boat and filling it with men started out to take over the *Speaker*. Her captain called them to come back as he had a word to offer. George Booth asked what he had to say, which was, it appears, that they would not be able to take the ship. "Then," said Booth, "we will die alongside of her." He then advised them not to board on the starboard side, as a gun loaded with partridge shot commanded the deck from that point and would exterminate them. They thanked him for this considerate information and proceeded to the ship, where the mate was keeping vigilant guard. The ship's own boat was sent ahead and her crew instructed to use the watch-word "Coventry" which had been set for the night on behalf of those ashore who might return in the darkness. When hailed they gave this word, which the mate accepted, but soon seeing the twelve-oared boat following he called to know its mission. One answered that it was a raft with water, another that it was a boat with beef. These divergent replies roused the mate's suspicions. He at once raised the alarm of pirates and called his men to arms. They stood to the guns, but Hugh Man having wet the priming according to agreement, there was no response from the carronades and the watch was soon mastered without loss of life on either side.

The following day the brigantine was provisioned and given to the captain of the *Speaker,* with leave for him to depart with such of his hands as desired to keep him company. Among those who chose to go was the traitor Man, who had wetted the priming and made the

capture of the ship possible, the pirates keeping his secret. The
brigantine sailed to Johanna where her captain died, as much from
mortification as from fever. The *Speaker* was now made ready for sea
and moved to St. Augustine, where some seventy odd men from the
Alexander, Captain James, were added to the company, making in all
two hundred and forty men, including twenty black servitors. The
Alexander guns were also transferred to the *Speaker*, giving her fifty-
four in all.

It was now planned to make a raid on the Indian seas, but first the
Speaker touched at the Arabian settlement of Zanzibar for supplies.
Captain Booth went ashore with fourteen men to negotiate with the
Sultan, but once inside the walls of his palace they were cut down.
The alarm was at once given and others of the pirates who were on
shore made for the ship's longboat, lying at a grapple off the beach.
The boatkeepers, seeing their flying comrades, at once moved in and
while not more than six were armed they put up such a stout defense
that most were saved. The quartermaster, separated from the others,
fought his way to a canoe, sword in hand, and in her made the longboat, which had pulled away from the strand. The fort at Zanzibar
fired upon the ship, which returned the bombardment with interest.
Those who reached the longboat were safely taken aboard, but Captain
Booth and twenty men lost their lives. Pickering, the quartermaster,
who so bravely defended himself from the Arabs, was named for captain
but declined to serve and the choice fell on John Bowen, while
Pickering succeeded him as master. Samuel Herault, a Frenchman,
became quartermaster and Nathaniel North captain-quartermaster.

When the *Speaker* made the mouth of the Red Sea, thirteen sail hove
into sight, which were at first taken for a Portuguese convoy and as
such pretty certain to be well guarded by frigates. So the adventurers
held off. Bowen's apprehensions were not shared by many of the crew,
who sought to depose him in their desire to engage. Yielding to the
pressure the *Speaker* assailed the fleet, which it found to be Moorish,
and took the foremost, which gave up a treasure of £500 per man.
Two of her crew were killed in the action, but the pirates escaped all
harm. Night saved the other vessels.

Thus enriched, the *Speaker* now sailed for the Malabar coast, where
one of her first prizes was an English East Indiaman, commanded by
Captain Conway, taken near Callicoon, into which port she was openly
taken and sold in three shares, one being awarded to a local merchant,

another to a speculator from Porca, and the third to a Dutch trader named Malpa. Home-bound for Madagascar with their riches, the pirates by mischance ran the *Speaker* upon St. Thomas's reef at Mauritius so effectively that she was lost, but Bowen and most of his crew made the shore where the Dutch governor received them with great kindness, placing the sick in the hospital at the fort and entertaining at his own mansion. Three months were spent here recuperating under sunny circumstances when, determining to regain Madagascar, the company purchased a sloop and, converting her into a brigantine, sailed from Mauritius in March, 1701, not failing to show the governor substantial testimony for his hospitality in the form of a purse of 2,500 pieces of eight and all the salvage of their ship, in return for which his polite excellency provided them with all the needed stores for their short voyage, at the same time cordially inviting them to come again should they desire a place of refreshment after their next adventure.

Coming to Madagascar they settled at the place called Maratan, on a pleasant plain beside the river. Here they fortified the mouth of the river and built a stockade on the landside to protect themselves from native raids. Between the bastions they erected their town, this effort taking up the rest of the year of 1701. The plain work of sowing and reaping proving tedious, it was planned by the restless spirits to seek again a harvest on the sea.

The brigantine, now called the *Content*, was overhauled but before it was fit for service they were unexpectedly provided with a better vessel. The ship *Speedy Return*, Captain Drummond, belonging to the Scotch-African and East India Company, came to anchor in their harbor, having as consort a brigantine, which Drummond designed to fill with slaves to sell to the Portuguese cocoa planters in Africa. Drummond, with Andrew Wilke, his surgeon, and a number of men came on shore with no suspicion of the nest they had entered, whereupon Bowen with a party of bold fellows paddled out to the ship and seized her without resistance. The signal of their success brought forty or more of their followers on board, with whose aid the brigantine was at once captured, all being done without bloodshed. The brigantine was burned as useless and the ship refitted for cruising against commerce. The old brigantine brought from Mauritius was rigged up as a consort and the pair began their cruise. The first night out the brigantine ran on a ledge.

Unaware of her plight, Bowen continued his voyage heading for the Mascarenes, where he had expected to find the *Rook Galley,* Captain Honeycomb, her presence there having been reported by some of the *Speedy Return's* people. She had, however, gone and after provisioning Bowen steered for Mauritius where he again hoped to find the *Rook.* Instead, a number of ships were in the harbor at that port, and not feeling strong enough to tackle such a fleet which might contain some bulldogs, Bowen returned to Madagascar, first putting in to Port Dauphin and then proceeding to St. Augustine. Not long after their arrival the brigantine *Content,* which they had thought lost or a deserter came in. There was a joyous reunion, but a survey showed the *Content* to be worthless. A council was held the result of which was that she was condemned and burned, her crew taking quarters on the *Speedy Return.* They now came into contact with the band of adventurers under Thomas Howard, whose story follows.

Getting together at Mayotta during the Christmas holidays of 1702, the two companies concluded an agreement to operate together, neither at the time possessing sufficient force to attempt anything ambitious. They idled at this port waiting for a ship to come along, it being more convenient and about as certain as cruising. Early in March the East Indiaman *Pembroke* came in to fill her water casks and was attacked and taken, losing her first mate and one seaman in a vain defense. The prize was plundered, then released with all her crew save the carpenter and captain. The pirates next came to New Methelage, whence it was planned to cruise on the Indian coast, for which they had detained Captain Woolley, of the *Pembroke,* to be a forced pilot. A quarrel rose between the two pirate companies as to which he should travel with, and so intense became the feeling that it was proposed to settle the dispute by the simple process of knocking him on the head. Bowen interfered, saving the captain's life and permitting him to remain on Howard's ship, the *Prosperous,* where he had been since being taken prisoner. The *Speedy Return* was found weighted with barnacles and needing repairs. She accordingly put into St. Augustine to clean and rig.

It was arranged that the *Prosperous* should take in water and provisions and meet the other at Mayotta. The *Prosperous* came accordingly to that port but after waiting for Bowen, who did not appear, went off on to Johanna. The *Speedy Return,* having been delayed

[53]

by slow work and contrary winds, could not make Mayotta and also turned toward Johanna, to learn that the *Prosperous* had been there and gone. Bowen now tried for the Red Sea, but the wind, proving contrary was compelled to sail for Surat, where it was his fortune to fall in again with Howard. Four ships came into view but, on observing the pirates, shifted their course in pairs, one to the north, the other south. The rovers followed one to each two of the fugitives. Bowen pursuing to the south took the stoutest ship, which proved to be a richly laden Moor, of 700 tons bound from Mocha to Surat. She was taken into Rajapore and her cargo sold to local merchants. Though having but little native gold on board, she carried a fat treasure of £22,000 of English money which went speedily into the pockets of her captors.

The *Prosperous* followed her prey to the mouth of the River Surat and there overtook one of the ships, which she overwhelmed with a broadside. The prize yielded 84,000 sequins, of the value of about $2.50 each. Having helped themselves to coin and cargo they set the hapless Hindu loose without anchor or cable to gain a harbor as best she could.

The *Speedy Return* and the *Prosperous* were judged to be in unsafe condition, so their stores and valuables with both crews were transferred to the 700-ton trader and they were set on fire. The joint company numbered at muster one hundred and sixty-four able-bodied men, of whom forty-three were English, who were outnumbered by Frenchmen. The rest were Dutch, Swedes, and Danes. Seventy Lascars were added to do the drudgery for the pampered pirates, and the Moor, rechristened *Defiance,* sailed out of Rajapore late in October, 1703, heading for Malabar.

North of Cochin, pursuant to arrangements made with a Dutch trader, they fired a gun for a lighter to come off with supplies, but there was no response, whereupon the quartermaster went within hail of a town on the province and announced their wish to buy supplies. The trader was Malpa who has been mentioned before as liking to deal with pirates. He caused to be sent off a boat loaded with cattle and swine, not to mention other essentials. What is more, the amiable Malpa informed them that a ship called the *Rime* lay in Mud Bay, not far distant, whose cargo he would be glad to purchase should she be taken. The *Defiance* was now a trading center, being visited by many people who sought to buy her wares and to sell their own. She was deemed too deep to make the venture suggested by Malpa, who then offered to sell them a lighter craft more fit for the enterprise. This deal did not go through because of the attitude of one Punt, the Royal Dutch Company's agent at the factory, who denounced the proposed transaction as villainy and prevented the delivery of the ship. The attempt on the *Rime* was therefore abandoned and the ship sailed for Mauritius where a long season was spent in enjoyment of the spoil. The only incident on the way was the recapture of the unlucky *Pembroke*, which yielded a supply of sugar. Here Bowen died.

Out of the capture of the *Speedy Return* grew a strange and deplorable tragedy. Captain Drummond and the *Speedy Return* hailed from Leith. As they failed to return, there was naturally much interest in their whereabouts. There was much feeling in Scotland, growing out of the hard fate of the Scotch colony at Darien, and the Scotch trading company, which owned the *Speedy Return* was ready to join its countrymen in any anti-English demonstration, as its invasion of the India trade had been hampered by its well-established John Company rival. Coincidently a Scotch Indiaman, the *Annandale*, had been seized in the Downs at the instance of the English corporation, in a claim for an infringement of the monopoly in the East. Therefore, in July, 1704, when it happened that the East India ship *Worcester*, Captain Thomas Green, home-bound, was sent to the northward by strong southerly winds and instead of making London put into Leith to await a favorable wind, she was seized in reparation. Having come from the same region where the *Speedy Return* was last supposed to be, much question was raised as to her whereabouts, to which of course Captain Green could make no answer. His insistence that he had neither seen nor heard of such a ship, by the strange contrariness of the human mind, put him under suspicion, and when George Haines, a romancing member of his crew, in his cups, sought to impress a silly girl with his adventures by recounting mysteriously a fight he had witnessed between two unnamed ships, the gossips at once jumped to the conclusion that the affair had been between the *Worcester* and the *Speedy Return*, to the piratical destruction of the latter. This was heightened by the alleged utterance of the carpenter, Henry Keigle, in a quarrel with Andrew Robertson, the gunner's mate, in which he darkly hinted at some wickedness in which they had shared during the voyage. These things were enough to put Green and his men under arrest. The authorities then began putting on pressure

[55]

to produce evidence. Two half-caste Portuguese servants on the *Worcester* were frightened into a confession that confirmed the invented suspicion and as a result Captain Green and his men were placed on trial before a High Court of the Admiralty. It seems incredible that upon such flimsy evidence any case could have been made out, for behind it there was not one word of truth. Yet Green, his officers and men, to the number of fourteen in all, were found guilty and sentenced to be hanged on the sands at Leith, which sentence was carried out in all its unjust horror, save for Thomas Linstead, the supercargo, who was reprieved. John Reynolds, the second mate, it was shown could not have been on the ship at the time of the alleged piracy. He therefore escaped conviction. The captain, James Simpson, Henry Keigle and George Haines, the babbling sailor, were first hanged on the 4th of April, 1705. The others followed on April 11th and 18th.

Every effort was made by Captain Green's friends and employers to save the unfortunate men without avail. When Bowen and Howard put in at Mauritius, two of the *Speedy Return's* men who had been pressed, Israel Phipeny and Peter Freeland, hid themselves until she sailed and made their way to Portsmouth on board the *Roper* galley, reaching harbor in March, 1705, just before the executions. John Green, brother of the captain, learning of their coming, secured affidavits from them as to the true fate of the *Speedy Return* before the Mayor of Portland, and hastened with them to Scotland but was unable to secure any rehearing of the case. The dour Scotch had made up their minds to be revenged and so slaughtered the innocent by due process of law.

The fate of Captain Drummond of the *Speedy Return* is not without interest in completing this history. It is told in the narrative of Robert Drury, who, when a sixteen-year old boy, was wrecked in the Indiaman *Degrave*, Captain William Young, on Madagascar in 1701. Some of the survivors were hailed by a man calling himself "Sam," who was sent by the King to lure them into his hands. He had been, as he said, an unwilling pirate and escaping had been taken into the King's service and bespoke their good treatment. They accordingly followed him to the ruler's town and there found Drummond and Captain Stewart of the brigantine which had been his consort, with a number of the crew who had been released by Bowen and after some wandering were now held captives. Upon being joined by the *Degrave's* people, Drummond, being a bold and determined man, resolved to make his escape with such as were willing to risk the attempt, following a notice from the King that he planned to scatter the white men among his villages. To effect his purpose Drummond proposed seizing His Malagasy Majesty and forcing him to set them free. Going in a body to attend the morning audience held by the King, the white men suddenly seized his person and that of his son and his queen. They were bound and put under guard while the palace and arsenal were rifled. Plenty of arms were found and soon were needed, for the natives rallied and began an attack, wounding one man. At this Captain Young warned the King to call off his minions under pain of death, which he did. Guarding their royal captives, the handful of English, together with the Lascars, made for the Mandenia River, the boundary of the kingdom from which they were trying to escape. They were pursued but stood off their foes. The wounded man had to be abandoned and on the third day pursuit quickened so that, when within a mile of the river after a toilsome march, they were cut off. With them was a woman who had been saved from the *Degrave*. She was killed, as were many others. The survivors kept on in four divisions, one under each captain and one under John Bembo, son of the admiral, who had been second officer on the *Degrave*. They defended themselves gamely until their shot were expended, when a parley was called. The Malagasy demanded the return of the arms as well as the captives. To this Drummond demurred and in the night with Stewart and Bembo made his escape. Young, who remained behind, was killed as were all the whites except Drury, who was held captive, and the man called Sam. Drummond and his fellows reached Port Dauphin, where they roused the rival monarch into making a raid against their late prisoners' forces, in which the allies got the worst of it. The whites little bettered their condition by the change. Benbow, after four years of captivity, succeeded in getting home. Drummond was killed by the natives. No trace can be found of the fate of the others. Drury at the end of fifteen years fell in with some of the pirates who had settled on the island and, after varied adventures in their company, reached England and wrote his most interesting "Journal," first published in 1729 with some help it is to be suspected from Daniel Defoe.

VI

OF NATHANIEL NORTH

NATHANIEL NORTH was the son of a sawyer in Bermuda, who at the age of seventeen took to the sea from his native island, in the prosaic position of cook on board a sloop sailing to Barbadoes. She was Bermuda-built, the cedars of the island furnishing an admirable timber, with the design of being fitted out for a privateer, and was on her way to be delivered to her owners for the purpose when North became one of her crew. Reaching Barbadoes at a time when His Majesty's ships on the station were short of men, all the sloop's hands were impressed according to the unjust custom then and long prevalent in the British Navy, North and his companions being entered on board the man of war *Referee*. The master complained to the governor and secured the release of all his men save North, who, being but a lad, was not considered worth petitioning for. He accordingly remained with the *Referee*, which was assigned to Jamaica, on which station the boy found means to desert, transferring his talents to a sugar drogher, on which he sailed for two years, improving his seamanship until he was offered the post of master, which he declined. King William's war being well under way, he entered on a Jamaica privateer, which did some profitable cruising against the French. Each man had a fat share in the spoil in the shape of good hard dollars, which went as easily as it came. Money gone, he again joined a privateer, with continuing success, so much so that it became for a number of cruises his sole occupation. Tired at last, or the picking becoming poor, he shipped under Captain Reesby in a brigantine loaded for the Spanish main, a trade that smacked much of smuggling with a side line of privateering, and was deemed so profitable that men served on half wages, trusting in their shares to make much more than good. Ill luck followed this venture, however, for no prizes came in their way and the trading was interrupted by a Spanish *guarda costa*, of forty guns and a crew of three hundred and fifty Frenchmen, hired by Spain, with a French captain. When returning to Jamaica, off Bluefields they fell in with two French privateers, who failed to note the brigantine's teeth. Captain Reesby met them with such resolution that one hauled down its colors and the other took to its heels. Ten of Reesby's men were slain in the combat and seven wounded. These he put ashore at Bluefields with the best arrangements for their care and then took his brigantine into Port Royal.

Reesby rewarded his crew well and was especially partial to North, who was an able seaman and good swimmer beside being an expert at handling a canoe. He signed for a new voyage at $17 a month with no share. The brigantine now ran a cargo of slaves to the Spanish coast, three hundred in number, and these with the goods carried enabled them to trade with the Spanish profitably. Four months were spent in this business. Returning to Jamaica and content with his success, Reesby laid up and North once more took up privateering. This turned out well, but on getting ashore from the cruise he was impressed on the frigate *Mary*, which took a turn along the Spanish main, and on again reaching Jamaica fitted for England. Having no mind for more man-o-war's work, North endeavored to swim ashore, but was caught as he was poised on the cathead for the plunge and whipped at the gangway. This did not improve his love for the British navy and he contrived to make his escape, finding refuge on the privateer *Neptune*, a sloop commanded by Captain Lycence. He had been lieutenant on the *Referee*, whose captain, Moses, came with the sloop for "diversion," of which he soon found plenty, for encountering a French privateer off Hispaniola, a sharp engagement followed in which Moses was wounded and carried below. Lycence now ordered an effort to board, but the quartermaster at the helm made a mis-turn of the tiller so that the *Neptune* fell off instead of chasing and gave the Frenchmen a chance to send in a volley of small shot, which killed Lycence. Moses ordered North to take the helm and with his wound dressed took command. He at once laid the sloop on board, and in the conflict at close quarters the French captain was killed, upon which she yielded.

Ten of the *Neptune's* men lost their lives and twenty were wounded. The Frenchman had fifty killed and wounded. Brought into Jamaica the prize was identified as the Bristol-built *Crown*. Her owners claimed half her value in the prize count and were awarded a third, which included cargo. Moses, though a captain in the regular service, the

UNDER THE BLACK FLAG

Referee not being in order, made another try at privateering, taking North with him. At the end of this cruise Moses renewed his command of the *Referee*, but North, who was on shore was impressed by a gang from the *Assistance*. He appealed to Captain Moses, but the best that friend could do was to give him such high reference that he was "handsomely treated" and made one of the barge's crew, a mark of man-o'-war distinction.

He remained with the *Assistance* until she was ordered to England, when, fearing that a cold climate would not agree with him, he remained ashore in concealment until the frigate departed. More privateering followed, but two of the prizes were recaptures, and the suits brought by their English owners for their return cut down the profits, so North decided to sail no more under his country's colors but went into service with a Dutch trader working out of Curaçao to the Spanish shore. From this he was taken by a French privateer and though not ill-used ended his employment. A Spanish privateer next enlisted the adventurer, operating against French commerce as far up as the Newfoundland banks with some success. Putting into Rhode Island to dispose of the prizes, the captain of the privateer an Englishman named Lovering died, the ship was broken up, and an accounting sent to the owners.

One of the prizes, a Bristol-built boat called the *Pelican*, retaken from the French, was bought by the ship's company, who procured a commission to cruise to the southward for eighteen months, "for certain" with two years allowed in case of accident. The "commission" was evidently a very elastic affair, for the *Pelican* was equipped for a long voyage and stoutly armed. One defect, the fact that no iron hoops could be had, forced them to take casks bound with wood instead, which proved a bringer of ill fortune. The crew who were the owners selected the course to steer which was for the popular Madagascar route. The *Pelican* doubled the Cape of Good Hope in June, and in late July they watered and refreshed themselves at St. Augustine. Their design as now revealed was to rob the Moors, as all dark-faced people were called, whether Hindu or Arab. It now having come August it was deemed too late to carry out the program, by which it was proposed only to rob the heathen and return home with clear consciences and great wealth, within the time fixed by the commission. They therefore dropped down to Johanna.

Discovering there that their provisions were spoiling, they plotted kidnapping the King and holding him for ransom. This was stopped by the refusal of the master to navigate the *Pelican* along an unknown coast. Cruising further, a landing was made at Comoro and the town ransacked. It yielded only some checkered linen and a few silver chains. Proceeding to Mayotta they here found a marooned Frenchman who had been well kept by the King, whom they consulted about surprising and taking the town, to which the exile was averse, because of his good treatment. The company would not listen to his scruples and forced him to comply. Accordingly they surrounded the King's house and made him captive, though his son cut his way to freedom, which was only his for a brief moment, as he was afterwards shot. As a justification for this ribald act it was charged that the King had poisoned the crew of another ship which they made pretense was their consort, the whole being false, as there was no other vessel with them. The King was carried captive aboard the *Pelican*, while the members of his household were corralled in a temple under a guard of thirty-six men. The outrage aroused the natives, who came to His Majesty's rescue in great numbers, but the ship opened upon the naked mass with grape shot and dispersed it with great slaughter. The King now freed himself by paying a ransom in silver chains to the value of $1,000 and further swore allegiance to the rogues, who, to establish their excuse, exhorted from him a promise not to poison any more white men,

These performances occupied a fortnight, after which they sailed for St. Augustine, taking with them twenty of the natives as slaves. A sickness now afflicted the crew so fatal in its character as to take the lives of the master and thirteen men. When the others recovered it was determined to again put to sea, but an examination of the water casks showed the wooden hoops so worm-eaten and defective that the voyage could not be undertaken, until the carpenter went into the woods and found some lithe creepers with which he bound the casks. Rejoiced at this the crew made the carpenter captain and elected Nathaniel North quartermaster. The crew was recruited among the beach combers at St. Augustine up to one hundred and five men, all of whom were voted an equal share in what might be taken. The Red Sea was chosen as cruising ground.

Here they met Captain Culliford of the Mocha frigate, and another ship called the *Sallada*, commanded by one Shivers. To their hail from both came the same reply. "From the sea." They accordingly agreed to act together and share and share alike in all spoil for the period of two months to come. Ten days later a Moorish ship came into range and was first encountered by the *Sallada*. The Moor fired one broadside, killing two men on the *Sallada*, though two shots hulled her. She was promptly carried by boarding, despite the fact that her passengers and crew numbered a thousand. The money was taken on board the Mocha frigate where it was divided between the two crews, to the exclusion of those on the *Pelican*, and despite the agreement. Naturally there was much expostulating, especially as but for wood and water spared by the *Pelican* the Mocha frigate could not have kept upon the ground. To this they were roughly ordered to begone. The Pelicans replied that they would not go without a return of the wood and water they had spared. The quarrel was at length adjusted by a grant of $1,000 and some water from the Moor, with word to buy wood where they could.

After this gross act of bad faith the two sailed for Malabar, where the provisions were put on shore, Culliford and the other knaves returning to St. Augustine, where a division of the plunder took place. There were three hundred and fifty pirates in the two crews, each of whom received a thousand pounds per man in silver and gold, beside a share in the goods. The *Pelican* remained in the Red Sea, where she overhauled one unsuspecting Moor and fired into her with small arms, killing several. Just as their prey seemed within grasp, the Moor set his studding sails and catching a little of the light air moved in time to escape being lashed to the *Pelican*. The latter tried to ram the Moor's stern and so disable the rudder, but the wind still favored and she got safely out of reach.

Maddened by this ill luck, the company became of a disordered mind and of differing purposes, all cursing the ship as a slow sailer and others urging that she be taken to Madagascar and broken up. They cooled off shortly, however, and determined to cruise off Malabar, where in a little time three of the Mogul's ships were taken, one of which yielded $6,000. The second, equipped with twenty-six guns was renamed the *Dolphin* to replace the *Pelican*, which was set adrift, while the third they sold for $18,000. Heading for Madagascar they were well nigh wrecked in a hurricane near Mauritius, losing all their masts. By working under jury rig they reached St. Mary's. Here they found Culliford and Shivers with their prize and a number of ships from New York trading with them, one being the *Pembroke*, commanded by Samuel Burgess and owned by Frederick Philipse, both of whom will be heard from again. The captain of the *Dolphin* —the unnamed carpenter—and some of the men "being weary of this life" returned to New York with the traders, the crew selecting Samuel Inless, a pirate residing at St. Mary's, as commander in his stead. They once more made for Malacca and took a few prizes of little value. North was given command of one of the captures and, having with him the Moorish owner of another, secured from him a pilot's chart which enabled him to make a small island near the Dutch possessions for water, in return for which valuable information he secured the release of the Moor's vessel. Nicobar was the next region scoured. Here a Danish ship was despoiled and taken to Madagascar, where they divided between three and four hundred pounds per man.

Three English frigates, the *Anglesea*, the *Hastings*, and the *Lizard* now appearing off St. Mary's, the *Dolphin* was hauled up so high and dry that she could not be floated again and burned. The men-of-war came, however, with lenient intent, Captain Littleton of the *Anglesea*, the Acting Commodore, bearing the King's pardon for all pirates who might care to retire from the profession. Culliford and Shivers at once took advantage of the clemency and returned to the world by the merchant ships. North, though accepting, did so with misgivings, as the date was past that covered by the pardon which would have included the *Dolphin's* men. He accordingly took her long boat and, with some other doubtful ones, endeavored to reach the mainland of Madagascar. They were upset in a squall and all were lost save North and a negro slave woman, whom he placed on the bottom of the boat. North himself swam four leagues to the land, arriving stark naked, the negroes taking him for the devil when he emerged from the sea. One woman more courageous than the rest gave him half of her petticoat to cover his limbs and with a male companion whom she reassured assisted him to a white settlement sixteen miles distant. Here he was clothed and cared for until well recovered, when he attached himself to the court of a native prince, where he remained for a year. North then served with Fougerre, Booth, Bowen, and Howard, with corresponding adventures in the Red Sea, narrowly missing wreck in the Gulf of Persia on one voyage. The death of Bowen at Mauritius, before noted, caused the promotion of North to his position, for which he was uncommonly well trained, few men on the station having had a more venturesome experience or being better fitted for the sea. He was installed after the manner of the pirates with much ceremony, thus:

[63]

"The Ceremony of this Instalation is, the Crew having made choice of him to Command, either by an unanimous Consent, or by a Majority of Suffrages, they carry him a Sword in a very solemn Manner, make him some Complements, and desire he will take upon him the Command, as he is the most capable among them. That he will take Possession of the great Cabin; and, on his accepting the Office, he is led into the Cabin in State, and placed at a Table, where only one Chair is set at the upper End, and one at the lower End of the Table for the Company's Quarter-Master. The Captain and he being placed, the latter succinctly tells him, that the Company having Experience of his Conduct and Courage, do him the Honour to elect him for their Head, not doubting his behaving himself with his usual Bravery, and doing every Thing which may conduce to the publick Good; in Confidence of which, he, in the Name of the Company, promised to obey all his lawful Commands, and declared him Captain. Then the Quarter-Master takes up the Sword, which he had before presented him, and he had returned, puts it into his Hand, and says, 'This is the Commission under which you are to act, may you prove fortunate to your self and us.' The Guns are then fired, round shot and all; he is saluted with three Chears; the Ceremony is ended with an Invitation from the Captain to such as he thinks fit to have dine with him, and a large Bowl of Punch is ordered to every Mess."

North, with his new command, leaving Mauritius steered for Madagascar and touching near Cape Dolphin for water and supplies, was forced to sail by the rising wind, leaving fifty men behind. He kept on to the east side of the island, putting in at Ambonavoula where some of the cargo was landed and a settlement effected, houses being erected for their better comfort. The Moorish prisoners were kept on the ship, though their boatswains were quietly advised by North to slip away in the night, which they did to the surprise of the company. North kept his own counsel, observing that if the ship was gone the fault lay with themselves for keeping so poor a guard. He suggested patience and gradually brought them to his mind, which was to forsake piracy and become honest settlers. Much land was cleared and tilled and many cattle raised, the settlement thriving in this estate for five years. North ruled the colony and, taking sides with a neighboring prince, was active in the native wars and equally so in making peace. An occasional pirate made a call, notably Halsey. North having no great longing for the old trade but being in need of clothes and funds, joined Halsey for a voyage as quartermaster, while some of the others went along as gentlemen adventurers, going into the Red Sea, where North took over Halsey's brigantine. Getting back to Madagascar, North laid up his vessel now old and worm-eaten. He took up residence with the King of Maratan, who alternately caressed and bullied him, North making peace by paying His Majesty 100 sequins for having persuaded the King's sister "to pass her solitary hours with him," this conduct being judged too free for royalty. He lived here a year when, with his companions, he built a fifteen-ton sloop, voyaging in it to Manangaro, thirty leagues to the northward, where with the help of another pirate settler they moved their effects to Ambonavoula. For the rest of his life North remained in Madagascar accumulating property, influence, and a family. He made an occasional slaving trip to Johanna and traded with Mauritius, all going pretty well, until, mixing in one of the frequent native quarrels, he was seized and murdered by the agents of one faction. Few careers were more extraordinary than this of Nathaniel North.

VII

OF JOHN HALSEY

JOHN HALSEY is described as having been a "Boston man of New England," commissioned to cruise against the French, as captain of the brigantine *Charles*. He raided the fishing banks of Newfoundland and there captured a fisherman from Brest and, putting a prize crew aboard, designed to meet her at Fayal in the Azores. When the prize failed to appear he dropped down to the Canaries, pillaging and sinking a Spanish Barcelona en route. Pausing at the Cape Verde Islands, he put his lieutenant ashore, evidently as the result of a disagreement. Several of the crew took advantage of the stay to decamp, but were returned by the Portuguese governor, Halsey's commission enabling him to make an orderly demand on the authorities. The lure of Madagascar now operating, Halsey stood away for the Cape of Good Hope and made for the island, putting in at the Bay of Augustine for wood and water and here picking up a few castaway seamen from the *Degrave*, the lost Indiaman commanded by Captain Young.

From Augustine he turned toward the Red Sea, falling in on the way with a Dutch ship of sixty guns, outbound from Mocha, whose company he kept for a week. Though planning piracy, Halsey had determined at the beginning to take only "Moorish" ships. This did not content his crew, who insisted upon attacking the Dutchman. Upon Halsey's refusal, both he and the gunner who wished no harm to European vessels were deprived of office and placed in confinement, while the crew manœuvered to board the Hollander. The latter, aroused by the suspicious action of his neighbor, fired a shot, which unstripped a swivel gun on board the *Charles,* grazed the man at the wheel and smashed the toprail. The quality of this reception dismayed the amateurs, who sheered off. Some hid hurriedly in the hold, to the disgust of the surgeon, who, though opposed to piracy, could not forbear "pricking" the cowards with his sword.

The officers were now reinstated, and the *Charles* sailed for the Nicobar Islands. The *Buffalo,* a "Moorish" ship, commanded, however,

OF JOHN HALSEY

by Captain Buckley, an Englishman, with two of his countrymen as
mates, was taken, the ownership being sufficient justification for the act.
The *Buffalo* was bound for Achin, well-laden with butter, rice, and
cloth, all of which was handy spoil. The two mates were "forced,"
but the captain and the "Moors" were left in their ship at Nicobar,
while the *Charles* took a further turn at sea, where she picked up a
country sloop bound also for Achin, with Captain Collins and two
English mates in charge, the crew being Lascars. She was taken into
Nicobar to join the *Buffalo*, to find that Captain Buckley had died
during their absence.

Neither prize had yielded any money or treasure and as a result a
dispute arose, some of the company desiring to return to the West Indies, others to adventure further in the Indian Ocean. The disaffected
seized the sloop and making one Rowe captain and a Frenchman named
Myers, who had joined at Madagascar, master, made for that island.
Buckley's two mates, who had been forced, were allowed to depart for
the mainland in a canoe, while Halsey and the others in the *Charles*
steered to the Straits of Malacca, intending to lie in the way of ships
bound for Manila, which usually carried treasure in their cargoes.
One European-built craft came into sight, but as she bore thirty-six
guns the company lacked the courage to attack, fearing her to be another Dutchman, such as had scared them en route to the Red Sea.

They next chased a large ship, which proved to be a well-armed Indiaman, the *Albemarle*, and at once fired up on the brigantine. The
Charles turned tail and fled, the *Albemarle* following, but the brigantine
proved fleet enough to get away. Water being low and food scarce,
and the luckless lot not daring to land at Malacca for fear of being
seized by the Dutch, it was determined by vote to return to Madagascar. They put in at Mauritius, where the governor, not being squeamish, allowed them to secure the needed supplies in return for a small
present. Sailing from Mauritius they now made a port in Madagascar,
called Hopeful Point by the pirates, or "Harangby" by the natives, not
far from St. Mary's Isle. Here they met their late companions in the
Buffalo and the *Dorothy*, a prize that had been taken by Captain
Thomas White, a talented member of the profession, who had built up
a considerable community, as related in his part of this history. The
Charles was repaired and provisioned and her crew recruited up to one
hundred men and then she headed once more for the Red Sea. They
halted at Johanna and took on some live goats and coconuts in the

way of fresh provisions and eleven days thereafter reached the straits of Bab el Mandeb. Lying here, they had but a short wait before twenty-five of the Mogul's fleet, sailing for Mocha, came into view. Hopes were high for some rich captures, but it falling a dead calm, the "Moors," by using their oars got safely away and the *Charles* for lack of wind was unable to follow. A petty prize in the form of a grab from Mocha was taken a few days later. She had a cargo of drugs and some two thousand dollars, the first real money taken since the venture began.

Three days later four English ships came within view and ill luck having banished all scruples it was determined to attack. Night was near but the pirate kept close to the others, each blowing a trumpet through the night to keep apprised of their several whereabouts and avoid collision. In the morning the English captains, suspicious of their neighbor, fell in line to receive him, and hailed: "Who are you and where from?" To which the only answer was: "From the sea." With this reply the brigantine sheered off, at which one of the ship-masters, deeming her in flight, urged Captain Jago, who commanded the vessel nearest in the line and carried twenty-four guns and seventy-six men to pursue. His mate, who knew it was but an attempt to lure one of the vessels out of the keeping of the others, advised against it. Just then the pirate, turning, singled out the *Rising Eagle*, a ship of sixteen guns as her prey, she being farthest astern. Her master, Captain Chamberlain, put up a hard fight for three quarters of an hour, boarding the pirate. In the conflict his first mate and several of the crew were killed and the purser, wounded, leaped into the sea and was drowned. Captain Jago, under the urging of the others coming somewhat gingerly to the rescue, was raked by a roundshot, fore and aft, and needing no more of this sharp medicine took to his heels, though especially equipped to fight pirates. The two others also abandoned their consort and the *Rising Eagle* became a prize. Although the crew had cried for quarter and the fight was supposed over, the second mate, firing from the forecastle, avenged his chief by killing two of the *Charles's* men, one of whom was the gunner's mate. It was proposed to kill him at once, but "several Irish and Scotch" together with one Thomas White who had once been a pirate captain, interposed and his life was saved. The belligerent second officer, it appears, was an Irishman.

From prisoners on the *Rising Eagle* the pirates learned that one of the fleeing vessels, the *Essex*, carried some treasure. She was pursued and surrendered at the firing of a single gun, though well manned to resist boarding. The two others were passed in the pursuit and were so timid that men stood by to lower the colors if assailed. The captain bore the rather appropriate name of Thomas Punt, and knew Nathaniel North, quartermaster of the *Charles*. As a result of this acquaintance Punt was civilly treated, as were his passengers, several English gentlemen. The *Essex* had £40,000 in coin aboard and £10,-000 was found on the *Rising Eagle*. The former was allowed to proceed, but the latter was taken back to Madagascar. Here the cash was divided and a period of life on shore enjoyed, during which some of the *Essex's* passengers came in a small sloop called the *Greyhound*, from India, seeking to buy back the goods that had been taken. They loaded the sloop with necessaries, thinking these would be in demand and that the trade would not end so badly for themselves. They were received amiably and their purpose promised to turn out fortuitously.

While this was going on, a Scotch ship called the *Neptune* came into St. Mary's Isle, expecting to procure a cargo of slaves to market among the Dutch planters of Batavia. She was a strong vessel with twenty-six guns and a crew of fifty-four men, James Miller, captain. He had a good cargo of wines and other luxuries on his ship and struck up a rich trade with the pirates, thus competing with the Madras merchants, who, much miffed at the outcome, covertly suggested that the Governor of Madras would be well pleased if they seized the slaver, to which the reply was made that if the men got started they might not stop with the *Neptune*. At this juncture a tremendous hurricane blew, in which the slaver was dismasted and the pirate ships wrecked. Being without vessels, the rogues now conspired with Samuel Burgess, mate of the *Neptune* to seize and re-equip her for their own purposes. This was accordingly done. While she was fitting, Halsey, who appears to have had no part in the disorderly proceedings, died of fever. He was buried with much ceremony to the rites of the Church of England. The colors were draped at half mast and Halsey's sword and pistols lay on his coffin.

With the captain's death all restraint vanished. The *Greyhound* had escaped the storm but, manning the *Neptune's* pinnace, they took her at anchor and restored to themselves all the money and goods they had given the merchants in return for their wares. Putting two hogsheads of brandy and ten pipes of Madeira on board the *Greyhound*, they turned her over to Captain Miller and his second mate and boat-swain and ordered them to sea. The rest of the *Neptune's* crew they detained as likely recruits, but most of them died from drink and fever.

The refitting of the *Neptune* with the few materials at hand and the desultory sort of labor provided by the dissolute men took nearly a year, and when it was about done, another hurricane blew and she was completely wrecked. The company never found another ship, but scattered or died on the island. Thus ends the tale of Captain Halsey and his crew.

VIII

OF SAMUEL BURGESS

SAMUEL BURGESS was one of those rarities, a born New Yorker who achieved distinction. Well educated, he took a turn at privateering against the French in the West Indies during King William's war. He held an elastic view of his commission and was in a way guilty of piratical acts because of this practice, which was overlooked in the easy days of Benjamin Fletcher's governorship of the Colony. The excuse for privateering ending with the war, Burgess became mate on one of the ships of Frederick Philipse, the New York merchant who sent a number of vessels to Madagascar engaged in the very profitable trade with the pirates centered there. On one voyage the ship was lost and Burgess had to remain eighteen months on the island, until compelled to leave on board an English pirate at the behest of the king, who wearied of entertaining the shipwrecked crew. They were quite content to remain in happy, well-fed idleness, but His Majesty would have none of it and they had either to leave or starve. The name of the captain who carried them off is not given, but they made a successful cruise in his company. Returning to America they sold their illicit wares to traders along the Spanish Main and then made for New York, clearing their characters by purposely losing the ship on Sandy Hook, after carefully landing the cash.

Burgess now married a relative of his employer, Frederick Philipse, who built another ship called the *Pembroke* and sent her under Burgess to Madagascar. He paused at Delagoa on the African coast and picked up some ivory, proceeding thence to St. Augustine. Here he found some of his former companions with whom he trafficked hospitably and then proceeded to Methelage, where more trading was done with pirates. Cruising around the island to St. Mary's he found some more acquaintances, with money to spend and slaves to offer. A number took passage with him to New York, where he returned without fear and without reproach, the voyage netting a clear profit of £5,000. These ventures of Burgess and Philipse turn up frequently in the cor-

[71]

respondence of the Earl of Bellomont, Governor of New York and Captain Kidd's partner, with the Lords of Trade, notably on one instance under date of July 22, 1699:

"When Frederick Philipse's ship and the other two come from Madagascar (which are expected every day) New York will abound in gold. 'Tis the most beneficial trade that to Madagascar, with the pirates, that was ever heard of, and I believe there's more got that way than by turning pirates and robbing. I am told this Shelly (Giles, one of the trading captains) sold rum, which cost but two shillings per gallon at New York for fifty shillings and three pounds per gallon at Madagascar, and a pipe of Madeira wine, which cost him £19 was sold there for £300. Strong liquors and gun-powder and ball are the commodities that go off there to the best advantage, and those four ships last summer carried thither great quantities of those things."

Philipse had a clever plan for evading the scrutiny of his cargoes. He owned a sloop, the *Frederick*, of which Humphrey Perkings was master, in which his son Adolph met the incoming barks from Madagascar, off New York, out of sight of land, taking on the pirate goods and letting the ship come in with nothing on board but slaves. On one occasion Adolph came back with the slaves, while the sloop under "one Jay, a Frenchman," proceeded across the Atlantic and around Scotland to Hamburg, where Sir Paul Ricaut, His Majesty's resident, seized her and sent the men back to New York, who there made known under oath the contraband nature of the cargo, without seeming to destroy the status of Philipse as a leading citizen. "One Jay" would appear to have been the forefather of the celebrated John, who made our first treaty with England and founded the distinguished New York family of that name.

Philipse, highly pleased with this success, allowed Burgess to pick his own cargo for the return trip and he selected mainly wines and liquors, which were safely landed at the pirate ports on Madagascar and brought a net return of £10,000 beside 300 slaves, who afforded a return cargo. A third voyage was equally profitable and was made in company with a consort under the same ownership. Both cargoes were favorably disposed of and a passenger list of some twenty ex-pirates was filled, these gentlemen having graciously accepted Commodore Littleton's pardon.

When they stopped at the Cape of Good Hope the captain of the

OF SAMUEL BURGESS

Loyal Cook, an East Indiaman, seized Burgess and his ship and took them to Madras in fair revenge for much that his company had suffered at the hands of the Red Sea men. The Governor of Madras, however, declined to countenance the seizure. While the passengers had accepted Littleton's pardon, some were not sure it would avail in Madras and accordingly escaped while at the Cape with Dutch connivance. Those who remained with the ship were kept in irons at Madras and died in prison. One of the scamps who escaped at the Cape had £1,700 in his chest, of which a comrade on shore held the key. When seeking to leave he would not break the chest, saying it was a pity to spoil a new lock and so left his cash to the captain of the Indiaman.

Philipse, learning of the capture of his vessel promptly sued the East India Company and won! Burgess was brought to London on the *Loyal Cook* and set at liberty. The captain, finding himself responsible for his conduct in seizing the ship, disappeared, but the company made good her value. Burgess in the meantime fell victim to the meanness of an old customer, Captain Culliford who had been jailed in London. He was tried and acquitted of piracy but was beggared by the costs. Culliford now swore a charge of pirating against Burgess, who was tried and found guilty. Philipse stood by him with money and influence and, succeeding in securing the interest of the Bishops of London and Canterbury, managed to have him pardoned by Queen Mary.

After this narrow escape Burgess made a voyage to the South Seas as lieutenant on a privateer, returning from which he lived a year in London. He then went out once more to Madagascar as mate of the *Neptune,* which ship was seized by Captain Halsey, as narrated in his life and whom Burgess joined. Following the death of Halsey Burgess became administrator of his estate, enjoying beside a considerable bequest of his own. This caused such dissatisfaction among Halsey's old followers that they took away £3,000 of the bequest and £1,200 of Burgess's own money, which had fallen to his share during the cruise. Yet, such was the fickle character of the company, that they now turned about and voted to make Burgess captain of the *Rising Eagle,* a Scotch ship taken by Halsey on his last cruise. While she was being fitted up, the company again became suspicious, quite justly, as Burgess fully intended to run away with her, and he was deposed. He succeeded, however, in persuading his old comrades

[73]

to give him back his money. He lived for five months at St. Mary's when, his house being destroyed by fire, he sailed with David Williams to Methelage and there lived with the king, who permitted him to share in that captain's property after his death. Burgess took to slave trading.

There now came to Methelage a sloop under Nathaniel North, manned by thirty men who had been with Burgess on Captain Miller's ship, who declared Burgess had made them turn pirates and demanded that he be plundered in revenge. North would not assent, whereupon the men seized him and kept him under guard, while they stripped Burgess of his money. Then, releasing North, they gave him £300 as his share and departed. But on North's return to Methelage he gave Burgess back his £300.

Burgess continued to reside for several years at Methelage, when his routine was interrupted by another rare adventure. Some eighty Dutchmen were set ashore from two Frenchmen, who had taken their ship belonging to the Dutch East India Company. Shortness of provisions caused them to release the captives, who were all seamen. The officers were carried to Johanna and there released. They then built a vessel and returned to Methelage after their men. Burgess proving of some considerable service they took him along, putting in at another port to rescue some other Dutchmen there marooned, but were next wrecked at a place called Youngoul. Burgess, again stranded, lived here a year and a half. The king, an uncle of the ruler of Methelage, then kindly sent him back to that port, where he remained for five years, during which a serious sickness deprived him of the sight of one eye. The *Drake,* a London slaver, came in at the end of the term and engaged to take Burgess home. Just then another slaver, the *Henry,* under the same ownership, came in and Harvey, her captain, being a stranger to the trade, asked his transfer, to which the commander of the *Drake* assented. Burgess accepted, with the understanding that he would be given a command in the West Indies, where the slaves were to be delivered. Harvey carried "a high hand" and fell into such disgrace with the King that nine months passed without securing a cargo. Harvey then sent Burgess to the King with his complaint, which his Madagascar Majesty much resented, coming as it did from the lips of one who had so long shared his bounty, and took him severely to task. Dining after the rebuke with some of the chiefs, Burgess drank copiously of native beer, which his friends believed to have been poisoned, for he was soon seized with an illness and died. Strange as it may seem, the honest chief mate of the *Henry* secured his property in cash and brought it intact to his wife and children in New York, from whom he had been so long separated.

Philipse, Burgess's employer, was a famous figure in the New York of colonial days and its richest merchant. He began life in Manhattan as a carpenter, but perceiving its commercial possibilities took early to trade, gaining privileges from the Government, first from Peter Stuyvesant, and continuing to enjoy favors from "the Hot Head's" English successors. For twenty years he was a member of the council, ending his term with the coming of Bellomont, in tacit acknowledgment of his relations with the Red Sea trade. The Philipse Manor House at Yonkers, N. Y., now the City Hall, was his creation and he was one of the builders of the Dutch church at Sleepy Hollow, in which he is buried. A fair descendant, Mary Philipse, was credited with warming the heart of no less personage than George Washington before he was captured by the Widow Custis.

IX

OF WILLIAM KIDD

AS the curate wrote of Henry the Eighth, that his last years were clouded with domestic infelicities, so it might be said of Captain William Kidd that he was unfortunate in business, having acquired his reputation as a pirate through untoward circumstances. A mariner of Greenock, Scotland, he came to America and served with much merit combating French privateers in the West Indies during King William's War. So pleased with his prowess were the planters and merchants of Antigua that they gave him a stout bark named after their island, with which he traded out from New York, where he became in the late years of the seventeenth century a citizen of importance who took part in local politics and was looked upon with favor by many persons of consequence.

New York in 1690, being the center of the Madagascar trade, it occurred to Kidd that instead of trading with pirates it might be more profitable to despoil them, and with this end in view he enlisted the support of Richard Coote, Earl of Bellomont, Governor General of the Colonies and Robert Livingston, a very enterprising young Scotsman, who had settled in the city and became founder of a long and eminent American line. Endorsed by the former, and accompanied by the latter, he visited London and there formed a close corporation which furnished the funds to carry out his design. Included in the affair were the Earl of Orford, Sir Edmund Harrison, the Earl of Romney, Somers, the Lord Chancellor and the Duke of Shrewsbury, beside Livingston, Bellomont and others, while King William was to receive one tenth of any proceeds as foster-father of the expedition.

The *Adventure Galley*, newly built at Deptford, was secured for the voyage, sent to sea in April, 1696, and reached New York in June. On the way over a luckless Frenchman was captured, as a bit of practice, and one-tenth of its value went in due course to His Majesty, the King. There was long delay in New York in filling the crew, for the prospects had become less alluring, fewer cargoes coming from the

East, where the Mozambique Channel and the Arabian Coast were being better guarded by British, Dutch and Portuguese men-of-war. But finally the *Adventure* got away in September and headed for the Indies. The long voyage across the Atlantic and around the Cape of Good Hope tried the temper of the crew, on the whole little better than the pirates of whose treasures they were in search. Kidd had two commissions from the excellent King William, one a letter of marque against French shipping, and the other to take pirates, some of whom, notably Thomas Tew, heretofore mentioned, were named in the paper authorizing him to seize them and their vessels wherever found. As the whole enterprise was speculative, the crew was without wages, save as they should share in prize money. Quite naturally, after passing the Cape, these gentlemen kept their eyes skinned for spoil. Kidd and Livingston alone underwrote the *Adventure*, agreeing to pay all outgo not met by results of the experiment. Should 100,000 pounds be secured, Captain Kidd was to have the *Adventure Galley* given him as a bonus. Everything therefore depended upon catching either Frenchmen or pirates.

After passing the Cape they sailed for a week in company with five British men-of-war, under Commodore Warren, society which would hardly have been selected had Kidd been a-pirating bound. Warren went on to Calicut, while Kidd steered for Madagascar to search out a rendezvous affected by gentlemen of easy fortune. None were to be seen. He therefore sailed for Johanna and there found four English East Indiamen with whom he exchanged greetings, and departed for Mohilla, where he beached the ship and scraped off the barnacles. His crew must have been in sorry shape, for fifty of them died within a week— probably of cholera. Kidd therefore made sail as soon as possible and concluded to cruise off the Red Sea, hoping for prizes. They had been out now a full year and had not laid eyes upon a pirate or any vessel other than British. The *Adventure* leaked and the men were miserable, having had no money or excitement.

On August 14th, the Mocha fleet came into view and taking Kidd for a pirate, opened fire on him. This was unfortunately returned in a hot moment and the fact was used against him later. Nothing further happened, however, and the *Adventure* worked back to Malabar. He held up, but did not plunder, a small Armenian vessel, and stood off a Portuguese warship which attacked him. A Dutch ship crossing their path caused a semi-mutiny led by the gunner, William Moore, who insisted that she be taken. Kidd was strong enough to keep the upper hand. In a quarrel that followed, Kidd struck Moore with a bucket and killed him. It was for this murder, and not for piracy, that he was subsequently sentenced to death.

A Moorish ship under French passes gave some small returns, which kept the crew quiet until February 5, 1688, when another vessel, well laden, the *Quedagh Merchant*, owned by Armenians, became their prey. She, too, had French passes, which gave excuse for holding her. The *Adventure* guarded her to Madagascar, where the *Adventure* sank, while most of the men joined a pirate and sailed away. Kidd and his few remaining companions boarded the *Quedagh Merchant* and brought her to Hispaniola.

Somehow, ill news of his doings had reached England and a word of warning must likewise have come to him, for he did not sail boldly back to New York as he should have done, but, buying a small vessel, with a few companions and such spoil as remained, of very modest value, he approached his home port cautiously. Some of the men went ashore on the Jersey coast and made themselves scarce. With the others and his sloop he put into Peconic Bay and buried a few chests on Gardiner's Island; hoping all the while for some word of assurance from Livingston or Bellomont. This did not come. Some of the dry goods from the *Quedagh Merchant* were shipped to Stamford, and the gold and jewels remained in the cache at Gardiner's Island, when Kidd, receiving what he construed to be a safe conduct from Bellomont, was lured to Boston. Here he was clapped into a new and strong prison, where he was held until taken to England for trial. There he was lodged in the Old Bailey with a couple of unlucky comrades. The House of Parliament tried to use him to asperse the King's ministers, but failing in this, lost interest in the case and left him to be tried in the customary way.

Under old English law the defense had few rights. Kidd believed he had covered his course by taking only vessels sailing under French passes, and these were in the possession of the Admiralty, which failed to give them up for evidence in his defense. His noble partners left him to his fate. It came about then that he was convicted. No wonder he cried out on hearing his doom: "My Lord, it is a very hard sentence. For my part, I am the innocentest person of them all, only I have been sworn against by perjured persons."

[78]

OF WILLIAM KIDD

The end came on Friday, May 23, 1701, for the incident was long drawn out. On that day he was taken to Execution Dock with Darby Mullins of his crew to keep him company in death. He climbed the ladder bravely as behooved him, but when it was withdrawn the halter broke and he must needs mount again. This time the hemp held.

So, having been unfairly tried, he was very badly hanged, and his poor estate, confiscated by the King, was used to found the Hospital for Seamen at Greenwich, which prevails until this day, and his widow, already twice wedded, took again a name, leaving his to live alone in undeserved infamy.

X

OF JOSEPH BRADISH

OF Joseph Bradish, who was sent to England in Kidd's company, there is little known outside of the brief official references. The Earl of Bellomont, Governor of the Colonies, records that Bradish was born in Cambridge, Mass., the seat of Harvard College. He ran away with a ship called the *Adventure*, an "Interloper"—free trader—from London, bound for Borneo, leaving her rightful commander, Captain Gulick, together with his officers and part of the crew marooned on Polonis, an obscure Indian island. Bradish, after some adventuring in Eastern seas, brought the vessel into Montauk Harbor, Long Island, New York, late in 1698 or early in 1699. The *Adventure* was a large ship for her day, measuring 400 tons. She was sunk by Bradish between Montauk Point and Block Island, and the crew scattered. Venturing to Boston, the pirate was taken prisoner, together with a companion, Tee Withersly. Both were lodged in Boston jail in June, 1699. The pair escaped by collusion with a maid servant employed by Ray, the jailer, who was accused of laziness. Bradish and his fellow were subsequently recaptured.

Bellomont, in his report to the Lords of Trade, gives these inklings concerning the case, under date of May 3, 1699: "I had no notice [of the *Adventure's* arrival] till a week after the ship was sunk, or if I had had notice I could have done nothing towards the seizing or securing of the ship or men without a Man of Warr, which the Lords of the Admirālty seem to think these Provinces unworthy of. I send your Lordships three or four depositions concerning the Pirate ship. The most material of these I have taken. The deposition of Symon Bonane, a Jew, goes (No. 1); that of Cornelius Schelinger (No. 3); that of Lieutenant Colonel Pierson (No. 4). This last the principal deposition, because with him Bradish had left £942-19-3 in money, the particulars whereof goes (No. 5). The bag of jewels mentioned by Pierson's deposition were opened before myself and the council, where I had ordered a Jew in their town to be present, he understanding jewels well. At first sight we had thought these to be £10,000 worth, but we soon found they were counterfeit, an inventory whereof goes (No. 6). My proclamation for the seizing of Bradish and his crew goes (No. 7). I seized three men in this town [New York], who I had notice were come from Block Island, and had concealed some of those pirates' money, and I secured them until I gave the governor of Rhode Island notice where the money was concealed, which I hear he has since secured; Block Island being in his government. That money I understand is near £1,000. Ten or eleven of the pirates are seized at New London by Colonel [Fitz-John] Winthrop, Governor of Connecticut, and £1,800 in money as he writes me word. At Boston they have taken fifteen or sixteen of the pirates I hear, and 5 or £6,000. The governor of Rhode Island is said to have discovered and seized another parcel of the money beside what I gave him notice of, so that 'tis supposed there may be in the whole near £10,000 secured for the owners in England, who, I hear are Sir Joseph Hearne, Mr. Sheperd and Mr. Heathcote. What I have received from Pierson is lodged with Colonel Courtland, the collector, and shall be forthcoming to the owners upon your Lordships' order, or such authority as I can be secure in. Lieutenant Colonel Pierson came frankly and voluntarily to me and owned Bradish had been at his house and left some bags of money with him and a bag of jewels. He has a fair character in the county and is a man of substance and a member of the present Assembly. I frightened him by telling him he would stand in need of the King's mercy, for by the statute of the 28th of Henry 8th, he was equally guilty with Bradish; which is a truth. I hope your Lordships will obtain the King's leave for me to pardon him, which is what I will not venture to do to him or anybody else without your leave, notwithstanding you are pleased to write me in your letter of the 25th of last October that I have a power by my commission to pardon pirates; and I assure your Lordships I do not intercede for him upon the score of reward, for I neither have taken nor ever will take any reward from him. I must observe to your Lordships that five or six of the men that ran away with this ship under Bradish are, as I hear, some of Colonel Fletcher's pirates that went out with Tew and other Pirates commissioned by Fletcher. Two or three of 'em have wives in this town and were actually, as I have been informed, in town. I laid out for them, but they are too well befriended to be given up to justice; and so I am apt to believe they are still here."

[81]

"Lieutenant Colonel Pierson" was indeed a person of consequence. He was Henry Pierson, of Southampton. His service as one of the two representatives to the Colonial legislature from Suffolk County began with the establishment of that body in 1691. He served in the second, third, and fourth legislatures continuously, acting as Speaker in the last named and was elected to the sixth and seventh. It was during the period of the sixth that the Bradish episode occurred. In the seventh session he took part in an exciting bit of political diversion. The death of the Earl of Bellomont had left no successor in the governorship. The assembly decreed that the power lay in the Council, but Willard Smith, President of that body, held that the pro tem rule was his. Pierson and Matthew Howell, his colleague, joined with a few other members in support of Smith's claim. For this Howell was expelled and the signers censured as having "offered the greatest scandal to the whole House of Representatives," and "liable to the severest rebukes . . . for their disloyalty and disobedience." Howell was sent back by his constituents, but William Nicoll, also a friend of the pirates, succeeded Pierson, who does not reappear again in the legislative annals.

The Lords of Trade of England reported to the Lords Justices, September 12, 1699, that Governor Fitz-John Winthrop, of Connecticut, had reported to them the capture of ten more of Bradish's men. In the same report the Lords of Trade humbly entreated the Lords Justices to direct the Earl of Bellomont to "use his utmost endeavors" to have "the Jaylor of Boston [Ray] in New England punished with the utmost severity of the law for the escape of Bradish aforementioned and that if the law of the colony be defective in that point he endeavor to get some more effectual act passed for preventing the like mischief in the future."

Apropos of Colonel Pierson's action in befriending Bradish, Bellomont remarked from Boston under date of October 20, 1699, in a letter to the Lords of Trade:

"I formerly acquainted your Lordships that Nassau Island, alias Long Island, was become a great receptacle for Pirates; I am since more confirmed 'tis so. Gillam, a notorious pirate (who came back from Madagascar with Kidd) was suffered to escape thither from Rhode Island, and 'tis believed he is still there, notwithstanding the Lieutenant Governor of New York published by my direction a reward of £230 for his apprehension, and at the same time £10 apiece for two

[82]

of Kidd's men that escaped from this town to Nassau Island. . . . The people have many of them been pirates themselves, and are sure to be well affected to the trade; but besides that they are so lawless and desperate a people that I can get no honest man that will venture to go and collect the excise among them, and watch their trade. There are four towns that make it their daily practice to receive ships and sloops with all sorts of merchandise, though they be not allowed ports."

He suggested as a remedy the quartering of one hundred soldiers among them under "discreet officers," as he knew of no other way to "bring those people to be obedient to the Laws and suppress piracy among them."

The Lords of Trade wrote soothingly to Bellomont April 11, 1700: "All that your Lordship has writ us in your several letters about pirates has been very useful. And we have accordingly laid before his Majesty divers representatives of your Lordships in the taking of Kidd, Bradish, Gillam and others . . . concerning all which matters His Majesty's directors have been sent you; and we doubt not of your continuing your endeavors for the suppression of Piracy so we hope (amongst others) to have some good account of the seizing of those pirates, which in your letter of the 22d of July were sheltered with a great deal of money on Nassau Island, though we are very sensible of the difficulty to do it in a place where they are so much favored.

"As for the desire you express in your letter of 3d May to have His Majesty's leave to pardon Lieutenant Colonel Pierson for having some pirates' goods in his hands, we have laid it accordingly before His Majesty by the Earl of Jersey, who has returned us answer: That His Majesty is pleased to allow your Lordship to pardon the said Colonel Pierson, provided he has delivered up all the effects he had in his hands belonging to the said pirates."

XI

OF THOMAS HOWARD

MUCH has been heard of Thomas Howard in the preceding account of Bowen. He was the son of a lighterman on the Thames, whose small estate he squandered and then took refuge from the results by shipping for Jamaica, the favorite resort of the ne'er-do-well. Deserting his ship upon arrival, he joined with a few others and embarked in a canoe for Grand Cayman, a clearing house for those piratically inclined. On arrival they found enough others of their kind to make up a company of twenty men, whose next act was to seize a turtling sloop and with her hunt for better prey. For a time they took only turtle hunters, whom they impressed in their crew, under threat of marooning. A brigantine from Ireland, with a hold full of convict "servants" was then taken and retained. The rejoicing "servants" joined, and all the crew but five were impressed. The Captain, with five hands, was given the sloop and enough provisions to carry him to Jamaica. Having now a vessel of force, the pirates extended their range, taking a sloop with six guns, which had been trading on the Spanish main. Being a better ship than the brigantine, she was exchanged and a number of her crew were forced to join.

Being now strong enough to venture far the company sailed for Virginia, stopping on the road a sizeable New England brigantine, carrying provisions to Barbadoes. The guns were shifted from the sloop and the latter given to the Yankees, who were allowed to depart less a few of their number who were forced. There were now eighty men on board with ten guns. One James acted as Captain and Howard became quartermaster. Off the cape several inbound ships from England were taken, which gave a profitable return, being well laden with wines, wares, and clothes for the planters. They also carried some convict "servants," who rejoiced at the change in fortune and joined forthwith. The number of impressed men was also increased, so that they had now a formidable company, well provided for in every way. Soon a still better English ship with more transported hands was taken and exchanged for the brigantine. A man of war coming into view, it was deemed wise to depart from the neighborhood and they steered accordingly for the African coast, with an eye out for Guinea traders. Here they were more than successful in seizing ships and replacing the unwilling members of their crew with others more inclined for the business. This good fortune continued for several months. At the end of that period they encountered a Portuguese three-decker carrying thirty-six guns. Her captain, a Portuguese, would make no resistance, but her mate was an Englishman named Ruland, who had once before been taken by pirates and who put up a stiff fight, with the help of the English, French, and Dutch in the crew. The Captain hid below, where most of his own countrymen followed him. The defense had finally to yield after several hours of fighting. The pirates, finding the captain hiding in the powder room, dragged him to the light and whipped him about the deck as a cowardly dog. Ruland and his fighters were forced to join. They took over the Portuguese ship, abandoning their own and by cutting down her upper deck and gunwale made a deep, long vessel which they named the *Alexander*. They now totaled one hundred and eighty men and were fit to meet the strongest ships at sea. Working down the coast they took numerous prizes, some of which were turned over to forced men who wished to depart. Such men were replaced by others more willing, but carpenters, caulkers, armorers, and musicians were always kept.

Near Cape Lopez they found a large Bristol ship lying at anchor, her crew being too depleted by sickness for her to move. This seemed a better vessel than the *Alexander* and an exchange was planned. A survey showed her to be unsound and she was left where she was found, after being rifled of valuables. At Cape Lopez the *Alexander* was cleaned and repaired. Their first encounter after leaving Lopez was with an English ship, which refused to yield. A severe fight followed, and Howard and a number of men boarded her, but the boatswain having neglected to lash the *Alexander* alongside properly she fell astern, leaving Howard and his fellows unsupported. With great address they hauled up a boat, which the Englishman had towing behind, and got back to their ship, but the latter being deep, struck on a bank and the valiant Britisher got safely away. The pirates were compelled to empty their water casks and throw their supply of firewood overboard in order to lighten the *Alexander* so she would float.

This done, it was necessary to return to Cape Lopez for a new supply of both essentials. When these were secured they again went cruising toward the Cape of Good Hope. Two Portuguese brigantines were taken, despoiled, and burned, their crews being set on shore.

Doubling the Cape the *Alexander* steered for Madagascar and had the ill luck to strike on a reef about forty miles from St. Augustine. The captain was ill in his berth and the majority of the men put ashore to a small island, carrying a large stock of supplies in the boats in order to lighten the ship, and leaving only Howard, who was still quartermaster, and eleven hands on board, beside the prostrate commander. Howard and the others now took the treasure and abandoned the vessel, making for the mainland of Madagascar, with all the ship's boats. The captain noting the silence managed to crawl to the deck, in time to observe their departure. He fired two guns which roused the men on the island, who were helpless to pursue, being without a boat. The ship was now high and dry with the lowering tide and could be walked to from the island. She was not injured and could have been kedged off had there been boats to carry out the anchors. There being none, the *Alexander* was dismembered and her timbers used to construct another smaller craft of sixty tons on which it was designed to escape from the island. In fear for their provision supply, the English and Dutch among the castaways, being the most forceful and in the majority, forced the Portuguese and French, thirty-six in all, to entrust themselves on a raft and so seek the shore. The day the remainder were ready to launch their new vessel a pirate brigantine came along and rescued them all.

Howard and his companions had a mixed adventure. They lingered along the west side of the island working toward St. Mary's and one day perceiving the *Angelsea, Hastings,* and *Lizard,* Commodore Littleton's squadron which had brought out the pardon for the pirates who would give up the trade and punishment for those who persisted, made the mistake of thinking they might belong to brethren and accordingly made a smoke signal from the shore. Boats were sent off, but being recognized as belonging to warships, caused the gang to hide in the bush until they departed. The party now remained on shore. Food was plenty until one day when Howard was wild-hog shooting, the eleven took to the boats and left him to shift for himself. Howard was in due time picked up by the pirate Fourgette, who is mentioned in White's career. He was well treated by a native prince.

Howard now joined the *Speaker* and remained with her until she was lost at Mauritius, when he again returned to Madagascar, settling down at St. Augustine.

While he was living here the *Prosperous*, of thirty-six guns, Captain Hilliard, came in and was seized by Howard and other pirates rendezvousing at St. Augustine. Hilliard, his mate, and several men were killed. The ship was fitted for pirating and Howard elected commander. Going with her to Maratan, Howard there found some of the *Speaker's* men who were taken on board, making a complement of seventy. Continuing to St. Mary's they there careened, cleaned the ship, and took on some recruits. While at St. Mary's an invitation was received from a retired Dutch pirate, Otto Van Tuyl, to visit his plantation in the mainland and attend a celebration held in honor of the christening of two of his children. The company accepted and were hospitably entertained. Word having been passed round by some one envious of his prosperity that Van Tuyl had once killed some pirates, the fickle rascals, without any facts to justify the fancy, pillaged his house and in all violation of the laws of hospitality took him prisoner. Such goods as they could not transport in cases they burned or threw into the river, and it was decided to take Van Tuyl to the ship and hang him from the yard-arm.

This exquisite piece of villainy was defeated by a friendly pirate who managed to cut Van Tuyl's bonds, so that he fled to the woods and, rallying a force of natives, waylaid his late guests on their way down the river in a canoe and Howard's pinnace, in which they were transporting their host's goods, a number of women and some of his children. The women were set to paddling while the men fired in defense from the canoe. The latter was upset on the bar. All but two of the rogues swam the river and escaped. One, who was wounded, and a comrade, who stood by him, were taken by Van Tuyl. The women also got safely ashore. Van Tuyl then attacked the pinnace as she came along, wounding Howard in the arm. There was no further damage out of the excitement.

Curiously enough, Van Tuyl afterwards came to New York as a passenger with Captain William Kidd, and his affidavit, labeled as that of "an old pirate," was part of the documentary evidence sent to London against the captain. One of the charges of Bellomont's enemies was that he had held in prison one Buckminister, another of Kidd's passengers, while releasing Van Tuyl on bail. His after fate does not appear, but he probably became a respectable resident of New York.

Howard's company, having made the neighborhood too hot for comfort, now sailed for Methelage where they took on supplies for a cruise to Bengal waters. A Dutch adventurer of forty guns coming in, the rival captains took each other's measure but wisely concluded not to test their strength; Howard, leaving the Dutchman the field, went on to Mayotta. How he here met Bowen and joined his fortunes has been fully related in the history of that worthy. Howard retired from the sea, took a native woman for a wife and, being "a morose, ill-natured fellow," was put to death by members of her family.

XII

OF THOMAS WHITE

THOMAS WHITE was a Devon man, born in Plymouth. His mother, early widowed, kept a public house and having fair means gave him a good education. Like many Plymouth lads, he took an early turn on a man-of-war, leaving the sea to settle at Barbadoes where he married. There being considerable shipping out of Bridgetown, he was able to continue his occupation of mariner by becoming master of the brigantine *Marygold*, in which he made two prosperous voyages to Guinea, bringing back cargoes of slaves for the island planters. On a third venture to the African coast White was captured by a French pirate, who transferred his company to the brigantine and forced her master to remain, as previously noted in the life of John Bowen. His adventures for a considerable period following this will be found in the preceding account of Bowen, with whom he cruised as a common sailor, still maintaining the position of a forced man.

Upon the dispersal of Bowen's company at Mauritius, White made his way to Methelage in Madagascar and lived for a season upon the charity of the king. Here he remained until Captain Thomas Howard came in with the *Prosperous,* seeking recruits. Others who were stranded in Methelage joined as did White, in the hope of somehow finding in the service a way of reaching home, rather than of advancing in the profession. He was soon selected as quartermaster, but his service was short. While he was ashore with twenty-six men at Port Dolphin, the *Prosperous* was blown out to sea. White, presuming she would make for the west side of Madagascar, sought to follow in his boat. The party reached St. Augustine, where they delayed expecting the *Prosperous* to appear. She did not come and after a week the King ordered them to be gone, not believing that they had any ship and thinking they might prove to be dangerous vagabonds. He did not deny them provisions and, stocked up, they went on to Methelage. Here the King who knew their story treated them with kindness. The boat was raised a streak to make her more seaworthy and an effort was made to reach St. Mary's in the hope of finding the *Prosperous* anchored there.

This required a trip around the north end of Madagascar, where they found the current too strong to breast and so abandoned the attempt and put into a small native harbor, where they idled for nearly a month. Many of the men wished to burn the boat and make a march overland to the dominions of a king they knew to be friendly. To this White would not agree as being too risky. After much contention, in which he saved the boat with difficulty, half of the reckless fellows took their share of the provisions and marched away, White and the others escorting them a day's journey. He then returned and, taking the boat, returned once more to Methelage.

Here he remained three months, putting a deck on his boat and awaiting a favorable opportunity to depart. During this time three pirates who had been captives on the frigate *Severn* and had escaped at Mohilla came in. They had made their way from Mohilla to Johanna in a canoe and then from Johanna to Mayotta, where the King gave them the boat in which they came to Methelage. These joined their fortunes with White and his companions. The current having somewhat abated, it was determined to attempt once more rounding the island. On trial the current was found still too strong to breast, so they went ashore for a month and lived as best they could on wild hog and native fruits and vegetables. They then succeeded in getting around and about forty miles below the extremity of the north point put into a little port, where they found a piece of cloth that had belonged to the jacket of the carpenter of the *Prosperous* who had been among those who went into the wilderness. It had evidently been torn off to protect his feet. When they reached St. Mary's a canoe came off with a note addressed to "any white man" written by one of their former companions, which warned them to be on their guard against native treachery. Here, too, they learned of the disbanding of the company of the *Prosperous*, who were described as living on shore "like princes." Under guidance of one of the canoe men, White and the others were taken to a point called Olumbah, where they found a dozen of the *Prosperous* people living in a large house guarded by a redoubt containing twenty pieces of ordnance. The others were settled in similar groups according to nationality in divers places near by. The wanderers found that their shares in the takings of the *Prosperous* had been very justly laid by and were at once given them. White, not wishing to remain, asked to be given the boat, but the others insisted that it be put up for sale and he bought it for 400 pieces of eight. Others who wished to depart joined him in the boat and returned to Methelage.

Here they found a French ship, of which Herault, who had been Bowen's quartermaster, was captain and which had been abandoned by her people to some English survivors from the wrecked *Degrave*, who were not strong enough to man a vessel of fifty guns, but were too strong for Herault. War being on between England and France, he feared they might take her anyway without its being an act of piracy, and, having been guilty himself, concluded to retire gracefully. The English therefore chose White captain and put the ship into shape for sea. Proceeding they touched at Doñ Mascarene, where a surgeon was added to the company and going again to Madagascar stopped at Ambonavoula, where more men were picked up, raising the company to sixty. Being now well-equipped, he proceeded to Mayotta to await there the season for operations in the Red Sea. The delay was improved to clean the ship and to fill her with provisions.

In due time he then proceeded to the straits of Bab el Mandeb and, making harbor, lay in wait for the Mocha ships. Two Arab grabs were taken which yielded provisions, some drugs, and a little money. One large stranger that appeared proved to be Dutch and too stout to tackle. Indeed, the company rejoiced that she was willing to go her way without testing them. Abandoning the straits, where their presence was perhaps too well known, they cruised on the African coast where it was their fortune to encounter the *Malabar*, of nearly a thousand tons, and carrying six hundred people. She was taken after a fight, in which the boatswain was killed and three of the pirates wounded. The strain of the battle so ill used their ship that she was filled with prisoners and abandoned, White taking over the huge *Malabar*.

Feeling their strength, they next pursued a Portuguese man-of-war, but were halted by the parting of the maintop. Four days after they overhauled a Portuguese ship, who, misled by their English colors into believing they were a British frigate, sent a boat aboard with a present of sweetmeats for the captain. The boat was detained. Another with an armed force was sent on board the Portuguese and took possession of her, explaining to the astonished captain that "war" had broken out between England and Portugal. Two days later the English ship *Dorothy*, Captain Pennruddock, was taken after a chase. She had a Lascar crew, the officers alone being white. Pennruddock's cash and his ship were taken from him and he was given the Portuguese vessel, with the choice of such goods as he wished from the *Dorothy*, with leave to go and mend his fortunes as best he might. The *Malabar*, being cumbersome, was now exchanged for the *Dorothy*, after being well rifled of valuables and coin to the amount of £200 per man. In their search the pirates missed 50,000 sequins that had been hidden in a jar under a stall occupied by a cow, which gave milk for the Hindu supercargo, an elderly man with a weak stomach. The prisoners, Hindu and Portuguese, were put on the *Malabar*, to go where they pleased.

A day after the exchange an English ketch of six guns, Captain Benjamin Stacy, was taken. Some money and the goods on board were commandeered. Included in the cash was five hundred dollars, beside a silver mug and several spoons, property of two children, who were being conveyed home to England under Stacy's care. The children wept bitterly over their loss and on being asked the cause of their emotion Stacy replied that the property was all the children had in the world, being orphans and dependent upon it for their bringing up. At this White made a speech to his company reciting the facts, at which the men voted to restore the property, to which they added $120 from their own store, beside presents to the mate and junior officers of the ketch, which was then released.

In the bay of Defarr, a ketch was overhauled at anchor and helpless, her master and some of the crew being taken ashore by the natives. A passenger on board was one Monsieur Berger, a French gentleman whom the pirates took with them, together with $2,000 in cash. The ketch they allowed the native chief to keep in return for provisions.

It was now seasonable to return to Madagascar, which they did by way of Mauritius. The booty, reaching £1,200 per man, was here divided and several taking their share left the ship. The others on their way to Madagascar stopped at Hopeful Point, where they landed their goods and made a settlement. White laid out something of an estate, bought cattle, and set himself up comfortably. Meanwhile he cut down the *Dorothy* to make her a better sailer in preparation for another cruise. John Halsey coming in with a better vessel, it was decided to join him and White entered before the mast. He kept with

Halsey for half a year, when, on retiring to Port Hopeful, he was taken with what proved to be his last illness. Before his decease he appointed three of his old associates as guardians for a son by a native woman, with the instruction that he be sent to England, educated, and brought up to be "a better man than his father," all of which was faithfully performed and with the desired result.

XIII

OF JOHN EVANS

JOHN EVANS was one of several Welshmen who followed more or less modestly in the footsteps of their countryman, the great Sir Henry Morgan. Seeking fortune in the West Indies, he was for a time mate of a sloop sailing out of the Island of Nevis. Feeling that the prospects were poor in honest seafaring, he, with a number of others of like spirit, commandeered a canoe at Port Royal in Jamaica and went buccaneering along the coast, though to tell the truth their efforts were no more than housebreaking, as in this fashion they plundered a number of residences on the remote plantations making headquarters in their boat and hiding in the creeks, hoping for the gratification of a larger ambition, which was to seize some vessel and go genuinely to pirating.

Finding a small sloop from Bermuda anchored in Dun's Hole they took possession, Evans making himself captain. After a day of roistering ashore they returned at night to rob the inn, which had taken their money for food and drink, taking such cash and valuables as were discovered on board the sloop and making sail in the morning. Four guns were mounted on the vessel, which was then named the *Scourer* and headed for Hispaniola. A well-furnished Spanish sloop was the first prize and yielded the encouraging sum of £150 per man, though as their numbers were few the total was not great. Beating up for the Windward Islands, the New England ship *Dove*, Captain Diamond, crossed their path near Porto Rico. Her mate and three of the crew were forced to join and the *Dove* was dismissed, less some of her valuables. They now rested among the islands until refreshed and on again making sail captured the *Lacretia and Catherine*, Captain Mills, a vessel of two hundred tons. The crew in a spirit of exhilaration set up an inquiry as to the manner in which Captain Mills had used his seamen, as a preliminary perhaps to justifying their own ill usage of him, but Evans stopped the play with the terse remark, "What have we to do to turn reformers? What we want is money," and set his gentry

[94]

to rummaging the ship, contenting himself in the interest of Justice by asking the men if Mills gave them enough food and, finding this true, observed: "Then he ought to give you work enough."

The *Lacretia and Catherine* was held for the purpose of using her to help haul down the sloop for cleaning, but before they undertook the work a Dutch sloop was taken which yielded £50 per man, and as it proved better for the hauling it was detained and the New Englander released. The cleaning took place at Ruby Island, from which spot they steered for Jamaica, off the coast of which they took a sugar drogher and ran thence to Grand Cayman.

Their prosperity was now destined to come to a sudden end. The boatswain, a surly fellow, made "ill words" with the captain, and challenged him to a duel on shore, with pistols and cutlasses, according to the code of the sea. This Evans accepted and when reaching Grand Cayman, invited him to the shore to settle their dispute by arms. The boatswain declined to fulfill the challenge he had made and Evans accordingly beat him with a cane. The surly fellow drew a pistol and shot him through the head, then jumping into the sea made for the shore. He was caught and brought back, the pirates planning dire torture for his punishment, which came to naught because the gunner hot with rage shot him through the body, but not fatally. The wretch begged for a week's mercy, which was not granted, another pistol ball ending his life.

They now desired the mate of the *Lacretia and Catherine*, who had been pressed, to take their dead captain's place, but he declined the honor. It was decided to break up and give the sloop to the New England mate, who with the aid of a boy brought the vessel and the story to Port Royal. The rogues dispersed at Grand Cayman, after dividing £9,000 among the thirty persons who then constituted their number.

XIV

OF DAVID WILLIAMS

DAVID WILLIAMS was a Welsh-born seaman, who shipped before the mast on board the *Mary* an Indiaman bound from London to Madras. Running short of water when off the east coast of Madagascar, in latitude 20, the captain sent the longboat with a crew to procure some of the needed fluid, Williams being among the number. The surf ran too high to permit a landing, so Williams and a companion stripped and swam to the beach to seek a water supply. The wind coming up and the surf growing heavier, they were unable to breast it and the boat, after waiting a while, pulled back to the ship, which sailed without any further effort to secure the seamen, putting in at St. Augustine's Bay for water and then proceeding on her voyage.

The castaways, without food or clothing, managing to subsist on fruit, wandered along the coast until they fell in with some natives, who treated them with compassion, clothing their nakedness and supplying them with subsistence. William's companion died from hardship and homesickness. Warfare later broke out between the chief under whose protection Williams lived and a more powerful neighbor, who was victor in the struggle, and among the prisoners captured the young Welshman. The conqueror was kind to the captive and gave him a musket to carry, as more worthy of the arm than a native, and promised that he should fare as well as himself if he would aid him in his battles. For a considerable period he lived pleasantly, but a coalition of the tribes against his prince brought on a new conflict, in the course of which Williams fell prisoner to the other side. The victor, noting Williams's prowess in the fighting, showed no resentment but treated him as a valued acquisition and so he lived again in high favor. A new war led to the destruction of this prince's power and in the rout Williams took refuge in a tree, from which he was compelled to surrender to his pursuers.

His captor, the King of Maratan, used him even better than either of his former protectors. He became a trusted leader of raiding parties and his success was such as to spread his fame throughout the island. This repute reaching Dempaino, a ruler of great power, some two hundred miles distant, caused him to send an ambassador with orders to bring the Welshman to his court. He met the ambassador, who formally demanded his surrender from the prince, who declined on the ground that he yielded only to supereminence and thought himself of fully as much consequence as Dempaino. With this reply he dismissed the envoy. Williams had been five years in Madagascar when he became the subject of this dispute, which soon grew serious, for Dempaino sent one of his best generals with six thousand men to bring him to his capital, with the promise that he would follow himself with a greater array if the white man was not given up. The force was too formidable to be opposed and the King of Maratan yielded. He was also compelled to pay one hundred slaves and five hundred herd of cattle toward the expense of the expedition, to ward off worse punishment for his haughtiness. Williams was sent alone to the commanding general, which caused the latter to ask if he were a slave, to come so unattended. The King answered that he had never been so considered, but taking the hint gave his former guest a slave. Dempaino received him as one worthy of being sent for with six thousand men, and clothed and lodged him most handsomely.

He lived uneventfully with the King as an ornament to his court, for several years, when a pirate craft, the *Bedford Galley*, commanded by Achen Jones, a Welshman, came to the coast and his royal master, perhaps tired of his European toy, allowed him, Williams, to depart as a member of the ship's company. The pirate put into St. Augustine, where by careless handling in careening the galley's back was broken. The pirate *Pelican* now came in and some joined her for a cruise to the East Indies, including Williams, who left her to join Captain Culliford, in the Mocha frigate. Culliford had success in the Red Sea and returning to St. Mary's divided the proceeds. Williams did some venturing on various pirate craft and at length returned to His Majesty the King of Maratan, who instead of being overjoyed asked him what presents he had brought him. Williams retorted that he had more than paid all obligations in the past, which angered the royal gentleman so much that he ordered the adventurer to leave his territory.

He now joined Captain Howard, of the privateer *Prosperous*, who went to St. Mary's, whence a descent was made on the Dutch at the Cape of Good Hope with poor results, as numbers were taken in an attempt to carry off Ort Van Tyle, a rich Hollander. Williams, with one Thomas Collins, was kept at hard farm labor for six months, in virtual slavery.

Collins was crippled by a broken arm and unable to follow Williams when he ran away at the end of that period. A Kaffir chief sheltered him for half a year, when he left to live with John Pro, another, but friendly Dutchman, near the shore where he lived for six months more. A British fleet putting in under Commodore Richards carried off both Pro and Williams in irons to Johanna. The captives were kept on the *Severn*. Her captain making an attack on Mohilla, some of the men-of-war's men were killed and the two prisoners contrived to get away.

By canoe they reached the island called Mayotta, where with the aid of the local ruler they built a boat staunch enough to bear them to Madagascar. There at Methelage they found Captain Thomas White and his pirate crew. They lay at Methelage for three months, when, burning their boat, they joined White's company and went with him to Ambonavoula where Williams remained ashore until White, bringing in the ship *Hopewell*, fitted her for a Red Sea trip, in which Williams took part, becoming quartermaster toward the end of the voyage. Returning, the *Hopewell* paused at Mauritius for provisions and about half the company abandoned her. The others continued to Hopewell Point, on Madagascar, where dividing the spoil they made themselves homes on shore. Captain Halsey coming in Williams joined him for a cruise and returning landed at Maratan, where he made up with the crusty King and aided him in a war with his brother. This ending in favor of the King, Williams boarded another pirate Ambonavoula, who sent his longboat to Maratan, after his companions. Three months later he became captain of one of Halsey's consorts, taking over a Scotch vessel captured by the latter and compelling its crew to fit her out. When about ready she was wrecked by a hurricane.

Williams now built a sloop and sailed with a company of ten for Mauritius, but missing the port they came around Madagascar to Methelage, where the sloop was laid up and her crew lived a year, or until Williams had outstayed his welcome with the King, who was of morose temper, and finally ordered the whites away. They sought to sail around the north end of the island, but the contrary wind sent them into Boyne, a port ten leagues from Methelage and in the same king's dominions. Only five men were with Williams on the sloop and with three of these the captain went ashore in a canoe that was paddled by some negroes of his crew, together with David Eaton and William Dawson. Two of the men asked for a guide to the king's town and were furnished one by the governor, who also ordered them to be waylaid and killed, which was done from ambush. Williams and a Frenchman named Myers, looking about the town to buy some agate beads, were seized by the governor's police, who killed Myers at once but bound Williams and put him to torture, pouring hot ashes over his head and setting boys to beating him with sticks. He begged for his life and offered the governor two thousand dollars for ransom, but the Malagasy made answer that he would have both his life and his dollars. The uphappy Welshman was then speared to death.

The single white man on the sloop now came in for the governor's attention. He sent Williams's boat off, filled with goats and some calabashes of native beer, with twelve of his armed retainers, using the two negroes who had come ashore with her to paddle out. Six natives and several slave women were on the sloop, who had come with Williams. When hailed and asked where the captain was, one of the governor's men replied that he was drinking beer with the governor and was sending them provisions. One of the women warned William Noakes, the white man, not to let them on deck, suspecting treachery. Noakes abused her for her pains and was soon dead as the result of his desire to secure the beer in the boat.

This massacre caused the pirates in the King's domains to demand the punishment of the governor. The latter offered to let them take such vengeance as they pleased, to which the wise ruler made reply that justice was his prerogative, not theirs. The murderous chieftain was then speared to death. So ended the strange story of the Welsh boy who swam through the breakers and into the recorded adventures.

XV

OF JOHN QUELCH

THE Boston *News-Letter* in its fifth issue, published May 29, 1704, contained this item of marine intelligence:

"Arrived at Marblehead, Captain Quelch, in the Brigantine that Captain Plowman went out in, are said to come from New Spain and have made a good voyage."

She had indeed, made a "good voyage" and had come home to a bad ending. It had its beginning in July, 1703, when the brigantine, named the *Charles*, property of Charles Hobby, Colonel Nicholas Paige, William Clarke, Benjamin Gallop, and John Colman, leading citizens and merchants of Boston, was commissioned by Governor Joseph Dudley as a privateer to go against the French in Acadia and Newfoundland. On the first of August, fully manned, the *Charles* lay off Marblehead but was delayed in sailing by the illness of her captain, Daniel Plowman. The crew showing signs of disorder and discontent, Plowman wrote to his owners discovering his plight and urging them to come at once to "take some speedy care in saving what we can." Two of the owners to whom this message was directly addressed proceeded forthwith to Marblehead, where they found the captain, as alleged, too ill to receive them and apparently were barred from boarding the vessel, from which Plowman again wrote urging them to have her brought to Boston and there to remove all things on board to prevent embezzlement by the turbulent crew. He also advised against sending the ship to sea under another captain, adding: "It will not do with these people"—meaning his men.

Before this advice could be heeded, Captain Plowman was locked in his cabin and the crew took possession of the ship. This done John Quelch came on board and was chosen captain. The *Charles* at once put to sea. When she was well out on the Atlantic, Plowman was thrown overboard, though whether alive or dead the record does not state. Instead of proceeding under her commission, the *Charles* was headed for the coast of Brazil, where an active career of piracy began. It was late in the year when the objective was reached, but between November 15, 1703 and February 17, 1704, nine vessels were taken, five of them being brigantines, one a ship of two hundred tons and the others shallops of minor measure. The ship carried twelve guns and thirty-five men. Like all the others, she was under the Portuguese flag. That kingdom being at peace with Britain, the seizures were rank piracy. Though most of the craft taken were small the spoil was considerable, including beside provisions, cloth, silks, sugar, rum, several slaves, gold dust and coin to the value of £1,000.

The owners of the *Charles*, naturally uneasy during the absence of their vessel, had sent a circular letter to six of the West India colonies advising of their interest and seeking information. None came, however, until the item in the *News-Letter* told of the ship's return. She appears to have been abandoned when once brought into Marblehead and her crew scattered. That they had been pirating was soon made clear by their own admissions. As the owners of the *Charles* were liable under the Act as accessories, Messrs. Colman and Clarke took steps to clear themselves by laying information against Quelch and his companions, applying to Isaac Addington, Secretary of the Province of Massachusetts Bay, and Paul Dudley, the Attorney General, on May 23, 1704. Dudley at once began hunting the rascals down. Judge Samuel Sewall notes in his diary meeting Dudley at Lynn in "egre pursuit of the Pirates" and as already having caught one, whom he turned over to the judge who sent the rogue to Boston. Lieutenant-Governor Povey now made the hunt general, issuing a proclamation calling for the arrest of the pirates wherever found and for seizing their treasure. The names listed beside that of Quelch included those of John Lambert, John Miller, John Clifford, John Dorothy, James Parret, Charles James, William Whiting, John Pitman, John Templeton, Benjamin Perkins, William Williams, Richard Lawrence, Erasmus Peterson, John King, Charles King, Isaac Johnson, William Lawson, Daniel Chevalle, John Way, Thomas Farrington, Matthew Pimer, Anthony Holding, William Rayner, John Quittance, John Harwood, William James, Dennis Carter, Nicholas Richardson, James Austin, James Patterson, Joseph Hutnot, George Pierce, George Norton, Gabriel Davis, John Breck, John Carter, Paul Giddens, Nicholas Dunbar, Richard Thurbar, Daniel Churley and Christopher Scudamore.

A number were reported as taking refuge in Rhode Island, five of whom bought a small sloop and successfully evaded arrest by sailing for Long Island, in New York's jurisdiction and there, well-hidden, they defied the law. One only was caught and by Governor Cranston's order sent to Boston. On May 29th Governor Dudley issued a proclamation warning against concealing the fugitives or their money. He gave a list of forty-two names as men wanted. This was published in the *News-Letter* June 5th. By the 6th of June some superlatively honest New Englanders had turned in several ounces of gold to the Council Board as part of the contraband wealth taken by Quelch. As a result, Governor Dudley appointed a Commission of Inquiry, under which Samuel Sewell, Acting Chief Justice of the Superior Court, Nathaniel Byfield, Judge of the Admiralty, and Paul Dudley, the Attorney General, were directed to repair to Marblehead and "to send for and examine all persons of whom they shall have information or just grounds of suspicion [that they] do conceal and detain" gold and treasure brought in by the pirates, "either at Marblehead, or parts adjacent, and to take what they shall find into their hands, as also to secure any of the Pirates."

Colonel John Legg of Marblehead and Colonel John Wentworth of Ipswich were called upon to summon the militia of their several regiments to hunt the fugitives. Hearing that some had joined one Captain Larramore on a privateer lying at the Isle of Shoals, Sewall, with twenty men in the sloop *Trial* and a pinnace, proceeded thereto and caught seven, four on the vessel and three on Starr Island. In all twenty-one were rounded up. They were taken to Boston and there lodged in custody of Daniel Willard, the keeper of the jail, and placed on trial on June 13, 1704. Quelch, John Lambert, Christopher Scudamore, John Miller, Erasmus Peterson, Peter Roach and Charles King were convicted and sentenced to death. The others were held for a time and allowed to go their ways.

Following the conviction of the seven, great competition resulted between the clergy to save their wretched souls, the Rev. Cotton Mather being foremost in the endeavor. According to the *News-Letter:* "There were sermons preached in their hearing every day and prayers made daily with them. And they were catechised and had occasional exhortations."

The execution took place below high-water mark on the back of the Charles River, off a point of land below Copps Hill on June 30, 1704, on a gallows for the erection of which John Barnard was paid forty pounds. The culprits were escorted from the prison to Scarlet's Wharf by forty musketeers, the Provost Marshal and the Town Constables, together with Cotton Mather and other clergymen, where they embarked on their last voyage to the gallows. Mather had prayed with or rather at the men in prison on the preceding Tuesday. He now repeated the performance with renewed unction, inspired by the presence of a great audience, the scene being thus described by Samuel Sewall in his diary:

"But when I came to see how the river was covered with people I was amazed. Some say there were one hundred boats. One hundred and fifty boats and canoes saith Cousin Knoody of York. . . . When the scaffold was hoisted to a due height the seven malefactors went up. Mr. Mather (Cotton) prayed to them standing upon the boat. Ropes were all fasten'd to the gallows (save King, who was repriev'd). When the scaffold was let to sink there was such a scream of the Women that my wife heard it in our Entry next the orchard and was much surprised at it, yet the wind was sou'west. Our house is a full mile from the place."

The prisoners, as usual, were permitted to make "farewell remarks." John Lambert begged his hearers to avoid bad company, but the unrepentant and somewhat indignant Quelch added that "they should also take care how they brought money into New England to be hanged for it." The reprieved King was edified by seeing his companions neatly swung off, having traveled with them to the foot of the gallows before his luck was made known.

On the occasion of the execution the *News-Letter* issued the first "extra" in American newspaper annals—one quite worthy of the successors, being "An account of the Behaviour and last Dying Speeches of John Quelch, John Lambert, Christopher Scudamore, John Miller, Erasmus Peterson and Peter Roach, the six Pirates that were executed on Charles River, Boston side, on Friday, June 30, 1704." Half of the space was given to the "exhortations to the malefactors" by the Clergymen and Cotton Mather's prayer, "as near as it could be taken in writing in the great crowd."

In its next regular issue the *News-Letter* observes "that as they had led a wicked and vicious life, so to appearance, they dyed very obdurately and impenitently, hardened in their sins."

[103]

XVI

OF THE BAHAMA PIRATES

M UCH lawless history finds its seat in the group of islands called
the Bahamas, more than 3,000 rocks and keys stretching from
near the coast of Florida to the Island of St. Domingo, where
Columbus came into touch with the New World. The Spanish settled
first upon San Salvador; there it is related they remained until the
natives, who wore gold plates upon their lips, being asked whence the
gold came pointed across the Caribbean and so led to the great forays
of Cortez and Pizzaro against Mexico and Peru. In the meanwhile
they treated the poor Caribs with such hideous cruelty as soon to exterminate them and then, forsaking the islands themselves, left their
houses and chapels to crumble into shapeless coral. The Bahamas were
rediscovered by Captain William Sayle and included in the grant of the
Carolinas, made by Charles II, March 24, 1663, to the Duke of Alber-
marle, Sir George Carteret, Lords Berkeley, Ashley, Craven, and four
others, as rewards for their services to the Restoration. The lordly
proprietors did nothing for this much of their new estate, but with
the rise of buccaneering the islands began to gather inhabitants, so
much so that in 1670 they were favored with a governor, Capt. John
Wentworth who, striving to reform the settlers in matters affecting
meum and *tuum*, was seized by his subjects and bundled off to Jamaica
with a warning to stay there if he desired to preserve his head. They
did as they pleased until 1671, when Robert Clarke was set over them.
His was a worse fate than that of his predecessor for the Spanish from
Cuba, smarting under their wrongs, descended on New Providence,
which had been happily named in view of the shelter it afforded and the
kind of men who received its protection, and destroyed the settlement
carrying off the governor in chains, together with such inhabitants as
failed to hide in the scrub. Clarke was tortured to death and his body
roasted after the most approved fashion set by the Inquisition.

Upon the departure of the Spaniards the settlers pulled themselves
together again and a new governor, Mr. Lilburn, came out from Eng-

[104]

land. In 1684, the Spanish made another descent, destroyed all the improvements, and repeated their former barbarities. Again, such as could concealed themselves in the woods and were left without governmen or protection until 1687. The survivors meanwhile elected Rev. Mr. Bridges, a Presbyterian pastor, as their head and he acted until 1690 when the Lords Proprietors sent out Jones to be governor. He contrived to exasperate the people by his petty tyrannies and was secure only so long as Every the pirate protected him, as noted in the life of that worthy. No sooner had Every departed than the people rose and put Jones in jail, selecting one Ashley as governor. He held on until Every, returning unexpectedly, released Jones, who took vengeance on his persecutors with the pirate's aid and ran things with a relentless hand in this strange partnership. Word of his performances at last coming to England, the Proprietors sent out Governor Trot, who superseded Jones in 1694, freeing the political prisoners and permitting Jones to depart. He winked at Every, whose crew, disbanding, added many enterprising men to his government, now populous enough to build a town of 160 houses, which was named Nassau.

Trot retired in 1697 and Governor Webb became his successor. He became so obnoxious that he deemed it wise to depart hastily for Philadelphia, which he did in 1699, leaving a mulatto called Elding in charge of his principality. Elding, by co-operation with freebooters, held on until 1701, when the Lords Proprietors again asserted themselves, sending out Mr. Hasket to act as governor. His was but a brief authority, for in five weeks after his arrival his efforts to curb his subjects, led them to place him in irons and put him on board a ketch in the harbor whence they dispatched him to England with warning never to return. They now elected Litchwood to serve in his stead. He ruled liberally, according to the public desires, until 1703 when, the war of the Spanish Succession being well under way, an expedition from Havana surprised the island, burned and plundered the town and carried such inhabitants as failed to flee, away to Cuba. Returning on a second raid they collected all the people, white and black, who had not been prudent enough to leave for Carolina and bore them to Cuba, leaving Nassau a desolate ruin. The Lords Proprietors, ignorant of these transactions, had now found time to send a successor named Birch to replace the exiled Hasket. He found his dominion desolate and returned to London.

It remained in such a state until 1716, when it was repopulated in this strange fashion: While the Peace of Utrecht, concluded in 1713, had brought respite between nations it had by no means reconciled races. The frictions of a century were not easily removed and the West Indies, Cuba, and the Spanish main were still on guard against each other and with good reason. It chanced in 1714 that the Spanish plate fleet from Mexico to Havana was wrecked by a Norther in the Gulf of Florida. The ships carried many millions in pieces of eight and being located were salvaged by a number of vessels sent out from Havana with a corps of engineers equipped for the purpose. Much of the coin had been recovered before news of the latent treasure reached the ears of the ex-privateersmen and potential pirates of the West Indies, who were stirred to act.

One Henry Jennings gathered recruits at Jamaica and fitted out two ships and three sloops for an expedition against the salvors. While the coin was transferred to Havana, at convenience, it was being recovered daily by the divers and stored in a camp on shore. When Jennings and his squadron reached the scene of the wrecks, about 350,000 pieces of eight were in hand awaiting shipment. Two government commissaries and sixty soldiers guarded the treasure. Jennings brought his fleet to anchor and, landing five hundred men put the guards to flight without a battle, seized the treasure and sailed for Jamaica. *Enroute* he met with a Spanish ship, Havana bound, which was overhauled and searched. Finding 60,000 pieces of eight on board as well as valuable cochineal dye, indigo, and the like, he plundered and released her. The pillaged ship followed in their wake and, noting them coming in to Jamaica, hastened back to Havana and roused the governor to action. He sent a vessel to Jamaica, carrying the just complaint against Jennings and his company, demanding the return of the treasure and justice against the rascals. This was not forthcoming, but decorum forbade giving the expedition further shelter.

To avoid embarrassing His Excellency of Jamaica, who had given the Spaniards no redress, Jennings and his flotilla departed, not, however without marketing their stolen wares and putting on board full supplies of food and ammunition. Once at sea they began an open career of piracy, turning to the Gulf of Honduras and operating mainly against Spain. Here they fell in with nineteen crews of logwood cutters whose vessels had been seized by the Spanish authorities and who had been packed off for home on three small sloops. These gladly joined Jennings in revenge. Being now strong and in need of a shore station, Jennings and his venturesome followers picked upon New Providence as a likely spot and going thither set up their colony. News of their prowess soon reached England, where it caused due alarm as being likely to strike a spark which would begin war anew, and of war the world was weary. Accordingly, his high mightiness, George the First, having by Grace of God then assumed authority over British dominions, on September 15, 1716, issued from Whitehall "a pronounciamento" to the effect "that complaint having been made to his Majesty by great numbers of merchants, masters of ships and others, as well as by several governors of His Majesty's islands and Plantations in the West Indies, that the pirates are grown so numerous that they infest not only the seas near Jamaica but even those of the Northern Continent of America and that unless some effective means be used, the whole trade of Britain to those parts will not only be obstructed but is in imminent danger of being lost" and further provided for the increase and consolidation in the number of ships overseas in an effective force for the purpose. These included the forty-gun ships *Adventure, Diamond,* and *Ludlow Castle,* the twenty-gun *Winchelsea* and the sloop *Swift* at Jamaica, the *Scarborough, Seaford,* and sloop *Tryal* at Barbadoes, and a call upon the station ships at Virginia, New York, and Boston.

As an experienced hand was needed to manage affairs, Woodes Rogers, of Bristol, who in two ships, the *Duke* and *Duchess* of that city, had not long before concluded a marvelous privateering voyage around the world, taking great wealth from Spain in the Pacific, having that gifted ex-buccaneer, William Dampier, as his pilot and among other things rescuing Alexander Selkirk from Jean Fernandez, was selected for the command. He was given two men-of-war to convey himself to Nassau and commissioned Governor of New Providence with power of life and death. As a warning of what was to come in the way of justice, very much tempered with mercy, the royal George favored Nassau with an advance copy of this proclamation:

"Whereas we have received Information, that several Persons, Subjects of Great Britain, have since the 24th Day of June, in the Year of our Lord 1715, committed divers Pyracies and Robberies upon the High-Seas, in the West-Indies, or adjoyning to our Plantations, which hath and may Occasion great Damage to the Merchants of Great Britain, and others trading into those Parts; and tho' we have appointed such a Force as we judge sufficient for suppressing the said Pyrates, yet the more effectually to put an End to the same, we have thought fit, by and with the Advice of our Privy Council, to Issue this our Royal Proclamation; and we do hereby promise, and declare, that in Case any of the said Pyrates, shall on or before the 5th of September, in the Year of our Lord 1718, surrender him or themselves, to one of our Principal Secretaries of State in Great Britain or Ireland, or to any Governor or Deputy of any of our Plantations beyond the Seas; every such Pyrate and Pyrates so surrendering him, or themselves, as aforesaid, shall have our gracious Pardon, of and for such, his or their Pyracy, or Pyracies, by him or them committed before the fifth of January next ensuing. And we do hereby strictly charge and command all our Admirals, Captains, and other Officers at Sea, and all our Governors and Commanders of any Forts, Castles, or other Places in our Plantations, and all our other Officers Civil and Military, to seize and take such of the Pyrates, who shall refuse or neglect to surrender themselves accordingly. And we do hereby further declare, that in Case any Person or Persons, on, or after, the 6th Day of September, 1718, shall discover or seize, or cause or procure to be discovered or seized, any one or more of the said Pyrates, so refusing or neglecting to surrender themselves as aforesaid, so as they may be brought to Justice, and convicted of the said Offence, such Person or Persons so making such Discovery or Seizure, or causing or procuring such Discovery or Seizure to be made, shall have and receive as a Reward for the same, viz. for every Commander of any private Ship or Vessel, the sum of £100 for every Lieutenant, Master, Boatswain, Carpenter, and Gunner, the Sum of £40; for every inferior Officer, the sum of £30 and for every private Man, the Sum of £20. And if any Person or Persons, belonging to and being Part of the Crew of any such Pyrate Ship or Vessel, shall on or after the said sixth Day of September, 1718, seize and deliver, or cause to be seized or delivered, any Commander or Commanders, of such Pyrate Ship or Vessel, so as that he or they be brought to Justice, and convicted of the said Offence, such Person or Persons, as a Reward for the same, shall receive for every such Commander, the Sum of £200 which said Sums, the Lord Treasurer, or the Commissioners of our Treasury for the Time being, are hereby required, and desired to pay accordingly.

"Given at our Court, at Hampton-Court, the fifth Day of September, 1717, in the fourth Year of our Reign.

"God Save the King."

Instead of being confounded, the community was first amused at
the receipt of this notice and went about its business as before, having
snapped its finger at many governors, *and made a prize of the ship
which brought the document!* A summons was sent to the adventurers
at sea and a grand council held as to the best course to pursue.
There was so much confusion at the meeting that nothing was determined upon. Some were for fortifying and fighting, or at least treating with the government as one commonwealth with another. Others
favored a middle course, in order if dispersed they might be in shape
for pardon, without the pain of restitution. It was left for Captain
Jennings to make up their minds for them, as he personally determined
to accept the terms. This disconcerted the belligerents, who did not
know how to turn. Jennings and one hundred and fifty others embarked for Bermuda where they received certificates from the governor.
He had been a man of good character before the desire to buccaneer
seized him and readily resumed his status, but many of his followers
drifted back to Nassau. The other captains involved included Benjamin Hornigold, Edward Teach, John Martel, John Arthur Davis,
James Fife, Christopher Winter, Nicholas Brown, Paul Williams,
Thomas Carter, Charles Bellamy, Oliver La Bouche, Edward England,
Howel Davis, Major Penner, Thomas Burgess, Thomas Cocklyn, Robert Sample and Charles Vane. Winter and Brown were not in port
and subsequently surrendered to the Spanish in Cuba rather than face
the new régime.

Rogers arrived late in May or early June (the dates differ), coming
off the inner harbor at dusk. He had picked up as a pilot Richard
Turnley, who was to pay later for his service. It was dusk and the
channel so difficult that Turnley advised lying by for the night.
Charles Vane, who had just come in with a prize, having no mind to
reform or lose his possession, made use of the darkness to get away.
The harbor being blocked and his ship drawing too much water to escape by the east passage, he transferred all hands and valuables to a
lighter craft and departed. Then, double charging all the guns on the
deserted ship, he fired the vessel in the thought that, should the warships attempt to cut him out, with both parties they would meet mischief. On the fleet the cannonading and glare of flames created the
belief that the pirates were celebrating their pardon; Captain Whitney
thereupon sent a boat in under one of his lieutenants to note the celebration. He was promptly seized by Vane, the boat stripped and of-

ficer and men held until daybreak when their captor departed, flaunting a black flag and firing a derisive gun in farewell. When the ships got in and Rogers heard the lieutenant's story, the sloop *Buck* was hurriedly sent in pursuit but being overladen could not match the light pirate and was recalled.

The ships now worked in and fixed their anchorages, spending the day in getting themselves in order. The next morning Rogers came ashore, where he was received with proper ceremony by his subjects. The pirate captains drew their men up in double file, between which he marched with his naval escort to be met by Thomas Taylor, president of the Council and Thomas Walker, the Chief Justice. Steps were taken to provide port officers, of whom Richard Turnley, the pilot, was chief, to examine ships and see to orderly clearings. A military council was held to arrange proper guards against the lawless and the Spaniards, from whom there was still danger. Hornigold, Arthur Davis, and others received commissions while George Featherston, Dennis Macarty, and James Bonney, were appointed to minor places. The fort was repaired, the streets cleaned and civilization and law were put to the fore.

When Rogers had restored some semblance of order at Nassau, with what seemed to be good judgment he set out to find occupation for the restless spirits, one being the enterprise of fitting out a number of vessels for trading down the islands. These included the schooner *Bachelor's Adventure*, Captain Henry White, the sloop *Lancaster*, Captain William Greenway, and the sloop *May*, Captain John Augur. There being need of provisions, the flotilla were directed by arrangement to trade first with Porto Principe on the island of Cuba, where there was an abundance of hogs and cattle, which live stock were needed in the Bahamas, as furnishing a certain supply of meat. The three departed from Nassau on the 5th of October, 1718. The next day they put in at Green Key, an island southeast of New Providence, where wild hogs abounded, for the purpose of procuring some fresh pork. The hunters were out during the day and at night Greenway and White came on board Augar's sloop to discuss the time for sailing. After it had been agreed to start at ten o'clock the next morning, the captains returned to their several vessels.

Later Phineas Burch, Dennis Macarty, and a considerable number of others came on board Augur's sloop, making the pretense that they wished to see Richard Turnley, the chief Pilot, and James Carr, a former midshipman in the Royal Navy, who, being deep in Rogers's, confidence, had been made supercargo of the fleet. Knowing there was a supply of beer on board, the crowd called for some of this plain refreshment, which had been brought along as a gift for the Spanish merchants at Porto Principe. Mr. Carr cheerfully went to the store-room for some bottles, which were served to the company as they sat about Captain Augur on the poop. When the liquor had circulated the talk fell upon the good old days of piracy, with much boasting of former adventures, until, fired by beer and excitement, some who had been outlaws proclaimed that the life of a pirate was the only one for a man of spirit. Suddenly Burch sprang up and announced with an oath that he would become captain of the vessel, to which Augur answered that one captain would suffice and he was the man. The furor died down for a time. Then Burch began to boast of the bright arms on his vessel and as if to confute him some one brought up the cutlasses belonging to the crew that had that day been cleaned, among them the supercargo's silver-hilted sword. Burch asking whose it was. Mr. Carr replied it was his own, whereat the ruffian, now well stimulated, took it from the scabbard and, swinging it over Carr's head, resumed his vaporings and coming near the supercargo struck him with it. Turnley warned him to desist. During the confusion thus caused Macarty and some others seized the cabin where the arms were stored, while others struck up a song: "Did you not promise me that you would marry me?" which was the signal for revolt. Burch responded by shout-ing, "By G— that I will, for I am a parson." With that he again struck Mr. Carr with his sword. Carr and Turnley seized him, but the armed men poured out of the cabin and at once overpowered them and took the sloop. Greenway was now hailed to come on board and, suspecting nothing, obeyed. He was led into the cabin by Macarty and told he was a prisoner. His sloop was next captured and Captain White was lured on board the *May* by the same stratagem and made captive. His crew was agreeable to the new undertaking and Augur now showed his old colors by joining with the men, perhaps having been in the conspiracy from the start.

Some of the gang wished to kill Turnley, the honest pilot, but the majority were for marooning him that he might "die like a dog" for having been the man to guide Rogers into the harbor of New Provi-dence. This was accordingly done. Turnley, Carr, and several others who were not of their kind, were stripped naked, tossed into a boat without oars, and commanded to begone. They contrived, however, to land on the island where, being discovered the next morning, they were invited on board, Macarty being the messenger. Thinking the rascals had relented they returned, but only to meet with brutal treatment designed to force the discovery of some items of value they had failed to extract, including Mr. Carr's silver watch and snuff-box. Thomas Rich, one of the honest men, was threatened because he had once been seen at Nassau with a gold watch which could not now be found. He was able to prove that it belonged to Captain Gale of the guardship *Delicia,* on which he had been a seaman, and so escaped more torture. They vainly tried to persuade Greenway to join as he was a good navigator but, being obdurate, he was put with the other officers and unwilling men to the number of eight in a boat and set adrift. The rogues then rifled Greenway's sloop. He having got on shore and seeing them row away, ventured to his vessel, but when the pirates perceived this, they assumed that he had returned to join and turned back to talk with him. They were in a half-drunken state and he wheedled them into such good humor that he was told to keep the sloop, which had little left in it. Accordingly, Greenway swam ashore to tell the others also, bringing word that they must not depart until the pirates sailed, that being their final decree.

In the afternoon Burch and some others came ashore with wine and food, endeavoring to tempt the naked fellows back, but after much talk they drank all the wine themselves save a glass for each of the marooned, with a bit of biscuit to wash down. A turtle hunter named Hutchins now came in and under threat of marooning joined the gang. On October 9th they ordered Greenway and his companions on board his sloop and made them set the foresail to the bowsprit for a jib and reef the mainsail close to the boom, with orders so to leave them. Later Burch and Macarty in drunken frolic came on board and, cutting the sails and rigging to pieces, ordered them not to sail until permitted; then departed taking away the boat. Thus abandoned in a worthless vessel, they began to improvise makeshifts with the help of a worn hatchet, the only tool on board. With this they cut up an old cable, and twisted the fiber into rope-yarns, with which they mended the sails. The pirates departing, they made a raft of logs and on reaching the shore cut wild cabbage and found berries and prickly pears; also they caught a few fish and were getting into shape to sail when the pirates appeared again. The party at once paddled ashore on their raft, fired at by the villains, but succeeded in getting away unharmed. The brutes then cut down the *Lancaster's* masts and turning her to deep water sunk her. Then they went on shore to hunt the fugitives, who had in the meantime concealed themselves in tree tops where they remained unobserved. After this useless search the pirates again departed. The maroons having no fire dipped fish in sea water and let them dry in the sun until they were hard, and so more edible.

After eight days the pirates came back and showed some pity, sending a man into the woods to call them out, promising on their honor not to do anyone harm. This being accepted, they gave over some food, some blankets and thread and needles. George Redding, one of the crew who had been forced from the turtler, being a friend of Turnley's, contrived to hand him a tinder box. They now tried once more to force all hands to join and the eight still refusing, Greenway, White, and the captain of the turtler, Benjamin Hutchins, were held, the five others—Carr, Turnley, Rich, John Taylor, and John Cox— were again landed. After the departure of the fickle rascals the party got along well, thanks to the tinder box, but were soon alarmed to see them reappear. They hid again in the tree tops and, fearing treachery, refused to respond when called. This time the hearts of the rogues had again melted. On departing they left a good supply of food, beside several muskets, a keg of powder and some ball, an axe, a pot, a pan, and three hunting dogs from the turtler sloop. Again the pirates came and, surprising Turnley with a wild hog he had just shot, made Cox carry it to the boat, on which they gave him a bottle of rum and promised to go away and never trouble them more.

This promise was kept, but not necessarily of a purpose. Sailing away toward Long Island, they came upon three vessels at anchor, which they presumed were from New York or Bermuda. They bore down upon them to find instead they were Spanish privateers who at once defended themselves, first firing on the turtler sloop, which being the faster was first in range, killing and wounding many of her crew, the others leaping into the sea and swimming ashore. The commodore of the privateers was an Irishman nicknamed "Turn Joe." The Spaniards took the sloop, finding on her Phineas Burch, the braggart who had been captain. The second pirate came alongside and was riddled as the first had been and taken, as was the third, each thinking the other had been successful and eager to join in the promised pillage. "Turn Joe" picking out the men who had been forced, took

UNDER THE BLACK FLAG

the goods out of one of his smaller vessels, and gave her to them to take themselves home, together with some of the wounded scamps. They reached Nassau and turned in their prisoners, also apprising Rogers of the whereabouts of Turnley and his companions. He at once sent John Sims, a mulatto who owned a light boat, to their rescue, which he at last contrived after much difficulty in persuading them to come out of the tree tops in which they hid on his coming.

Rogers next sent Benjamin Hornigold, one of his reformed pirates, to Long Island to find the rogues who had reached the shore. Hornigold knew his business and managed it well. Taking Turnley along as pilot, he kept off the shore concealing all but a few men. The pirates with equal cunning kept mostly in ambush, a small company going to the beach and pleading as castaways to be taken off, the plan being for the others to rush from ambush and seize the sloop. Hornigold scented this and kept his boat well off shore, while listening to their pleadings, the crew being men picked as not likely to be known. As they begged for food, he sent some bread and wine off in the boat by a man who posed as her master, with a tender interest in the shipwrecked. He gave them the bread and wine, but accounted for himself as putting in after salt for New York. They pleaded to be taken on as passengers, to which the man replied that their number, sixteen, was too great, but he would take a few and leave food for the others until they could be succored. Several entered the boat and were taken to the sloop. Led down into the cabin, they were properly astonished to see Hornigold and to be promptly clapped in irons. The boat now returned and invited a few more to come. In this way all were trapped, shackled and taken to Nassau, where they were tried. Ten, John Augur, Dennis Macarty, William Cunningham, William Lewis, Thomas Morris, George Bendal, William Morris, George Bendal, William Ling, George Rogers, and George Roundevil, were convicted. Six were found to be forced and let go.

They appear to have gone unrepentant to their doom, after vainly striving to stir their former friends to attempt a rescue, crying out from the gallows "that they never thought to have seen the time when ten such men as they should be ty'd up and hanged like dogs, and four hundred of their sworn friends and companions quietly standing by to behold the spectacle."

When called upon to repent their wickedness, one answered from the platform: "I do heartily repent; I repent I have not done more

[114]

mischief and that we did not cut the throats of them that took us, and I am extremely sorry that you ain't all hanged as well as we." Dennis Macarty, calling out that some friends had often said he would die in his shoes, declared he would make them liars, and kicking them off was soon dangling.

Roundevil was reprieved at the last moment but made to witness the fate of his companions. He later went privateering with Joseph Burgess, and the sloop striking a rock south of Green Key, he leaped into the boat with five others, leaving Burgess alone on the poop. The captain begged not to be abandoned but the others refusing to return Roundevil jumped into the sea, swam back to the wreck "and there perished with his friend since he could not save him."

To complete the tale, save as it is continued in the careers of those who refused to surrender or backslid, it may be said that Hornigold, like Burgess, was lost in a wreck from which only five of his crew escaped.

XVII

OF JOHN MARTEL

OF those pirate leaders rendezvousing at New Providence in the Bahamas, when that port was a center of the trade, John Martel was a conspicuous member. Like others of his craft, he had begun with privateering out of Jamaica during the French war and, finding it much to his taste, kept on after all commissions had expired or had been revoked. He is first located in command of a piratical sloop of eight guns and sixty men cruising off Jamaica, in September, 1716. A sloop named *King Solomon* was an early victim, giving a small return in goods, money, and provisions. Heading for Cardenas in Cuba, they took on the way two sloops and off the port a twenty-gun galley, the *John and Martha*, Captain Wilson, loaded with logwood and sugar. Wilson and his men, save a few of the more capable, were put ashore. The *John and Martha* was then altered into a cruiser, fitted with twenty-two guns and given a crew of 100 men under Martel.

A sloop from Barbadoes was taken and trade promised to thrive, when dissension arose on the *John and Martha* because of the arbitrary acts of the captain. He was deposed and given the sloop, together with those who preferred his company, one Kennedy, an Irishman born in Cuba taking his place in command of the larger vessel. On the 15th of October the *Berkeley* galley, Captain Saunders, was taken by Kennedy and on the 16th the *Greyhound*, a London galley, loaded with slaves from Guinea and bearing besides some gold dust and ivory.

John Evans, her captain, after the publication by Captain Charles Johnson of his "Lives of the Pirates," wrote him, correcting his sketch of Martel and giving a detailed account of his captivity, which is of more than passing interest. The capture was made ten leagues S. W. of the Isle of Mona. The pirate was observed at dawn and showed no colors or men save the one at the wheel. His course was such that he would soon be aboard the *Greyhound*, whose captain called

[116]

on the helmsman to halt, but getting no reply managed to get clear and crowded sail. At this the pirate came to life and followed fast—faster than the *Greyhound* could sail, she being very foul from her long voyage from Guinea, while the pirate was clean. She was soon brought to by a shot, which also saluted the unfurling of a black flag, on which was the figure of a man, sword in hand, an hour glass before him, and the skull and bones. A pennant blew out with the latter insignia. Evans refused to check his course until a second shot came through his mainsail, when, on the advice of his officers he halted and went aboard the pirate to be greeted by Captain Saunders, whom he mistook for the captain. Saunders corrected the mistake by escorting Evans aft where he met Kennedy, who welcomed him politely and drank his health in a can of wine. Some of the crew told Evans he was lucky in having escaped Martel, as he had once cut off the whole company of a ship laden with Madeira wine, who put him to too much trouble in its capture.

The pirates now boarded the *Greyhound* and knocked the shackles off the slaves, taking forty of the best to their own vessel and making free with the black women. Kennedy asked for his gold and was assured that he had none. At this he was taken to the great cabin and subjected to an inquisition, in which his mate shared. Pistols were clapped to their breasts and they were threatened with death unless they revealed all the gold on board. The mate was first questioned and denied all knowledge more than that he had seen gold brought on and taken out of the ship. He was sent away and preparations made to torture the captain by burning lighted matches between his fingers. He then thought better of his reticence and speaking privately to Kennedy told him where one hundred ounces were concealed. "He immediately," says Evans, "sent his boat on board the *Greyhound*, with my carpenter and a half a dozen of his own crew, who were so impatient to be at the gold, they made a mere pincushion of the fellow's breech, continually pricking his backside with their swords to hasten him."

The captain was confined to the hold and abused by sundry ruffians for confiding his secret to Kennedy, one knocking him senseless with a blow from the flat of his cutlass. Kennedy left the ship in his yawl at this manifestation of brutality and swore he would not remain in such company, but was persuaded to return. They anchored that night at Savona, where they were kept until the 20th, when both the *Weymouth* and *Greyhound* were permitted to depart.

"The *Weymouth*," adds Evans," had two women passengers on board; how they passed their time I need not say.

"Notwithstanding the melancholy situation I was in, I could not refrain from laughing when I saw the fellows who went on board the *Greyhound* return to their own ship, for they had, in rumaging my cabbin, met a leather powder bag and puff, with which they had powdered themselves from head to foot, walked the deck with hats under their arms, minced their oaths and affected all the airs of a Beau, with an awkwardness that would have forcd a smile from a Cynic."

Evans found his papers torn to fragments and the negroes free. He was without arms to subdue them, but summoning resolution, caused the crew to grasp handspikers and drive them to the hold. This done, they were called up one by one and shackled. In this way he made a fair delivery save of the forty taken on the pirate. Four of his men elected to remain in the free company. Though out of the larger ship, Martel seems to have cruised in common. Next among the Leeward Islands a number of profitable captures were made, including a twenty-gun ship called the *Dolphin* from Jamaica for Newfoundland, which was retained as a consort. In mid-December, the *Kent* galley, Captain Lawton, home-bound from Jamaica, was added to the list of captures. She was released and compelled to turn back to Jamaica for supplies, being emptied by her captors.

The ships needing cleaning, all were taken into Santa Cruz, where it was thought they would be safe from molestation, there being in the fleet beside the ship and brigantine originally employed, the twenty-gun ship and two sloops, or five vessels in all. Once at the island the several craft were warped into creeks for safety and the operations of cleaning begun.

It chanced that in November the activities of the pirates had caused Governor Hamilton, of the Leeward Islands, to instruct Captain Hume, of H. M. S. *Scarborough*, at Barbadoes to go in search of the marauders. The *Scarborough* had been much crippled by fever, having lost twenty by death, with forty in the sick bay. Captain Hume put his sick ashore and taking on twenty soldiers at Antigua, ten at Nevis, and ten at St. Christopher's, cruised among the islands. At Anguilla he heard that the pirates had been at Spanish Town, on one of the Virgin

[118]

Islands, but on reaching that port gained no intelligence of their plans, as they had put in about Christmas. It was then January 15th, 1717, and Captain Hume had decided to return to Barbadoes, when that same evening a boat came in from Santa Cruz with word of Martel's presence at the northwest side of that island. He got under way at once and by the next morning was off the creeks, where the pirates lay. They welcomed him with a liberal store of shot, some of them heated red, to which he replied with the frigate's full force. His pilot, however, would not risk taking the *Scarborough* in, but she was at length warped alongside the reef, which enabled her to return the fire more effectively. About 4 P. M. a sloop that guarded the channel through the reef went down under the bombardment. The *Scarborough* then turned her batteries on the ship, which lay behind an island. On the night of January 12th, fearing weather conditions, Captain Hume stood off the island, maintaining a blockade. On the 20th, being still compelled to keep at sea, the pirates tried to warp the ship out of the channel and make a run for it. Instead of clearing the reef they grounded, and the *Scarborough* now putting in, the ship was abandoned and set on fire, twenty negroes on board being allowed to perish in the flames. Nineteen of the pirates got away in one of the small sloops, but Martel and the remainder, with twenty more Africans, who were slaves on the ship, made for the woods where the man-of-war's men did not care to pursue. The prisoners left on the remaining vessels were rescued, but nothing further appears on record of Martel and his companions.

XVIII

OF EDWARD TEACH, CALLED BLACKBEARD

BRISTOL, as a seafaring port, took the lead in the seventeenth and eighteenth centuries in turning out pirates, one of the most eminent of whom was Edward Teach, called Blackbeard, from the flowing fronds of hair that decorated his chin and added ferocity to his visage. He went to sea like many another Bristol lad, and found adventure during Queen Anne's war in sailing out from Kingston on a Jamaica privateer cruising against the French. From privateering to piracy was a short and easy step. Teach became a member of the pirate crew under Captain Benjamin Hornigold and soon distinguished himself for strength and courage, so that he was made master of a prize ship. This was toward the end of 1716. Hornigold made New Providence in the Bahamas his headquarters. From this port, in the spring of 1717, the pair cruised toward the American coast, taking on the way a billop, from Havana, carrying 120 barrels of flour and a Bermuda sloop, commanded by one Thurber. Captain Thurber had only to part with his store of wine to secure release. A ship from Madeira to Charleston gave a better yield. Hornigold and Teach now put into a Virginia inlet and there cleaned their vessels, after which they once more sought the West Indies. In latitude 24 a French Guinea trader, from the African coast to Martinique, fell into their hands. She proved a rich prize and was retained as a cruiser, Teach becoming captain. With his pockets well filled, Hornigold now elected to return to New Providence, where, Woodes Rogers having arrived and set about the work of abolishing piracy, he accepted King George's pardon and turned pirate-taker as an aid to Rogers.

Teach, keeping the Guineamen, armed her with forty-nine guns and out of respect to her late Majesty named the ship *Queen Anne's Revenge*. He became active at once. Off St. Vincent a valuable ship called the *Great Allen*, Captain Christopher Taylor, was captured, her crew put ashore on the island, and the vessel burned. This roused the warships on the station and one of them, the *Scarborough*, of thirty guns, attacked the pirate but proved too weak for the undertaking and made off; Teach having defended himself valiantly for several hours, the *Scarborough* put in to Barbadoes to salve her wounds. Following this adventure Teach now fell in with Major Stede Bonnet, and the *Revenge*. When Teach found Bonnet ignorant of sea knowledge, he removed him from the *Revenge* with the consent of the crew, and put a trusty hand of his own named Richards in charge. Bonnet remained on Teach's ship during the eventful cruise that followed, where, as "he had not been used to the fatigues and cares of such a post" he would be relieved "and live easy and at his pleasure," not being "obliged to perform duty, but follow his own inclinations."

The two sail now put in at Turniff, "ten leagues short of the Bay of Honduras," where the water-casks were filled. While they were lying here a sloop was sighted inbound, at which Richards in the *Revenge* slipped his cable and, hoisting the black flag, overhauled the stranger, which proved to be the *Adventure,* from Jamaica, David Harriot, master. The crew and captain were placed on Blackbeard's ship, while a prize crew under Israel Hands took possession of the sloop. On the 9th of April, 1717, after a week at Turniff the squadron set sail for the Bay of Honduras, where they surprised a ship and four sloops at anchor. The ship was the *Protestant Cæsar,* Captain Wyar, from Boston. Three of the sloops were owned by Jonathan Bernard of Jamaica, and the fourth by Captain James, who commanded her. As Teach came sailing in at the head of his fleet he unfurled the black flag and fired a gun, at which Captain Wyar and his crew made quick haste to gain the shore. The ship was plundered and burned, out of spite against Boston, where some pirates had lately been hanged. Captain James also lost his vessel in flames. Bernard's three sloops were spared. Next the rovers made Turk's Island, going thence to Grand Cayman, where an unlucky turtle catcher furnished meager spoil. They then went to Havana, perhaps in some disguise, to sell their loot, and thence to the Bahamas. The next tack was to the Carolinas, picking two sloops and a brigantine on the way. The fleet hovered off the Charleston bar for nearly a week, during which time they took a London ship, outbound, Captain Robert Clark, with passengers for England, two pinks, a brigantine with fourteen slaves on board, and a second ship.

News of these exploits alarmed the coast, off which Charles Vane had just been operating very successfully. Eight ships lay in the harbor of Charleston, not daring to put to sea, and none came in. Trade was entirely interrupted and this misfortune, following the close of a costly war with the Cherokees, filled the province with gloom. To top the insolence of the performance, being in need of medicines Teach sent his empty chest aboard the *Revenge*, which under Richards entered the harbor, and using Mr. Marks, one of Captain Clark's passengers, as a messenger, he demanded of the authorities that it be filled and the *Revenge* be allowed to return unmolested to her consorts, under threat of the direst vengeance to the captives held in the flagship. During the delivery of this message, Richards and members of his crew walked the streets serenely, with no sign of fear. The town folks observed this bravado with deep but ineffective indignation, fearing as they did for the safety of friends held as hostages, one of whom was Samuel Wragg, a member of the Council. The chest was therefore filled with drugs to the value of £400 and the brazen emissaries returned unscathed to the fleet. Upon this Blackbeard released his captives, after taking all their money, above £1,500 and such stores as he needed.

Satisfied with his prowess, Teach now took all his vessels into Topsail Inlet and planned to accept the King's pardon. Not certain that this course would meet with the favor of all, he purposely grounded his ship and, summoning hands to his aid, the sloop also was grounded, so heavily that both were abandoned. Bonnet was returned to the *Revenge*, while Teach took the tender and, with forty hands who were devoted, marooned seventeen of the irreconcilables without food or water on a bar and, proceeding to the house of Governor Charles Eden, surrendered under the King's pardon. Eden, it was more than surmised, shared in some of Teach's treasure, for he gave him fair title to the *Queen Anne's Revenge*, and, construing the stranded sloop, her consort, as a "Spanish prize" although English owned, awarded that to the now "loyal" pirate. "These proceedings," observes the chronicle of the day, "shew that governors are but men."

The vessels, taken out of the ooze, were now anchored in Ocracoke Inlet, during which time Teach married a sixteen-year-old damsel, dazzled by his display of silks, jewels, and gold, whom he treated with surpassing brutality. By this time it was June, 1718. Forgetting his oath under the King's pardon, the pirate once more took to the sea, heading for Bermuda and robbing three vessels on the way. Near the islands two French ships for Martinique were held up. One, light-laden, was released. The other, filled with sugar and cocoa, was

[122]

taken back to North Carolina and her cargo sold, Eden sharing in the proceeds, classing the capture as a bit of "privateering." Sixty hogsheads of sugar went to his Excellency, and to Mr. Knight, his secretary and Collector of Customs, twenty. The pirates shared the rest of the pickings. Lest some one might come in who knew the ship, by the Governor's consent she was condemned as leaky and unfit and set on fire so, burning to the water's edge, she sank out of sight and with her the evidence of the crime. Secure in the shelter of the Governor's favor, Teach lay in Ocracoke between three and four months, trading off his spoil with the sloops that navigated the inlets, some of whom were willing and others unwilling customers. Some times he helped himself without pay, grimly advising the reluctant skipper to charge the account, "knowing well they dared not send him a bill for the payment."

Meantime he caroused with his companions, or made himself a welcome guest among the planters by his lavish entertainment and free gifts of rum and sugar. As his wares gave out he began treating the planters in the same manner as the sloop masters, helping himself to supplies and waxing insolent against protest. He even took a high tone toward the Governor, to which that involved official had to submit. The requisitions upon the sloops and planters becoming burdensome, the latter, feeling the uselessness of an appeal to Eden, sent a delegation to A. Spottiswoode, His Majesty's Lieutenant-Governor and Commander-in-Chief of the Colony and Dominion of Virginia, asking for relief from their oppressions and for the sending of an armed force to destroy the pirate and his crew. Two vessels of war, the *Pearl* and *Lime*, had been lying in the James River for ten months and it was arranged to employ a number of sloops, manned from these, to hunt out the rogues. Lieutenant Robert Maynard, commander of the *Pearl*, was placed in command of the expedition. The sloops carried no cannon, but were well equipped with men and small arms. As a prelude to the hunt Governor Spottiswoode issued this proclamation:

"Whereas, by an Act of Assembly, made at a Session of Assembly, begun at the Capital in Williamsburgh, the eleventh Day of November, in the fifth Year of his Majesty's Reign, entitled, An Act to encourage the apprehending and destroying of Pyrates: It is, amongst other Things enacted, that all and every Person, or Persons, who, from and after the fourteenth Day of November, in the Year of our Lord one thousand seven hundred and eighteen, and before the fourteenth Day of November, which shall be in the Year of our Lord one thousand seven hundred and nineteen, shall take any Pyrate, or Pyrates, on the Sea or Land, or in Case of Resistance, shall kill any such Pyrate, or Pyrates, between the Degrees of thirty four, and thirty nine, of Northern Latitude, and within one hundred Leagues of the Continent of Virginia, or within the Provinces of Virginia, or North Carolina, upon the Conviction, or making due Proof of the killing of all, and every such Pyrate, and Pyrates, before the Governor and Council, shall be entitled to have, and receive out of the publick Money, in the Hands of the Treasurer of this Colony, the several Rewards following; that is to say, for Edward Teach, commonly call'd Captain Teach, or Black-Beard, one hundred Pounds, for every other Commander of a Pyrate Ship, Sloop, or Vessel, forty Pounds; for every Lieutenant, Master, or Quarter-Master, Boatswain, or Carpenter, twenty Pounds; for every other inferior Officer, fifteen Pounds, and for every private Man taken on Board such Ship, Sloop or Vessel, ten Pounds; and, that for every Pyrate, which shall be taken by any Ship, Sloop or Vessel, belonging to this Colony, or North Carolina, within the Time aforesaid, in any Place whatsoever, the like Rewards shall be paid according to the Quality and Condition of such Pyrates. Wherefore, for the Encouragement of all such Persons as shall be willing to serve his Majesty, and their Country, in so just and honorable an Undertaking, as the suppressing a Sort of People, who may be truly called Enemies to Mankind; I have thought fit, with the Advice and Consent of his Majesty's Council, to issue this Proclamation, hereby declaring, the said Rewards shall be punctually and justly paid, in current Money of Virginia, according to the Directions of the said Act. And, I do order and appoint this Proclamation, to be published by the Sheriffs, at their respective County-Houses, and by all Ministers and Readers, in the several Churches and Chappels, throughout this Colony.

"Given at our Council-Chamber at Williamsburgh, this 24th Day of November, 1718, in the fifth Year of his Majesty's Reign. God Save The King.

A. Spottiswoode."

Maynard and his squadron sailed from Kicquetan on the James, November 17, 1718, and made Ocracoke on the evening of the 21st, where he found the pirate lying in plain view. The expedition had been moved with great secrecy but Teach had word of its coming through his friend, Governor Eden, Mr. Secretary Knight having been at the pains to send him a letter of warning. Other alarms had proven fruitless, and Teach took no pains to meet this one until he saw the sloops arrive at the mouth of the inlet. When aware of the presence of the war fleet, he spent the night in carousing with the captain of a trader with whom it was suspected he was on more than good terms. But twenty-five of his crew were on board. Maynard made no move during the night, but when the tide served in the morning he proceeded to the attack, sending his boats in to take soundings. These coming within gunshot were fired upon, at which the lieutenant weighed and moved in with his sloops, using sails and sweeps. Teach cut his cable and kept his carronades blazing, in an effort to make a running fight. Maynard, having no cannon, had to respond unavailingly with musketry. Teach ran aground and Maynard's vessels drawing more water were kept at a distance. Accordingly he anchored within half-gunshot to heave over his ballast and stave the water casks. This lightened the ship enough to enable him to steer up to the stranded pirate, who hailed him with:

"Damn you for villains! And, from whence come you?"

"You may see by our colors," called Maynard, "that we are no pirates."

Teach then invited him to send a boat aboard that he might see who they were. To this Maynard replied:

"I cannot spare my boat, but I will come aboard as soon as I can with my sloop."

Teach then quaffed a deep draught of rum to Maynard with these words:

"Damnation seize my soul if I give you quarters or take any from you."

Maynard answered that he neither expected nor intended to give quarter. The pirate, lifted a little by the tide, resumed steerage way so he was able to fire a broadside into Maynard's sloops with fearful effect, killing and wounding twenty of the sailors on the flagship and nine on her consort. Maynard kept the survivors resolutely at the oars, there being no wind, even though the men were completely exposed to the pirate's fire. The pirate now drifted broadside to the shore and Maynard's consort, the *Ranger*, being disabled, dropped astern. Maynard, finding his craft made way, ordered all hands to lie flat on the deck, to avoid a second broadside, he and the man at the helm alone remaining erect. Cutlasses were bared and pistols primed for boarding, and ladders placed at the hatches, so that those between

[125]

decks might make a quick exit. In this posture he ran alongside the pirate, who showered home-made grenades into the sloop, with such resulting noise and smoke as to convince Blackbeard that he had overwhelmed his foes. He accordingly called to his crew that "all but three of four were knocked on the head" and ordered them to follow him. With a pistol in one hand and cutlass in the other, the formidable ruffian leaped to the sloop's deck with fourteen of his men. Maynard met him with a pistol shot which wounded but did not disable his foe. He missed Blackbeard's fire and the two engaged at once in a fierce cutlass duel. Maynard's blade broke in guarding a blow and, swerving to cock a pistol, he would have fallen under the pirate's sword, but it was stopped by a slash from one of the sloop's seamen which might have severed Blackbeard's massive neck. Maynard had but twelve men in the fight against Teach and his fourteen. He fired his pistol at Teach with effect, but not enough to fell him. The robust rover kept his feet until he had received five pistol balls and twenty cutlass wounds in his body, and fell dead in the act of cocking his weapon. Eight of the fourteen were out of the fighting, dead or wounded. The remaining six leaped overboard and cried for quarter, which was granted. The sloops had drifted apart during the encounter, but the *Ranger* coming up engaged those remaining on board Blackbeard's vessel and soon forced their surrender.

It appears that before the fight Blackbeard had sent a faithful negro into the hold with a match to fire the powder, should Maynard and his men get command of his decks. Two prisoners below decks succeeded in preventing the black's carrying out this demonic purpose.

Maynard severed Blackbeard's head from his shattered body and, hanging it from the tip of the bowsprit, sailed in triumph to Bathtown. Letters found in the sloop showed the corrupt relations of the pirate with Governor Eden, and Secretary Knight; also his relations with some New York merchants. On reaching Bathtown, Maynard seized the Governor's storehouse, finding in it the sugar taken from the French ship, which had been presented to Eden and his secretary, as previously noted. Knight was taken ill and soon died, in the fear, it was believed, that he might be called to account. Israel Hands, late master of the sloop, was found at Bathtown and taken back with fourteen other prisoners to Virginia for trial. Maynard set sail with the head of Blackbeard still suspended from his bowsprit. The dead on the pirate vessel beside their captain were Phillip Morton, gunner; Garrat Gibbens, boatswain; Owen Roberts, carpenter; Thomas Miller, quartermaster, and John Husk, Joseph Curtis, Joseph Brooks and Nathaniel Jackson, seamen. Those taken, beside Hands, were John Carnes, Joseph Phillips, Joseph Brooks, 2d, James Blake, John Gills, Thomas Gates, James White, James Robbins, John Martin, Edward Salter, James White, Richard Stiles, Stephen Daniel, Richard Greensail, Samuel Odell, and Cæsar, the black man, who had been set to blow up the ship. Thirteen out of the fifteen captives were hanged. Samuel Odell showed that he was forced, and Hands, who had been shot through the knee by Teach in a drunken frolic and lamed for life, though convicted, was spared by the grace of a copy of the King's pardon coming to hand in a ship that arrived before the date set for his execution. He went to London and there begged his bread on the streets.

Teach was a striking figure, very tall and his beard black and long. He wore it in twisted pigtails, tied with ribbons and sometimes threw strands over his ears. In action he wore a string over his shoulder, carrying three brace of pistols, ready primed, and affixed lighted matches to his hatband, the burning glare of which added to the savageness of his appearance and gave him the aspect of a fury hot from Hell. Indeed, he cultivated this presence and once when drunk said, "Come, let us make a hell of our own, and try how long we can bear it." Accordingly the company adjoined to the hold where bars of brimstone were lighted, which they endured until almost suffocated, when the men cried for air. He then opened the hatches, "not a little pleased that he had held out the longest."

When asked the night before his death whether his wife knew where he had hidden his money, he replied that "nobody but himself and the Devil" knew and "the longest liver would take it all."

Yet the rascal kept a journal in which there was not a little wisdom and knowledge of human nature shown, one entry reading:

"Such a day! Rum all out! Our company somewhat sober! A damn'd confusion among us! Great talk of a separation. So I looked hard for a prize—took one with a great deal of liquor on board, so kept the company hot, damn'd hot; then all things went well again."

Beside the goods stored in Governor Eden's cache, there was found in the sloop and under a tent on shore, 25 hogsheads of sugar, 11 tierces and 145 bags of cocoa, a barrel of indigo, and a bale of cotton, the whole in value, with the governor's and secretary's share, being valued at £25,000. This was shared among the company on Maynard's vessel's, both those in the fight and those who remained on the warships in the James, together with Governor Spotswood's reward. Sad to relate some of them turned pirate and one at least was caught with Roberts's crew and hanged.

Whatever may be thought of Blackbeard's villainies, his fame was wide and long-lived; his end most becoming.

There was great rejoicing throughout the colonies over the destruction of the pirate. Benjamin Franklin, then an apprentice in his brother James's Boston printing office, composed what he calls in his autobiography, "a sailor's song on the taking of Teach (or Blackbeard) the pirate" which he was sent about the streets to sell. "Wretched stuff" Franklin calls it. No copy is known to be extant. Dr. Edward Everett Hale, in the Memorial History of Boston, cites a fragment of rude verse, given him from memory by Dr. George Hayward that may possibly have been part of Franklin's ballad. It reads:

> "Then each man to his gun,
> For the work must be done
> With cutlass, sword or pistol.
> And when we no longer can strike a blow
> Then fire the magazine boys and up we go.
> It is better to swim in the sea below
> Than to hang in the air and feed the crow,
> Said jolly Ned Teach of Bristol."

NOTE: Incidentally the precocious Benjamin's primary place in journalism was the outcome of a matter of piracy. The New England *Courant* of June, 17, 1722, published an item under a Newport, R. I., date concerning the activity of a pirate off Block Island, concluding with this comment: "We are advised from Boston, that the Government of Massachusetts are fitting out a ship to go after the pirates, to be commanded by Capain Peter Papillon, and 'tis thought he will sail sometime this month, wind and weather permitting."

Whether this was giving away information or sarcasm is not now clear, but it gave offense to the authorities. James Franklin was summoned before the council "to answer for the same" and upon his taking responsibility for the item "it was resolved that the publication of the said paragraph was a high affront to this government" and the sheriff was forthwith ordered to place the publisher in jail, where he remained, being given only the liberty of the yard to repair his health upon his assurance of contrition. While he was in prison his brother Ben ran the paper. July 5th, he was compelled to give bonds for good behavior and to submit all "copy" to the secretary of the council for approval. He did not proceed satisfactorily under this duress, though released after four weeks in confinement. He struggled under the hardship until the paper was suppressed in February, 1723, when on the 11th of that month it came out under Benjamin's name, the elder no longer being permitted to publish news in Boston.

Beside being exploited in song and story, "Blackbeard" was shown on the boards. There is record of a play and a spectacle inspired by his repute. The first was "Blackbeard; or, the Captive Princess," which had its initial performance at the Royal Circus, London, on Easter Monday, 1798 and was repeated for upward 100 nights. In 1811 "The Nautical Spectacle, Blackbeard, the Pirate" was presented at the Boston Theater. In 1820 the play was revived in London under the more magnificent title of "Blackbeard; or, The Desperate Pirate and Captive Princess."

Though two hundred years have passed since Blackbeard ceased to frequent the North Carolina sounds and inlets, his memory still haunts the vicinage. "Teach's Oak," under whose shade he was reputed to relax, still stands in gigantic old age near Oriental, N. C., and the fisher folk think that sometimes in a fog they see in the dark whorls that spot the mist, the pirate's head grimly grinning from the bowsprit of the *Pearl*.

XIX

OF CHARLES VANE

WE have been told the story in a preceding chapter of Charles Vane's escape from the Bahamas, and the gay manner of it. His history begins so far as known with that episode, save that he was one of Jennings's men in the purloining of the Spanish silver. Safe from pursuit, Vane lost no time in resuming operations. Soon a fishing vessel brought in to New Providence Captain King and a few seamen of the ship *Neptune*, a South Carolina vessel loaded with rice and naval stores bound for London, which the escaping pirate had taken, plundered and dismasted and Vane believed had sunk, because on leaving a gun had been fired into her hold for the purpose of blowing out the bottom. Some of the crew were impressed and King, with the others, given the canoe in which they had been moving from one island to another when picked up by the fishermen, their capture taking place near Green Turtle Bay. Governor Rogers at once fitted out a ship called the *Willing Mind*, with fifty men, and a sloop with thirty, and sent them in search of Vane. He was not discovered, but the *Neptune* was found still afloat, the shot having lodged in the ballast, thus doing no injury to the hull. She was brought in but the *Willing Mind*, being ill-steered, was broken on the bar.

Vane, continuing his cruise, caught a sloop from Barbadoes, which furnished him with a suitable consort and into her he put twenty-eight men under one Yeats as master. The pair next captured a smuggling trader bound for New Providence. She was called the *John and Elizabeth* and had some Spanish silver aboard, the proceeds of her contrabanding to Cuba. She was taken along to one of the Windward Islets where they cleaned the ship, divided spoil and lived riotously in the pirate way. Toward the end of May, being in need of supplies, they beat up toward the Windwards, where they took a Spanish sloop from Cuba to Porto Rico, whose crew was placed in their longboat and allowed to get ashore, if they could. She yielded little, but later, between St. Christopher and Anguilla, a sloop and brigantine filled all their needs. Being now supplied, they lay in the track of ships between Old and New England, with much success, taking what was valuable and letting the vessels go. At the end of August they ran down to the Carolinas and off the coast took an Ipswich ship, commanded by Captain Coggeshall, loaded with logwood from the Bay of Honduras. At first the capture was deemed useful for their own purposes and Coggeshall's crew was set to throwing the logwood overboard. The wind changing and with it their minds, the pirates returned the vessel to her commander and went on their way. A sloop for Barbadoes, another from Antigua, and a brigantine slaver with ninety blacks aboard, next fell prizes. All were pillaged and released, the slaves being placed on board the consort with Yeats, by which manner they were soon restored to their consignees, for Yeats, considering himself ill-treated by Vane, now made up his mind to desert. Within a day or two, while at anchor, and at evening, Yeats slipped cable and made sail. Vane perceiving this and sensing that it meant an effort to part company, raised anchor and went in pursuit. He was fast gaining when the sloop crossed the bar of the North Edisto, where the brigantine could not follow. Vane gave him a broadside as a farewell and sheered off. Yeats sent a petition to the Governor of South Carolina for pardon, which was granted and the negroes were duly delivered to those who had bought them. Vane lingered off the bar, hoping Yeats would come out again, and improved his time by capturing two ships outbound from Charleston for England.

By this time the authorities were aroused and two sloops were fitted out to take him, but they fell in with other quarry, as related in the history of Stede Bonnet. Vane, by giving a misleading account of his direction to one of the released ships, sent his pursuers in an opposite course and himself went north, where in Roanoke Sound he met John Teach, the famous Blackbeard, with whom he politely exchanged salutes. Finding the hunting ground so well occupied, after a few days of exchanging civilities with Teach, Vane tacked toward Long Island, off which he took a Salem brigantine returning from Jamaica, John Shattuck, Captain. This was on the 23d of October, 1718. A small sloop was also captured. It was now decided to cruise off Hispaniola between Cape Maysi and Mole St. Nicholas, the weather in the North Atlantic growing cold. A season of delight was spent in these waters. Food and liquor were plentiful. A descent on the shore yielded a liberal supply of plunder and provisions.

[131]

During February in the Windward passage, the *Kingston*, a large London ship was taken, having a cargo of value beside a number of passengers, men and two women. Passing north of Jamaica Vane stopped and robbed a turtle sloop and then put on her the people from the *Kingston*, save the two women, whose fate may be imagined, though it was not often the habit of the craft to detain females. The company had grown by recruits and impressment from the *Neptune* and *Kingston*, so that the latter was made a consort and Vane's quartermaster, John Rackam, given charge. Vane, running short of liquor, called on his colleagues for a supply. The quantity spared being considered meager, he went on board of Rackam and expostulated with him over his parsimony. In the resulting quarrel Rackam threatened to shoot him if he did not leave the ship and once on board his own to sink him if he did not part company.

They separated accordingly, Vane and his companions in the sloop sailing for the Bay of Honduras as the best spot for beginning over again. Off Jamaica a sloop and several perigues were overtaken, all of whose men joined. The sloop was taken along, with Robert Deal, who had been mate on the brigantine and sided with Vane, as master. The two came into the Bay of Honduras on the 16th of December, where they found the sloop *Pearl*, of Jamaica, Charles Rowling, master. He resisted, but was soon taken. Later another Jamaica sloop was also captured. Vane rendezvoused at the Island of Bonacco where the sloops were cleaned and then, departing on a cruise, were caught in a tornado which separated them. The one that bore Vane was wrecked, after two days' tossing in the gale, on a small island. She was dashed to pieces and nearly all of the men drowned. Here the survivors remained, enduring great hardship, succored by turtle catchers from the mainland to which they did not care to go and meet the tender treatment likely from the Spanish authorities. While they thus lingered a Jamaica ship put in whose captain, Halford, had been one of Morgan's buccaneers and knew Vane well. To his prayer to be taken away, Halford replied: "Charles, I shan't trust you on board my ship, unless I carry you as prisoner, for I shall have you caballing with my men, knock me on the head and run away with my ship a-pirating."

Vane protested on his honor but Halford refused again, saying there were ways enough for him to escape if he tried and, remarking that he was about to sail, added: "I am going down the bay and shall return here in about a month; and if I find you on the island when I come back I'll carry you to Jamaica and hang you."

"Which way can I get away?" asked Vane.

"Are there no fishermen's dories on the beach," answered Halford. "Can't you take one of them?"

"What," said Vane "would you have me steal a dory then?"

"Do you make it a matter of conscience," grimly replied Halford, "to steal a dory when you have been a common robber and pirate, stealing ships and cargoes and plundering all mankind that fell in your way? Stay there and be damned if you are so squeamish."

Thus abandoned, Vane awaited the next comer. A ship put in whose captain had no knowledge of him and he was allowed to enter before the mast. By ill fortune it chanced they fell in with Halford, who, being invited to dine on board, recognized him. He at once informed the captain of the identity of the smart seaman who had already won attention by his merits. The captain then said he would not keep him on board. Halford concluded his duty was to take Vane to Jamaica and sending an armed boat after him had him removed to his own vessel. He was carried to Kingston, tried, condemned, and executed. Deal had no better fortune for he, too, with the men in the sloop were earlier taken by a man-of-war and graced the greedy gibbets at Port Royal.

XX

OF STEDE BONNET

MAJOR STEDE BONNET was a citizen of substance in Barbadoes where he had been highly esteemed. Becoming obsessed with the idea that he was destined for a great career upon the sea, he abandoned his estate in the early summer of 1717 and, purchasing a sloop, he equipped the vessel with ten guns. Naming her the *Revenge*, he set sail by night upon his criminal course. His actions are inexplicable upon any basis of need, for he had ample fortune and his step was credited to a disorder of the mind, which, according to the chronicle of the day, in accounting for "this Humour of going a pyrating," was produced "by some Discomforts he found in the married state." To which the chronicle concludes: "Be that as it will, the Major was but ill qually'd for the Business, as not understanding maritime Affairs."

Upon leaving Barbadoes Bonnet headed for the Capes of Virginia, off which he despoiled the *Anne of Glasgow*, Captain Montgomery; the *Endeavor*, of Bristol, Captain Scot; the *Young*, from Leeds and the *Turbes* from Barbadoes. This last was burned. From the capes the *Revenge* stood for the New England coast and off Block Island captured a sloop bound for the West Indies. She then put into Peconic Bay at the east end of Long Island and, landing a boat's crew on Gardiner's Island, bought and paid for fresh provisions. Turning south, the *Revenge* lurked off the bar before Charleston, in South Carolina. Here Bonnet took a sloop from Barbadoes, Joseph Palmer, master, bound in with "sugar, rum, and negroes," and later a Down-East brigantine, Thomas Porter, master. The brigantine was robbed and released, but the Barbadoes sloop was taken into an obscure Carolina harbor and burned.

Bonnet had by this time demonstrated to the crew his lack of seaknowledge and there was much disorder and confusion on his craft. For the moment no course could be decided upon, when by chance they fell in with Edward Teach, the famous Blackbeard. Bonnet was deposed and one Richards made captain of the *Revenge*, while Bonnet went on board of Blackbeard's ship and there remained until she was lost in Topsail Inlet. On this disaster Teach took advantage of the King's proclamation to pirates and surrendered. Bonnet then regained command of his own vessel, took her into Bathtown in North Carolina and also took advantage of His Majesty's mercy. He received the certificate of pardon and cleared for St. Thomas, with the purport, it was stated, of privateering against Spain, war having broken out between the Triple Alliance and that country.

Returning to Topsail Inlet, presumably to recruit his crew from the ruffians left there with Blackbeard, he found all had departed with the goods and money that had been collected on joint account, and leaving seventeen men marooned on a desolate sandbar, without food, water, or any means of escape. The wretches had been thus deserted for two nights and a day when discovered by Bonnet, through two men who had escaped Teach's net and hidden in the village. He at once rescued the maroons and invited them to volunteer for his proposed venture against Spain, announcing his expectation of securing a letter of marque at St. Thomas. Learning from a market boat that came "with apples and cider to sell" that Blackbeard was at Ocracoke Inlet, and finding his crew eager for vengeance, he sailed in pursuit of that worthy, but found him gone.

They then turned to the Virginia capes and, being in need of stores, overhauled a pink and took from her what was needed, paying however, for the supplies, ten or twelve barrels of pork and 400 pounds of bread, with a quantity of rice and spare cables. Two days later a sloop was stopped six miles from Cape Henry, which yielded two hogsheads of rum, for which no compensation was made, and eight men were set aboard of her as a prize crew. These gentlemen not caring to risk their necks further in such crazy company departed with the sloop and were seen no more. Bonnet had now taken the conceit to call himself "Captain Thomas," and flinging his pardon to the winds began a career of active robbery. Two ships from Virginia to Glasgow were held up, but only 100 pounds of tobacco taken from them. The next day a small sloop bound for Bermuda yielded twenty barrels of pork and some bacon, for which they returned a hogshead of molasses and a quantity of rice. Two of the sloop's seamen joined the *Revenge*. Another Glasgow ship gave them nothing but a few combs, pins, and needles, for which Bonnet exchanged pork and bread.

They now worked northward to the Delaware capes, where in latitude 34 N. a New England schooner from North Carolina to Boston was stopped. She had to surrender nothing more than a few calfskins that were used as gun covers, but was held for several days. Two snows bound for Bristol from Philadelphia were next taken off the Delaware capes, together with a sloop headed for Barbadoes. These captures gave up a little money and a few goods of value. All were released. On the 29th of July, 1718, in the same latitude another Barbadoes sloop fell victim. Thomas Reed was her captain. Being well laden with provisions, she was retained and a prize crew placed on board. July 31st a sixty-ton sloop inbound from Antigua to Philadelphia, Peter Mainwaring, master, became prey to the pirates. Her worth in money, molasses, sugar, and cotton was about £500. Bonnet was fast learning the "trade." This vessel was kept and with the others headed for the Cape Fear River, whose complicated entrance afforded shelter as it did to the blockade runners in after years.

Here the *Revenge* was rechristened the *Royal James*, but required so much mending as to keep the company two months in port, and proved their undoing. Word reached Governor Robert Johnson at Charleston of the flotilla's presence in his dominions, causing much excitement and the matter was laid before the Council for action. Colonel William Rhett volunteered to proceed with two armed sloops and attempt the capture of the pirates. This offer was promptly accepted and a few days later the *Henry*, of eight guns and seventy men, Captain John Masters, and the *Sea Nymph*, Captain Fayrer Hall, eight guns and sixty men were ready, Colonel Rhett acted as commander-in-chief with the *Henry* as flagship, sailing from the inner harbor to Sullivan's Island on September 14th, to shape up for the expedition.

While they were lying here, a skipper came in with an empty ship from Antigua, having been plundered off the bar by Charles Vane. This made him an object of immediate interest to Rhett's squadron, especially as some of Vane's released captives stated that he was planning to rest in one of the inlets to the southward. Rhett went outside on September 15th and searched the region below Charleston, but finding no trace of Vane turned to the Cape Fear River, coming into it on September 26th. The masts of Bonnet's fleet were visible, but one of Rhett's sloops grounding held until dark before getting off, which made a delay until morning necessary. The pirates sent three canoes down stream to reconnoiter the newcomers and were disagreeably surprised to learn who they were. Bonnet spent the night organizing his defense and among other things wrote a letter threatening dire vengeance should he escape, which he showed to Captain Mainwaring, who was still his prisoner.

In the early morning the *Royal James*, full manned, all crews being taken from the prize, sailed down stream to meet the invaders. Rhett at once endeavored to interpose a sloop on either quarter, with the plan of boarding the pirate simultaneously. In this he was defeated by Bonnet's making for the shore, all the time keeping up a vigorous fire. However, the outlaw ran aground, being followed within pistol shot by the *Henry*, which was also grounded. The *Sea Nymph* too was caught by the bottom, dead ahead of the pirate and nearly out of range. The lowering tide left for the time an advantage with Bonnet, standing well above the *Henry's* level. This lasted during the ebb, but on the flood the *Henry* was first to float, and after five hours of disadvantages began to do effective execution. During the period of inaction the pirates hooted with derision at the colonists, inviting them to come aboard—if they could. To this ribaldry the latter, replied "with cheerful huzzars" and promises to speak with the rogues by and by. Rhett, when afloat, repaired his injured rigging, much cut up by Bonnet's fire, and prepared to board, when to his astonishment Bonnet raised the white flag and asked for a parley, the result which was surrender. Rhett was properly gratified to find he had cornered the right man—Major Stede Bonnet, alias "Captain Thomas."

The fight had not been an easy one. Ten of the *Henry's* men were killed and fourteen wounded, while two died on the *Sea Nymph* and two were injured. Seven were killed outright on the *Royal James*, or *Revenge*, two mortally and three slightly wounded. Rhett left Cape Fear on September 30th, with his prize and prisoners and reached Charleston on the 3d of October, 1718. There was great rejoicing in Charleston over the victory. After two days' dentention on the ships Bonnet and his crew were brought ashore. No proper prison existed at that day, so the crew were confined in the watchhouse while Bonnet was put in charge of the marshal, and kept at his house. Some days later David Hariot, master of the *Revenge* and Ignatius Pell, the boatswain, were also placed in the Marshal's custody and joined Bonnet at his residence. They were expected to turn State's evidence. While the Marshal's mansion was guarded by two sentinels and presumably precautions were taken to keep the captives in bounds, they proved

[137]

insufficient, however, for on the night of October 24th, Bonnet and Hariot made their escape. The boatswain declined to join. Much excitement ensued, together with the incidental scandal and open accusation of bribe-taking, in which the Governor was not spared. That official, however, acted promptly. By proclamation he offered £700 in rewards and sent armed boats to patrol the avenues of exit by water, north and south of the city. There was great fear that the adventurers might seize a ship and set out again on their enterprise. Indeed, Bonnet did depart by water in spite of the patrol, having obtained the use of a shallop, but was beaten back to Sullivan's Island by bad weather and lack of food.

Rumor of the presence of the refugees reaching the authorities, Colonel Rhett was sent in pursuit of them. A night search of Sullivan's Island was made by an armed force which came upon the fugitives, killing Hariot. A negro and an Indian in their company were wounded in the affray. Bonnet surrendered and was brought to Charleston on the morning of November 6, 1718. A Court of Admiralty had been established on the 28th of October for the purpose of trying the pirates, with Nicholas Trot, Chief Justice of the Colony, presiding. The following members of the crew of the *Revenge* were placed on trial: Robert Tucker, Edward Robinson, Neal Paterson, William Scot, William Eddy, Alexander Annand, George Rose, George Dunkin, Thomas Nicholas, John Ridge, Matthew King, Daniel Perry, Henry Virgin, James Robbins, James Mullet, Thomas Price, James Wilson, John Lopez, Zachariah Long, Job Bayly, John-William Smith, Thomas Carman, John Thomas, William Morrison, Samuel Booth, William Hewet, John Levit, William Livers, John Brierly, Robert Boyd, Rowland Sharp, Jonathan Clarke, Thomas Gerrard. All were convicted and sentenced to death, save Rowland Sharp, Jonathan Clarke, and Thomas Gerrard who were proven to have been forced to stay in their bad company. Short shift was allowed. The prisoners were hanged on the 8th day of the month at White Point, the present end of the Battery, at Charleston. The court continuing in session placed Bonnet at the bar on November 10th. He was found guilty and given a death sentence, the court adjourning on the 12th with its work thoroughly done.

Strenuous effort was made to save the convict from his doom. He had friends in Charleston who wished him sent to England where his case might finally be reviewed by the King. Colonel Rhett, twice his captor, offered to accompany him across the sea. The expense, however, promised to be considerable, and his guilt was so unquestionable, coupled with his flagrant violation of his pardon, that the result promised to be unchanged. He was therefore sent to the gallows on November 16th, in a pitiable state of collapse after a vain personal appeal in writing to Judge Trot, that made him out a craven of the greatest dimensions.

XXI

OF JOHN RACKAM

JOHN RACKAM, or as he was known in the trade "Calico Jack" from his habit of always dressing in light cottons, dates in history from his parting with Vane, which is set down as occurring on November 24, 1718. Upon quitting Vane, Rackam first made for the Isle of Princes, where they divided the rich cargo of the *Kingston* by throwing dice for lots, the highest numbers having the leading choice. This being done, they were much cumbered with goods, which were coopered up in casks and buried on the island. A turtle sloop coming in, Rackam learned from her master that war was on with Spain and that time still remained to surrender under the King's pardon. Being in some doubt as to their position, since they had fled from New Providence in the face of pardon, and had committed many acts of piracy, they engaged the captain of the turtle boat to request the governor of Jamaica to consider their status under the circumstances and to bring the answer. The Kingston people having reached that island, the Governor was already fitting out two sloops for a pirate hunt and was glad to learn so accurately of their whereabouts. These sailed at once and took Rackam at great disadvantage, his sails being down and his stores ashore. He therefore fled to the interior of the island with his men, leaving the two women on the *Kingston,* which was taken back to Jamaica with a good share of her cargo still on board. This included considerable gold concealed in bale goods, which the pirates had not discovered.

Rackam and his companions lived as best they could in the woods until the sloops departed, leaving some boats behind, in which it was resolved to go to New Providence and seek pardon under a pretense that they had been carried away by Vane against their wills. Fitting out the best boat with a sail and loading it with some of the concealed goods, with arms, ammunition, and provisions, they made their way to the Isle of Pines, then to the north shore of Cuba, where they took a stouter boat and, sinking their own, actually managed to get to New

OF JOHN RACKAM

Providence about May 15, 1719. Rogers saw fit to receive them and to grant immunity. The goods were sold and all were able to live generously for the time, especially Rackam, who had the larger share. While thus idling Rackam fell in with Anne Bonny, wife of James Bonny, one of the pardoned outlaws. She was reputed to have been born near the city of Cork, in Ireland, the illegitimate daughter of an attorney-at-law, her mother a serving maid in his wife's employ, with whom he emigrated to Carolina, after the dissolution of his domestic arrangements following the discovery of his relations by his better half. Here he practiced his profession and ventured in trade, the maid living with him as his consort until her death. The daughter, now of age, continued to keep his house. She was a vigorous person and hot-tempered, so much so as to cause queer stories to be told concerning her violent actions. Marrying James Bonny, a young sailor, without her father's consent, she was turned out of doors. Her husband, disappointed in the support he expected to receive from a well-to-do father-in-law, departed with his wife for New Providence in search of employment among the adventurers gathered there. Naturally, one of his type soon lost his appeal to the lady, who, being cast upon her own resources, became acquainted with John Rackam, who expended liberal sums upon her so long as his money lasted. This being gone, he volunteered with Joseph Burgees, one of the pardoned pirates, in a privateering cruise against the Spaniards. Two good prizes were brought in, the proceeds from which once more filled the pockets of Rackam, who proceeded to empty them again on Anne Bonny. The husband, though complaisant, was needy and it was proposed that he sell his interest in the lady, to which, indeed, he consented, but the scandal reaching the ears of Rogers the Governor cut the bargain off and ordered the pair to live together respectably or he would have both whipped and would make Rackam wield the lash. The pact was not kept, for the woman and Rackam could not keep apart and therefore resolved to run away together.

They plotted with some of the more reckless spirits, who did not take kindly to the dull life imposed by the King's graciousness, to seize a forty-ton sloop owned by John Haman, who lived on one of the little keys and had employed his small swift vessel in raids on Cuban coastwise trade with much success. Anne Bonny was employed to visit the sloop and spy out an opportunity for its seizure. She found that but two hands were employed and that Haman was always on shore at night with his wife and children. Picking a dark night, Rackam, Anne Bonny, and their chosen companions boarded the sloop. While the woman, in male attire, armed with cutlass and pistol, with one of the men entered the cabin and waking the crew told them to make no noise unless they wished their brains blown out, Rackam loosed the cables, and letting one slip for speed and hauling in the other, put to sea. They were hailed by the Fort and guardship as to where they were going, but replied that their grapple would not hold and accordingly went on until well away. The two men being unwilling, a volunteer was sent ashore in a boat with a message to Haman that his sloop would be returned when they were done with it.

Working among the keys they saw a turtle sloop belonging to Richard Turnley, against whom Anne Bonny held a grudge for a part he played in the scandal, he being a witness to the bargain with Rackam, and it was determined to take revenge upon him. Turnley, seeing the two men employed by Haman putting off for shore, surmised that something was amiss and did not await his callers but taking his son who was along ran and hid in the bushes. Rackam dismantled and sunk the sloop, after robbing it of its sails and other belongings, and induced three out of its four men to join him. These were Richard Connor, the mate, John Davis, and John Howell. David Seward, the fourth, had been an able pirate but was disabled by an old wound and so was left behind.

The pirates now stretched over to the Bay Islands, growing in numbers and getting a better ship by exchange from time to time until strong. As they worked toward Jamaica a vessel, wine-laden from Madeira, fell most gratefully in their thirsty way. She was detained and relieved of her cargo as far as desired and then dismissed, but Rackam took along Hosea Tisdell, an inn-keeper of Jamaica, who had been a passenger on one of the ships taken in Vane's time. The Madeira ship gave them cheer for the holidays, which were spent on one of the keys, with much carousing. After Christmas, the supplies of liquor running low, they cleaned ship and set out to assuage their thirst. Small inter-island sloops furnished the only prey for several months, until they made a queer capture in the shape of a ship bound from London for the plantations, filled with convicts going out in bondage to the farmers. These enjoyed but a few days of liberty in the hands of their captors, for, being a lubberly sailor, she was soon retaken by a British man-of-war.

Rackam now operated near Bermuda, taking a ship outbound from England and a pink from New England. These were taken to the Bahamas where, despite the presence of Rogers with his pardons and punishment, there was still shelter and a welcome. The naval stores on these captures enabled him to caulk and pitch the brigantine, but when he grew careless, word of their presence reached Rogers, who sent two sloops against them and retook the prizes; the brigantine being swift got away.

In his prosperity Rackam established a family headquarters at an obscure port in a small island south of Cuba, where Anne Bonny resided during periods of domestic indisposition, returning to the ship when the discomfort was past. He now paid a visit to the "family" and a stay was made until money and stores were gone. While he was clearing ship and preparing to depart, a Spanish *guarda costa* came in with an English sloop caught illegally trading on the coast. The Spaniard made bold to attack Rackam, who lay close to the island and well out of range. Therefore the *guarda costa* warped into the channel during the evening, with the certainty that the trap was thus shut and he could destroy the pirate readily in the dawn. Rackam soon perceived the desperate pass he was in and acted like a man of courage and resource. The captured sloop lay in such a position that she could be used for escape. Rackam, therefore, manned his boats in the dark and with muffled oars slipped from the brigantine to the sloop. Quickly mastering the prize crew and making her his own, he cut the cable and put to sea. In the morning the Spaniards opened with all their guns upon the brigantine, which to their amazement remained silent under the fire. Their chagrin may be imagined when it was discovered that the birds had flown with a valuable prize, leaving nothing but an empty and well-worn hull behind.

The pirates, rejoicing in the exchange, continued on their lawless career. In August, 1720, Rackam infested the north coast of Jamaica, but found only small returns from inter-island commerce. Some fishermen were robbed of their nets and tackle—no great spoil for the pirates who then went to Hispaniola where they landed and secured cattle and a reinforcement of several Frenchmen who were there engaged in curing wild hogs. Two passing sloops gave up some supplies and Rackam once more made for the north of Jamaica. Here he took a schooner, of which Thomas Spenlow was master, near Porto Maria Bay on the 29th of October. A day later he pursued a sloop into Dry Harbor Bay whose crew, on his firing a gun, ran ashore, leaving him their vessel and cargo. Finding his color they hailed and, volunteering to join, were duly enrolled in the crew.

Pausing to capture a canoe, whose occupants made for the shore at Ocho Bay, Rackam's presence became known to the Governor of Jamaica. He at once fitted out an armed sloop under Captain Barnes, who went in search of the rovers. He was soon to find them. Rackam, idling near Point Negrie, saw a pirogue near the shore containing nine men who, at the sight of the sloop, went ashore. They were hailed by Rackam, informed he was English, and invited to come on board and drink some punch. This the unlucky nine did, bringing with them muskets and cutlasses, which involved a suspicion of their own enterprise. However, while they were being regaled, Captain Barnes and his sloop came upon them and the wind being in his favor, he soon had the sloop at his mercy. She surrendered after a very short interchange of shot.

All were taken into Port Royal and on the 16th of November, 1720, were put on trial at St. Jago de la Vega, Sir Nicholas Laws sitting as Chief Justice. The following were convicted and sentenced to death: John Rackam, captain; George Featherston, master; Richard Conner, quartermaster; John Davis, John Howell, Patrick Cary, Thomas Earl, James Dobbin, and Noah Harwood. The next day Rackam, Davis, Howell, Featherston, and Cary were hanged at Port Royal, where a busy gallows was maintained for the accommodation of such gentlemen. Earl, Dobbin, and Harwood furnished a spectacle for Kingston a day later. After death Rackam was hanged in chains at Plumb Point, Featherston at Bush Key, and Conner at Gun Key, as crows are swung in cornfields to warn their kind. The nine who had boarded from the *piroque* were tried as having been guilty of piratical intent. The two Frenchmen taken on at Hispaniola escaped conviction as being pressed men, and these testified that the visitors had helped man the sweeps when the sloop first sought to escape from Barnes. They pleaded that they were innocent turtle hunters, but their muskets, cutlasses, and cheerful consort with the pirates proved their undoing. The luckless adventurers were all convicted and six were certainly hanged.

Two of Rackam's crew remained untried in prison. One it may be guessed was Anne Bonny. The other was also a woman and both were respited for the same maternal reason. Anne's story has been told. The career of Mary Read, the other was even stranger.

Mary Read was the daughter of a sailor's wife, who when her husband vanished, took on other favorites. She had a son while living with her sailor, but Mary appeared after he had been more than the due time absent. The son dying, to hide her shame the mother brought Mary up as a boy, deceiving her former husband's mother into the belief that this was her grandson and so receiving support that lasted until the elder woman died. Mary growing robust became a foot-boy at thirteen and when a little older and well grown enlisted on a man-of-war. Serving a term here, she joined the Duke of Marlborough's army in Flanders as a foot soldier and saw the several actions of the campaign, fighting as bravely as any of her male companions, so much so as to deserve a commission which she could not gain, through the practice of selling such promotions as then prevailed and not having the means to buy. The feminine instinct now asserted itself and she became more literally a companion in arms with a handsome young Fleming. Changing her uniform for the dress of her sex, she was publicly married, the unusual affair making a great stir in the army. Returning from the field the pair set up a public house near Ipswich, which prospered so long as the soldiers were near, but upon the signing of peace their custom disappeared, the Fleming died, and the widow found herself in need.

She accordingly again put on the uniform, closed the inn and joined a regiment of foot, guarding one of the frontier towns. Garrison life being dull and profitless, she now decided to seek fortune in the West Indies, and by strange chance the vessel in which she had taken passage was captured by English pirates. The others on shipboard being Dutch, she alone was impressed, being well hidden in her male attire. The pirates, however, took advantage of the King's pardon and Mary was disbanded with the others. Learning that Woodes Rogers, at New Providence, was fitting out some privateers against Spain, she joined with some of her late companions in journeying to the island for the purpose of enlisting in the enterprise. The crew of the particular vessel to which she was assigned rose and, taking her over, resumed the old trade.

In season she became a member of Rackam's crew, where Anne Bonny, taking her for a handsome young fellow and showing some favor, was made aware of her sex and became her protector so far as she needed one. Rackam, becoming jealous, was apprised of her identity but kept the secret. A handsome recruit being impressed from a captured prize, the story goes that she fell violently in love with him and discovered her secret to him. Engaging in a quarrel with one of the pirates, the lover *flame* agreed to go ashore and fight it out with cutlasses, at which in anxiety over her love Mary Read is credited with having anticipated the hour and fought the duel with such skill as to kill the challenger. The two agreed to be faithful to each other as man and wife, and so held the relation.

On the trial a number of men were acquitted as having been pressed, among whom was her husband, but she refused to make known his identity, saying only that he was an honest man with no liking for piracy, and that it had been their intention to leave the ship at the first chance and lead different lives. Yet it was shown that she had fought bravely at the attack made by Barnes and had urged the men who took refuge in the hold to stand to the defense like men and when they did not come up fired a pistol through the hatch, killing one of the cravens and wounding others. Her guilt was therefore plain. It was testified that when Rackam once asked her what liking she could possibly have for such a life that had only an ignominious death ahead if taken, she answered that as to hanging she thought it no great hardship, for, were it not for it, every cowardly fellow would turn pirate and so infest the sea that men of courage must starve.

While the respite saved Mary Read from the gallows it did not set her free. Death did that in prison.

Anne Bonny had fought valorously in the attack leading to Rackam's capture, while others dived below. Before his execution Rackam was allowed to see her in prison at Jamaica, but the cold comfort that fell from her lips was only this: That she was sorry to see him there, for if he had fought like a man he would not now be about to hang like a dog.

The woman's father was well known in Jamaica, many having traded with him in Carolina. Considerable influence was exerted to save her from the death sentence and in the end it was respited, though the records do not tell her ultimate fate.

XXII

OF CAPTAIN CONDENT

THIS worthy, a native of Plymouth in Devon, first appears at New Providence in the Bahamas at the time Woodes Rogers arrived in 1717 with the King's mercy for marauders. He became quartermaster on a New York sloop, owned by a Jewish merchant of that city, which had been engaged in trade with the pirates and left New Providence for America. They were not long out before an Indian, who was a member of the crew, taking umbrage at some ill treatment, manáged to secure most of the small arms and, taking possession of the hold, announced his purpose of blowing up the ship. This he would no doubt have accomplished but for the courage of Condent, who, taking a pistol in one hand and a cutlass in the other, made at the mutineer single handed. The Indian fired a shot which broke Condent's arm, but his return fire killed the savage, who was cut to pieces by the crew, the gunner, more savage than the victim, tearing out his heart and eating it as a choice morsel.

They now took openly to pirating, stopping a merchant ship, the *Duke of York*, about which such dispute arose that half the crew and the captain went aboard the prize, leaving the sloop to Condent and the others. He was at once made captain and steered for the Cape Verde Islands. *En route* a ship laden with wine for the tables of the West India planters was taken and despoiled. Coming now to the Isle of May, where he found some twenty vessels loading salt, Condent proceeded to lord it over the fleet, taking it upon himself to administer justice by instituting an inquiry among the ships as to how the men were used by their commanders, and whipping those captains who were accused of ill-doing. He also helped himself to the mast of one to make a boom for his mainsail and took such provisions and stores as he required. Then taking on some volunteers and some impressed men he sailed to St. Jago.

Here he found a Dutch ship, that was taken after a slight encounter and that proved much better for his purpose than the sloop and was accordingly exchanged and named the *Flying Dragon*. Condent presented the sloop to the mate of one of the salt ships, whom he had impressed at the Isle of May. He now turned across the Atlantic to Brazil, taking a number of Portuguese ships, which were released after giving up their portables. The *Wright* galley, Captain John Spelt, under charter of the South Sea Company to bring slaves from Angola to Buenos Ayres, was next captured. Spelt, being a Plymouth man, was treated civilly as became a fellow townsman. A Portuguese ship gave material for refitting the *Wright*, which was done. A Dutch ship of size now fell prey, the galley supporting the *Dragon* in a smart encounter, in which the Dutch captain was killed. He now put into Fernando de Noronha with the three sail and here cleaned the *Flying Dragon*. The *Wright* galley was returned to Captain Spelt with eleven Dutchmen, to make amends for the English who had been impressed from his crew, together with a liberal share of goods from the Portuguese. Condent also let the Dutchman go free, under promise not to sail for twenty-four hours after the departure of the *Flying Dragon*.

Seeking the coast of Brazil once more, they ran foul of a Portuguese warship and after a test of strength decided her too strong to be dealt with and, being the better sailor, got away. A Portuguese merchant taken a few days later informed Condent that forty men or more had been killed on the warship during the encounter. Continuing to the southward a French ship of eighteen guns, laden with brandy and wine and bound for the South Sea, fell victim, and was taken into the river Plate. A party sent ashore to hunt wild cattle were seized by a Spanish man-of-war, but their brazen story that they belonged to a Guinea slaver, with a cargo for the South Sea Company, secured their release. Five of the forced men ran away with a canoe, and the French ship, being stripped of her wet goods, was set adrift and stranded. Working up the coast of Brazil, Condent learned of the loss of a pirate ship and the imprisonment of her crew by the Portuguese authorities and accordingly maltreated all of the natives who fell into his hands, cropping their ears and slitting their noses. An occasional priest would be compelled to say mass at the mainmast, after which the pirates would ride him pick-a-back about the decks or, loading him like a beast, drive him about for a donkey.

Brazil being exhausted for the moment, the *Flying Dragon* flew to the Guinea coast, there making capture of the *Indian Queen*, an English ship commanded by Captain Hill. In Loango Bay, two ships, one Dutch, the other English, were run ashore to escape the pirate. The *Fame*, English, Captain Bowen, was lost. But Condent hauled the Dutchman off and took her as a consort. Captain Hill and his ship were then released and the *Flying Dragon* rounded the cape for the Indies. Near Good Hope he took the *Ostend*, a British East India-man, of which Mr. Nash, a noted merchant of London, was supercargo. A Dutch East Indiaman was next taken and the *Ostend* released. Condent then reached St. Mary's Isle, off Madagascar, where he picked up the remains of John Halsey's crew. Continuing toward Bengal, off Johanna, in company with two other pirates who joined at St. Mary's he took the East Indiaman *Cassandra*, James Macragh, Captain. The cruise to the East proved very successful. Returning to Mauritius, richly laden, they took a Portuguese frigate of twenty guns, having in addition to cash the Governor of Goa as a passenger. With the Portuguese as a reinforcement and many hands, they now descended upon a Dutch fort at Zanzibar, which was taken and destroyed. Such of the garrison as cared to were accepted as volunteers and the company returned to St. Mary's where the spoil was divided and the partnership dissolved. Many of the men settled with the natives. Others sent a petition to the Governor of Mauritius by the captain of a Bristol snow, who was well paid for his errand, bespeaking pardon. This His Excellency graciously granted on condition that they would destroy their ships. This was done and the *Flying Dragon* flew the seas no more. Condent went to Mauritius and, being rich, married the sister-in-law of the Governor and presumably lived happily ever after, leaving the island to live respectably in France as a merchant at **St. Malo.**

XXIII

OF SAMUEL BELLAMY

THE records of the time do not reveal the beginnings of Samuel Bellamy. He seems to have turned to the trade following disappointment in a lost treasure hunt, in which he engaged with an associate, Paul Williams. With two sloops the pair had been employed in a search for silver in the wreck of a Spanish galleon, inspired thereto by the success of Sir William Phipps. Determining not to lose the fruits of the enterprise, they used their vessels to waylay a ship called the *Whidaw*, Captain Prince, bound from Jamaica to London. The *Whidaw* had evidently carried a cargo of slaves to the West Indies, for she was found rich in cash, gold dust, and ivory, beside other merchandise. The adventurers mounted twenty-eight guns on the *Whidaw* and put aboard a crew of 150 hands, evidently doing some recruiting among the keys. This was late in February, 1717. Bellamy was chosen captain and with one of the sloops under Williams for consort, cruised off the Virginia capes, making several small captures. Here both were very nearly swamped in a great gale, which lasted three nights and four days, during which the *Whidaw* lost her mizzen mast and sprang a leak. Only the most desperate efforts saved the ship.

The battered vessels sought to make haven in some North Carolina inlet, but, the wind shifting, they bore for Rhode Island. The *Whidaw's* leak continued and kept the pumps in action night and day until it was discovered that the open seams were in the bow and within reach of a caulking iron. The carpenter soon filled the gaps and, rigging a jury mast in place of the lost mizzen, they proceeded in better spirit. The sloop lost only her mainsail, split by the first blast. Near Rhode Island in the month of April, a Boston sloop, Captain Beer, was the first captured. Bellamy and Williams were favorable to returning the ship to Beer after she had been plundered, but, the crews objecting, she was sunk. Bellamy treated Beer to a choice bit of objurgation, saying:

[150]

OF SAMUEL BELLAMY

"I am sorry they won't let you have your sloop again, as I have sworn to do no one a mischief when it is not to my advantage; but we must sink the sloop which might be of use to you, though you are a sneaking puppy, and so are all those who will submit to be governed by laws which rich men have made for their own security, for the cowardly whelps have not the courage otherwise to defend what they get by their knavery; but damn ye all together; damn them all for a pack of cowardly rascals, and you who serve them, for a parcel of pin-headed numbskulls. They villify us, the scoundrels do, when there is only this difference, they rob the Poor under the cover of Law, forsooth, and we plunder the Rich under the Protection of our own courage."

He urged Beer to join him instead of "sneaking after employment." To this Beer replied that his conscience would not permit him to break through the laws of God and man. To which the pirate retorted:

"You are a devilish conscientious rascal. I am a free Prince and I have as much authority to make war on the whole world, as he who has a hundred ships at sea, and an army of 100,000 men in the field; and this my conscience tells me, but there is no arguing with such snivelling puppies who allow superiors to kick them about the decks, and pin their faith on a pimp of a Parson; a squab, who neither practices nor believes what he puts upon the chuckle-headed Fools he preaches to."

Provisions and water being plenty, the pirates made merry during Captain Beer's stay on board. One of the crew had been a strolling actor who, turning highwayman in England, had the fortune to save his neck by being transported to Jamaica, from the bondage of which he escaped to become pirate. This merry rogue made up a play called "The Royal Pirate," which was performed with great spirit by a cast selected from the crew, which certainly knew all the "stage business." It was given on the quarter-deck with great applause, but unhappily the intoxicated gunner on hearing the lines uttered by Alexander, the Royal Pirate,

> "Knowst thou that death attends thy mighty crimes,
> And thou shalt hang tomorrow morn betimes"

construed it as meaning a real execution for the character addressed who was "honest Jack Spinckes" and sought to save him by clearing the decks, using a hand grenade for the purpose. He also called some equally drunken comrades to the rescue. In the confusion caused by the explosion King Alexander had his arm cut off by one of the inebriates and the explosion shattered Jack Spinckes's arm. The drunkards were seized but not until Alexander had killed the man who cut off his arm. The others were put in irons to sober off, but the play was thereafter tabooed. When sober the gunner and his companions were tried by court-martial, to be acquitted and commended for their zeal.

Beer was now freed from this mad company by being set ashore on Block Island. The vessels continuing on their cruise took a ship laden with wine off Cape Cod and put a prize crew of seven men on board, leaving her captain with them, but transferring the crew to the *Whidaw*. She was ordered to keep company while the squadron sailed to Penobscot Bay, whence they went up the river several miles to find a fit place to careen and clean their hulls. A point was found two miles and a half from the mouth. Here guns were landed, earthworks raised by the prisoners set ashore for the purpose, and huts erected. A magazine was also built, deep in the earth, with a roof to protect it from rain. All this was done in four days. The powder taken care of, the sloop was first careened and cleaned. The *Whidaw* was next put in order. The merry stroller suggested the spot as a fit one for founding a dominion and offered to become Secretary of State, "having been a servitor at Oxford before I turned stroller." Bellamy and Williams drily replied that they would consider his suggestion and should they find it expedient to found a monarchy would make him Prime Minister, or Quartermaster ashore, "and when he had enriched himself and family by placing their subjects they would pass an act of indemnity for his security."

The ships being in sea-shape they now steered for Fortune Bay in Newfoundland, taking a few fishermen which they sunk after impressing their crews. They were now separated by a storm. Off St. Pierre the *Whidaw* encountered a French thirty-six-gun ship carrying soldiers to Quebec. The pirate ventured an engagement and was twice boarded by the French, repelling each attack. After two hours of close fighting Bellamy made off, and thanks to night falling, escaped. He lost thirty-six men during the conflict, including the stroller, who found his dominion in the sea!

Working up to Newfoundland the sloop joined. The *Whidaw* was much cut up and it was resolved to return to New England to repair

[152]

and recruit. Cruising down the coast between St. George's Banks and Nantucket, they took a snow called the *Mary Ann*, whose captain they ordered to pilot them into Provincetown on Cape Cod. He was sent ahead in his own boat with orders to carry a light for their guidance. The captain was kept constantly at the helm, and one night, when both crews of the pirates were carousing and all hands drunk, he deliberately ran the *Mary Ann* ashore near Wellfleet. The pirates following the light soon struck on the reef and in their rage murdered the prisoners and pressed men; at least their mangled corpses came ashore. The sloop also struck and, both ships going to pieces, but nine men came out alive from either. Those who were seized were taken to Boston, tried, and six of them executed on November 15, 1717.

Captain Cyprian Southack, having been sent in pursuit of Bellamy and expecting to find him within the Cape, notes the existence of a passage through the elbow near Wellfleet at that time, for in a comment on his chart of "The Sea of New England," he refers to it as: "The place I came through in a whale boat, being ordered by ye government to look after ye Pirate ship *Whido*, Bellame commander, cast away ye 26 of April 1717 where I buried one hundred and two men."

The History of Wellfleet records that one hundred and two bodies were buried from the wreck and as late as 1793 Levi Whitman, the historian of Wellfleet, notes that coins of King William and Mary's time were found on the sand after a storm with occasional pieces of silver called "cob-money."

XXIV

OF CAPTAIN LEWIS

THERE is no history of the beginnings of this particular pirate beyond that he was found in the company headed by one Bannister, who was hanged at the yard-arm of a British warship off Port Royal, and being but a lad was let go. He had a talent for language and beside English knew French and Spanish and the Jargon of the Mosquito shore. As a seaman on one of the sloops smuggling to the Spanish islands, he was taken prisoner by the Spaniards and held for sometime at Havana from whence he escaped with six more in a canoe. Surprising a Spanish pirogue, they took possession of her, two of the crew joining. The nine now captured a turtle sloop, forced some of her men, and sent the rest ashore in the pirogue. Continuing to plunder fisher boats and turtle hunters, Lewis got together a sufficient force to capture a pink bound from Jamaica to Campeche, in which haven he adventured and where he made other captures.

Locating a fine ten-gun brigantine from Bermuda, Captain Tucker, he offered 10,000 pieces of eight for the vessel, suggesting that if this were refused he would take her without price. Other ships being at hand, Captain Tucker urged them to join him and take the pirate. All refused, but sailing from the bay together they came upon Lewis, when Tucker again urged them to lend him men and he would fight the marauders. Since they again refused, he left them to their fate, after treating the pirate to a broadside. The others were all taken. One speedy sloop might have escaped, but a gun shot brought her to. Lewis had the captain brought to him and reproved the craven for betraying his owners, telling him he would punish him as a coward. "For," he said, "you might have got off, being a much better sailor than my vessel." With that he beat the captain with a cane. The latter whining under the strokes said he had much money on board, having been trading for some months and proferred this for mercy, at which Lewis called him a rascal and redoubled his strokes. Then he sent to the sloop and took the money, together with a negro seaman.

Forty other black hands were taken and added to the crew, beside a white carpenter. One of the sloops of ninety tons was mounted with twelve guns and fitted as a cruiser, the company now numbering eighty of all colors.

The Florida channel was Lewis's next cruising ground; there he way-laid ships in the leeward passage, and took several. Running into a Carolina creek, he traded his sugar and rum to the country folks, though losing many of his impressed men who made good use of this contact with the coast to desert. The Virginia capes next furnished some good prizes, from which he recruited a number of unwilling sea-men and returned to the Carolinas. Becoming suspicious of the English members of his crew, he put them in a small boat ten leagues from land and dismissed them. They were never heard from again and presumably were lost. His company was now all French and negro. He next moved to the Newfoundland banks, making havoc among the fishermen and there put into shore to clean. This being done, he in-vaded Trinity Harbor, where a number of ships lay and seized the twenty-four-gun galley *Herman*. The captain of the latter cajoled Lewis into sending his quartermaster ashore under promise to give him provisions. This he did, but the man was seized at the instance of the other captains in port and taken to Woodes Rogers, the pirate-tamer, who happened to be then at Trinity. Rogers chained the fellow to a sheet anchor that lay on the shore and placed a gun on a point commanding the exit to the harbor to bar Lewis's escape. This proved futile for Lewis, abandoning the ship, worked his sloop out with the help of sweeps, though well riddled with shot from the cannon. The bold rover now lay off the harbor and demanded the release of his quartermaster, intercepting at the same time a fisher boat, of which the *Herman's* captain brother was master and holding him hostage. The quartemaster was returned forthwith. When he came on board Lewis asked him how he had been used and he replied civilly. To which Lewis rejoined that it was lucky as, had he been ill treated he would have slit the throats of the fishermen. They were then freed, but the quartermaster insisted that they join him in drinking the health of the gentlemen ashore, especially Captain Rogers. At the same time he whispered to their captain that had Lewis known of his being chained all night to the sheet-anchor he and his men would have been butchered. When they were well out of the way the quartermaster told Lewis what really had happened to him and was reproached for hiding it from him. The decent man rejoined that he did not think the innocent should suffer for the guilty.

Alarm was sent to Captain Tudor Trevor, of the *Sheerness*, man-of-war, lying at St. John's, of the pirate's presence and he came at once to Trinity, but missed the rover by four hours. Lewis continued along the Newfoundland coast, taking mainly fishing craft. Making a harbor in which a large French ship lay, which was filling with fish from several auxiliaries, Lewis was hailed with a warning to sheer off, as a pirate was on the coast and if he came nearer he would get a broadside. As the Frenchman had twenty-four guns, Lewis followed the advice, but was no less determined to have the ship. He accordingly went to sea for a fortnight to allay suspicion. The French captain in the meantime set up a battery on shore for better defense and was well prepared to welcome him on his return. The pirate showed too much talent for the merchant, however. He captured two of the shallops at sea and, loading them with his men, landed from one at early dawn and took the battery, while the other cut out the ship, just as the morning star came into view, because of which Lewis gave that name to his capture. In the fight the owner's son, who had come on a pleasure voyage, was killed. The captain told Lewis he assumed he only wanted his liquor and provisions, but the pirate blandly replied that he would take the ship. He gave the Frenchman his fish and the sloop, but took some of his hands, who, with others picked on the cruise, now gave him a company of two hundred men.

Being now in the first class, Lewis steered for the Guinea coast, taking numerous vessels, both French and English, including a Carolina slaver, commanded by Captain Smith. During the chase the fore and main topmast of the pirate were torn away by the press of sail and Lewis running to the top tore out a handful of his hair and tossed it to the wind, saying: "Good devil, take this till I come."

The ship seemed to move faster after this sacrifice, which greatly impressed the crew with their captain's influence with the Evil One. Smith was well treated and really given more than was taken in exchange, and then released, Lewis telling him he expected to come again to the Carolina coast and hoped he would find a friend.

The French under the leadership of one Le Barre, now became dissatisfied, the English again predominating in the crew and determined to part. A large sloop had lately been taken, to which the malcontents transferred themselves with stores of goods and ammunition. The sloop was warped under the shore to stow and arrange her affairs, when, the wind rising, Lewis determined to take advantage of the moment to curb their rivalry. He therefore ranged the ship alongside and ordered La Barre to cut away the mast or he would rake him. This was obeyed. They were then told to go ashore, allowing them only small arms and cartridge boxes. He then recovered the sloop, put her goods and guns on board the ship and sank the mastless hull.

The French begged to be returned on board, but were not permitted, though La Barre and a few were received and liberally supplied with liquor, Lewis himself drinking heavily. That night the French boarded the ship in canoes and sought to take her. In the fighting Lewis was killed, but the English, led by John Cornelius, the quartermaster, beat them off after an hour and a half of hand-to-hand fighting. The *Morning Star* then continued her course under command of Cornelius.

XXV

OF JOHN CORNELIUS

NOTHING more is known of John Cornelius, who succeeded to the mastery of the *Morning Star* in the manner noted in the story of Captain Lewis, save that he was of Irish birth. After the repulse of the French he continued along the Guinea coast, taking numbers of English and Portuguese vessels. The English he robbed and released. The Portuguese ships were invariably burned.

Two English slavers, loading at Whydah, when they learned of his presence decided to sail in company for mutual protection, one carrying twelve, the other thirty-six guns. The captain of the minor vessel was ill in his cabin when it came time to start and two hundred of the blacks leaping overboard from the larger, she was delayed, so that the small vessel, with 400 Africans in her hold, kept on, the sick captain being eager to get off the malarial coast. When two days at sea the *Morning Star* was sighted and her character guessed. Joseph Williams, a factor on the slaver who knew the negro dialect, told the blacks that the pirate would kill and eat them unless they fought to save themselves and fifty took up small arms and lances. Cornelius met them about ten in the morning, flying English colors, and hailing as a man-of-war hunting pirates, asked them to send a boat aboard. This being refused, a running fight began which lasted for ten hours, the negroes firing so steadily that the pirates could not board. In the night the slaver blew up astern and sank before the longboat could be cleared. Sixteen of the crew got into the yawl, which floated off the forecastle. Joseph Williams had his clothes caught in the rigging as the ship went down, but with rare presence of mind cut himself lose with his sheath knife, swimming to the yawl, in which the others had embarked. His comrades would not let him climb in, having already cut the hands or knocked in the heads of the blacks who tried to save themselves in this scene of horror. They allowed Williams to keep one hand on the gunwale while they rowed to the pirate and begged for rescue. This was denied unless they would join the ship, which was promised, and all were taken on board, dried, and clothed. One negro only was saved out of the 400. The sick captain went down in his cabin.

Two Portuguese ships were next overhauled, plundered, and dismissed. It was foggy and, minute guns being heard through the mist, Cornelius surmised that they denoted the death of an English captain and, proceeding in the direction of the sound, met the ship and took her without trouble. The men and officers of the lost slaver now asked for their freedom and to be allowed to go on the English prize, the officers pleading that they had large families and were now well-nigh ruined. To this Cornelius agreed and gave them a liberal amount of supplies from the spoil of the Portuguese. He limited his generosity to the married men, keeping Joseph Williams and all the bachelors, together with some men from the prize. Three Portuguese ships caught at anchor were next plundered and burned. Many men were impressed from captured slavers and forced to do drudgery about the decks, the lordly pirates refusing to turn their hands to anything more than working ship and fighting. Joseph Williams, being abused by one Robert Bland for refusing to take the whipstaff while they went to play, was beaten with a rope's end and asked the privilege of fighting his oppressor. Under pirate rules he had to volunteer in order to establish equality. This he did, choosing fists for weapons, but alas, he had sacrificed his true virtue in vain, the pirate Bland giving him a good beating.

Cornelius now doubling the Cape had a close call from meeting Commodore Littleton's squadron bound home from Madagascar, the *Lizard*, *Hastings*, and *Anglesea*, which he sought to survey at closer range. His men, being wiser and certain they were warships, refused to venture and the *Morning Star* went on her way to Madagascar, ending her voyage at Pombotoque, a native village near Methelage. On the quartermaster visiting the shore, the chief of the territory sent a couple of oxen on board and escorted the officer twenty miles up country to visit the King. He carried a blunderbuss and a pair of pistols as presents to His Majesty, explaining their want of provisions, coupled with the information that his company was very poor and was out seeking fortune. The King, with the magnificence becoming a potentate, replied that he required nothing from them; he regarded all white men as his children and sent 100 cattle to the shore from which the pirates culled ten fat oxen and salted them down. To this bounty

[159]

the generous prince added as much rice as one hundred of his subjects could carry on their backs. In return Cornelius sent the King two barrels of powder and offered more, with a further present of arms. The King said he needed neither, indeed would give them ten barrels of powder, but could accept nothing from his children while poor. Should they return rich he would be glad to accept any present they might send.

While remaining in this lap of luxury it went ill with the crew, who from over-much eating, drinking, and consorting with the Madagascar women were stricken with fevers and died to the number of seventy. Cornelius having heard that the *Speaker* was cruising toward the East sailed in the hope of joining her for a joint operation, but she was in the Red Sea while the *Morning Star* entered the Persian Gulf, so they never met. Here the *Morning Star* lay under Antelope Island and had good success with prizes. It was now necessary to clean ship. Most of the stores and water were out preparatory to careening when two Portuguese men-of-war came into sight, one of seventy and the other of twenty-six guns. There was great scurrying to get water and food on board and to unlash the sails which had been tied up with rope-yarn. Some semblance of order being brought to pass, the *Morning Star* ranged up to the larger warship and gave her a broadside, while the smaller ship came up so close that she was readily showered with hand grenades. Against such odds Cornelius manœuvered to escape rather than fight. Both of his foes missed stays in going about, the smaller running aground and the larger losing so much way in wearing that she fell far behind the pirate when pursuing. Finding her alone, Cornelius waited with all teeth showing, but the Portuguese not coming to risk the battle singly sheered off. When darkness came on Cornelius reversed his course, ran past the Portuguese and came again to the spot where he had fixed to careen. His enemies had been ashore and staved the casks. They had now gone in search of him, not dreaming of such audacity as a return.

He cleaned ship and, finding the coasters poor in cash and cargoes, sailed for Johanna, with the design of there marooning the negro members of the crew. Joseph Williams, the valiant pressed man of whom so much has been heard, feared that the French and Dutch members of the crew, who outnumbered the English three to one, would give them similar treatment, armed the blacks and with their help took possession of the ship, acting himself as captain and keeping control until they were all back in Madagascar. The ship was given to the son of their friend the King, who had died during their absence and the company disbanded. Cornelius settled at Methelage, but survived his great adventures only five months.

XXVI

OF RICHARD WORLEY

NOTHING is known of the antecedents of Captain Richard Worley, and fortune favored him with but a brief career. In the latter part of September, 1718, despite the hue and cry then prevailing against pirates and the proclamation of the King providing for their surrender under advantageous circumstances, he sailed from the harbor of New York with eight desperate companions in an open boat. Skirting the coast the adventurers passed the capes of the Delaware, turned and went up the river as far as Newcastle before meeting any opportunity for enterprise. Here they found a shallop owned by George Grant, loaded with household goods, including some plate which they purloined and let the boat depart for Philadelphia, for which port it was heading from Opequam. This act not being committed on the high seas did not rise to the dignity of piracy, being nothing more than plain theft, or housebreaking.

The shallop on reaching Philadelphia gave the alarm. Express was sent to New York to warn the cruisers to keep lookout for the crew, but after a few days' search the lookout was abandoned. One of the shallop's men joined and two negro slaves were also taken from her and added to the pirate crew. Pulling down the river, they encountered a sloop owned by a mulatto which they seized. One of its men, a negro, chose to remain with them and having now a good complement the pirates cruised in Delaware Bay, where a few days later a sloop outbound for Hull fell prey, from which they were able amply to provision themselves and to which they transferred their persons. These several operations renewed the alarm and Robert Hunter, the Colonial President of New York, issued a proclamation in the King's name, asking for their apprehension and that of all pirates who had failed to take advantage of His Majesty's mercy. The warship *Phenix*, of twenty guns was also sent to sea in search of them.

The Hull sloop was strong and newly cleaned, and being well-provisioned she sailed toward the Bahamas, thus unconsciously evad-

ing the *Phenix* and her twenty guns. In a six weeks' cruise W
took a New York sloop, which he sank, and a brigantine, which
released after being looted. He had increased his force to twenty
men and had six guns mounted. A black flag with the custom
emblems was now flown and his career seemed most promising.
crew was oath-bound to stand by each other and fight to the end, a
ing and giving no quarter.

Working back toward the Virginia coast, Worley now took a sh
the *Eagle*, inbound from London, having a large crew and many p;
sengers on board. With this vessel in convoy he made for Charlesto
where rumor had preceded him to the effect that another pirate, or
Moody, with a vessel of fifty guns and two hundred men was about t
descend upon the shipping. The Governor, Colonel Robert Johnston
at once commandeered the *Mediterranean* galley, Captain Arthur Loan,
and the *King William*, John Washington, Captain, and beside fitted
out Stede Bonnet's recently captured sloop *Revenge* and another sloop
that had just arrived from Philadelphia. John Masters was put in
command of the *Revenge*, and Fayrer Hall of the Philadelphia sloop,
both having distinguished themselves in the taking of Bonnet not long
before. Twenty-four guns were hastily put aboard the *Mediterranean*
and thirty on the *King William*. The *Revenge* was armed with eight
and the sloop with six carronades.

The Governor called for volunteers to man the vessels and offered a
liberal bounty to all who would go. The captains refused to sail on
the Governor's word of reward and he was compelled to call the legislature in special session, at which an act was passed guaranteeing
recompense for any vessel that might be lost and full satisfaction to all
concerned. These proceedings took upward of a week of time, during
which period the Governor kept a fleet of scout boats in the Ashley and
Cooper Rivers and among the islands in the harbor, to make certain
that "Moody" and his fifty guns did not descend unwarned upon the
shipping lying in port.

Several days before the legislation was completed a ship and sloop
appeared off the harbor signaling for a pilot, but as the port officials
believed them to belong to Moody, none was sent out. The two vessels rode off the harbor, several times sending a boat to Sullivan's Island
for water, but were warned off by the patrol. The Governor and his
squadron at last put to sea with three hundred volunteers, "from below
Johnson's fort, over night, and the next morning by break of day,

[163]

weighted anchor and by eight were over the bar." The pirate sloop at once slipped her cable and manœuvered to get between Johnson's flotilla and the bar, evidently having no guess as to its purpose and seeking to cut it off from retreat. Picking the Philadelphia sloop as the first victim, Worley hoisted his black ensign and made for her. During these proceedings Johnson had made no show of force. Coming now within half a gunshot he threw open all ports and the volunteers swarmed to the decks. At the same time he ordered the *Revenge* and the other sloop to follow the smaller pirate, while he, on the *Mediterranean* and the *King William* followed the ship which was making for the sea, assuming her to be Moody's fifty-gun craft, though he wondered why she fired from two and showed none of the fifty from her ports, though crowded with people. The *Revenge* and her consort made short work of Worley's sloop. Most of the pirates fled to the hold to avoid the fire, though Worley and a few others stuck to the deck and were killed. This was within sight of Charleston, where the populace crowded the roofs to observe the contest.

Johnson did not come up with the fleeing ship until three in the afternoon. The prize crew aboard wrapped their arms in their "jolly Roger" and threw the package into the sea. The *King William* was the first to overhaul the ship, which was the *Eagle*, and firing her chase guns killed several people on board. Her colors were soon struck and the *King William* boarded, to find many women as well as men aboard, and to learn with amazement the character of their captive. It had been part of the pirates' plan to take the women to some hidden key in the Bahamas and set up a colony. Shortage of water and food had impelled their rash captain to tempt fate at Charleston. The captured pirates were duly hanged, and so ended a promising project that began most modestly out of New York harbor.

Worley undoubtedly expected to be well received at Charleston as others had been before him, "the trade" being covertly encouraged in the town. Indeed, Moody duly appeared in accordance with expectations, having in his company the ship *Minerva*, Captain Smyter, laden with wine from Madeira, which Moody evidently intended to market at Charleston, it being a favorite beverage among the merchants and planters of the Carolinas. The Governor kept his squadron together and forbade any communication with ships outside the bar, but despite

this "some people from the shore were so wicked as to go off in the night and give him (Moody) a particular account of the ships, sloops and men, that were preparing to go out against him," and so enabled him to make good his escape. Taking the *Minerva* far out to sea he emptied her well of the wine, and after telling her captain how he had been warned—even to the names of the ships and their commanders, let him go back to Charleston. Moody himself then put into Providence, surrendered under the terms of the King's most kindly proclamation, and presumably lived happy ever afterward.

XXVII

OF EDWARD ENGLAND

EDWARD ENGLAND was perhaps the most prominent of the pirates sojourning at New Providence previous to its occupation by the Crown. He had been mate of a Jamaica sloop that fell into the hands of Christopher Winter, one of the Providence pirates, and being taken by him to the Bahamas, he soon adopted the customs of his captors, sailing out of the islands in a sloop that took whatever came in its way. Upon the coming of Woodes Rogers in May, 1717, with his powers from the King to punish and pardon, England was one of those who later resolved to put to sea, making for the slave coast of Africa, where he took a number of vessels, notably the *Cadogan* snow captained by one Skinner. The latter, it appears, had had some trouble with members of his crew on a previous voyage and caused a number of them to be taken on board a man-of-war at Sierra Leone, where they were promptly impressed. In so doing he neglected to give them the pay then due, not expecting ever to see the gentlemen again. They contrived to desert and in drifting about the world served in a Jamaica sloop, which was taken by a pirate from the Bahamas, where they too took up the trade and were now on England's ship. Skinner was no more on board when he recognized his former boatswain, who greeted him with elaborate mockery, saying: "Ah, Captain Skinner! Is it you? The only man I wished to see! I am much in your debt, and now I shall pay you all in your own coin."

At this the trembling captain was placed on the windlass, where the company being called together, he was pelted with empty bottles until cut and bleeding. Then the wretched man was compelled to run a gauntlet about the decks until he fell under the beatings of ropes ends. This done, as he had been "a good master to his men," he should have an easy death and thereupon he was shot through the head. The *Cadogan* was then presented to Howel Davis, the mate, and the crew who started on their own career as will be related in the life of that hero.

England now taking a ship named the *Pearl* from Captain Tyzard, exchanged her for the sloop and stoutly refitted, named her the *Royal James*, complimenting his late Majesty of England and showing his scorn of the Hanoverian George then reigning. The rest of the winter was spent in the regions of the Azores and Cape de Verde Islands, with fair success. In the spring England returned to the river Gambia and operated down the coast from there to Cape Coast Castle taking a number of good prizes, viz: the *Eagle*, pink, of Cork, Captain Ricketts, 6 guns and 17 men, on March 25th; the *Charlotte*, of London, Captain Oldson, 8 guns, 18 men, May 26th; the *Sarah*, of London, Captain Stut, 4 guns, 18 men, May 27th; the *Bentworth*, of Bristol, Captain Gardener, 12 guns, 30 men, May 27th; the *Buck*, sloop of Gambia, Captain Sylvester, 2 guns, 2 men, May 27th; the *Carteret*, of London, Captain Snow, 4 guns, 18 men, May 28th; the *Mercury*, of London, Captain Magott, 4 guns, 18 men, May 29th; the *Coward*, galley, of London, Captain Creed, 2 guns, 13 men, June 17th; the *Elizabeth and Catherine*, of Barbadoes, Captain Bridge, 6 guns, 14 men, June 27th. The *Eagle*, bound for Jamaica, the *Sarah* for Virginia, and the *Buck* for Maryland, were allowed to depart. The *Charlotte*, *Bentworth*, *Carteret* and *Coward* were burned while the *Mercury* and the *Elizabeth and Catherine* were fitted up as consorts. The *Mercury* was renamed the *Queen Anne's Revenge* out of a faint memory of that recently deceased lady, while the *Elizabeth and Catherine* became the *Flying King*, after no potentate in particular. One Lane become captain of the first and Robert Sample of the second.

Out of all the captives fifty-five of the hands elected to serve with England. These set out for Brazil in November on an independent venture. They had considerable success in working mischief with Portuguese shipping until the *Flying King* was driven ashore by a Portuguese man-of-war. Out of her company of seventy, twelve were killed in the fight and thirty-nine were taken and hanged, of whom thirty-two were English born, three Dutch, two French, and one Portuguese. The *Queen Anne's Revenge* escaped, only to be lost on the coast not long after.

England, continuing as he had begun, took the *Peterborough* galley of Bristol, Captain Owen, and the *Victory*, Captain Ridout. The first was retained, the second plundered and released. At Cape Coast Castle two possible prizes took refuge under the guns of the fort, where they could not be safely assailed. These were the *John*, Captain Rider and the *Whydah*, Captain Prince. England essayed to smoke them out by turning one of his captures into a fire-ship and sending it all ablaze against them. This failed and the Castle used its guns so well that they departed for Whydah roads, where they met Oliver de La Bouche, an ex-Bahaman also, of the *Indian Queen,* a French pirate of twenty-eight guns which had reaped such harvest as there was. England now went into a creek to clean his ship and while idle the men debauched the negro women and roused such anger among the natives that fighting resulted. Some of the blacks were killed and one of their villages burned. The *Peterborough* was outfitted as a cruiser and new-named *Victory.*

When ready for sea a vote was taken as to the next course and, a majority favoring the East Indies, sail was made for Madagascar, which was reached early in 1720. Taking on board wood and water, they made for Malabar. Several native vessels were taken and one Dutch trader, after which the company returned to Madagascar. Here the conceit took some of them to search for any of Every's men who had been there nearly a quarter of a century before, but whose fame still lived, but no trace of any such could be found. The ships were cleaned and Johanna made the next port. Coming to the harbor they met two Indiamen, one English, the *Cassandra,* the other Dutch, which they at once attacked and took after a fight of the utmost ferocity. There exists a first-hand account from the pen of John Mackra, captain of the *Cassandra* written at Bombay, November 16, 1720, to the Honorable East India Company which is here repeated:

"We arrived the 25th of July last, in Company of the Greenwich, at Juanna, (an island not far from Madagascar) putting in there to refresh our Men, we found fourteen Pyrates that came in their Canoes from the Mayotta, where the Pyrate Ship to which they belong'd, viz, the Indian Queen, two hundred and fifty Tons, twenty eight Guns, and ninety Men, commanded by Capt. Oliver de la Bouche, bound from the Guinea Coast to the East-Indies, had been bulged and loft. They said they left the Captain and 40 of their Men building a new Vessel to proceed on their wicked Design. Capt. Kirby and I concluding it might be of great Service to the East-India Company to destroy such a Nest of Rogues, were ready to sail for that Purpose the 17th of August, about Eight o'Clock in the Morning, when we discovered two Pyrate Ships standing into the Bay of Juanna, one of thirty four, and the other of thirty Guns. I immediately went on Board the Greenwich, where they seem'd very diligent in Preparation for an Engagement, and I left Capt. Kirby with mutual Promises of standing by each other. I then unmoor'd, got under Sail, and brought two Boats a-head to row me close to the Greenwich; but he being open to a Valley and a Breeze, made the best of his Way from me; which an Ostender in our Company, of 22 Guns, seeing, did the same, though the Captain had promised heartily to engage with us, and I believe would have been as good as his Word, if Capt. Kirby had kept his. About half an Hour after Twelve, I called several times to the Greenwich to bear down to our Assistance, and fir'd Shot at him, but to no Purpose. For tho' we did not doubt but he would join us, because when he got about a League from us, he brought his Ship to, and look'd on, yet both he and the Ostender basely deserted us, and left us engaged with barbarous and inhuman Enemies, with their black and bloody flags hanging over us, without the least Appearance of escaping being cut to Pieces. But God, in his good Providence, determin'd other wise; for notwithstanding their Superiority, we engaged 'em both about three Hours, during which, the beggest received some Shot betwixt Wind and Water, which made her keep off a little to stop her Leaks. The other endeavoured all she could to board us, by rowing with her Oars, being within half a Ship's Length of us above an Hour; but by good Fortune we shot all her Oars to Pieces, which prevented them, and by consequence saved our Lives.

"About Four o'Clock, most of the Officers and Men posted on the Quarter-Deck being killed and wounded, the largest Ship making up to us with all Diligence, being still within a Cable's Length of us, often giving us a Broadside, and no hopes of Capt. Kirby's coming to our Assistance, we endeavoured to run ashoar; and tho' we drew four Foot Water more than the Pyrate, it pleased God that he stuck fast on a higher Ground than we happily fell in with; so was disappointed a second time from boarding us. Here we had a more violent Engagement than before. All my Officers, and most of my Men, behaved with unexpected Courage; and as we had a considerable Advantage by having Broadside to his Bow, we did him great Damage, so that had Capt. Kirby come in then, I believe we should have taken both, for we had one of them sure; but the other Pyrate (who was still firing at us) seeing the Greenwich did not offer to assist us, he supplied his Consort with three Boats full of fresh Men. About Five in the Evening the Greenwich stood clear away to Sea, leaving us struggling hard for Life in the very Jaws of Death; which the other Pyrate, that was afloat, seeing, got a-warp out, and was hauling under our Stern; by which time many of my Men being killed and wounded, and no Hopes left us from being all murdered by enraged barbarous Conquerors, I order'd all that could, to get into the Long-Boat under the Cover of the Smoak of our Guns; so that with what some did in Boats, and others by swimming, most of us that were able got ashoar by Seven o'Clock. When the Pyrates came aboard, they cut three of our wounded Men to Pieces. I, with a few of my People, made what haste I could to the King's Town, twenty five Miles from us, where I arrived next Day, almost dead with Fatigue and Loss of Blood, having been sorely wounded in the Head by a Musket Ball. '

"At this Town I heard that the Pyrates had offered ten thousand Dollars to the Country People to bring me in, which many of them would have accepted, only they knew the King and all his chief People were in my Interest. Meantime, I caused a Report to be spread, that I was dead of my Wounds, which much abated their Fury. About ten Days after, being pretty well recovered, and hoping the Malice of our Enemies was nigh over, I began to consider the dismal Condition we were reduced to, being in a Place where we had no Hopes of getting a Passage home, all of us in a manner naked, not having had Time to get another Shirt, or a Pair of Shoes.

"Having obtained Leave to go on Board the Pyrates, and a Promise of Safety, several of the Chief of them knew me, and some of them had sailed with me, which I found of great Advantage; because, notwithstanding their Promise, some of them would have cut me, and all that would not enter with them, to Pieces, had it not been for the chief Captain, Edward England, and some others I knew. They talked of burning one of their Ships, which we had so entirely disabled, as to be no farther useful to them, and to fit the Cassandra in her room; but in the end I managed my Tack so well, that they made me a Present of the said shattered Ship, which was Dutch built, called the Fancy, about three hundred Tons, and also a hundred and twenty nine Bales of the Company's Cloth, tho' they would not give me a Rag of my Cloathes.

"They sailed the 3d of September; and the Jury-Masts, and such old Sails as they left me, I made shift to do the like on the 8th, together with forty three of my Ship's Crew, including two Passengers and twelve Soldiers, having but five Tons of Water aboard; and after a Passage of forty eight Days, I arrived here October 26, almost naked and starv'd, having been reduced to a Pint of Water a Day, and almost in despair of ever seeing Land, by Reason of the Calms we met with between the Coast of Arabia and Malabar.—We had in all thirteen Men killed and twenty four wounded; and we were told, that we had destroyed about ninety or a hundred of the Pyrates. When they left us, they were about three hundred Whites and eighty Blacks in both Ships. I am persuaded, had our Consort the Greenwich done his Duty, we had destroyed both of them, and got two hundred thousand Pounds for our Owners and selves; whereas to his deserting us, the Loss of the Cassandra may justly be imputed. I have delivered all the Bales that were given me into the Company's Warehouse, for which the Governor and Council have ordered me a Reward. Our Governor, Mr. Boon, who is extreme kind and Civil to me, has ordered me home with this Pacquet; but Captain Harvey, who had a prior Promise, being come in with the Fleet, goes in my room. The Governor hath promis'd me a Country Voyage, to help make me up my Losses, and would have me stay to go home with him next Year."

England, indeed, had to exercise the utmost address to save Mackra from the wrath of his company. One Taylor, a great favorite in the forecastle because of his brutal strength, was persuaded to think well of the captain and when well mellowed with punch allowed the proposal to give Mackra a ship and some bales of cloth to go through undisputed. Another ruffian with a wooden leg and much display of whiskers sought the captain with a pistol in hand, which made him think himself doomed. Luckily the fellow had once sailed with him and swore no one should dare do him harm. He got away before the whimsies changed. England's friendliness to Mackra was of disadvantage to himself with the crew, and on an invented rumor circulating that Mackra was coming against them with an expedition, England was deposed from command and together with some of his intimates landed at Mauritius. Here they built a boat and crossed to Madagascar, where at the last account they were left living on the bounty of a native king. The brutal Taylor became captain in his stead, taking the Victory and the Cassandra and keeping some of the latter's officers on board.

The pirates now sailed for India. On reaching the coast and sighting several sail Mackra's men, still prisoners, were ordered to set the private signals of the East India Company to lure them into reach. This they refused to do, though threatened with death. The ships proved to be of the country, carrying horses. The captains and the

merchants aboard were brought to the pirate and tortured to make
them reveal their money. Getting nothing and being in sight of land
they were puzzled to know what to do with their prizes, especially as
many ships were seen standing off. So much objection was made to
the cruelty of drowning the horses that the ships were finally dismasted and allowed to drift. The next day the fleet bore toward them
flying English colors, to which the pirates answered with a red ensign
and coming up with them on a land breeze sailed through the fleet,
firing in all directions, causing much consternation but no resistance.
On their part the pirates took the fleet for that of Angria, a celebrated
pirate chief of the neighborhood. Not knowing just what to do, the
pirates took a small gallivat and sought to extort some knowledge of
the fleet from its crew, who swore they knew nothing of it. They were
put to torture, with no better results.

The wind coming up, the captives were tossed into their boat and the
pirates cruised to the southwest in the vicinity of the Portuguese colony
at Goa. Having ill-luck here and not daring to land for water they
went on to the Laccadive Islands, landing at Melinda, where they
found water and barbarously misused the native women, whose brothers
and husbands had fled to the bush, leaving them defenseless behind.
Then to add to the sum of villainy they cut down the coconut trees and
burned many of the houses, including a mission church built by the
Portuguese in their day. The gale rising, the ship was forced off the
island leaving seventy men and the water casks ashore. It was ten
days before she returned to their rescue. Provisions being scarce, they
resolved to go and trade for some with the Dutch at Cochin. Off Tel-
lecherry they took a small vessel, the property of the Governor, John
Tawke, master. He was very drunk and coming on board told the
tale of Mackra's fitting out against them, rousing great wrath in the
company, who cried: "A villain whom we have treated so civilly as to
give him a ship and other presents and now to be armed against us, he
ought to be hanged."

Coming to Calicut they endeavored to take a Moorish ship in the
harbor, but she was saved by the guns of a battery on the shore. Out
of malice one of Mackra's officers, Mr. Lasinby, was forced to man the
braces with the idea of exposing him to the shot. He was slow at
coming from below to this post and was unmercifully beaten for ex-
cusing himself and asking to be set ashore. When they met a Dutch
galiot the next day, Captain Tawke was allowed to depart, but the

brutes would not release Lasinby, though a number of the more decent interceded for him. Once at Cochin they established relations with the shore, saluted the fort, and received a plentiful supply of liquors and fresh provisions, but were advised to run a little to the southward, where they would receive the more substantial supplies needed. This move made, they were well stored with essentials, the Governor sending them sixty bales of sugar. His compliments were returned with Captain Mackra's clock and a gold watch for his excellency's daughter. John Trumpet, agent for the trader who supplied them, received about £6,000 for his wares. The pirates then departed. It was now Christmas, 1720, and the holidays were celebrated in drunken wastefulness, so that when the company sobered up after all their spending they had to be put on an allowance to reach Mauritius without starving, having no luck by the way.

From Mauritius they continued toward Madagascar, stopping at Don Mascarene, where a disabled Portuguese ship on which the Portuguese Governor of Goa, the Conde de Ericeira, was a passenger, became easy prey. She was one of the richest prizes on record, having according to the count between three and four million dollars worth of diamonds on board! The Governor of Don Mascarene, taking them for English privateers, came off and was seized. He was let go, in view of the lost diamonds, in which he had an interest, on a ransom of $2,000 and the promise to give them a ship, the *Victory* now being leaky and unsafe. Meanwhile, word coming of an Ostend ship at one of the island ports, she was taken and a number of the men sent in her to Madagascar to tell the story of their success and to get out masts for the prize. Then, putting two hundred Mozambique negroes on board the Portuguese ship, they sailed to the great island. Coming in they found that the crew of the *Ostender*, who had been left on board when sent to bear the message of rejoicing, while the latter were drunk, had retaken the ship and carried her into Mozambique, where the Governor sent her to Goa.

The diamonds were now divided, forty-two going to the men graded according to size, a lesser number where of greater weight than average. One silly fellow broke a large one in a mortar, swearing that he thus had a better share by owning forty-five sparks. Some now decided to take no more risk at sea. The *Victory* was burned. Taylor and the others fitted out the *Portuguese* and the *Cassandra* for another essay at fortune-finding, with the Indies in view. Before sailing they heard four warships were out after them and sailed instead for Africa, putting in at Delagoa, where they thought to find refuge but were greeted with a shot from the fort, which had been established without their knowledge by the Dutch a few months before. They battered it down. The fort destroyed, the place surrendered to Taylor but of 150 men left at the beginning of the settlement two thirds were dead from fever or fighting. Taylor remained four months and departing left some goods and stores with the poor Dutchmen, who seemed to have been forgotten by their backers at home. Sixteen joined the pirates. It was now late December, 1722. Not knowing what to do, a number took the Portuguese prize and went back to Madagascar. The others in the *Cassandra* made for the West Indies, where, finding no safety they surrendered at last with all their riches to the Spanish Governor at Porto Bello on the Isthmus of Darien, where Morgan had so distinguished himself half a century before. Taylor took a commission in the Spanish naval service. The others scattered: And so the Viceroy's diamonds were strewn to the four winds of the world.

XXVIII

OF HOWEL DAVIS

HOWEL DAVIS was a Monmouthshire man born at Milford Haven. Making the sea his occupation, his last honest voyage was to the coast of Guinea in the *Cadogan*, snow, of Bristol, Captain Skinner. The vessel being taken by the pirate England as related in his history and Captain Skinner slain, Davis joined the rovers. His pretense was that, England urging him to become one of his company, he refused in such high terms that the pirate sent him back to the snow as her captain with a deed of gift, under orders to proceed to the Brazils and there sell the vessel, dividing the returns man for man. Upon reading this generous document to the crew and urging its acceptance, Davis was surprised to find it was not agreeable to the majority who insisted that, as most of the cargo had been consigned to merchants in Barbadoes, they should deliver it there. Their will prevailed. On reaching Barbadoes the crew related the circumstances of Captain Skinner's death and the conduct of Davis, who was accordingly placed in prison where he remained for three months, but no act of piracy being provable against him he was finally released without trial. Davis was now barred from employment because of his part in the affair and determined to join the free companions at New Providence. He managed to make his way thither only to find that Woodes Rogers had come from England and suppressed the trade under orders from the Admiralty.

Rogers, having fitted out two sloops, the *Buck* and the *Mumvil Trader*, for business use in 1718, Davis joined the *Buck* and was sent with a cargo of European goods to Martinique, many of the ex-pirates being his companions in the forecastle. Davis conspired with five others to seize the sloop, which was done, and those who objected to joining were put aboard the *Mumvil*, after they had taken such property out of the consort as seemed most useful. Besides Davis the five included three others who became notable, viz: Thomas Anstis, Dennis Topping, and Walter Kennedy, of whom more will be heard.

[175]

The other two, unnamed, gave up their evil ways and returned respectable in time to England. But to proceed:

The company now celebrated with a huge bowl of punch and held an election at which Davis was made commander. He drew up articles for all to sign, with a declaration of war against the world, and put the ship in order for a cruise at Coxon's Hole at the east end of Cuba. The spot chosen was perfect for the purpose, entrance to the harbor being so narrow that one ship could defend itself against a hundred. Having no carpenter, the crew had much trouble in getting the sloop cleaned and into shape, but she was finally got to sea and her course laid for Hispaniola. His men numbered thirty-five. A French vessel of twelve guns was first taken and a prize crew placed on board. This was hardly done when another sail hove in sight to the windward. Ordering his capture to follow, Davis stood for the newcomer and summoned her to strike. To this a reply was made that they admired his impudence. Davis accordingly treated them to a broadside which was returned. The prize coming up, her crew ordered all the prisoners to the deck in white shirts to make a show of force and hoisted an unclean bit of cloth as the best they could do in the way of a black flag. So alarmed at this show of force were the people on the ship, who were French, that they struck. Davis then ordered the captain to come on board with twenty men, which the deceived gentlemen did, thus weakening his ship beyond recovery, should he discover his mistake, for he had sixty in his crew and carried twenty-four guns. All but the captain were at once put in irons and a prize crew took the ship in hand.

When the French commander discovered how he had been duped by a much inferior force and that the pirate's consort was totally unarmed, his rage and chagrin were without measure. Davis, finding his prize slow and cumbersome, took out her valuables and restored her to the captain who, when once more on his own deck, became hysterical and sought to throw himself into the sea, but was restrained by his crew. Davis now abandoned the smaller prize also, but amply outfitted with arms and ammunition from the Frenchman, made for the Azores, taking a Spanish sloop on the way. The Azores not proving fruitful he turned to the Cape Verde group, coming to anchor at St. Nicholas. He hoisted the English colors and passing for a British privateer was civilly treated. The visitors remained a week with growing popularity, fed by their liberal purchases and Davis was even re-

ceived by the Governor with due distinction. Opportunity was taken
to clean the ship and this done she put to sea, less five of her crew who
decided to stay on the island. One of them, Charles Franklin, a
Monmouthshire man, married and made the place his residence for life.

Boa Vista was next visited, but her harbor producing no prizes they
proceeded to the Isle of May, where many vessels were found lying in
the roadstead. These were ruthlessly plundered, while many fresh
hands were recruited by voluntary enlistment and impressment.
They also seized a vessel with twenty-six cannon and called her the
King James, in pleasant memory of that deposed monarch. The water
supply being poor Davis moved to St. Jago where it was plentiful.
Here the Governor, suspecting their character, put Davis through a
sharp examination, to which he responded with much hauteur and
turned his back on His Excellency, but despite his bearing lost no time
in getting on board his ship. Feeling rankled at his treatment, he
consulted with the ship's company about surprising the port by night,
being confident that it could be done. The men consented to the enterprise and when darkness came down the boats bore a formidable attacking party to the shore. The guards were remiss and as a result the
fort was taken, after a brief assault in which three of the pirates were
killed. The garrison fled to the Governor's palace and there bar-
ricaded themselves. It was a strong building and its doors and walls
could not be broken. The windows and roof were showered with hand
grenades, which did much mischief to the furnishings but failed to
overwhelm the defenders, though several of these were slain. By daybreak the country was aroused and the invaders took to their boats,
having done much damage with no advantage to themselves.

On putting to sea the roll was called and the company found to be
seventy strong. The next course to be pursued was now discussed and
the majority favored Gambia Castle as a point of attack, Davis being
a leader in this opinion. As he had been engaged in the Guinea trade
he told his companions from knowledge that much money was always
kept in store at the castle and proposed an assault upon it. This
seemed a doubtful enterprise against a garrison in a place well-fitted
for defense, but on his exhorting his followers to leave the details to
him they acquiesced and he worked out a clever stratagem.

The crew were first instructed to keep out of sight, so that no more
than a modest number would appear on deck. Running the ship close
under the fort, he caused a boat to be manned by six seamen in poor

attire while he, himself, uniformed as captain, with the master and the surgeon dressed as merchants, went as passengers. The men were instructed in the story that was to be told; namely, that they were from Liverpool, bound to trade at Senegal for gums and ivory, but had been driven off the coast by two French men-of-war from whom they had had a narrow escape. They had therefore put in at the castle in an effort to make the best of it and trade as they could. This having been well rehearsed they reached the landing-place where a file of musketeers were posted, through which the make-believe merchants passed into the presence of the Governor who received them courteously and listened to the concocted tale. On inquiring the nature of their cargo the Governor was informed that it consisted of iron and plate, articles much in demand, at which the Governor offered them full value for it all and also offered to purchase any spare spirits that might be on board. With this he invited the trio to dine with him. Davis replied that he, as captain, was compelled to return to the ship. The others accepted and Davis agreed to return later with a supply of liquor.

All this while the daring rogue made good use of his eyes, noting the beats of the sentries, the location of the guardhouse, and other items of value in considering the steps to be taken. Coming on board, he requested the crew to keep sober and to watch for the striking of the flag over His Excellency's residence, at which event they would know he was in control of the situation and to then send twenty good men ashore. But one other craft was in port and she was ordered seized, while her captain and crew were taken on the pirate lest, in noting the unusual bustle that would accompany the proceedings, they might make trouble. He now picked a boat's crew, giving each two pairs of pistols to be hidden under their waistcoats, with instructions to loiter in the guardroom and on hearing a pistol shot to secure the men and arms held therein.

Dinner had not been served when Davis made his return to the shore, so the Governor proposed that they should pass the time with a bowl of punch. This was duly brewed, the coxswain of the pirate acting as servitor. This gave him a chance to observe conditions in the house and to report when it was well cleared of all beside the Governor and his servants. He whispered to Davis that the proper moment had arrived, at which the latter covered the Governor with a pistol and told him to surrender with his house and all it contained else he were a dead man. The amazed Governor could only submit. His walls were decked with muskets. These were taken from their hangings and loaded. Davis then fired a pistol as a signal to his men in the guard-room, who at once stepped between the unsuspecting soldiers and their stacked weapons, seizing the arms and threatening their owners with loaded pistols, so that they stood passive while one of the pirates carried the muskets out of reach. Then the soldiers were locked in, while guards were posted outside the room. The flag was now hauled down and the boats came ashore as per program. In this manner the fort was mastered without a blow; all was done neatly and in order.

Davis addressed the captives and invited them to join his company, which some of them did. The others he removed to the captured sloop and, to save the bother of guarding them, took away her sails and cordage so that they had no means of getting away. Much frolicking followed, the guns of the fort being employed to salute the rogues on the ship, who replied thunderously. The rejoicings lasted far into the night, but with day the serious work of securing the plunder began. The result was far out of proportion to the risk, most of the treasure having been lately removed from the castle, so that there remained no more than three thousand pounds in gold bars and a considerable quantity of goods. All portable articles of value were taken to the ship, though some were given to the captain of the sloop to reward him for his scare and all the trouble they had caused him.

It was now time to depart and just as they were weighing anchor a ship appeared in the offing. She came in under sail, evidently expecting a prize and Davis made ready a warm welcome. The new arrival was astonished to see so many men and guns on his expected victim and feared he had unwittingly run upon a British ship of war. He was too near to back out and resolving upon a bold course hoisted the black flag, fired a gun, and ran in expecting to board. To his surprise a gun returned his salute and a black flag floated from the mizzen of the ship, to the mighty relief of the captain, Oliver La Bouche, a French pirate and ex-Bahama man, who was now greeted as a brother. Much visiting and civility passed between the captains and their crews, it being agreed that they cruise down the coast together on the chance of securing a better ship for La Bouche. At Sierra Leone a tall vessel at anchor promised to fill the bill and Davis, having the better ship, sailed smartly up, though feeling some misgiving because she made no effort to be off. Instead she treated him to a broadside and hoisted the black flag. Davis sent his banner to the mizzen and fired a gun to leeward, so ending the episode. It appeared she was a pirate of twenty guns, commanded by Thomas Cocklyn, another recalcitrant Bahama man who had fled from New Providence after submitting to Rogers. He had put springs on his cable and awaited their oncoming in the hope of easily taking two prizes in the trap thus set.

"The satisfaction was great on all sides at this juncture of Confederates and Brethern in iniquity," says the Chronicle. After a social period the three captains agreed to unite in a joint attack upon the fort. On the third day La Bouche moved his brigantine at high water and began the assault. The fort opened on her and she replied with a brisk bombardment, in which the two others soon joined. The combined effort was too great to be withstood and the garrison abandoned their guns, leaving the fort to the pirates. Possession was taken and held for seven weeks, during which time the ships were cleaned and refitted.

We get a vivid glimpse of the doings at this juncture from "A New Account of Some Parts of Guinea," published by Captain William Snelgrave, an experienced African trader, in 1734, when he set down the tale of his adventurous life. Captain Snelgrave was master of the *Bird* Galley of London, and under orders from his owner, Humphrey Morrice, sailed in November, 1718, for Holland, where he loaded with a cargo of bale goods, wines, liquors, etc., for the Guinea coast. His ship was held by storm and grounding and it was not until late in January, 1719, that he made his final start, only to be badly baffled by the winter gales, which sent him into Kinsale, Ireland, where repairs and weather kept him until the 10th of March, when he made a good clearing, followed by a swift voyage to Sierra Leone, reaching harbor on the first day of April, his pace being somewhat accelerated by a Sallee rover which chased him past the Canaries.

By the time of Snelgrave's arrival the piratical squadron had gathered ten ships, which had innocently come into Sierra Leone, never dreaming into what hands it had fallen. Cocklyn's story was interesting. He, with others had been on a pirate craft under Moody, one of the Bahama Island group that evaded or broke faith with Rogers. This was a fast sailing brigantine which, in the course of business, took a ship called the *Rising Sun* and when a dispute broke out in the company, a part of them, including Cocklyn, were forced on board of her and sent away with a small store of food and ammunition. Cocklyn was elected captain and they lost no time in bettering their condition. Running into the river at Sierra Leone they surprised a sloop owned by a wealthy native, Señor Joseph, so called, who had been in England and, as Snelgrave says, "was a person of good account in this country." He gave up in ransom a sum sufficient to supply the *Rising Sun* with munitions and supplies. Other vessels were soon added to the score so that, with the captures made by his colleagues, the ten noted above were in hand at the time of Snelgrave's arrival.

Le Bouche had also been one of Moody's company and after the split, with others, took umbrage at the captain, with the result that the latter and twelve others were evicted from the brigantine and turned away in an open boat, which had been taken from some Spaniards near the Canaries. The unlucky scoundrels were never heard from more. Le Bouche becoming captain, the brigantine reached Sierra Leone about a month after parting from the *Rising Sun*. She was not warmly greeted at first, but when it was known that Moody had been marooned the brethren refraternized and Davis, coming along the same day, accomplished a unique reunion of Bahama outlaws. It might be said that Moody had the reputation of being a humane and gentleman-like commander, which was the cause of his undoing, Cocklyn and Le Bouche being both unvarnished brutes and much more in temper with their fellows. Davis was also considerate and humane and kept his one hundred and fifty rascals within reasonable bounds. This was somewhat unusual in the craft, for the captain's authority was slight, except as a leader in the fighting, the quartermaster being the real representative with the crew.

Snelgrave's misfortune befell him in this wise. It falling calm in the afternoon when he made land, and seeing smoke on the shore off the river Sierra Leone, he requested Simon Jones, his first mate, to take the pinnace and to locate the smoke-makers, presuming them to be natives, and so find out if it was clear upstream. Jones was familiar with the region and dissented as to going, arguing that no people lived near the point whence the smoke came and that it was probably caused by some wanderers roasting oysters, who would have departed before he could reach the shore. Yielding to this argument, Snelgrave started for the river's mouth and, a sea breeze setting in, beat up stream at sunset, noting farther up a ship at anchor. Snelgrave dropped his mud-hook inside the bar and piped all hands for supper, dining himself with the officers. About eight o'clock the officer in charge of the deck passed word down the companion-way that he heard "the rowing of a boat." Snelgrave at once went on deck and ordered lanterns lighted in the thought that some "gentlemen that lived there as free merchants" might be calling, but, as a precaution against other gentry less respectable, sent Jones to the steerage to put things in order and to have twenty of the crew armed with cutlasses muster on the quarter-deck. Upon hailing the rowers, they replied they were from the *Two Friends*, Captain Elliot, of Barbadoes. One of Snelgrave's officers knew such a ship and captain, but Snelgrave, still suspicious, ordered a second hailing, in the meantime hastening the armed men from below. The answering cry from the boat was to the effect that they were from America, which was largely true, followed by a volley from small arms.

Though Snelgrave had a crew of forty-five men and sixteen guns and the boat a crew of only twelve, it was soon over, Simon Jones proving rascal and holding back the men his captain had ordered to come armed to the quarter-deck. The captain vainly called to "some brisk fellows" who had been on a former voyage with him to avoid the shame of being so easily taken, but without response, for the excellent reason that the rascal Jones had sequestered the arms. One man was killed by the fire of the pirates. Some grenades were thrown among the men, which added to the consternation and, no one responding to Snelgrave's orders to fire, the *Bird* was soon a capture. Hearing a demand for the captain, Snelgrave came forward, to be greeted with a pistol thrust against him. This he parried as it went off, the bullet passing between his body and his arm. He was threatened with instant death for daring to attempt the defense of his ship. Leaping to the quarterdeck Snelgrave there encountered the pirate boatswain, who "was a bloody villain" and aimed a deadly blow with his cutlass at the captain, who stooped low enough and quickly enough to avoid it, while the blade broke on the rail. Some of the crew now surrounded the captain and begged for his life. For this they were abused and beaten, several being savagely slashed with cutlasses. While this was happening the pirates' boat, which had been suffered to lie loose, drifted upstream and Snelgrave was ordered to send some of his men after her. The rascally Jones offered to go, departing under the threat that if he did not soon return his comrades would be cut to pieces. He was back in a short time, when the quartermaster told Snelgrave he was safe unless his men should complain against him, it being a piratical practice to punish cruel captains. The pirates belonged to Cocklyn's crew and, hearing the firing, that worthy cut his cable and drifting down to the *Bird*, treated her to a broadside without the trouble of asking questions, assuming offhand that the boat's crew had been taken.

Snelgrave urged the quartermaster to take the trumpet and inform his colleagues of the facts, to which that personage angrily asked "whether I was afraid of going to the Devil by a great shot, for as to his part he hoped he should be sent to Hell one of these days by a cannon ball." Snelgrave hoped that this would not be his road, but the trumpet was then used to tell Cocklyn that they "had taken a brave prize with all manner of good liquors and fresh provisions on board."

There now followed an orgie of wanton waste. Cocklyn ordered a feast to be at once prepared, though it was already far into the night. A considerable number of geese, turkeys, and fowl were in the coops and a large hog in the pen. These, roughly slaughtered and half picked and dressed, the hog not being skinned, were thrown into the large cauldrons designed to boil rice for five hundred slaves and set to bubbling. The quartermaster sent word by a messenger to Snelgrave asking the time. The latter, deeming this a polite way of demanding his watch, sent it back by the man. At this the ruffian kicked it across the deck. One of the pirates caught the timepiece and put it in the common chest to be sold at the mast.

Snelgrave was now transferred to the *Rising Sun*, where Cocklyn told him he would be well treated if it were shown he had not abused the crew and would answer truthfully all questions. He was anxious to know the *Bird's* sailing qualities, with the view of taking her over as his vessel. The questioning over, a tall fellow with four pistols in his girdle came up and introduced himself as James Griffin, an old schoolmate, which was indeed the case, though Snelgrave delayed recognition until certain that his old acquaintance was not one to do him harm by the relationship, finding him to have been forced out of one of the Bristol ships, Captain James Chrichton, then held in the river. Griffin offered to stand guard over him the rest of the night, saying he would be in danger from the wretches, who were fast getting drunk on the ample supplies of liquors on the *Bird*. He suggested that punch should be prepared and then escorted Snelgrave to the great cabin where Cocklyn joined in emptying the bowl, toasting "King James the Third," whereby the captain found "they were doubly on the side of the gallows, both as traitors and pirates." At midnight Griffin secured a hammock for his friend and mounted guard beside it, which proved to be a well-taken precaution, for about two in the morning the boatswain came along from the prize determined to "slice" Snelgrave's liver. Though warned off, he persisted in attacking when Griffin used his cutlass so valorously that the rogue ran away. The boatswain's conduct was reported in the morning and reprehended by the crew, who were for whipping him, but Snelgrave, pleading that the man was in liquor, secured the remission of the punishment, despite which the ungrateful villain later once more attempted his life.

The next morning Simon Jones, the treacherous mate, came shamefacedly to Snelgrave and announced that he, with ten others, would join the pirates, as his "circumstances were bad at home; moreover he had a wife whom he could not love," and for these reasons had signed the articles. The captain later learned that Jones had been hoping to find the pirates at Sierra Leone, for the very purpose of becoming one of them, which explained his pusillanimous conduct at the time of the capture. The next morning, April 2d, Jones went with the pirates to the *Bird* and the orgy continued. Valuable goods were tossed overboard. Any package that required care in unpacking went into the sea. Bottles were not uncorked, but had their necks knocked off with cutlasses. Claret was drawn from the pipes in bucketfuls and these as often tossed in the faces of each other as drunk by the tipsy toughs. By night value to the amount of three thousand pounds was thus destroyed.

All this while Snelgrave remained in Cocklyn's hands and in considerable danger. It chanced that Captain Henry Glynn, a trader at Sierra Leone, who knew Snelgrave, hearing of his capture, persuaded Davis, and Le Bouche to go with him to the *Rising Sun*, upon which Davis apologized for the rough treatment and told the ruffians that both Snelgrave and his employer were most worthy people, well noted for their fair treatment of seamen. They all visited the *Bird* together where Snelgrave was shocked at the destruction and waste. All the fine goods were gone and two boxes of books had been thrown into the stream through the cabin windows, one of the pirates observing that there was "jaw enough" in them to serve a nation, and he feared there might be something in them "to prevent some of their comrades from going on in their voyage to hell, whither they were all bound."

OF HOWEL DAVIS

One of Davis's crew, a lad of eighteen, caught helping himself, was set upon by the quartermaster, but defended himself with the plea that he was within his rights as they were all pirates. This did not assuage the wrath of the quartermaster, who cut the boy's thumb with his cutlass, at the same time scratching Davis, who had intervened, holding that he alone should mete out punishment. He went back to his own ship in high dudgeon, whereupon his crew resolved to trounce Cocklyn and his company, slipping their cable and preparing to run down the brigantine. Cocklyn, perceiving this, asked Glynn to call in Davis and proffer his amends. This he did and so averted a conflict to which Snelgrave at least looked forward with pleasure. The quartermaster was made to apologize and Davis was awarded a full share of the prize. That night the boatswain made his second attempt against Snelgrave's life, narrowly missing killing the ship's carpenter by mistake, for which the latter beat him within an inch of his life. During the days that followed the crews of Davis and Le Bouche were allowed on the *Bird* and continued the reckless destruction of cargo and waste of wine and provisions. Snelgrave sought and secured permission to go ashore and remain with Captain Glynn. Cocklyn wanting to make use of the *Bird*, the three companies voted to give the brigantine to Snelgrave, with such goods as remained and enough more from the other prizes to make up his losses. They were quite unable to understand a protest he made against receiving stolen wares, volunteering to escort him down the coast, where he might trade and pick up a slave cargo and offering to give him the best of any African they might take out of prizes.

The men were wrathy at Snelgrave's squeamishness and were on the point of recanting their generosity when Davis intervened, saying:

"I know this man and can readily guess his thoughts concerning their master; for he thinks if he should act in the manner you have proposed, he shall ever after lose his Reputation. Now I am for allowing everybody to go to the Devil in their own way; so desire you will give him the remnants of his own cargo, with what is left of his private adventure and let him do with it what he thinks fitting."

This was granted and the brigantine run alongside of the *Bird* galley for the purpose of transferring the remaining cargo. It turned out that Captain Elliot and the *Two Friends of Barbadoes* were among the captures and Snelgrave procured the privilege of remaining with her, while the transferring went on. One amusing incident illus-

[185]

trating the democracy of the pirates is this related by Snelgrave: "Among my adventure of goods I had in a box three secondhand embroidered coats. One day the three pirate captains, coming on board the prize together, inquired for them, I told them they were in a Box under the bed place in the state room, so they ordered them out and immediately put them on. But the longest coat falling to Cocklyn's share, who was a very short man, it almost reached as low as his ankles. This very much displeased him and he would fain have changed with La Bouche or Davis. But they refused, telling him: 'As they were going ashore among the negro ladies who did not know the white men's fashion, it was no matter. Moreover, as his coat was scarlet, embroidered with silver, they believed he would have the preference of them, (whose coats were not so showy) in the opinion of their mistresses.' This making him easy they all went on shore together . . . The pirate captains having taken these clothes without leave from their quartermaster, it gave great offense to all the crew, who alleged: 'If they suffered such things, the captains would for the future assume a power to take whatever they liked for themselves.' So upon their returning on board next morning, the coats were taken from them and put in the common chest to be sold at the mast."

The quartermaster, one Williams, finding that Snelgrave had a hand in giving the coats to the captains, showed much hostility. He had once been a captain himself and Elliot tipped off Snelgrave to so address him. He did so and the flattery proved so potent that it dissolved his wrath and bought a present of a keg of claret, as well as a friendship that served until they parted. A French ship now coming in unsuspectingly, it was captured by Cocklyn and his crew, who punished her captain for not yielding promptly, by hauling him up to the yardarm, neck in noose, until he became unconscious. He would have lost his life in this merry diversion had not La Bouche interferred. He highly resented this abuse of his countryman and swore "he would remain no longer in partnership with such barbarous villains." The captain became his guest, but the company vented their fury on the ship, cutting her masts by the board and running the hull ashore.

On April 20th, Snelgrave was invited to the rechristening of his ship, now called the *Windham* galley. Punch was served in the great cabin and Cocklyn, as a toast, cried: "God bless the *Windham* galley," at which the guests drank their liquor and broke the glasses while a

[186]

salute was fired from the ship's guns. The ceremony was marred by an explosion of several boxes of cartridges into which a spark found its way, and narrowly missed touching off a store of 20,000 pounds of powder. Upon referring to this danger Davis was answered by Cocklyn with: "He wished it had taken fire for it would have been a noble blast to have gone to Hell with."

Snelgrave was allowed to land his goods and, being given his full liberty, took up quarters on shore with Captain Glynn. A bonfire was made of the *Rising Sun*. Elliot, who was being held with his ship as a tender, managed to slip away one night in a storm and regained Barbadoes, where he soon after died. Snelgrave had another narrow escape, when invited to dine on Davis's ship. Again the careless crew set the ship on fire to the peril of 30,000 pounds of powder. Most of the men were drunk and great confusion followed, the sober ones taking to the boats alongside. Snelgrave took a hand in having these recalled and with the help of Goulding, the gunner's mate, "a brisk, active fellow" and Taylor, the master, saved the ship. This Taylor was destined to perform later one of the greatest coups in the history of piracy and to go scot free into Respectability!

The *Dispatch*, Captain Wilson, belonging to the Royal African Company, came in the river and the renegade Simon Jones, who once having served the company and deeming himself abused, desired her destruction in revenge. One John Stubbs, "a witty, brisk fellow," proved that to destroy the *Dispatch* which was old and worthless, would really favor the company, by way of giving it her insurance money, so Jones failed in his revenge and the vessel was restored to Captain Wilson.

On April 29th an auction was held on Snelgrave's belongings, many of which were bought for him by friendly rogues and returned. His watch being put up, Captain Davis bid and in spite of others ran it up to £100, which he paid. A row followed, one of the fellows declaring the watch to be a base metal and threatening its late owner with punishment as a cheat, and was for sending to Glynn's house and haveing him brought on board for the purpose. Davis headed off this impulse, while Griffin sent him word to hide in the woods until the ships sailed, which would be soon. This proved correct. The next day they were gone. The friendly Griffin succeeded in escaping at Annamboa and went to Barbadoes where he died unscathed of law.

Soon after sailing Davis discovered a conspiracy led by Taylor, the master, to depose him and went on board Cocklyn's ship, only to find that gentleman had inspired the plot. This brought matters to a crisis and Davis dissolved the partnership, declaring himself in these terms:

"Hark ye, Cocklyn and La Bouche! I find by strengthening you I have put a rod in your hands to whip myself, but I am still able to deal with you both. But since we met in love let us part in love, for I find that three in a trade can never agree."

At this they parted, each holding a different course. Davis kept on down the coast to Cape Appollonia, plundering one English and two Scotch ships *en route*. Five days later he met off Three Point Bay a stiff antagonist in a Dutch trader, armed with thirty guns and carrying ninety men, of whom half were English. The Dutchman secured the advantage of the first broadside, killing nine of Davis's men. He returned the fire and a long fierce combat followed, lasting from one o'clock in the afternoon until nine the next morning, when the brave Hollander hauled down his flag. The ship being much stouter and better than that of Davis, it was taken over and refitted. Thirty-two guns were installed and twenty-seven swivels. Making the *King James* a consort, Davis sailed for Anambo. Three English traders, the *Hink*, Captain Hall; the *Morrico*, Captain Finn and the *Princess*, Captain Plumb were found in the harbor busy bartering goods for gold dust, ivory, and slaves. All three were taken without resistance and the *Princess* furnished a recruit in the person of Bartholomew Roberts, her second mate, of whom much more will be heard in this history. Some negroes, in canoes, who were trading with the ships got to the shore unmolested and at once notified the commander of the fort of the presence of the pirates. He therefor opened fire, but had not weight of metal sufficient to reach the visitors, who threw out their black flags and returned his volleys to no more purpose than returning the compliments, adding the *Hink* and the *Princess* to their squadron. Davis sailed for the Isle of Princes, encountering on the road another Dutch ship, deeply laden and having the Governor of Acra on board as a passenger. She yielded £15,000 in cash and a great store of rich merchandise. Hale and Plumb now got back their empty ships, and the plundered Dutchman was also allowed to go.

The *King James* springing a leak, Davis took all hands out of her and left her anchored at High Cameroon. With the rest of the company he came to the Isle of Princes, flying English colors, and when the Portuguese Governor's launch came off to hail, Davis informed her coxswain that his ship was a British man-of-war in search of pirates. He was welcomed as an honored guest and to lend éclat to his character he saluted the fort, which returned the discharge as he came to anchor under the guns. Ordering out the pinnace, Davis went ashore in true man-of-war style and was received by a file of musketeers who escorted him to the Governor's mansion, where he was handsomely entertained and promised any supplies he might require: To which Davis replied by thanking the Governor heartily and assuring him that the King of England would pay for all that was taken. The formalities being over, he returned to his ship. A French ship coming in, Davis had the audacity to plunder her under the Governor's very nose on the pretext that she had been trading with pirates. For this exploit he was actually complimented by His Excellency. The Frenchman's goods, he explained, he confiscated for the King's use!

The rascals even went so far as to make an excursion, to the number of fourteen, with Davis at their head, to visit the village in the hills where the Portuguese ladies of the colony spent the hot season. Fortunately the dames and damsels fled at their approach, but made no report to the heads of their families, not knowing who the callers were. The crowd returned unmolested to the ship, which was now cleaned and prepared for further adventures, while Davis plotted to persuade the Governor, the priests, and leading citizens to pay a hospitable visit on board and then seize them for ransom in the sum of £40,000. This was a fatal program. One night a Portuguese negro, who had been pressed on the ship, swam ashore and revealed their identity to the Governor, informing him of the visit to the village which had so alarmed the ladies and of the purpose of the plot. The Governor gave no intimation of possessing this knowledge, but graciously accepted the invitation. One of the whimsies of the pirates was to take on the names of Lords, which they used when called in council or upon important occasion. To make the visit more impressive Davis went ashore, accompanied by some of these "Lords" to escort his guests to the ship. They were invited into the Governor's house for some refreshment, which accepting, they were fired upon from an ambuscade and all fell either dead or fatally wounded except one who with singular address got to the boat and off to the ship in time to warn his comrades. Davis was shot through the bowels. He fell but rose and attempted to flee to the shore, firing his pistols at his pursuers who pounced out from their concealment, "Thus like a Game

Cock, giving a dying blow that he might not fall unavenged" says the old narration. He moved but a few yards then fell again to rise no more. Of all the gentlemen of Fortune hailing from the sea his career was one of the boldest and most notable.

. The several captains left behind at Sierra Leone under Snelgrave's leadership patched up their affairs as best they could and, taking two vessels that were left in usable shape, the *Bristol* snow and the *Elizabeth* of London, worked back home with all hands, Snelgrave landing safely in Bristol on August 19, 1719.

Of La Bouche, it may be noted that his real name was Oliver Levasseur and that he hailed from Calais. We are indebted to M. Bernardin de St. Pierre, the gifted author of "Paul and Virginia," for a final glimpse of him. M. de St. Pierre, visiting the Isle of Bourbon, in 1770, picked up some memories of its past. It would appear that many pirates were domesticated there in the early eighteenth century and it was always hospitable to them. The Portuguese Viceroy of Goa, the Comte d'Ericeira, coming to anchor at St. Denis, the capital, on April 8, 1721, arranged to dine with the French Governor M. Desforges Boucher. He had no more than landed when La Bouche came sailing in with a fifty-gun ship, ran alongside of the Viceroy's vessel and took possession of her. Then landing, he invited himself to a seat at the Governor's table, where he placed his person between the latter and the Viceroy and informed his Portuguese excellency that he was a prisoner. The pirate having been put in good humor by wine and good cheer, Boucher asked him to set the Viceroy's ransom.

"I must have a thousand dollars," replied La Bouche.

"That is far too little," replied the shrewd governor, "for a brave freebooter like yourself to accept from a grand lord like the Viceroy. Ask something handsome or ask nothing."

"Well," answered La Bouche, "I shall ask nothing. The Viceroy is free to go."

According to St. Pierre, the Viceroy at once departed. M. Millard's "History of Bourbon," however, disposes of this fanciful tale to the contrary. Instead, the thousand not being forthcoming, La Bouche departed with the Portuguese ship after putting its crew ashore, scorning to accept an amnesty which was proclaimed for such as he, and, being subsequently apprehended, was hanged for his impudence on the 17th of July.

XXIX

OF BARTHOLOMEW ROBERTS

BARTHOLOMEW ROBERTS, who ranked even above Every in the extent of his exploits, if not in fame, entered the profession by way of that popular route, the slave trade, according to the record, embarking from London as an honest seaman on board the ship *Princess*, Plumb, master, ranking as second mate, in November, 1719. However honest Roberts may have been, the *Princess* went on an ill errand, for she was chartered to take a cargo of blacks from Annamboa for the West Indian market. Arriving at Guinea in February 1720, the *Princess* fell prey to the pirate, Howel Davis, who pressed Roberts into his crew after the fashion of his kind. It is represented that Roberts was in the beginning "very averse to this sort of life," but his reluctance soon gave way under the preference that was always before him as an able seaman, and on the death of Davis it befell the crew to select a successor. The leaders among them, as before noted, having taken on fanciful names and causing themselves to be dubbed Lords, held caucuses around the punch bowl to consider candidates. One Dennis suggested sapiently "that, while we are sober we pitch upon a Man of Courage, skilled in Navigation. One, who by his Council and Bravery seems best able to defend this commonwealth, and warn us from the Dangers and Tempests of an unstable element, and the fatal consequences of Anarchy and such a one I take Roberts to be—a fellow I think, in all respects worthy of your esteem and favour."

Roberts received the most votes, though but six weeks in the company, and "the choice was confirmed both by the Lords and Commoners." He accepted the honor and responsibility by grimly remarking that "since he had dipped his hands in muddy water and must be a Pyrate, it was better being a commander than a common man."

The first act of the new administration after making the needed promotion was to organize an attack upon the fort as a measure of revenge for the death of Davis and their comrades. Thirty determined ruffians, led by an Irishman named Walter Kennedy, who had been a

[191]

London burglar, noted for his reckless valor, made the assault and, though the work was well defended by artillery and the slope of a hill, its Portuguese garrison fled to the town when the pirates appeared. The latter threw the guns into the sea and returned in triumph to their ship. Fired by this, the men were anxious to burn the town, but Roberts persuaded them against the risk. The forest behind it would give a ready shelter to forces that might overwhelm them and it was a poor satisfaction merely to destroy houses. So the idea was dropped, the fierce souls contenting themselves with lightening the French ship, so that she could approach the town in shoal water, and, after a brisk bombardment that did some damage, they came away, their road being illuminated by the blaze of two Portuguese ships in the harbor which were set on fire.

The first prize taken by Roberts was a Dutch Guineaman, which was restored empty to her skipper. An English ship, the *Experiment*, Captain Cornet, was next overhauled at Cape Lopez. Her crew joined the pirates to a man, save the captain. Steering now to St. Thome they found no victim, and departed thence to Annamboa, where they filled with water and provisions and considered their next course. Some were for making the Mozambique cruise, or proceeding to Bengal; others favored the Brazils. These won the toss and they accordingly sailed to the west, making Fernando de Norhona in twenty-eight days. Here they watered and "boot-top'd their ships" and "made ready for their designed cruise."

For nine weeks the rovers hovered along the Brazilian coast without ever sighting sail. The company then voting to proceed to the West Indies, an inshore tack was made preparatory to the long leg to the eastward, by which chance they fell in with a convoy of forty-two Portuguese ships in the Bay of All Saints, all richly laden for Lisbon and guarded by two men-of-war, each mounting seventy guns. With immeasurable audacity Roberts blended his ship with the fleet and, working alongside one of the heaviest loaded, ordered her master to come aboard, threatening no quarter if any signal was set or hail given for help. This accompanied by a due flourish of cutlasses so astounded the Portuguese that he at once complied. Once on board Roberts saluted the dazed captain politely and informed him "they were gentlemen of Fortune," but their business with him was only to be informed which was the richest vessel in the fleet. By furnishing this information he would be restored to his ship; if dumb he died.

On this the luckless captain prudently, in more ways than one, pointed out one carrying forty guns and one hundred and fifty men—a much weightier force than that of his captors—as the fattest prospect. Contemptuous of Portuguese, the pirates laid close to the heavy ship and invited her captain to come on board to have "a matter of consequence" imparted to him. To this the Portuguese replied that he would attend presently, but the stir on his ship indicated plainly that he knew the character of his caller and was delaying for time. Roberts at once favored the Portuguese with a broadside, closed and boarded. She was promptly carried with the loss of but two men and, although the struggle alarmed the fleet, "the men of war, who still rid at anchor made but a scurvey haste" in coming to the assistance of their countrymen. One indeed, did get under way, but being menaced by Roberts, who was determined to hold his prize, turned tail and the pirates made off unmolested. The victim was very richly laden with sugar, tobacco, and skins and, more important than all, had 40,000 gold moidores in her treasure chest, beside much jewelry, including a cross set with diamonds, designed for the King of Portugal. Gleeful at their success, the rovers now sought a safe place in which to luxuriate and divide the spoil. It was decided to make for Surinam and they picked upon Devil's Island, off the mouth of the river on the Guinea coast of South America, as a favorable spot and there proceeding made themselves at home. This island won ugly repute in after years as the prison of Captain Albert Dreyfus of the French army, unjustly convicted of selling military secrets to the Germans, and remains a colony for the most desperate of French criminals. They were received civilly by the then Dutch governor of Surinam, to whom they presented the Portuguese King's diamond cross. The populace were equally friendly and their wives "exchanged wares and drove a considerable trade with them."

Their sea stores running short, they learned from an American sloop seized in the river that a brigantine from Rhode Island with a cargo of provisions was due. She was sighted one afternoon and Roberts, "imagining that no one could do the business as well as himself," went with forty men on the sloop to bring her in. He took no thought as to how well the sloop was provided with food and water, nor of the mischances of the sea. The brigantine outdistanced him and the contrary winds and currents wore them thirty leagues to the leeward in eight days of drifting and contending. Provisions being almost exhausted, the sloop was anchored and her only boat manned to seek aid of the company at Devil's Island. This lack of forethought had now well-nigh fatal consequences. Without water and no means of reaching shore until the return of their boat, the pirates finally fabricated a raft of cabin flooring and an old tub, on which shore was reached and water and food brought to the sloop. After some days' absence the boat came back with most unwelcome news, for Walter Kennedy, whom Roberts had left behind as Lieutenant, had departed with both the *Rover* and her prize.

In "grievous passion" Roberts and his companions projected further adventures with the sloop "but, finding hitherto they had been but as a rope of sand," they drew up a set of Articles to be signed and sworn to as a better warrant for fealty to each other "excluding all Irishmen from the Benefit of it, to whom they had an implacable Aversion on account of Kennedy."

Summarized, these Articles provided:

I. Every Man has a Vote in Affairs of Moment; has equal Title to the fresh Provisions, or strong Liquors, at any Time seized, and use them at pleasure, unless a Scarcity (no uncommon Thing among them) make it necessary, for the good of all, to vote a Retrenchment.

II. Every Man to be called fairly in turn, by List, on Board of Prizes, because, (over and above their proper Share,) they were on these Occasions allowed a Shift of Cloaths; But if they defrauded the Company to the Value of a Dollar, in Plate, Jewels, or Money, Marooning was their Punishment. [This was a Barbarous Custom of Putting the Offender on Shore, on some desolate or uninhabited Cape or Island, with a Gun, a few Shot, a Bottle of Water, and a Bottle of Powder, or subsist with, or starve. If the Robbery was only between one another, they contented themselves with slitting the Ears and Nose of him that was Guilty, and set him on Shore, not in an uninhabited Place, but somewhere, where he was sure to encounter Hardships.]

III. No Person to Game at Cards or Dice for Money.

IV. The Lights and Candles to be put out at eight o'Clock at Night: If any of the Crew, after that Hour, still remained inclined for Drinking, they were to do it on the open Deck; which Roberts believed would give a Check to their Debauches, for he was a sober Man himself, but found at length, that all his Endevours to put an End to this Debauch, proved ineffectual.

V. To keep their Piece, Pistols, and Cutlasses clean, and fit for

Service; In this they were extravagantly nice, endeavouring to outdo one another, in the Beauty and Richness of their Arms, giving sometimes at an Auction (at the Mast,) 30 or 40l. a Pair, for Pistols. These were slung in Time of Service, with different coloured Ribbands, over their Shoulders, in a Way peculiar to these Fellows, in which they took great Delight.

VI. No Boy or Woman to be allowed amongst them. If any Man were found seducing anny of the latter Sex, and carried her to Sea, disguised, he was to suffer Death; so that when any fell into their Hands, as it chanced in the Onflow, they put a Centinel immediately over her to prevent ill Consequences from so dangerous an Instrument of Division and Quarrel; (but then here lies the Roguery; they contend who shall be Centinel, which happens generally to one of the greatest Bullies, who, to secure the Lady's Virtue will let none lye with her but himself.)

VII. To Desert the Ship, or their Quarters in Battle, was punished with Death, or Marooning.

VIII. No striking one another on Board, but every Man's Quarrels to be ended on Shore, at Sword and Pistol, Thus; The Quarter-Master of the Ship, when the Parties will not come to any Reconciliation, accompanies them on Shore with what Assistance he thinks proper, and turns the Disputants Back to Back, at so many Paces Distance: At the Word of Command, they turn and fire immediately, (or else the Piece is knocked out of their Hands:) If both miss they come to their Cutlashes, and then he is declared Victor who draws the first Blood.

IX. No Man to talk of breaking up their Way of Living, till each had shared a 1000l. If in order to this, any Man should lose a Limb, or become a Cripple in their Service, he was to have 800 Dollars, out of the publick Stock, and for lesser Hurts, proportionably.

X. The Captain and Quarter-master to receive two Shares of a Prize; the Master, Boatswain, and Gunner, one Share and a half, and other Officers, one and a Quarter.

XI. The Musicians to have Rest on the Sabbath Day, but the other six Days and Nights, none without special Favour.

As for the rascally Kennedy and his comrades, they sailed for Barbadoes, where they took a Virginia ship commanded by a Quaker named Knot, who true to his faith, had neither pistol, sword, nor cutlass on board. Feeling secure in his passive society, eight of the pirates decided to become passengers with Brother Knot back to Virginia. In earnest of their good intent they gave the captain goods, gold dust, and moidores to the value of £250. They proved, however, drunken bullies on the passage to port, constantly threatening the captain with their weapons. Once in sight of the capes four put off in a boat and found a friendly reception among the planters. Knot succeeded in getting word to Governor Spottiswoode. All were caught, tried, and hanged. Two Portuguese Jews who had been brought along were the chief witnesses, these having somehow survived the voyage to and from Surinam. Kennedy cruising off Jamaica took another sloop, in which some of the better men decided to make for home. Kennedy hid himself with them and was threatened with being thrown overboard as a natural-born traitor, but finally swearing loyalty was allowed to go along. They reached Scotland and separated. By their free manner of spending they were soon marked men. Two were found murdered on the road, seventeen were arrested in Edinburgh and two of these turning State's evidence, fifteen were convicted and hanged. Kennedy hid in Ireland for a time but coming to London opened a house of ill fame and was betrayed by one of the inmates to whom he had made himself known. He tried to save himself by naming others, but of the list only one man was arrested and he proved that he had been forced and was released. Kennedy was hanged at Execution Dock, July 19, 1721. So much for the renegades!

Roberts and his small company now proceeded toward the West Indies to retrieve their fortunes. In the latitude of Désirade, a small island near Guadeloupe, two unlucky sloops supplied them with provisions and later they captured a Rhode Island brigantine. Proceeding to Barbadoes a Bristol ship, voyaging out, was next captured. From her they took an abundance of clothes, some money, twenty-five bales of goods, five barrels of powder, and considerable provisions. Five of her crew were also impressed. After a three days' detention she was allowed to depart and carried the alarm to Bridgetown. A galley and sloop then in harbor were hastily fitted out, the former with twenty guns and eighty men, the latter with ten guns and forty men. Woodes Rogers, of Bristol, who had a fame of his own then and later, commanded the galley and Captain Graves, the sloop, Rogers being commodore. They sailed against Roberts, who did not suspect their design but ordered them to come to. A broadside was the reply and an engagement followed in which the pirate, perceiving himself outclassed, manœuvered successfully to escape. He was compelled to sacrifice some of his guns and provisions to lighten ship and ever after held Barbadoes and all comers therefrom in great aversion.

Roberts now headed for the island of Dominica where he was well received and secured water and supplies. Much needing recruits, he found here thirteen men set ashore from a French *guarda costa* who had been taken out of two New England ships. These gladly joined his fortunes. Word of his presence reaching the Governor of Martinique, the Frenchmen sent two sloops in pursuit. Fortunately Roberts had left Dominica as affording no good place to clean the ship and had gone for that purpose to the lagoon at Corvocoa in the Granadillas. Making quick dispatch of this task in a week he sailed one evening, nicely avoiding the French who arrived off the harbor the next morning. This haste was not due to fear, relates the current chronicler, but "as they had the impudence themselves to own, for the want of Wine and Women."

Roberts now headed for Newfoundland to despoil the fishing fleets, arriving at Trepassy late in June, 1720. They entered the harbor with the black flag flying, drums beating and trumpets sounding. The crews of twenty-two vessels at anchor abandoned their craft and took to the shore. Except for a Bristol galley which they seized and armed with sixteen guns, the pirates destroyed all the shipping, the nets drying upon the shore, the fish-stages, and in short acted "like mad men, that cast Fire-Brands, Arrows and Death and say, 'are not we in sport!'"

The Bristol galley was sent to the fishing banks, where it destroyed eight French ships and took another, which Roberts manned and equipped as an addition to his squadron. She was named the *Fortune* and the Bristol galley given to her crew. The sloop and the *Fortune* now cruising together took among other ships the *Richard* of Biddeford, Jonathan Winfield, master; the *Willing Mind,* of Biddeford Poole; the *Expectation,* of Topsham—all Devon craft, it would appear by the names. The *Samuel,* Cary, master of London, was a fourth victim. This last was full of valuable cargo and carried several passengers, who were tortured to make them discover their money. The ship was wrecked in the search for hidden cash. From the *Samuel* they garnered sails, guns, powder, cordage, and goods to the value of some £9,000. Some of the latest news of the active moves against their profession had reached them, for they assured Captain Cary that "They should accept no act of grace; that the King and Parliament might be damned for their acts of grace for them; neither would they go to Hope Point to be hang'd up, a sun-drying, as Kidd's and Bradish's company were; but that if they should ever be overpowered they would set fire to the powder, with a pistol and go all merrily to Hell together."

The sight of another sail caused them to leave the *Samuel* and make for the newcomer, which was a snow from Bristol, Captain Bowles, Boston bound. Him "they used barbarously, because of his country, Captain Rogers who attacked them off Barbadoes being of the City of Bristol."

Two days after, on July 16th, they took a Virginia vessel, the *Little Turk*, James Phillips, master and the *Love*, of Liverpool. Both were plundered and released. A Bristol sloop, the *Phenix*, John Richards, master, shared the same fate, as did a brigantine and a sloop called the *Sudbury*. The crew of the brigantine were forced to join. They now turned again toward Désirade, where they expected to meet some provision sloops from New England, ostensibly loaded for Africa, but really, it is believed, sent out for the secret purpose of trading with the pirates. They missed their accomplices and, supplies running low, put into St. Christopher, which port proving hostile they fired on the town and burned two ships lying in the road, one from the hated Bristol, and turned to St. Bartholomew. Whether the kinship in name was a benison is not known but they were well received by men and women alike and remained until sated with dissipation.

It was now decided to make for the African coast. *En route* they fell athwart a French ship, better than the one taken on the Newfoundland banks. She was accordingly exchanged and called the *Royal Fortune*. They were planning to touch at the Cape Verde Islands, but a stupid error in navigation sent the squadron so far to leeward that they could not make Africa and had to beat back to the West Indies to gain the trade wind again. The only course left seemed to be to steer once more for Surinam, seven hundred leagues away. This was done amid great suffering for but a single mouthful of water per day was allowed each man and many were killed by drinking sea brine. Bread was also reduced to a few crumbs per man. When the last drop of water was gone, land came into view and they found themselves at the mouth of the Meriwinga River in Surinam. The longboat went ashore after water and soon returned with a supply. With full casks, but a meager food stock, they now turned toward Barbadoes. On the way a ship was taken; also a brigantine from St. Christopher's, for Philadelphia, the mate of which, James Skryme, signed the articles and will be heard from again. Watering at Tobago and being now well-provisioned, Roberts planned to pay his compliments to the French Governor at Martinique, who shared his hatred with his English contemporary at Barbadoes. He caused a new flag to be made, showing himself standing upon two skulls, with the letters A. B. H. and A. M. H. under them—meaning "a Barbadoes Head" and "a Martinique Head" respectively.

This stay in the West Indies was very active. At Dominica a Dutch adventurer, carrying twenty-two guns and twenty men, surrendered after a fight and a Rhode Island brigantine, Captain Norton, gave up its cargo. Proceeding to Guadeloupe, a sloop and a French fly-boat, sugar loaded, were added to the prey. They now moved to Sanama Bay in Hispaniola, where ships were cleaned and their crews refreshed on shore. Two sloops came in whose masters humbly besought Roberts to give them some instructions in his art, which the captain did, supplying them with powder, arms, and essentials and wishing them good luck on their way. Three deserters, were here brought to boot Harry Glasby, who had been mate of the *Royal Fortune*, "a reserved, sober," and therefore distrusted man, and two others. A court was set up in the steerage of the *Royal Fortune*, and with a brimming punch bowl at hand, the deserters were brought to the bar. It looked ill for Glasby, until one Valentine Ashplant, with two loaded pistols, took his place as counsel for the accused, who had been denied one at the opening, and declared that Glasby should not die, or that if he did he would go with him, plainly indicating that some members of the court would precede them. Glasby was acquitted, but the seamen received only the consideration of being allowed to select their own executioners and were shot at the mainmast.

The Rhode Island brigantine now replaced the well-used sloop and became the *Good Fortune*, Captain Norton being sent away on the Dutchman "not dissatisfied." They were again short of food and sailed for Désirade. A ship under Captain Higstone came in their way and supplied all needs from her cargo. Numbers of French craft were taken on this tack and provisions were more than plentiful. It was therefore, voted to venture again to the gold coast of Africa and they set out at once on the voyage, taking a number of prizes *en route*. There was much discontent on board both vessels, growing for one thing out of the killing of a drunken sailor by Roberts while the squadron was in port. One comrade, named Jones, thereupon boldly

assailed Roberts and despite a cutlass thrust threw him across a gun
and was beating him handsomely when he was pulled off by others and
after trial well flogged for his offense. Soon after Jones and others
from the *Royal Fortune* made a visit to the *Good Fortune* under
Thomas Anstis, who felt resentment against Roberts for lording it as
commodore, and it was decided to desert and set up for themselves.
This was done one night when about four hundred miles off the African
shore.

Roberts, alone, now made for Sierra Leone and reaching the coast
was assailed by two French coast guards, one of ten guns and sixty-five
men, the other of sixteen guns and seventy men. He hoisted the black
flag and beat them both to a quick surrender. When he put into the
Sierra Leone River one of the prizes was equipped as a consort and
named the *Ranger*, James Skryme becoming captain. Here befell an
amusing adventure. One Plunkett, a truculent Irishman, was the English governor of the island, which had some time before been wrested
from the Portuguese. William Smith, who was sent to the West Coast
in 1726 to investigate conditions for the Royal African Company, records this incident in his book "A New Voyage to Guinea":

"Sierra Leone was first discover'd by the Portuguese, but I cannot
be rightly inform'd at what Time the English became masters of it,
nor indeed is it very material, since they had it, a number of years in
their Possession unmolested 'till Roberts, the famous Pirate took it in
the Year 1720, when old Plunkett, who was blown up in Gambia
Castle, was governor, which he effected in the following manner:
'Roberts having then three good stout ships under his command, put
into Sierra Leone for fresh Water and finding a trading ship in Frenchman's Bay, he took her from thence and carried her into another Bay,
with a long, narrow entrance near the Cape, and where there was a
great Depth of Water. This, in my Survey, I have call'd Pirates Bay,
because when Roberts had rifled her, he set Fire to her: Part of her
Bottom was to be seen at Low Water when I was there. The next
Day, he sent up a Boat well mann'd and arm'd with his humble service
to Governor Plunkett desiring to know if he could spare him any gold
Dust, or Powder and Ball. Old Plunkett returned his word that he had
no Gold to spare; but as for Powder and Ball, he had some at Mr.
Robert's service if he would come for it. Roberts, having receiv'd
this answer, brought up his three Ships next Flood before Bense Island,
and a smart Engagement soon follow'd between him and the governor,

which lasted several Hours, till Plunkett had fir'd away all his Shot and Iron Bars; upon which he betook himself to his Boat, row'd up the back Channel to a small Island call'd Tombo; but they quickly followed, took him and brought him back to Bense, where Roberts was, who upon first sight of Plunkett's swore at him like any Devil, for his Irish Impudence daring to resist him. Old Plunkett, finding he had got into bad Company, fell a swearing and cursing as fast or faster than Roberts; which made the rest of the Pirates laugh heartily, desiring Roberts to sit down and hold his Peace, for he had no share in the Pallaver with Plunkett at all. So that by meer Dint of Cursing and Damning, Old Plunkett, as I am told, sav'd his Life.

"When they had rifled the Warehouses they went aboard their Ships and sail'd out of the River the next Ebb, leaving Old Plunkett once more in the quiet Possession of his Fort, which the Pirates had not damag'd greatly."

The Sierra Leone traders were friendly to the pirates. Some indeed had been members of the profession, notably one old fellow called Crackers, who had served with the Buccaneers. He lived at the Royal African Company's fort on Bense Island, where he had three small cannon before his door, with which he was wont to salute his friends the pirates when they appeared in the offing. Roberts picked up two recruits from the Royal African Company's employees and, finding that the two warships on the station, the *Swallow* and *Weymouth*, were on a cruise and would not return before Christmas, proceeded to make himself at home. It was late in June when Roberts became master of Sierra Leone and for six weeks he lay idle, repairing and resting his men; also indulging in the customary dissipations.

Early in August marauding was resumed, in a cruise down the coast as far as Jaquin, pillaging many ships and wantonly destroying such goods as could not be readily turned into cash. On August 8th, the old French ship taken on the Banks was exchanged for a "fine frigate-built ship" called the *Onslow*, property of the Royal African Company, Captain Gee, then lying at Sestos. His company included a number of English soldiers bound for Cape Coast Castle, some of whom joined the pirates and were coyly accepted "after much solicitation," rather than deprive them of a share in "our charity" and leave them to starve on a barren rock. Many of the sailors also volunteered. Among the passengers on the *Onslow* was a clergyman of the Church of England, going out to be chaplain at Cape Coast Castle. "Some of the pirates were for keeping him, offering him a share in the plunder and requiring no harder work than to "make Punch and say Prayers," but out of respect for his order declined to force him. The parson respectfully declined the post and was well treated, getting back some items belonging to other passengers and all of his own possessions except three prayer books and a corkscrew. James White, a crippled musician, taken from an English ship, the *Cornwall*, was not so fortunate, being compelled to remain and "play their time or be beat."

Captain Gee was given the old French ship, while his own became a new *Royal Fortune*, mounting forty guns. About October 1, 1720, the two rovers reached Old Calabar, where they remained to clean their hulls, safe from warships behind the bar. Several Bristol ships were taken at Calabar, but the company was not welcome, the negroes even fighting shy of them, refusing to trade with pirates. At this forty men were sent against the blacks, to force an alternation in their attitude. The reckless forty went against two thousand who failed to stand their ground after the first fire, when three of their number fell. The pirates then burned the town and returned to their ships. By reason of this conduct they were cut off from all supplies and, having finished cleaning the ships, sailed for Cape Lopez. Off Appollonia January 4th, a league to the leeward, the pirates espied the ship *King Solomon* at anchor and being unable to work up to her by sail sent a boatload of volunteers to cut her out. Captain Joseph Trahern, of the *King Solomon*, fired a musket as the boat came under his stern. He was answered with a volley, at which William Phillips, his boatswain, led the men to refuse to fight. John Walden, one of the pirates, ordered the anchor disposed of by cutting the cable, as hoisting it would be needless trouble. The *King Solomon* was then taken alongside the *Royal Fortune* and her cargo rifled, much being thrown into the sea. The same day a Dutch ship, the *Flushingham*, of Flushing, was held up and stripped of her spars and stores. But what angered Gerrit de Hæn, the Dutch skipper, most of all was their taking some fine sausages his wife had made. After wearing them as garlands about their necks, the playful rascals threw the delicacies into the sea. They also chopped off the heads of his fowls, ordered him as "landlord" to dress them for supper and to provide wine, which the poor man was compelled to do, and "as they grew drunk, to sit guilty" and hear them sing ribald French and Spanish songs out of his Dutch hymn books.

Warnings were now sent along the coast to the trading stations of both Dutch and English companies and it was no longer safe to make shore, and so kept off until they came to Whydah, into which port they sailed flying the Roberts flag with its two skulls marked A. B. H. and A. M. H. Eleven sail of various nations were in the harbor, English, French, and Portuguese, several of which had thirty guns and crews of one hundred or more men, yet none would resist Roberts, and they surrendered at discretion, one reason being that a good part of the crews were ashore trading. With one exception, that of the *Porcupine*, all were ransomed for eight pounds of gold dust per ship, Roberts and Glasby, who was still in favor, signing receipts, of which this is a sample:

"This is to certify whom it may or doth concern, that we *Gentlemen of Fortune*, have received eight Pounds of Gold-Dust, for the Ransom of the *Hardey*, Captain Dittwitt Commander, so that we Discharge the said Ship,

Witness our Hands, this   Bart. Roberts.
13th of Jan. 1721–2.   Harry Glasby."

The *Porcupine* was in the roads loaded with slaves. Her captain, Fletcher, was on shore and declined the proposition to ransom her. As a result she was boarded and set on fire, the eighty chained negroes being left to their dreadful fate. Some were released and jumped into the sea, only to be killed by sharks. The hurry and inhumanity were partly due to haste enhanced by a letter Roberts had intercepted from General Phips to Mr. Baldwin, the Royal African Company's agent at Whydah, warning him to guard the ships and stating that the *Swallow* was in pursuit. Roberts read the letter to the crew of the *Royal Fortune*, asking them not to be frightened but at the same time "it were better to avoid dry blows, which is the best that can be expected if overtaken." Two days—from Thursday to Saturday only— were spent at Whydah and it was voted to go to Anamabo, but the wind not holding fair they were forced to Cape Lopez and to their final fate.

The *Swallow*, indeed, was on the way, having sailed for Cape Corso on January 10th, but was delayed at Accra for a few hours and a whole day at Apong, enjoying the hospitality of "Miss Betty," a resort-keeper much in favor at the time. This was January 13th, on which day Roberts sailed from Whydah with a fair wind. Reaching Whydah, Captain Chaloner Ogle of the *Swallow*, was annoyed to find only the ransacked ships and the half-burned wreck of the *Porcu-pine*. Word came that the pirates were at Jaquin, seven leagues down the coast. The pirates had in the meantime taken another ship, the *Sandwich* galley, and had burned the sloop *Whydah* on the 15th. On January 11th, Ogle sailed on the hunt. He found only two scared Portuguese captains at Jaquin, who took him for a pirate, and he returned that night. They were much chagrined on the *Swallow* at the prospective escape of their foes, especially as it was believed that Roberts had an arms-chest full of gold locked with three keys, which they had hoped to have the pleasure of opening. On the 19th, rein-forced by thirty volunteers from the ships at Whydah, French and English, including some men from the *Porcupine*, Captain Ogle set forth again on the 19th, figuring to find his quarry either at Calabar Principe, the River Gaboon, Cape Lopez, or Anamoba.

He reached the Gaboon on February 1st, but finding no one, beat up to Cape Lopez, where at dawn on the 5th of February, he found his foe, with flags flying serenely, awaiting events. By an error in naviga-tion the *Swallow* was compelled to keep off to avoid a sand-spit and this being mistaken for flight caused Roberts to send the *Ranger* in chase. Ogle noting this move and rightly interpreting it, kept to sea, the *Ranger* briskly following. When in range Captain Skryme hoisted his black banner and shifted his spritsailyard alongships to clear for boarding, when the warship suddenly came to and showed her teeth at pistol shot. The black flag was hastily lowered and all haste made to get away. Having made a good start, the pirate again showed the flag and began firing, while a group on the poop, where they had gathered for the boarding, brandished their cutlasses defiantly. An effort to board was considered but the crew, disorganized, did not dare to attempt it. The combat kept on for two hours when the maintop of the pirate was shot away and she surrendered. Ten of her men were killed and twenty wounded. None were hurt on the *Swallow*. The *Ranger* had sixteen French, twenty negroes, and seventy-seven English-men in her company. The black colors were thrown over before sur-render, "that they might not rise in Judgment, or be displayed in triumph over them." John Morris, one of a desperate group in the main cabin, fired his pistol into some powder but the quantity was too small to do more than make a great flash. Skryme lost his leg, but continued to direct the fighting, such as it was. The captives were gorgeously clad and wore watches and much jewelry, but their gold dust had been left on the little *Ranger*, their consort in the harbor, along with Roberts and the *Royal Fortune*. One of those blackened by the powder flash was William Main, Roberts' boatswain. When questioned as to the powder explosion, Main replied that the men were "all mad and bewitched" and that he had lost a good hat by the explosion, it having been blown out of the cabin gallery into the sea. The wounded were cared for by the *Swallow's* surgeon and the unwounded were shackled. The *Ranger* was badly cut up, so that two days were spent in repairs when she was sent into Principe.

On the evening of February 8th, the *Swallow* again made Cape Lopez and with much satisfaction Ogle saw the masts of the *Royal Fortune*, with a prize alongside, the *Neptune* of London, Captain Hill. Holding off until morning to save alarm, the *Swallow* entered the harbor. Roberts was at breakfast with Captain Hill and refused to be alarmed at her appearance, declaring she must be either Portuguese or the *Ranger* returning. When fully apprised by Thomas Armstrong, a deserter from the *Swallow*, of her true identity, he cursed his alarmed men as cowards and at once got under way. He sought to pass the *Swallow* at the risk of a broadside and make the sea, trusting to superior speed for safety, thus failing to run ashore and make the best of his escape. He rigged himself handsomely in true pirate style with scarfs and jewels and a diamond cross depending from his neck and gave orders "with spirit." The broadside was received and returned. Armstrong, knowing the sailing points of the *Swallow*, had advised him to go before the wind, but essaying to tack her lost way and the *Swallow* came so close that a fight to the death remained the only resort. Before the issue could be fairly tried a grape shot struck Roberts in the throat and he fell dead over the tackle of a gun. Many of the crew were drunk, and leadership died with the commodore. His body, full-decked as it was, was at once tossed into the sea, as he had always requested should be done should he fall in action. There followed only a confused and desultory effort at defense and the mainmast falling from a shot, Henry Glasby, the master, struck the colors and the ship surrendered.

The *Royal Fortune* was a strong ship. Her forty guns and 157 men should have made a braver show. But three were killed; none on the *Swallow*. Some £2,000 in gold dust was found aboard and the black flag, caught under the mast, became a trophy. The little *Ranger* was found empty and deserted, the pirates having left her to strengthen the

Royal Fortune. Captain Hill was not unjustly accused of recouping himself out of the gold dust (£2,000) and goods in her hold, for he sailed away in the *Neptune* without waiting for the warship to come in. He later reached Barbadoes and there admitted he had looked out for himself, turning in fifty ounces of gold to the governor. Captain Ogle reported the gold found to be £3,000 in all, and intimated that an early division would be appreciated. He said nothing about restoring the treasure to its rightful owners. The captives were taken to Cape Coast Castle, where Captain Ogle established a Court of Admiralty for the purpose of trying the pirates, under authority granted him before leaving England. As the captain of the *Swallow*, he could not sit as a member of the court and accordingly Captain Herdman, of his consort, the *Weymouth*, presided. John Atkins, surgeon of the *Swallow*, who has left an interesting account of the voyage, though saying little of the pirates, was Register. A general indictment was prepared of the *Ranger's* crew, setting forth that in conformity to evil and mischievous intention, "ye have twice been down the coast; once since the beginning of August and a second time in January last, Sinking, Burning and Destroying the Goods and Vessels that happened in your way."

This applied to: James Skryme, Rich. Hardy, Wm. Main, Henry Dennis, Val. Ashplant, Rob. Birdson, Rich. Harris, D. Littlejohn, Thomas How, Her. Hunkins, Hugh Harris, W. Mackintosh, Thomas Wills, John Wilden, Ja. Greenham, John Jaynson, Chri. Lang, John Mitchel, T. Withstandenot, Peter la Fever, Wm. Shurin, Wm. Wats, Wm. Davis, James Barrow, Joshua Lee, Rob. Hartley, James Crane, George Smithson, Roger Pye, Rob. Fletcher, Ro. Hartley, Andrew Rance, Cuthbert Goss, Tho. Giles, Israel Hynde, William Church, Philip Haak, William Smith, Adam Comry, William Graves, Peter de Vine, John Johnson, John Stodgill, Henry Dawson, William Glass, Josiah Robinson, John Arnaught, John Davis, Henry Graves, Tho. Howard, John Rimer, Thomas Clephen, Wm. Guineys, James Cosins, Tho. Stretton, William Petty, Mic. Lemmon, Wm. Wood, Ed. Watts, John Horn, Piere Ravon, John Dugan, James Ardeon, Ettrien Gilliot, Ren. Marraud, John Gittin, Jo. Richardeau, John Lavogue, John Duplaissey, Peter Grossey, Rence Frogier, Lewis Arnaut, Rence Thoby, Meth Roulac, John Gumar, John Paquete, Allan Pigan, Pierce Shillot.

The prisoners all pleaded not guilty, in rebuttal of which Isaac Sun, Lieutenant; Ralph Baldrick, Boatswain and Daniel Mac Laughlin,

Mate, all officers of the *Swallow*, deposed that the men had been taken after an action on Monday, the 5th of February, lasting from eleven in the morning until three in the afternoon, during which they had fought under the black flag, their vessel "being a French-built ship of 32 guns called the *Ranger*."

A similar indictment was prepared against the survivors of the *Royal Fortune*, that on "the 10th of February last, in a ship ye were possessed of, called the *Royal Fortune*, of 40 guns, made a Hostile Defense and Resistance for some hours," and did it "under a Black Flag, flagrantly by that, denoting yourselves common Robbers, Opposers and Violators of all laws, Human and Divine" and as "Traytors, Pyrates and Enemies of Mankind." Those indicted were: Mich. Mare, Chris. Moody, Mar. Johnson, James Philips, David Symson, Tho. Sutton, Hag. Jacobson, W. Williams, Wm. Fernon, W. Williams, Roger Scot, Tho. Owen, Wm. Taylor, Joseph Nositer, John Parker, Robert Crow, George Smith, Ja. Clements, John Walden, Jo. Mansfield, James Harris, John Philips, Harry Glasby, Hugh Menzies, Wm. Magnus, Joseph Moor, John du Frock, Wm. Champnies, George Danson, Isaac Russel, Robert Lilbourn, Robert Johnson, Wm. Darling, Wm. Mead, Thomas Diggles, Ben. Jeffreys, John Francia, D. Harding, John Coleman, Charles Bunce, R. Armstrong, Abra. Harper, Peter Lesley, John Jessup, Thomas Watkins, Philip Bill, Jo. Stephenson, James Cromby, Thomas Garrat, George Ogle, Roger Gorsuch, John Watson, William Child, John Griffin, Per. Scudamore, Christ. Granger, Nicho. Brattle, James White, Tho. Davis, Tho. Sever, Rob. Bevins, T. Oughterlouney, David Rice, Rob. Haws, Hugh Riddle, Stephen Thomas, John Lane, Sam. Fletcher, Wm. Philips, Jacob Johnson, John King, Benjamin Par, William May, Ed. Thornden, George Wilson, Edward Tarlton, Robert Hays, Thomas Roberts, John Richards, John Cane, Richard Wood, Richard Scot, Wm. Davison, Sam. Morwell, Edward Evans, John Jessup. All pleaded not guilty.

There were on board a number of officers and men from the recently plundered ships who were called as witnesses on behalf of many who had been "forced" or who were counted among rogues with whom they had declined to serve, though, numbers alas, had taken readily to the new conditions.

Henry Glasby, master of the *Royal Fortune*, who had once tried to desert Roberts, was acquitted, though he had been two years with the pirates, it being shown that he had been kept a prisoner for his skill in navigation and forced to do duty. Richard Scot, carpenter of the *Porcupine*, another capture of the pirates, whom he served with his tools, was also regarded as a forced man. As a result of the several trials ninety-one of the captives were adjudged guilty. Of these James Skryme, captain of the *Ranger*, was hanged, together with Thomas Sutton, gunner; William Magnes, Richard Hardy and David Sympson, Quartermaster, and forty-seven seamen, viz: Christopher Moody, Valentine Ashplant, Peter de Vine, William Philips, Philip Bill, William Main, William Mackintosh, William Williams, Robert Haws, William Petty, John Jayson, Marcus Johnson, Robert Crow, Michael Maer, Daniel Harding, William Fernon, Jo. More, Abraham Harper, Jo. Parker, Jo. Philips, James Clement, Peter Scudamore, John Walden, Jo. Stephenson, Jo. Mansfield, Israel Hynde, Peter Lesley, Charles Bunce, Robert Birtson, Richard Harris, Joseph Nositer, William Williams, Agge Jacobson, Benjamin Jeffreys, Cuthbert Goss, John Jessup, Edward Watts, Thomas Giles, William Wood, Thomas Armstrong, Robert Johnson, George Smith, William Watts, James Philips, John Coleman, Robert Hays, and William Davis.

Two, Thomas Oughterlouney and George Wilson, respited to await the King's pleasure, were sent home and there pardoned. Seventeen were returned to England to serve time in the Marshalsea. Of the remainder, twenty accepted seven years' servitude on the plantations of the African Company. In all ninety-one were convicted and seventy-four set free, of whom eighteen were members of the crew of the captured Frenchman, the rest men from the English merchant craft taken during the recent cruises. The death sentence prescribed that the culprits should be taken "to the place of Execution without the Gates of the Castle, and there within the Flood-marks to be hanged by the Neck, 'till ye are Dead, Dead, Dead—" which seems somewhat redundant, to say the least. The gallows at the edge of the tide claimed all but one of those who died. Thomas Armstrong, deserter from the *Swallow*, was taken on board the *Weymouth*, where, as an example to the crew, whom he invited to join with him "in singing two or three latter verses of the 140th Psalm"; he was, at the firing of a gun, tied up at the Fore-Yard Arm.

Some of the more hardened culprits were cut down after execution and hanged in chains on gibbets erected upon adjacent hillocks. The skeletons were still rattling in the wind in 1726 when William Smith, the agent of the Royal African Company, visited Cape Coast Castle.

He also saw one of the indentured men "and was told he behaved very quietly and well."

It might be noted in passing that the *Weymouth* had for one of her lieutenants the celebrated Alexander Selkirk, whose strange story as a solitary on Juan Fernandez remains one of the romances of adventure. He died on the ship in 1723.

XXX

OF THOMAS ANSTIS

A S we have before narrated, Thomas Anstis was one of the five who joined with Howel Davis in seizing the sloop *Buck*, bound out of New Providence for Martinique in 1718 on an errand for Woodes Rogers. We have also noted his parting from Bartholomew Roberts on the Guinea coast on April 18, 1721 to go his own bent, a-pirating in the *Good Fortune* brigantine, whence he made his way to the West Indies and began his independent career.

A ship commanded by Captain Marston was encountered between Jamaica and Hispaniola from which Anstis took clothing, provisions, and all the liquor, but left the cargo untouched. He also impressed five of the crew in approved man-of-war style. Several other merchantmen were forced to give up food and men. One of these carried Colonel Doyley, of Montserrat, and his family as passengers. The colonel was beaten and wounded in his efforts to save a woman passenger from the brutal treatment of the crew. She was horribly maltreated and her back broken, after which the poor creature was cast into the sea. Following this villainy the ship rested at one of the keys to clean her hull and then sailed toward the Bermudas. The Guinea trader, *Morning Star*, from Africa to Carolina, was taken and being a strong vessel was held for use. Another ship from Barbadoes for New York furnished guns for the trader, which was equipped with thirty-two carronades and given a crew of one hundred men. John Fern, who had been gunner, was made captain. This made her superior in force to Anstis, but he was so much in love with the brigantine that he preferred to keep his flag aboard of her.

Though they were now formidable, dissension broke out in the company, many were for seeking the King's pardon and retiring from the trade. One Jones, the boatswain of the *Good Fortune*, was the leader in this and urged that, pending pardon, they should retire to a safe retreat on an uninhabited island near Cuba, which he had frequented on a privateer during Queen Anne's War. This was agreed to and a round robin drawn up in these terms:

[210]

OF THOMAS ANSTIS

"To his most sacred Majesty George, by the Grace of God, of Great-Britain, France and Ireland, King, Defender of the Faith, &c.

"The humble Petition of the Company, now belonging to the Ship Morning Star, and Brigantine Good Fortune, lying under the ignominious Name and Denomination of Pyrates.

"Humbly sheweth,

"That we your Majesty's most loyal Subjects, have, at sundry Times, been taken by Bartholomew Roberts, the then Captain of the above said Vessels and Company, together with another Ship, in which we left him; and have been forced by him and his wicked Accomplices, to enter into, and serve, in the said Company, as Pyrates, much contrary to our Wills and Inclinations: And we your loyal Subjects utterly abhoring and detesting that impious way of Living, did, with an unanimous Consent, and contrary to the Knowledge of the said Roberts, or his Accomplices, on, or about the 18th Day of April 1721, leave, and ran away with the aforesaid Ship Morning Star, and Brigantine Good Fortune, with no other Intent and Meaning than the Hopes of obtaining your Majesty's most gracious Pardon. And, that we your Majesty's most loyal Subjects, may with more Safety return to our native Country, and serve the Nation, unto which we belong, in our respective Capacities, without Fear of being prosecuted by the Injured, whose Estates have suffered by the said Roberts and his Accomplices, during our forcible Detainment, by the said Company: We most humbly implore your Majesty's most royal Assent, to this our humble Petition.

"And your Petitioners shall ever pray."

An accommodating merchant captain bound from Jamaica to England promised to deliver the petition to the authorities and on his return voyage to signal the result to the pirates at their island retreat. This unnamed key lay to the southwest of Cuba, and contained a well-concealed lagoon in which the ships could lie, without being visible from the sea. Here they remained for nine months. Being provisioned for only two, they took to turtle catching to eke out their food, which consisted mainly of rice. This, with the turtle flesh and eggs, sustained them. During all the time they had no other sort of meat.

They idled away their time with dancing, mock trials, and turtle hunting. So matters rested until April, 1722, when the brigantine was fitted out to lay in the track of the Jamaica ship to learn the result of

[211]

their plea. She was met according to program, but brought no answer. Returning to their island with their ill news, they resolved to resume cruising. Both vessels accordingly put to sea, but the first night out, the *Morning Star*, through the carelessness of her navigator, was wrecked on Grand Cayman. Most of the crew were saved and in the morning Anstis came to anchor and sent a boat to their rescue. He brought off Fern, Phillips, the carpenter, and a few men, when two British war ships, the *Hector* and *Adventurer*, came upon them. Anstis cut his cable and ran, pursued by the *Adventurer*. He was so closely followed that his capture seemed certain, but, the wind failing, the pirates manned their sweeps and the brigantine, being a light vessel, thus got safely away. The *Hector* sent a landing party ashore where forty of the *Morning Star's* crew voluntarily surrendered, claiming they were forced men. The rest hid in the woods and escaped. Later a sloop from Bermuda touched at the island and George Bradley, the master of the *Morning Star*, together with three seamen, surrendered and were taken thither. Anstis, in the *Good Fortune*, reached the Bay of Honduras and lay at one of the small islands, where he cleaned the ship, taking on the way a Rhode Island sloop, Captain Dursey, master, and several other small craft. All these were destroyed and the crews added to that of the brigantine. Dursey plotted with some of the prisoners to take the pirate, but was betrayed before he could complete his plan, but he and five others succeeded in getting ashore in a canoe with arms and ammunition. When a little later a boat came ashore for water, Dursey seized her and her crew. At this Anstis sent a boat with thirty men ashore after the fugitives, but the valiant Dursey and his companions gave them so warm a welcome that they retreated to the *Good Fortune* and made no further effort to recapture him.

Return was now made to the West Indies in December, 1722, taking a ship commanded by Captain Smith, which was armed and given over to Fern, late of the *Morning Star*. Cruising together, they took a few island craft, but turning toward the Bahamas captured a Dublin sloop, the *Antelope*, loaded with supplies, which were most welcome. They now had need of cleaning the ships and picked Tobago as a good place to careen. Here when the guns and stores were landed and the ship at heel, the man-of-war *Winchelsea* pounced upon them and all took to the woods after setting both the ship and sloop on fire. Anstis got away in the *Good Fortune*. But most of his best followers were on the island and his crew was mainly composed of pressed men and malcontents, who rose against Anstis and shot him in his hammock. The quartermaster and a few of the faithful, resisting, were also killed. The mutineers then took the *Good Fortune* and their prisoners into Curaçao, where they surrendered the outfit to the Dutch authorities, the pirates being tried and hanged.

The men of the *Winchelsea* searched the jungle at Tobago, taking Fern, his gunner, and several men who were taken to Antigua and hanged in chains. The others evaded the hunters and after hiding some weeks succeeded in seizing a small sloop, on which they voyaged to England, reaching Bristol Channel in October, 1723. Here they sank the sloop and scattered. There is no record that any were brought to justice.

XXXI

OF GEORGE LOWTHER

GEORGE LOWTHER was second mate of the Royal African Company's ship the *Gambia Castle*, Charles Russel, captain, sailing from London to the Guinea coast. Part of her company included some soldiers under Captain John Massey, sent by His Glorious Majesty George the First, to guard the interests of his nation at James' Island. She made port in May, 1721, when Massey landed, as did Colonel Whitney, the Governor, who arrived at the same time on another ship.

The governor and the captain soon found affairs were very ill arranged for their satisfaction, the merchants and factors whom they were sent to protect providing very poorly for them in a material way, provisions being especially scant and bad. Massey was greatly displeased at this and told the community to its face that he was not there as a guinea slave; he had promised his men good treatment and provisions fitting for soldiers. If both were not forthcoming, he would take suitable measures for the preservation of so many of his countrymen and companions. Colonel Whitney was now taken ill and for better accommodations was removed to the *Gambia Castle*, still lying in port. He was too sick to take part in the dispute, but had already decided not to remain in a place where he could have so little credit.

Ill feeling had now risen between Captain Russel and Lowther, who, for some infraction on the part of his second officer, ordered him to be punished. Lowther stood well with the crew and when Russel gave this command the men picked up handspikes and stood to protect him. Russel desisted at this show of force but hated Lowther the more. Massey in his discontent found sympathy with Lowther, with the result that the two aggrieved men undertook to improve their condition in their own way. The Governor, who had recovered and gone ashore, took no note of Massey's attitude, though it was quite plain that trouble was in the brew. The sailors were in open rebellion on the ship, refusing to obey either Russel or his first mate. In this pass the captain went ashore to hold council with the Governor as to the best means of restoring discipline on his ship, but Lowther, suspecting this, sent a note to Massey asking him to come on board, as it was time to act. The captain at once told his men that if they wished to return to England now was the time. He then broke open the storerooms and proceeding to the Governor's apartment removed his bed, plate, and furniture, expecting that he would join them and go home, as indeed he had promised to do, but now refused, in the fear that the ship would "go a-pirating." Lowther had taken possession and locked up the first mate. He had also loaded the guns and put the ship in trim for sailing. Massey in the meantime dismantled the guns in the fort, removed all the provisions and eleven pipes of wine to the ship, and came on board himself with his men and the Governor's son in the afternoon. Lowther weighed one anchor but, fearing it was too late to go down the river, slipped the other, with the resulting mishap of getting the ship aground. Massey at once took two men ashore, remounted the guns and stood guard all night in the fort. He also forced some of the shore people to aid in floating the vessel, which was done in the morning.

Russel now came off and offered Lowther any terms to let him have the ship back. The mate refused to consider any suggestion. Massey and his men again dismantled the cannon in the fort and came once more on board. The Governor not joining, his son and several others, who were not willing to leave him behind, went ashore. The *Gambia Castle* then put to sea. When well out Lowther called the ship's company together and told them it would be great folly to proceed to England, where powerful influences would convict them of mutiny, a capital offense, and it was better to look out for themselves. Such as were unwilling to follow would be put ashore in a place of safety. All agreed to join. Steps were taken to alter the ship for rough service and black colors rigged. The vessel was renamed the *Delivery*. All told she mustered some fifty men, who subscribed to the following articles on the ship's Bible:

1. The Captain is to have two full Shares; the Master is to have one Share and a half; the Doctor, Mate, Gunner, and Boatswain, one Share and a quarter.

2. He that shall be found Guilty of taking up any unlawful Weapon on Board the Privateer, or any Prize, by us taken, so as to strike or

abuse one another, in any regard, shall suffer what Punishment the Captain and Majority of the Company shall think fit.

3. He that shall be found Guilty of Cowardice, in the Time of Engagement, shall suffer what Punishment the Captain and Majority shall think fit.

4. If any Gold, Jewels, Silver, &c. be found on Board of any Prize or Prizes, to the Value of a Piece of Eight, and the Finder do not deliver it to the Quarter-Master, in the Space of 24 Hours, shall suffer what Punishment the Captain and Majority shall think fit.

5. He that is found Guilty of Gaming, or Defrauding another to the Value of a Shilling, shall suffer what Punishment the Captain and Majority of the Company shall think fit.

6. He that shall have the Misfortune to lose a Limb, in Time of Engagement, shall have the Sum of one hundred and fifty Pounds Sterling, and remain with the Company as long as he shall think fit.

7. Good Quarters to be given when call'd for.

8. He that sees a Sail first, shall have the best Pistol, or Small-Arm, on Board her.

The ship steered for the West Indies, leaving Gambia on the 13th of June and sailing with such celerity that on the 20th they were within twenty leagues of Barbadoes. At this point they met a Boston brigantine, the *Charles*, James Douglas, master. She was taken, despoiled, and released. Proceeding on to Hispaniola, a French sloop laden with wine and brandy was halted. Massey went on board of her in the guise of a merchant and after some time spent in fencing whispered to the captain that they would have it all without money. Monsieur perceived clearly his condition and reluctantly gave up thirty casks of brandy, five of wine, some piece goods and £70 in coin. Lowther returned him £5 of this for his civility.

The company grew restless and Massey, being a soldier, chafed for active service. He accordingly asked Lowther for thirty men with whom to attack the French settlements on Hayti, promising to bring back "the devil and all of the plunder." Lowther attempted to dissuade him from this hazardous purpose, but without avail and the matter was placed before the company. The large majority were against it, but the defeat bred a schism which promised open conflict on board, which was stayed by the sighting of a sail. She was a small craft from Jamaica, easily taken and having little of value on board.

Lowther wished to sink her, together with some passengers, but this cruelty Massey would not permit. A smuggling sloop was taken the next day and Massey, becoming more hostile, Lowther gave the sloop to him with permission to depart. This he did with ten companions and went directly to Jamaica. There he laid his case before the Governor with such address, insisting he had acted only to save the lives of his men, that his course was condoned and he was sent home to England.

Reaching London, he wrote a long letter to the Royal African Company reciting his adventures, owning that he deserved death but appealing to them that if forgiven he would still be of good service to them as a soldier. Meeting with the response that he could not be forgiven but would be fairly hanged, Massey surrendered himself, but so little interest was taken in him that he was released on £100 bail. July 5, 1723 he was brought to trial. Captain Russel and the Governor's son were witnesses against him, but he really insisted on giving the testimony himself that forced his conviction and was properly hanged three weeks later at Execution Dock.

Lowther, continuing his cruise, caught two small ships near Porto Rico. They proved to be a Spanish pirate and a British ship, Captain Smith, that had just been taken. Lowther rated the Spaniards well for their villainy, until they were seriously discomposed at the prospect of the yard-arm, when they were relieved to discover their captors were greater rogues than themselves and they were allowed to depart in their launch, Lowther burning both vessels. The English crew joined. A sloop from St. Christopher's was captured and taken along to a small island, where they careened and cleaned the *Delivery* and after a period of debauching sailed again at Christmas time, with the Bay of Honduras in mind but making a stop at Grand Cayman, when Edward Low, a person who was to become eminent in the trade, was met with. Low's vessel was small and poorly manned, so he was invited to sail in company. Low's sloop was sunk and he came on board the *Happy Delivery* as Lieutenant to Lowther, his men becoming part of the crew.

On January 10th they came to Honduras and captured a ship called the *Greyhound* of 200 tons, Captain Benjamin Edwards, sailing from Boston, after an hour's conflict in which the New Englanders gave a good account of themselves. When he struck, the pirates boarded and maltreated the brave members of the crew with cats and cutlass pricks but killed no one. All were removed to the *Happy Delivery* and the

Greyhound burned. Two Boston brigantines were found in the bay. One was burned, the other sunk. A Connecticut sloop was also fired and one from Jamaica taken and kept. A Virginia sloop was plundered and returned to her captain, while another from Rhode Island was retained and armed with eight carronades and ten swivels. Lowther now set up as Admiral, with Low as captain of one sloop and Charles Harris, who had been mate of the *Greyhound,* captain of the other. Bringing the fleet to Port Mayo, they landed sails and stores and put the ships on keel for rubbing down. While busy at this work they were attacked by the natives in such force that they were compelled to flee to the ships, abandoning their stores, which were large and valuable, and setting the *Happy Delivery* on fire. The largest sloop, now called the *Ranger,* became the home of the company, which abandoned the smaller at sea. Short of provisions and in much ill-humor, they made the West Indies where early in May they took a brigantine whose cargo supplied their needs. She was emptied and sunk. The *Rebecca,* a brigantine from Boston to St. Christopher, was the next capture. Friction between Lowther and Low made it agree-able to part from the latter, who was given the brigantine and allowed to depart on his own motion, forty-four men going with each ship, and Harris going with Low. They separated on the night of the 28th of May, 1722.

Lowther headed for New York and captured a few minor prizes June 3d. A small trader for New England back from Barbadoes resisted, but was taken with a fair cargo of West India goods and rum. They now dropped down to the Carolinas. Here a ship called the *Amy,* Captain Gwatkins, not only refused to surrender at the raising of the black flag, but used her broadside so effectually that Lowther tried to evade a further battle. In the manœuvering, however, the *Amy* put the *Ranger* between herself and the shore, at which Lowther ran aground and landed his men. Gwatkins thought he could board and fire the pirate and proceeded in a boat for that purpose, but was fired upon and killed. His mate withdrew, leaving Lowther free to escape. He succeeded in floating the sloop, but she was badly shattered and many of her men were killed by the *Amy's* fire. She was worked into an obscure inlet and there laid up through the winter.

In the spring of 1723 they managed to get to sea and took to the banks of Newfoundland to prey upon the fishermen. A schooner called the *Swift* yielded some supplies and was allowed to go free, after pressing three of her men. Some small prizes were looted, then the company in August decided to cruise in the West Indies. A Boston vessel, the *John and Elizabeth,* Captain Richard Stanny, fell victim on the way. Two of her men were pressed. Success was slight on the cruise until a Martinique vessel afforded food and the *Princess,* a Guinea slaver, yielded up some coin. They found it necessary to careen and fixed upon Blanco, a little island near Tortuga, as a fit place. Here in a sandy bay Lowther took refuge in October and put his guns and stores on shore, in which posture he was observed by the *Eagle,* a sloop of Barbadoes, whose captain, scenting a pirate, resolved to attack. The pirates, caught at a disadvantage, cut cable and hauled the *Ranger* ashore by her stern, but, on the *Eagle's* closing in, struck. Lowther and twelve of the men escaped through the cabin windows. The sloop and the others were taken. The *Eagle* sent twenty-five men ashore to hunt for Lowther, who was not found. She therefore proceeded with the sloop to Comena, on the Spanish main, whence the Spanish Governor sent a force to Blanco to catch the pirates in hiding. Four were found, taken back and condemned; three to life in the galleys and one to the castle of Araria. Lowther, three men, and a boy were not discovered, though it was said that later his body was found in the bush, self-slain, with a pistol burst by his side. Sixteen men taken by the *Eagle* were brought to St. Christopher's, where they were put on trial March 11, 1722. Thirteen were convicted and three freed. Two of the thirteen received pardon. The others were hanged on the 20th of March.

XXXII

OF EDWARD LOW

EDWARD LOW, a most vigorous and successful member of the piratical profession, had Westminster, in the heart of London, as his birthplace and began his practice of thieving when a lad at the very gate of the Parliament House, gaming with the proceeds among the footmen who loitered at the gates of the Commons.

The tideway of the Thames led him readily to the sea, to which an elder brother had already taken and was followed in due season by Edward, who is recorded as having sailed in his company for three or four years. When they parted the younger took up his residence in Boston, in New England and there followed the occupation of a rigger. Here he worked for six years, making then a brief return to London, where he saw his mother for the last time and returned to Boston and the rigging loft. A year or two longer at this work led to a disagreement with his employers and the rigger abandoned his avocation to take a berth on a Boston sloop trading to Honduras for logwood. Being masterful in character, he was made foreman of the woodcutters (patron being the local term). This required courage and decision, for the logwood cutters were mainly trespassers against Spain and Low, with a force of twelve men, went ashore to the forests. The captain of the sloop being in a hurry to fill and sail one day ordered the logging crew to return for another load without their dinner, which was then ready. Incensed at this the twelve and their leader revolted, with the result that Low felled the captain with a musket shot, and with his companions left the ship in the longboat and started out to improve their condition. The next day a small sailing craft was seized, with which the thirteen began their career under the skull and crossbones.

The crew made sail for Grand Cayman, already an important piratical center, expecting there to join others or fit out more completely. Here they fell in with Captain George Lowther, with whom a working alliance was soon arranged, and operations were begun on a large scale, account of which is had under Lowther's career. The first capture by the new company, after parting with Lowther, came on the 3d of June in the shape of a vessel from Amboy in New Jersey, John Hance, master, trading to the West Indies. Captain Hance escaped with nothing more than the loss of his provisions. A Rhode Island sloop commanded by James Colquhoun, taken later in the day, was not so fortunate. Her sails and rigging were cut and bowsprit taken off, to leave her helpless after the cargo was rifled, and Colquhoun was wantonly wounded to render him useless in making port. This was not far distant, for the sloop managed to make Block Island at eleven o'clock at night. The longboat went ashore and roused the inhabitants. A drum was beaten and soon two sloops were equipped and put to sea under Captains James Headland and John Brown. The vessels carried fourteen guns, two swivels, and one hundred and forty men, and such haste was made that they were at sea in search of the pirates before sunset on the next day. Low's ship was in plain sight but evaded pursuit during the night and his pursuers, after cruising several days, returned to Block Island empty-handed.

In the meantime Low moved to the eastward, coming on the 15th of June to Port Roseway (or Rossaway) in what is the harbor of Shelburne, Nova Scotia, then and now a famous shelter for fishermen. Here he found fourteen or fifteen sail, unarmed and helpless, which he proceeded to pillage and from which to impress hands. A vivid account of this incident survives in the "Memorial" of Philip Ashton, published in Boston by Samuel Gerrish in 1725. Ashton had been on a fishing trip out of Marblehead in a small schooner with a crew of four men and a boy. He came in to Port Roseway about four in the afternoon and noted what was taken to be a brigantine from the West Indies among other previous arrivals. After three or four hours a boat from the brigantine pulled alongside of Ashton's vessel, from which four men armed with pistols and cutlasses leaped on board and presenting these weapons took her in hand. Carried to the brigantine, Ashton and his men were strongly urged to join and, showing no willingness, were taken to Low on the quarter deck, who wished to know if any of them were married. All were too frightened to speak, when Low, clapping a pistol to Ashton's head, cried out:

"You dog! Why don't you answer?"

At this Ashton found voice enough to say that he was single, which mollified the pirate, whose policy it appears was to impress no married men. Ashton records that Low's wife had died some time before in

Boston and that when recovering from a revel he would weep over her memory; also that he had a young child in that city.

A new Marblehead schooner of eighty tons, taken from the fleet, was exchanged for the brigantine on the 19th of June, and loading the latter with prisoners Low sent her to Boston. Ashton begged to be allowed to depart with her, but was roughly refused, seven others sharing his captivity.

Putting to sea, Low now encountered two sloops bound for Boston with provisions for the British garrison. These he attacked, but they made a good defense and after a two days' chase evaded their pursuers in a fog. Low now steered for the Azores Islands. On the way to the Western Islands late in July Low took a French ship of thirty-four guns and, making her keep company, entered St. Michael's Harbor on the 3d of August, 1722, where he looted seven vessels, including the *Dove*, Captain Cox; the *Rose Pink*, Captain Thompson; the *Mére de Dieu*, Captain Roche. So sudden was his descent that all surrendered without resistance and suffered themselves to be plundered. The *Rose* had been an English warship and, though having a British captain, was now a Portuguese possession and laden with wheat. Being stoutly built and carrying fourteen guns, Low took her over and made her flagship, increasing her armament to thirty-six cannon, taken from the Frenchman. The schooner was given over to John Lopez, a Portuguese, claiming to be English born and using the name of John Russel. Being short of provisions, Low now made a demand for supplies upon the Portuguese Governor of St. Michael's, with which that official thought it well to comply, presumably being amply compensated for his courtesy. The Chronicle says the French ship was burned after the removal of all her crew but the cook, who "being a greazy fellow, would fry well in the fire" and was accordingly bound to the main mast and burned with the ship "to the no small diversion of Low and his Mirmidons."

The schooner under command of Russel, lying by Low's orders between St. Michael's and St. Mary's Isle about the 20th of August took the *Wright* galley, Captain Carter. He with his crew and some Portuguese passengers showed fight, and they were brutally slashed and maltreated. Two Portuguese priests were run up to the yard-arm until insensible and then released. This was repeated several times as sport. Another Portuguese was wantonly killed by a pirate who did not like his looks and severed his body at the abdomen with a cutlass stroke.

One rogue striking at a prisoner miscarried his weapon and cut Commodore Low's lower lip so his teeth were bare, which did not improve his appearance, especially as the drunken surgeon, with whose work he found fault, struck him and disturbed his stitches and then "bid him sew up his Chops himself."
They now sailed past Madeira with no better prey than a fishing boat and made the Cape Verde Islands. Here they had much success, capturing in rapid order a Liverpool ship, Captain Scot, commander; two Portuguese sloops, an English craft, of which James Pease was master, and three sloops from St. Thomas bound for Curaçao. One of these sloops Low fitted out, under Farrington Spriggs, as Ashton calls him, or Francis, as he is generally known, who was quartermaster, and sent them to the Azores to intercept the *Greyhound*, Captain Glasgow; the *Joliff*, Captain Aram, credited with piratical ambitions, with an invitation to join his fleet. Instead, landing at St. Michael's for water, some of the men were recognized by passengers from Carter's sloop and put under arrest in the castle, "where they were provided for as long as they lived"—a short period, it is to be feared. The sloop rejoined, less the luckless ones.
We are able to get an interesting portrayal of Low and his proceedings from the "Voyages of Captain George Roberts," published in 1726. Roberts was master of a sloop called the *Dolphin*, bound from Barbadoes to London, who, pausing to do a little trading among the Cape Verde Islands, noted on the morning of October 10, 1722, three vessels seemingly in company, lying off Carrisal, Isle of St. Nicholas, where he rested at anchor. As the sun rose "the middlemost of the three" stood in toward the *Dolphin*. Roberts, using his glass soon made her out to be "a schooner, and full of Hands, all in their white shirts" and "likewise a whole tier of Great Guns." He suspected what they were but had no way of escape save by running the sloop ashore "which would have been meer madness" as he observes. The schooner called *Ranger* came in under the day breeze "fast as the wind," flying English colors, to which Roberts responded by hoisting his own. She hailed and asked that a boat be sent aboard, which Roberts complied with, manning it with two of his crew. Roberts remained on his own deck, lightly dressed, barefooted, and wearing a mottled shirt of Holland cloth. Russel called to him from the schooner:
"You speckled-shirt dog! Why did you not come aboard with the boat? I will drub you within an inch of your life and that inch too."

[223]

Roberts replied politely that he had not known his society was desired but if the gentleman "pleased to send the boat" he would "wait upon him on board." To which Russel responded: "Ay, you dog, and I will teach you better manners." Upon this an armed boat's crew came from the pirate to the sloop, several of whom ferried Roberts back, the remainder seizing his vessel. Russel met him at the gangway with drawn cutlass, and Roberts fully expected a slash from the blade. This might have occurred had not the gunner of the pirate intervened, when Russel contented himself with further abuse for not coming with the first boat. To which the poor Roberts humbly replied that if he had "done amiss" it was through ignorance and from not knowing "who or what they were."

At this Russel roared: "Damn you, you dog, what or who do you think we are?"

The captain answered falteringly that he believed they were "Gentlemen of Fortune ranging the sea."

"You lie, by G—," was the rough response. "We are pirates, by G—."

Roberts added to the length and humbleness to his apology for lack of perception, and was then harried further because of his scant costume. He volunteered to go back and don better clothes, not having known he should have to pay a visit to "such gentlemen as they were." He was informed that the clothes he had on were all he could keep. The rest as well as the sloop and its cargo were to become the pirates' spoil.

Low, in the *Rose Pink* now came within hail when, to quote Roberts, "Russel gave him an Account of what had passed, and of his design of landing that Evening upon the Island of St. Nicholas in order to take the Priest and Governor." To this the "Commodore" agreed and sent reinforcements in his "great launch" to aid in the venture. The raid was made that night and in the morning Russel returned with the priest, the Governor's son, and half a dozen negro servitors. These were taken aboard the *Rose Pink* and with them Captain Roberts to pay his respects "to the great Captain Low, then Commodore." The gunner acted as master of ceremonies, escorting Roberts to the cabin, where he was civilly received by Low, who expressed himslf as sorry for his misfortune, preferring, he added to despoil others than his countrymen. "But, however," says he, "since Fortune has ordered it so that you have fallen into our hands, I would have you be of good

[224]

cheer and not cast down." Roberts expressed the faint hope that he was in the hands of "gentlemen of Honour and Generosity; it being still in their power to determine whether to make this, their capture of me, a misfortune or not." To this Low made answer: "It did not lie in his particular Power; for he was but one Man, and all Business of this nature must be done in Publick and by a majority of Votes by the whole company, and though neither he, nor, he believed, any of his company, desired to meet with any of their own Nation . . . Yet when they did it could not be very well avoided, but that they must take as their own what Providence sent them; and as they were Gentlemen who entirely depended upon Fortune, they durst not be so ungrateful to her, as to refuse any Thing which she put in their way, for if they were to despise any of her Favours, tho' never so mean, they might offend her, and thereby cause her to withdraw her Hand from them; and so, perhaps, they might perish for want of those things, which in the rash folly they slighted."

This philosophy Low recited while perched on one of the Great Guns, though at the end he politely asked Roberts to be seated on one of the chairs in which the cabins abounded. The captive thought Low's position on the gun was a pose—to appear more martial and hero-like than if he sat in a commonplace chair.

The commodore's next remark was to ask Roberts what he would have to drink. He replied that he would take what was offered, to which Low rejoined, "It would not avail me any Thing to be cast down. It was the fortune of war, and grieving or vexing myself, might be of no good Consequence in respect to my Health; beside it would be more taking with the company to appear brisk, lively and with as little concern as I could."

With this Low rang the cabin bell and on the appearance of the servant thus summoned ordered a bowl of punch. It came in sparkling in a rich silver vessel holding two gallons, to which was added two bottles of claret. Low drank to the captain's good fortune in the punch while he reciprocated with the claret. Mellowed by the punch Low regretted that they had not met ten days earlier, when he might have loaded the sloop with goods, now disposed of, either by giving them to other prizes or "heaving the rest into Davy Jones's Locker." He might meet him again and be able to give some restitution for the present loss.

The visit was now interrupted by the coming of Russel, with his ac-

UNDER THE BLACK FLAG

count of the raid on St. Nicholas Isle, in which thirty-five pirates took part, surrounding the Governor's house, so no one could escape and then capturing that of the priest, where they demanded and received refreshment, for the poverty of which the Father apologized, saying he could not entertain properly at that hour, but would do better should his guests remain during the day. To this Russel replied that from good authority the priest and the Governor were reported to have "a good store of dollars as well as gold, hoarded up and that we were come to share it with them, it being one great Branch of our Trade not to let money lie rusting and cankering in old bags or chests, but to make it move or circulate whenever we could come at it."

The priest said the report was false and lighted a candle so they might see all. They found but twenty dollars in money, which Russel did not think worth taking; there was even less in the Governor's house. So they returned empty-handed save for the prisoners, "for his more ample satisfaction."

Captain Low, says Roberts, sat "as demure and attentive" as a judge during the detailed narrative, then started up with:

"Zounds! What satisfaction is this to me or the company? We do not want these fellows, damn them. No, we wanted their money, if they had any; and if not, they might have stayed ashore or gone to the Devil!"

The punch bowl was now liberally tapped, Roberts alone being allowed to drink claret, and Russel went on with his tale, which was that he brought the captives aboard for further pressure as to the truth of their lack of money. The islanders were then put ashore and Roberts was held to await the vote of the company.

Three members of the pirate crew made themselves known to Roberts as once having sailed with him in the ship *Susannah*, of which he was master in 1718. These exerted themselves in his favor. His mate, however, enrolled with the pirates, and, save for two boys, the rest of his crew were taken on board the *Rose Pink*. Russel was for pressing Roberts aboard the fleet, as an experienced navigator both for the Gold Coast and the Brazils, but Low was against it, and the three men from the *Savannah* told much to the credit of Roberts, beside his being married and having four children. The punch bowl was pretty brisk during all this negotiating, and Roberts had many philosophical talks with Low, on all manner of subjects, the rogue's interest in human nature being very deep. Finally Low ordered a consultation

[226]

signal set to summon the crew to settle the fate of Roberts. This was done by hoisting what the pirates called their green trumpeter · at the mizzen-peak, this being a green silk flag with the yellow figure of a man blowing a trumpet embroidered on it. The boats soon brought the several crews to the *Rose Pink*. Roberts was sent into the cabin, while the deliberation went on upon the decks. No decision was then arrived at, the crews dined forward and the officers in the cabin, both having abundant supplies of liquor. The men ate in a very disorderly fashion, "more like a kennel of hounds than like men, snatching and catching the victuals from one another." This was disgusting to Roberts, but the men deemed it one of their chief diversions, being "martial like"

A further effort was made the next day to have Roberts stay with the fleet, Russel offering to replace the empty, leaking sloop with the first good prize taken, with which he could recoup himself for his losses. This did not appeal to Roberts, who was next exhorted to stay as chaplain, some of his philosophizing having been quoted about the ship. To this there was dissent, it being remarked that pirates "had no God but their money and no Saviour but their arms." Others said "that I had said nothing but what was very good, true, and rational and that they wished that godliness, or at least some humanity, were in more practice among them; which they believed would be more to their reputation and cause a greater esteem to be had for them, both from God and Man."

In the end, Spriggs as well as Low being friendly, the company voted for his release. Russel took him from the *Rose Pink* to the schooner "to treat me with a sneaker of Punch" before parting. The "sneaker" developed a full bowl into which Russel poured two bottles of claret. Not liking the mixture, Roberts asked to drink his libations in unmixed claret. He was ordered to swallow his full bumper in turn if it killed him and prudently obeyed. Russel in his cups did his best to pick a quarrel and drew his pistol in great umbrage when Roberts drank to the health of King George; the captain verily believed he would have killed him but for the gunner who had interfered when he first came to the ship. He drew another when this was struck up and the master of the schooner diverting its aim, the weapon went off without damage. A bitter row followed among the officers with the result that Russel was overborne and his arms taken from him. The ruffian dropped off into a drunken sleep about two o'clock in the

morning, but the other officers remained up and kept guard. In the morning they conveyed Roberts back to the *Rose Pink*, when Low apologized for Russel's conduct and promised that the agreement would be kept. Incidentally, at this stage, Roberts reveals that Francis Spriggs was the captain of the third ship—the old brigantine. He was then told that all his men had joined the pirates and that he would have none but the boys to help him home; he therefore asked that he be set ashore. Russel then said that his fate was decreed and back to the sloop he would go.

"I was going to make him a reply," writes Roberts, "but casting my eye on Captain Low he wink'd at me to be silent and taking a bumper, drank to the success of their Proceedings."

After much more wrangling it was agreed to restore Roberts to his sloop in the afternoon. All dined together with the commodore, who once more filled the great punch bowl and set a dozen of claret on the table for Roberts's special delectation, "and that they said," observes the captain "was for me to take my leave of them and part sailor-like."

Not until ten o'clock at night on October 29th was Roberts sent back as promised. Russel, drunk again, had ordered the sloop stripped of sails and her water casks stove. The gunner remonstrated at this brutality.

"Pish," said Russel, "the same miraculous power that is to bring him provisions can also bring him a sail."

As Roberts rowed away the mate called after him that he was "pressed" and in a low voice begged he would write his brother in Carlingford of his misfortune. The captain found his sloop well-looted, a hatful of biscuit crumbs and some tobacco alone remaining for sustenance. With the aid of his boys he worked the sloop back to Carrisal, catching a shark *en route* for food and thence got safely back to England.

With Roberts's story Russel seems to disappear from the combination, whether taking the sloop and going on some other course or what not, for we find Low heading next for the Triangles, three small islands of the coast of Surinam, Ashton, who is minute at this point, mentioning only the schooner as in their company. Reaching the Triangles in bearing down the *Rose Pink* on careen Low overloaded the shrouds and yards with men, so that the ports came under water and the sea pouring in she completely capsized. Low and the ship's

surgeon were in the cabin when the flood rushed through the ports. With swift presence of mind he leaped through the after window. The surgeon who tried to follow was pressed back by the sea, when Low reaching in caught him by the collar and pulled him out. The men in the rigging, including Ashton, were thrown into the water, whence they were rescued by a boat which luckily was at hand. Two hands, John Bell and Zana Gourdon, lost their lives by the mishap. The schooner, though near, had all its men busy mending sails and knew nothing of the accident until the boat brought the survivors alongside. The pink sank in six fathoms. Being now short of supplies, and calms and currents being contrary to a design for Tobago, they steered for Grenada, then a French colony, where Low, concealing his crew below, pretended to be from Barbadoes, needing water. The French, taking him for a smuggler, thought it would be a neat stroke to capture the schooner and accordingly filled a sloop with thirty hands for the undertaking. Low, though unawares, when first attacked called all hands and soon made himself master of the sloop and its astonished crew. Seven or eight prizes were now taken in rapid order on a stretch to Santa Cruz where two more were added to the bag. Needing medicine, Low sent four Frenchmen from one of the captures in one of the small craft to St. Thomas, twelve leagues away, promising that if they returned with a full chest he would restore all the vessels, if not he would burn them and slaughter their crews. The errand was faithfully performed and Low on his part kept his word.

Cruising toward the Canaries they next encountered a fine Portuguese ship, *Nostro Signiora de Victoria*, bound home from Brazil. She was taken after a short resistance. When they failed to find any specie on board, it was revealed under torture of some of the crew that the captain had hung a bag with 11,000 gold moidores from a cord out of the cabin window and cut it loose when the ship surrendered. Low, according to the tale of the time, ordered the captain's lips to be cut off and broiled before his own eyes, and in the end put all hands to death, to the number of thirty-two. Working back on the route from New York and New England to the West Indies, Low took inside a month a snow bound from New York to Curaçao, Robert Leonard, master; a sloop bound for New York, Captain Craig; a snow, from London, via Jamaica, for New York; the *Stanhope*, pink, Andrew Delbridge, master, from Jamaica for Boston. This last they burned "because of Low's irreconcilable aversion to New England men."
[229]

They now sailed down to the Spanish main and between Porto Bello and Carthagena descried two large ships, one of which proved to be H. B. M. S. *Mermaid*, the other a Guinea trader. The pirates pursued until the heavy teeth of the *Mermaid* were seen, when they turned tail and fled, pursued by the warship, which gained rapidly. Ashton, then on the schooner, who tells the tale, confesses himself filled with terror at the prospect. The pirates, finding themselves outsailed, separated, Spriggs in the schooner standing in from the shore. The sloop, with Low, appearing the larger, was selected by the *Mermaid* as the one to follow, but a member of the crew who knew the water piloted her over a shoal which was too high for the *Mermaid* to pass and on which she grounded. Spriggs and his companions drank together a mighty bumper and swore to blow out each others' brains rather than be taken. They managed to get into Picaroon Bay and so escaped danger.

The pirates joined at Utilla seven or eight leagues to the leeward of the island of Roatan, where there, being but twenty-two men on the schooner, Ashton and seven others plotted to seize her and escape. Spriggs got some word of the plan and visiting Low informed him of it, getting into a great passion when that worthy declined to take it seriously. Returning to the schooner, Spriggs made pretense of picking out four to be shot and denouncing Ashton as deserving to be hung at the yard-arm. The latter disclaimed any thought of doing anyone injury, saying he only wanted to depart in peace, and, as he says, "the flame was quenched." They next lay in at Roatan, where landing was made on Port Royal Key, huts set up and much carousing indulged in. Water being needed and found on one of the lesser keys, Ashton asked to be allowed to become one of the party sent after it. He had often begged Low's permission to go home, but had always been told that he should do so when Low did, and never until then touch land. The cooper who was in charge of the water party assented to his going, so on Saturday, March 9, 1723, Ashton with five others and the cooper went ashore to get water in the longboat. Pretending that he was in search of cocoanuts, Ashton wandered away from the beach and hid five days in the thickets of the island, when to his great joy he saw the ships depart. Here for the moment let us leave him and return to Low.

During the latter's operations in the Bay of Honduras a Spanish sloop was encountered, which had just despoiled five English sloops and a pink that had put in after logwood. Low lured the Spaniards into reach by hoisting the banner of Spain, and then raised the black flag and, coming to close quarters, made her captive, without resistance. The vessels that had suffered were commanded by Messrs. Tuthill, Norton, Newbury, Sprafoot, Jeremiah Clark, and Parrot. Low's ruffians massacred the Spanish crew and released the English captives found in the hold and restored them to their vessels, taking some of their crew as volunteers. He would not, however let them steer for Jamaica, but made them agree under pain of death to make New York their next port. As Low needed a carpenter, he who had served the pink was forcibly taken along. The Spaniard was burned after being stripped of booty.

Cruising now between the Leeward and the Spanish main, Low took two snows bound from Jamaica to Liverpool and one from Jamaica to London, Budds, master. A ship from Biddeford for Jamaica, John Pinkham, captain, and two sloops from Jamaica for Virginia, were also gathered in. He now turned again toward the American coast, and off South Carolina on the 27th of May in swift order he chased and captured in turn "three good ships," the *Crown*, Captain Lovereigne; the *King William*, and the *Carteret*; a brigantine also was added to the prey. Off Cape Antonio, on the 8th of May, the Amsterdam *Merchant*, Captain John Welland, was taken, *en route* to Boston from Jamaica. She yielded small spoil—three barrels of beef, £150 in gold and silver and a colored slave called Dick. Her people were at first transferred to the *Ranger* and then to Low's ship, the *Fortune*. Here, out of his hatred for New England, Low treated Captain Welland with great cruelty, causing him to be slashed with cutlasses and to have his right ear cut off. Bleeding and exhausted he was thrown into the hold, where he lay for two or three hours until Patrick Cunningham, one of the crew, brought him some water and called the ship's surgeon, by which means he was saved from bleeding to death. He lived, however, to collect ample revenge. The next day, the *Kingston*, of Piscataqua, Captain Eastwick, was taken and after being plundered was released. Captain Welland and his men were sent away with her. The *Ranger* was now in charge of Charles Harris, Spriggs having again become quartermaster on the *Fortune*.

They were now in the path of trade and made frequent captures. A sloop for Amboy, N. J., Captain William Frazier, seems to have made some trouble for the pirates, who were credited with having burned the men's fingers with matches, slashed their persons with cutlasses, and

UNDER THE BLACK FLAG

then set them ashore on an uninhabited spot. Further victims included another ship, Barrington, master; two Carolina brigantines bound for London; a Virginia sloop headed for Bermuda; a ship from Glasgow to Virginia; a sloop from Philadelphia for Surinam; and a pink from Virginia to Dartmouth. These were all robbed and allowed to go, which led to the partial undoing of the pirates.

The mate of one of the Virginia vessels on June 7th encountered His Majesty's man-of-war, *Greyhound*, in latitude 39, and informed Captain Peter Solgard that he had been overhauled by Low the evening before, giving his opinion that the pair of marauders were headed for Block Island. Solgard at once made sail in pursuit and on the 10th of June, when fourteen leagues off Long Island, sighted the squadron. The *Fortune* and *Ranger* at once joined in chasing. To lure them on, Solgard, sizing up the two eager gentry, tacked and filled in a clumsy appearance of flight until he got the two into hailing distance when the black flag ran up on both. Each fired a gun, at which the *Greyhound* hauled up her mainsail and kept close up to the wind, contriving to keep her antagonists from running to the leeward. The pirates were good seamen and edged away under the man-of-war's stern, when a running fight followed for an hour. The sea was calm at the beginning of the action. Such wind as there was failed to stir the cruiser, but was of slight help to the pirates, who put out sweeps and crept away, lowering their black colors and hoisting red instead. Though Low, it appears, had planned to lay the *Fortune* alongside and shower grenades, Harris to come next in the *Ranger* to board over the deck of the former, he was unable to attempt this, the twenty guns of the *Greyhound* being too well served to permit the approach. They were out of range by three o'clock in the afternoon, when Solgard, also putting out sweeps, gained on them and by four had again come within striking distance, managing to place his vessel between the two, when, his fire causing the mainyard of the *Ranger* to drop, she lay helpless on the sea, and called for quarter and surrendered at discretion.

Low, instead of standing by and fighting as he could have done, with a fair chance of rescuing his consort, and as he was oath-bound to do, made good his escape. Despite his ferocity in dealing with merchant captains and their crews, Low showed himself, according to the language of the day, to be "a base, cowardly villain." Seven were wounded on the *Greyhound*, none fatally. The *Ranger* lost a dozen or more in killed and wounded. Her officers and crew were taken into

[232]

Newport, locked up in jail, and put on trial for their lives July 10, 1723. The court which tried the wretches was headed by William Dummer, Lieut-Governor of Massachusetts Bay, and included in its distinguished body: Nathaniel Paine, Esq.; Addington Davenport, Esq.; Thomas Fitch, Esq.; Spencer Phipps, Esq.; John Lechmere, Esq., Surveyor-General; John Valentine, Esq., Advocate-General; Samuel Cranston, Governor of Rhode Island; John Menzies, Esq., Judge of the Admiralty; Richard Ward, Esq., Register; Jahleel Brinton, Provost Marshal. Robert Auchmuta, Esq. acted as counsel for the defense by assignment of the Court.

The pirates were brought to the bar in three separate batches, taking as many days to try. The first included Charles Harris, Captain; Thomas Linnicar, Daniel Hyde, Stephen Mundon, Abraham Lacy, Edward Lawson, John Tomkins, Francis Laughton, Owen Rice, William Read, John Wilson and Henry Barnes. The two last proved that they had been forced men and were acquitted. The others were found guilty. The next lot put on trial were Thomas Hugget, Peter Cues, Thomas Jones, Edward Eaton, William Jones, John Brown, Joseph Sound, Charles Church, John Waters, William Beades and Thomas Mumford, a Gay Head Indian. The Indian had been taken with five others of his tribe the year before, while fishing off Nantucket. Two of his fellows had been hanged on the ship near Cape Sable. The fate of the others was not recorded. He was acquitted as forced, as was Thomas Jones, who was but a boy seventeen. The others were condemned on June 11th. The next day, June 12th, John Kencate, surgeon of the *Ranger;* Thomas Russell, Thomas Hazel, John Bright, John Fletcher, Thomas Child, Patrick Cunningham, Joseph Sweetser and Joseph Libbey were brought to the bar. Kencate showed that he had been impressed from the *Sycamore* galley, Captain Scott, in the previous September at Bonavista, one of the Cape de Verde Islands, and was acquitted. Sweetser also showed that he was a forced man and was freed. The others were found guilty. On July 19, 1723 the twenty-six condemned men were taken to Bull's Point, near Newport and hanged "with the flux and reflux of the sea." The bodies were then carried to Goat Island and buried on the shore between low and high water mark.

Captain Solgard of the *Greyhound* was greatly honored for his exploit. The City of New York at the hands of Robert Walter, Esq., the Mayor, presented him with its freedom the same being "handsomely engrossed on parchment" while the whole corporation waited upon him to present the same. The document related the pirates had caused "this city and Province" not only "very great trouble" but "considerable expense." The captain's action was described "as it is glorious in itself, so it is glorious in the public benefits and advantages that flow from it." The honor was conferred on the 25th of July, 1723, the parchment being signed by the Mayor and countersigned by William Sharpes, Clerk.

Vexed and vanquished, Low took vengeance on a sloop caught whaling off Nantucket, stripping and lashing Nathan Skiff, her master, with barbarous cruelty, following the flogging up by cutting off his ears. He was at last mercifully shot through the head, and the terrified crew set adrift in the whale boat in which they safely reached Nantucket. Skiff was a "fine, brisk young man" and his fate made Nantucket shudder. Later, taking a Block Island fishing boat, Low cut off her captain's head. Two whale boats taken near Block Island furnished further victims. The captain of one was disemboweled; the other Low compelled to eat his own ears "with pepper and salt" which "hard injection he comply'd with, without making a word." The crews of the whale boats who were released reported that Low would have killed them all "but Humanity prevailing in the tender Hearts of his companions, they refused to put his Savage Orders in Execution."

Low now headed for Newfoundland and off Cape Breton took more than twenty French fishing vessels, one of which, mounting twelve guns, he equipped in place of the lost *Ranger* and with her raided the fishing banks, taking some sixteen sail. Late in July he again waylaid the paths of commerce, one of his first victims being a large ship, the *Merry Christmas*. This he turned into a pirate, mounting thirty-four guns and making it a flag ship, and proclaimed himself Admiral under the black flag. Another victim was a Virginia ship, Captain Graves, to whom Low made welcome with the punch bowl as he had Roberts, drinking to him with a hearty: "Here's to you!" The poor captain, feeling too depressed to respond with aquatic heartiness begged to be excused, at which Low pointed a pistol at him with one hand and the flagon with the other, telling him to take his choice. Graves chose the punch.

In September Low and his fleet were again at the Canaries. An English sloop, recently bought by some Portuguese, with half of her old crew on board, was taken; the Portuguese were hanged in reprisal for the men executed at St. Michael. He set the English adrift in an open boat and burned the sloop. Then, proceeding to the Azores, he sent some boats into the road at St. Michael and with incredible audacity "cut out" a London ship of fourteen guns, Thompson, master, who had been taken by him the year before in the pink off the Carolinas. Thompson had a large crew, but the cowards would not fight as he wished. Taken to Low, Thompson had his ears cropped. His ship was burned, but the cowardly crew were set ashore in one of their own boats. A Portuguese ship was taken, but the crew were only pricked with cutlass points, though the ship was fired. One Richard Hains, a forced man on Low's ship, succeeded in getting away with the boatload of Portuguese and carried with him a silver tankard as a souvenir of his residence on the pirate.

Low now drifted down to Sierra Leone, where the ship *Delight*, a former man-of-war, Captain Hunt, was taken and, adding four guns to her equipment of twelve, he put sixty men aboard and placed her in the squadron with Spriggs as captain. Two days later, after a quarrel with Low for refusing to execute as a murderer a pirate who had killed one of his fellows, Spriggs deserted and set out on a career of his own.

Of Low's ending we have no record. In January, 1724, he took an English ship, the *Squirrel*, Stephenson master, and disappeared from history.

XXXIII

OF FARRINGTON SPRIGGS

SPRIGGS left Low in the night and was formally elected captain by his crew the next day. A black flag was prepared and hoisted at the peak following the design affected by Low, of a skeleton holding a dart in one hand and an hourglass in the other, the dart striking at a bleeding heart. This pleasant ensign being hoisted and saluted with a broadside of all the guns, the *Delight* headed for the West Indies.

Their first victim was a Portuguese bark, well laden, which gave great satisfaction, but for entertainment the pirates treated the captured crew to a "sweat," a curious form of running the gauntlet, by which the victims, one after the other, were compelled to run until exhausted, within a circle of candles set up and lighted between decks, while the pirates grouped around armed with forks, and, like pointed tools, picked the wretch until he sank exhausted. The "sweating" over, the Portuguese were dismissed in an open boat with a small store of food and their fine ship was given to the flames.

Near Santa Lucia, a sloop from Barbadoes gave some plunder. A few of the crew signed up, others were forced, and a few of the most obdurate were beaten and slashed, then put into a boat in which by some rare fortune they managed to make their way home. A French sloop from Martinique next fell into their hands, followed by a Jamaica ship laden with logwood. On March 22, 1724, stores, arms and powder were taken out of the latter and her fittings cut and destroyed. The two mates, Burridge and Stephens, with several hands, were forced to join, but the Captain, Hawkins, was given back his mutilated ship after a week's detention. On March 27th, a Rhode Island sloop was added to the spoil. Captain Pike and all his crew were forced on board, with the exception of the mate, "a grave, sober man," who showed such disapproval that he was sentenced to ten lashes for each of the pirates, which was duly carried out, with the mocking remark that he would thus have his discharge written on his back. The impressed Burridge signed the articles on the 28th, and, being an experienced navigator, was made master. This occasion was received with loud acclaim, all the guns being fired in a salvo and the day was spent in a wild carouse. The second of April developed a hoax worthy of the first. Coming upon a ship they fired and brought her to, with great expectation, finding on boarding that she was the vessel belonging to Captain Hawkins, which had been dismissed a few days before. Enraged at this, fifteen of the ruffians surrounded Hawkins and began stabbing at him with their cutlass points. He soon fell to the deck under the torture and would have been cut to pieces but for Burridge, the master, his ex-mate, who came to his rescue. The ship, however, was set in flames. They continued to harrass the unhappy Hawkins, sending him to supper in the cabin, but providing him only with a dish of tallow candles, which he was compelled to devour, a pistol being held at his breast and a cutlass over his head as appetizers. He was then buffeted about and sent forward with the other captives, who had been treated to the same delicacies.

Two days later, on April 6th, the pirate came to anchor at the island of Roatan, in the Bay of Honduras. Here Hawkins and some of his men, together with a passenger on his vessel, were put ashore with a small provision of ammunition and a solitary musket to shift as best they could.

We now have to recur to Philip Ashton, who had lived a Crusoe-like life on the island for nine months, when an English fugitive from the mainland, who had been long a Spanish prisoner, joined him. He had fled with the intent of making the island his home. On the third day his friend went canoeing among the islands and never returned. He had left five pounds of pork with Ashton, a bottle of powder, tongs, and flint, by which the marooned man was able to have fire for the first time and greatly improve his condition. Two or three months later Ashton found a small canoe on the beach and in this he escaped to Bonacco, an island six leagues from Roatan. Here he ran into some Spaniards, but fled at sight of them and paddled back to Roatan, where he continued his solitary life until the early summer of 1723, when he was discovered by a party under John Hope and John Ford, who had a company of logwood cutters on the Bay of Honduras and maintained a plantation on one of the islands as a place of refuge.

They were kind but rough—little better in manners Ashton found than the pirates.

At the time of Spriggs's arrival Ashton and three companions were returning on a moonlight night from a wild-hog and turtle hunt on Bonacco, well loaded with pork and tortoise meat, when they saw a gun flash and heard a loud report coming from a large pirogue near Castle Comfort, the small key where Hope and Ford had their headquarters. Musket firing followed from the shore. Certain that an attack by Spaniards or pirates was under way, Ashton and his companions rowed away as fast as possible toward an island a mile distant. The pirogue, noticing them, followed and gained until a swivel shot passed over their heads, but the fugitives got to land before she came within musket range. The pirates called to them that they were not Spaniards and would give good quarter, but the fugitives preferred to hide in the thickets. They then carried off the canoe with its supply of game. Ashton and his fellows were more fortunate than Ford and Hope, for they and all their people were taken from Castle Comfort, including a child and an Indian woman who was shamefully abused. One of Hope's people turned traitor and informed Spriggs that he had much of value hidden in the woods. At this Hope was brutally beaten until he revealed his treasure, which was taken and carried away.

After holding Hope and his fellows on the ships for five days, Spriggs gave them a flatboat on which to reach the mainland, under oath not to go near Ashton and the others on the island. They in the meanwhile kept hidden and, being without fire, had to eat raw provisions, which was no great hardship after all they had endured. When the pirates sailed at the end of that time, Hope, disregarding his enforced oath, came after them. Hope now decided to return to the bay and Ashton wished to go with him, but as the flat boat had twenty leagues to navigate and small provisions it seemed wiser for Ashton to remain. This view was held by another, John Symonds, who preferred to stay and trade with the Jamaica ships which came to Roatan. Ashton therefore lived with Symonds and his black servant for several months, ranging the islands in a canoe. When the time for the Jamaica traders to come after tortoise-shell arrived, they located at Bonacco near the mainland, where soon a brigantine ran in after water. She turned out to be a Salem ship commanded by Captain Dove, who lived but three miles from Ashton's father's house. They sailed late in

March, 1725, via Jamaica, Ashton reaching home in Marblehead two years, ten months, and fifteen days after his capture by the rovers. Hawkins and his marooned companions remained nineteen days on Roatan, during which time the passenger died of hardship. The musket supplied them with food until rescue came in the form of two men in a canoe who had been marooned on another island, to which Hawkins and the others were now borne, living and water being better there than at Roatan. Twelve days later a logwood sloop was sighted, which responded to a smoke signal. She proved to be the *Merriam*, Captain Jones, who had just escaped from the Spaniards of Honduras and bore Hawkins and his seamen home.

After cleaning ship at one of the keys, Spriggs headed for St. Christopher, hoping to fall in with that Captain Moore, of the *Eagle*, who had played false to Lowther, as related in his story, with the resolve of killing him in revenge for that act. Instead, he met a French man-of-war from Martinique, who took such an interest in the pirate that he was compelled to run for it and would have been overtaken but for the loss of the Frenchman's main-top-mast, which went by the board under an overload of sail and stopped the pursuit. After this narrow escape Spriggs turned toward Bermuda, where he took a Boston schooner, which he sank. To the captain he announced his impudent purpose to proceed to the fishing banks of Newfoundland, where he would reinforce his crew and then seek out Captain Peter Solgard and the *Greyhound* man-of-war, which had destroyed Low's consort, the *Ranger*, under Charles Harris, and fight him to a finish. Spriggs wished to know if the captain knew Solgard, and upon his thrice denying the acquaintance, ordered him "sweated" in the manner earlier described. The program, however, was not attempted. Instead, the course was laid toward St. Christopher, to the windward of which island, on the 4th of June, a sloop from St. Eustacia, Capt. Nicholas Trot, was taken. The vessel was plundered, several men impressed and, for diversion, others were hoisted to the rigging and allowed to drop, with resulting damage to skin and bones. Then they were allowed to depart.

The mad company next took a ship from Rhode Island, laden with provisions for St. Christopher's, and carrying beside a few horses. These the drunken pirates mounted in turn and galloped about the deck, with such recklessness that the frightened animals soon threw their

[239]

burdens, at which in great wrath they fell upon the crew of the Rhode Island, cutting and beating them barbarously for their failure to bring riding boots and spurs so that they might have been equipped to ride more successfully.

No record remains to show to what end came Spriggs and his company, but it is easily predicated upon their record.

XXXIV

OF JOHN PHILLIPS

THE career of John Phillips was more notable for its ending than for any achievements during the period of his lawlessness. It was his fate to fall at the hands of John Fillmore, great-great-grandfather of Millard Fillmore, the thirteenth President of the United States. Phillips was English born and a carpenter by occupation. Sailing from the west of England on a ship bound for Newfoundland, it was his mischance to be taken by Thomas Anstis in his brigantine, the *Good Fortune*. He at once became carpenter for the pirate, artisans and surgeons being men much needed by the outlaws, and remained with Anstis until his company broke up at Tobago. He was one of those who returned in the sloop sunk in Bristol Channel as related in the life of Anstis. While visiting his former haunts in Devonshire, he learned of the apprehension of some of his companions in the lost sloop and their incarceration in Bristol jail. Making a quick departure for Topsham, he found immediate employment on a vessel bound for Newfoundland, commanded by Captain Wadham.

Though hired for the round trip, he left the ship without leave at Peter Harbor in the spring of 1723 and worked at the task of splitting codfish during the curing season. The love of piracy was in his blood and he conspired with sixteen others to seize a stout fishing boat and improve their fortunes on the sea. Only five kept their appointment, but these sufficed to man the craft, Phillips promising that they would augment their numbers out of their captures. Phillips was chosen captain, John Nutt, master; James Sparks, gunner; Thomas Fern, carpenter. The only man without office was William White, a vagrom tailor from Boston, who had tried a fishing voyage as a remedy for some moral ills that made his home town uncomfortable. It is to White that Phillips owed his final undoing, though not from any purposeful act on the part of the tailor. The adventurers drew up a code of articles and swore fealty to them on a hatchet, in lieu of the Bible, the same reading:

"Every man shall obey civil Command; the Captain shall have one full Share and a half in all Prizes; the Master, Carpenter, Boatswain and Gunner shall have one Share and quarter.

"If any Man shall offer to run away, or keep any Secret from the Company, he shall be maroon'd, with one Bottle of Powder, one Bottle of Water, one small Arm, and Shot.

"If any Man shall steal any Thing in the Company, or game, to the Value of a Piece of Eight, he shall be maroon'd or shot.

"If at any Time we should meet another Marrooner (that is, Pyrate), that Man that shall sign his Articles without the Consent of our Company, shall suffer from such Punishment as the Captain and Company shall think fit.

"That Man that shall strike another whilst these Articles are in force, shall receive Moses's Law (that is, 40 Stripes lacking one) on the bare Back.

"That Man that shall snap his Arms, or smoak Tobacco in the Hold, without a Cap to his Pipe, or carry a Candle lighted without a Lanthorn, shall suffer the same Punishment as in the former Article.

"That Man that shall not keep his Arms clean, sit for an Engagement, or neglect his Business, shall be cut off from his Share, and suffer such other Punishment as the Captain and the Company shall think fit.

"If any Man shall lose a Joint in time of an Engagement, shall have 400 Pieces of Eight; if a Limb, 800.

"If at any time you meet with a prudent Woman, that Man that offers to meddle with her, without her Consent, shall suffer present Death."

Several small fishing vessels fell easy prey, but out of one they gained an accomplished recruit, John Rose Archer, who had been a follower of the great Blackbeard. Because of this he was made quartermaster, to the displeasure of the others, particularly that of Fern, the carpenter. Some other seamen also joined, but the crew was still small and not fit for large ventures.

One of those taken was the sloop *Dolphin*, Captain Haskell, the capture coming about in this wise, to quote from John Fillmore's narrative:

"The pirate soon came up and sent a boat aboard our sloop, demanding who we were and where we were bound, to which our captain gave a direct answer. By this boat's crew we learned that the noted pirate captain, Phillips, commanded their ship. This intelligence, it will readily be perceived, gave us great uneasiness, most of our crew being quite young. Having often heard of the cruelties committed by that execrable pirate, made us dread to fall into his hands. "The pirate's boat soon boarded us again, demanding the name of every hand on board. In this boat came White, the tailor, with whom I had been acquainted during his apprenticeship, as before mentioned. I was greatly surprised to find him employed in so criminal a course of life, though I said nothing of the matter to him. On the return of the pirate's boat with a list of our names, White as I was afterwards informed, acquainted Phillips of his knowledge of me, informing him, that if he could engage me in his service, he would gain a good, stout, resolute fellow, every way, he supposed, such a hand as he wanted.

"On receiving this information, as he stood in need of a hand, and found we had no property he wanted on board, he sent his boat once more, with orders to Captain Haskel, to send me on board his ship., and the rest of his crew, with the sloop, might go free. My worthy commander, with much visible concern in his countenance, took me aside, and informed me of Phillips' orders, adding that although it would be exceedingly disagreeable and painful to him to let me go, yet as we were entirely in the power of a bloody, merciless ruffian, and no hopes of escape, but by giving me up, I believe, says he, you must go and try your fortune with them.

"The thought of being sacrificed, as it were, to procure liberty for the rest of the crew, operated greatly upon my spirits, and the conclusion I drew up was, that I would not, on any conditions, agree to go on board the pirate. I therefore told my captain that I had ever been faithful to his interest and commands, that I had always wished to do my duty punctually and well, but that I was determined not to go on board the pirate, let the consequences be what it would. Our conversation ended here, for that time, and the boat returned without me.

"Phillips was greatly incensed when the boat returned without me, and sent again, with orders to bring me either dead or alive. My Captain took me aside again, and told me the pirate's resolution and message, adding, that he believed I should do well to go with them, for if I refused to go, and made resistance, it would be inevitable death to me, and probably to our whole crew. He urged further, that my submitting would prove the certain release of the rest of the crew, and there would be at least a probability of my making an escape from them at some time or other; but if I could not find a way to escape, it was not impossible but Phillips might discharge me, for he had sent word, that if I would agree to serve him faithfully for two months, he would then set me at liberty.

"Those only who have been in similar circumstances can form an adequate idea of the distress I experienced at this time. If I obstinately refused to join the pirates, instant death stared me and my comrades in the face; if I consented to go with them, I expected to be massacred for refusing to sign their piratical articles, which I had fully determined never to do, though I should be put to the extremith of torture for refusal. Into so critical a situation had my bad fortune plunged me, that inevitable destruction seemed to stare me in the face from every quarter.

"I took the matter however into serious consideration, and after the most mature deliberation, determined to venture myself among them, rather than bring the vengeance of the pirates on my comrades: I therefore went with them, seemingly contended, and the Captain renewed his promise to set me at liberty in two months. I engaged to serve him to the best of my abilities during that term.

"I was likewise agreeably disappointed in their not urging so strenuously as I expected, to the thing I most dreaded, viz: the signing of their articles.—To induce me to join them, they used more arguments of a persuasive than a compulsory nature, judging, I suppose, that youth would be more easily enticed than compelled to join in sharing their ill-gotten gain.

"When I first went on board the pirate, their crew consisted of ten men, including the Captain, and the whole of them I think, as stout, daring, hardy looking fellows as ever I saw together. As I then was the only hand on board who had not subscribed their articles, the Captain assigned to me the helm, where I kept my station, during the greatest part of the time I stayed with them."

This was in August 1723. During the two months that followed the pirate had but poor pickings. Fillmore now reminded Phillips of his promise to let him go, to which the latter "in tolerable good humor" replied "that we had done but little business since I had come aboard; that he could not well spare me yet, but if I would stay with him three months longer he would set me at liberty, upon his honor; and I was obliged quietly to comply with his demands, and trust to his honor, though it turned out in the end he did but mock me."

The pickings continued poor. Making the West Indies in October, 1723, they drifted about for three months without ever sighting sail and almost starved, being reduced to one pound of meat per day, divided among ten. At length they spied a French *guarda costa* from Martinique, of twelve guns and thirty-five men. Desperate as were the chances, they were taken. Making good the adage that "Hunger will break down stone walls," they ran alongside with the black flag flying and so intimidated the Frenchmen that they gave up without firing a gun. Four of the crew joined Phillips and the pirate was well provisioned from the Frenchman, which was then allowed to depart.

The ship being foul, Phillips steered for Tobago to careen, hoping to find there six or eight of his old companions and three negroes who had been left behind on the breaking up of the Anstis crew. The island was easily made. None of the old crowd were found but one negro, who said the men had been taken by a warship, carried to Antigua and hanged. This black man, Pedro by name, was taken on board, the ship was careened and cleaned, but was hardly back on the water before a man-of-war came spying into the harbor. Phillips lost no time in getting clear, warping out, and sailing to the windward. The four Frenchmen, to their good fortune, were left behind.

Fillmore now ventured to remind Phillips of his promise "and handsomely requested that he set me ashore, . . . that I might go to my mother who had not heard from me since my first captain returned from his fishing voyage.

" 'Set you at liberty! damn you. You shall be set at liberty when I'm damned and not before,' replied Phillips in a rage more compatible with the diabolical disposition of an infernal fiend than a being endowed with a rational soul, susceptible of human sensations."

Fillmore now lost hope of any voluntary liberation but awaited the chance of their capture by some stronger vessel; or the taking of more prisoners with whom he could concoct a plan for release before Phillips was finally damned.

After leaving Tobago a snow was now captured and Thomas Fern, the carpenter, with William Phillips, and two other men, Wood and Taylor, went on board the prize. The group decided to flee with the vessel, but when Phillips perceived this he gave chase and, firing upon them, killed Wood and wounded Phillips in the leg so severely that it had to be cut off, which Fern the carpenter, who had surrendered with Taylor, did with his saw "in as little time as he could have cut a deal board in two." He cauterized the stump with his axe, heated red in the galley fire, but despite such rude surgery the man recovered.

Standing away to the northward they then took a Portuguese ship bound for Brazil and some sloops from Jamaica, in one of which Fern, the carpenter, again attempted to escape, and was killed by Captain Phillips, while another member of the crew shared the same fate for like reason several days later. This terrorism curbed the desires of others to flee for the moment, though Fillmore continued to watch and wait. On March 25, 1724, two ships for London from Virginia came in the pirate's way. One of these had a John Phillips for captain; the other was Robert Mortimer, a fine young sea-master. The pirate Phillips, and two men were on Mortimer's vessel, when, hearing a call that was mutiny on their captor's craft, Mortimer essayed to retake his own. He struck Phillips with a handspike, bruising him badly, but failed to fell the pirate, who ran him through with his sword. The two pirates coming to his aid, Mortimer was hacked to pieces and his body thrown into the sea. His own men made no move to aid him. This was his first voyage as captain. Mortimer had a brother on the ship and he was sought for to be slain, but a fellow-townsman in the pirate crew concealed him until the wrath of Phillips had passed. Fern, the carpenter being dead, Edward Cheeseman, who held a like position on the honest Phillips's ship, was pressed into his place.

Phillips now turned toward Newfoundland, expecting to reinforce his crew from captured fishermen, of whom a number were taken. On April 4, 1724, a sloop was captured off Sable Island, which he kept in custody, giving poor Mortimer's vessel back to the mate and crew. In the afternoon of the same day a schooner was overhauled. Finding her the property of Mr. Minors, from whom he had stolen his first vessel, Phillips remarked that he had done him enough injury and allowed her to go her way. Another fisherman gave them a chase and when taken proved to be in command of Dependence Ellery, "a New England saint," whom the pirates caused to dance on the deck until he fell with weariness, as a slight return for the trouble he had caused them. Ten other fisher boats were plundered in rapid succession during the first fortnight of April, but naturally yielded little of value.

On the 14th an event occurred which led to the ending of Phillips.

He took the sloop *Squirrel,* of Cape Ann, of which Andrew Harridon, of Boston, was master. The crew were sent away on one of the captured fishermen, but Harridon was pressed on board. He declined to sign the articles, as Cheeseman, the carpenter, a Spanish Indian, Fillmore, and a young American whom the latter does not name, but who was an old acquaintance, had also refused to do. This made five who were without the pale. The last-mentioned man being placed with a prize crew on board the *Squirrel,* Phillips conceived the notion that he was planning mischief and going on the sloop accused him of conspiring with Fillmore and ran him through the body. Calling for Fillmore, he voiced the accusation and threatened him with death; indeed, snapped a pistol at his breast, but the weapon failed to fire. When a second time presented, Fillmore struck it up and the shot went into the air. Phillips, after flourishing a cutlass over the sailor's head, ordered him back to duty, saying he had only done this to try him.

Renewed demands were made upon the four to sign the articles, but they resolutely declined, despite threats against their lives. The four now determined to free themselves. Only five of the original crew were now on board and it was believed they could be dealt with. Harridon's courage failed him, but he agreed not to discover their plan and, had it not been for him, according to Fillmore "our plot would most probably have failed in its execution." What followed is best told in the words of his narrative:

"Cheeseman, the Indian and myself, got together, and agreed that Cheeseman should leave his broad-axe on the main deck when he had done using it, and when I saw Cheeseman make ready the best use of it I could, cutting and slashing all that offered to oppose me, while the Indian was to stand ready to help, as occasion might require. And each one of us, in the meantime, was to do every thing he could think of to forward the design.

"Our plan being thus concerted, I went down into the caboose, where White and John Rose Archer, a desperate fellow who had been taken in one of the prizes, and immediately joined the pirates, laid on the floor, as before mentioned, drunk as beasts. I took fire and burnt these two villains in the feet, while they lay senseless, so badly as to render them unable to be upon deck next day. There were only four now left of the old pirate gang, and five who had joined them since, besides the two I had rendered incapable of injuring us.

"We were up early in the morning, and Cheeseman used the broad-axe, and left it as agreed. It was very late in the morning, and the pirates were none of them up, and we were afraid they would not arise until too late to take an observation, and our plan of consequence must fall through. To prevent this, about ten o'clock I went to the cabin door, and told the captain the sun was almost up to the meridian. 'Damn you,' said he, 'it is none of your business.' This was all the thanks I got, and indeed all I expected for my service. However, it answered the end designed, for the Captain, Master, Boatswain, and Quarter-Master, came upon deck a little after eleven o'clock. Enquiry was made for White and Archer, and their burns imputed to accident. Harridon was nearly dead with fear, and the Indian became nearly as white as any of us. Phillips took notice to Harridon's paleness, and I cloaked the matter by informing him, that Harridon had been sick all night, and I believed a dram would help him. Phillips told me to go to his case and get a bottle of brandy; which I did, and we all drank heartily, except the Indian, who refused to taste a drop, though something apt to drink at other times.

"The important crisis drew near, when three of us were to attack the whole crew; the Master prepared to take his observation, and Cheeseman was walking the deck with a hammer in his hand. The Quarter-Master was in the cabin, drawing out some leaden slugs for a musket, and the Spanish Indian stood close by the cabin door. The Captain and Boatswain stood by the mainmast, talking upon some matters, and I stood partly behind them, whirling the axe around with my foot, until my knees fairly smote together.

"The Master being thus busied, I saw Cheeseman make the motion to heave him over, and I at that instant split the boatswain's head in twain with the broad-axe, and dropped him upon the deck to welter in his gore. Before the Captain had time to put himself into a posture of defense, I gave him a stroke with the head of my axe, which partly stunned him; at which Cheeseman, having dispatched the Master over board, came to my assistance, and gave the Captain a blow with his hammer, on the back side of his head, which put an immediate end of his mortal existence.

"The Quarter-Master hearing the bustle, came running out of the cabin with his hand up to strike Cheeseman with his hammer, and would probably have killed him, had not the Indian caught him by the elbow, as he was bringing the hammer down, and there held him, until I came up and gave him a blow upon the back side of his head, cutting his wig and neck almost off, so that his head hung down before him.

"We had now dispatched all the old pirates except White, and demanded a surrender of the vessel, which was granted, and the poor Frenchmen and negroes came to us and embraced our legs and feet, begging for their lives.

"We carried the vessel safely into Boston, where White, Archer, and one more of the pirates were tried, condemned and executed; the three other pirates were sent to England, with the vessel, with whom my friend Cheeseman and the Indian went likewise, whom government liberally rewarded for their services, and gave Cheeseman an honorable berth in one of the king's shipyards; the three pirates who went home with the vessel, were hung at Execution Dock, and the vessel was made a prize of by government.

"I never saw any of the human species more spiteful than White was, from the time he was taken until he was executed. I believe he would have killed me any time, in that interval, had it been in his power.

"The honorable court which condemned the pirates, gave me Captain Phillips' gun, silver hilted sword, silver shoe and knee buckles, a curious tobacco box, and two good rings that the pirate Captain Phillips used to wear.

"When we came in sight of the castle near Boston, we hoisted our pirate's colors and fired a gun, as a signal for them to come off to us. At this time some of the pirates were on deck, and one of them asked leave to fire another gun, which being granted, he would not swab the gun out nor have the vent stopped, but put in the cartridge, and stood directly before the muzzle to ram it down, by which means the cartridge took fire and blew him into pieces; it is supposed that he did this purposely, in order to escape the punishment which he knew must be his lot in case he was carried into the harbor."

The court which tried the pirates convened at Boston on the 12th of May, 1724. All the survivors on the ship save Harridon had to pass in review. John Fillmore, Edward Cheeseman, John Coombs, Henry Giles, Charles Ivymay, John Bootman, and Henry Payne were cleared as either pressed men or prisoners. So were three Frenchmen, John Baptis, Peter Jafferey, and Isaac Lassen, and three negroes, Pedro, who had been kidnapped from Tobago, and Francisco, and Pierro, taken from the French *guarda costa*. John Rose Archer, William

White, William Phillips, and William Taylor were condemned. Rose and White were hanged at Boston on June 2, 1724. The two others were respited for a year and a day, but were eventually hung at Execution Dock. The vessel became the property of the Crown. Rose and Taylor are recorded as having "dy'd very penitently." In addition to the distinction of being taken by the great-great-grandfather of a President, the wretches were favored with the religious consolation of that distinguished divine, the Rev. Cotton Mather, who exhorted them in prison a few days before their doom, his discourse being prettily preserved in a pamphlet with this engaging title: "The Converted Sinner. The Nature of a Conversion to Real and Vital Piety. A Sermon preached in Boston, May 31, 1724. In the hearing of certain Pirates, a little before their Execution. Added, a more Private Conference of a Minister with them."

XXXV

OF JOHN GOW

JOHN GOW, celebrated as the original of Captain Cleveland in Sir Walter Scott's novel "The Pirate," was a native of Wick in the Orkneys, born in 1697, son of William Gow, a respectable merchant and Margaret Calder, his wife. Little is known of his life up to the time of his taking the freedom of the seas, the only account of his career being that published by Daniel Defoe, of which but one original is in existence, this being in the files of the British museum. Facts were of no particular account to this ingenious gentleman, and such certain knowledge as we have must be gleaned from the legal records of the day. Mr. Alan Fea, whose ancestor caused the capture of the outlaw upon his return to the Orkneys in his pirate craft, has given us a painstaking account in his "Real Captain Cleveland" published in 1912, from which this digest is mainly taken.

In August, 1724, Gow signed aboard the Guernsey galley, *George*, at Amsterdam for a voyage to Santa Cruz in North Africa, for a cargo of leather, wool, and beeswax to be delivered at Genoa. The Captain, Oliver Freneau, taking note of the sailor's talents, appointed him second mate and gunner of the vessel, which was of about 200 tons burden. She reached Santa Cruz in September and lay there two months receiving cargo. Periods of idleness in harbor always breed discontent among seamen, and to this habit Gow lent himself and spread the idea of running off with the ship. The men lent a willing ear. These were William Melvin, an Edinburgh lad, Daniel Macauley of Stormway; James Williams, a Welshman; Michæl Moore, a young Irishman; John Peterson, a Dane, and two Swedes, John Winter and Peter Rollson, the last named being the ship's cook. None were older than twenty-four years of age, the youngest, Melvin, being seventeen.

By concerted plan Winter, Peterson, and Macauley began complaints to Captain Freneau about the food. The *George* sailed on November 3rd, and as part of the plot, the mutterings grew as soon as they were well at sea. Freneau, taking alarm, consulted with the chief mate,

Bonadventure Jelfs, and ordered Gow as gunner to load and prepare the small arms. To forestall him it was determined to attack that night. Following custom prayers were read to all in the cabin at eight o'clock, the watch was set, and by ten o'clock the officers other than Gow, viz, the chief mate Jelfs, supercargo Algier and the surgeon, all save the captain, were in their berths. The captain was on deck, but quit, unconscious of the pending action. Suddenly the sound of noise and pistol shots below startled Freneau, who called in alarm for the boatswain, who was not in the plot, asking what was the trouble. He replied that he was afraid someone was overboard. Running to the rail, the captain was seized from behind by Winter, Melvin, and Rolson, who tried to toss him over the bulwarks. Being a powerful man he resisted with all his strength, clinging to the shrouds. One of the mutineers stabbed him in the throat and Gow, coming to the deck, shot him twice with pistols. He was then pushed over the side, but clung to a rope which was severed, and the unfortunate man then fell into the sea. Jelfs and Algier had been killed by pistol fire and others not in the conspiracy hid as best they could. Gow now took command of the vessel; the members of the crew who had not joined, save one James Belbin who at once came over, were locked in the great cabin.

The mutineers spent the rest of the night carousing in celebration of their triumph. In the morning the prisoners were brought up one by one and told by Gow that they would come to no harm if they kept quiet and did their duty as formerly. Williams became lieutenant. Six guns that had been dormant in the hold were brought up and mounted, giving eighteen in all. "The George" was painted out on the stern and "The Revenge" lettered on instead. Then the course was altered from Italy to Spain. There was no delay in beginning operations as pirates. On November 12th, the first capture was made, an English sloop, the *Delight* of Liverpool, Captain Thomas Wise, from Newfoundland for Cadiz with a cargo of salted fish. The provisions, sails, cables, chains and anchors were removed and she was scuttled. Her captain and four men were set adrift in the boat. One of the crew, William Oliver, a fifteen-year-old boy was pressed into service as cabin boy. The second capture, made on November 21st, was a Scotch snow, the *Sarah* of Glasgow, Captain John Somerville, also with salted fish for Genoa, off the coast of Portugal. They were athirst for wine and this surplus of salt fish was aggravating. Two of the *Sarah's* crew, John Menzies, the carpenter, and Alexander Robb, a

Scotch lad of eighteen, joined the adventure with right good will. The rest were locked in the powder room. A French ship was next chased but outsailed the *Revenge*, the pursuit, however, leading her toward Madeira.

The water supply now became short and, anchoring off one of the islands, Gow sent a boat into the road to seize a ship or do some pilfering of wine or water. Gaining neither, he put into Porto Santo under English colors and sent his lieutenant in the longboat to ask the Governor for permission to take on wood and water. This was at once granted, and the Governor and staff followed the favor by making a call on the imposing-looking stranger. Gow entertained them for a time but, the food and water not coming off as speedily as desired, held the company prisoners until the next day when the supplies arrived. Then they were dismissed with presents and a salute. After they turned back toward Cape St. Vincent, an American sloop, the *Bachelor*, Captain Benjamin Cross surrendered. Her cargo was mostly timber, but some barrels of beef and bread came in welcome. Four of his hands were pressed, William Billes, John Reid, John Harris and William Harvey. A fifth, Robert Teague, volunteered. The prisoners of the *Sarah* were sent away on the *Bachelor*. William Oliver, the impressed cabin boy, wept as he saw them go, but was consoled by Gow with the promise that he would send him home with his pockets full of gold.

On December 27th, near the Spanish coast, a French vessel, the *Louis-Joseph*, Captain William Mens, was taken. She had a load of oil and wine, and was the first prize of any real value. Captains Cross and Somerville and the remaining prisoners were sent off on the Frenchman. Some of the cargo was left to requite them and they were given beside a quantity of beeswax from the hold of the *Revenge*, which had been part of her cargo when seized. A large French ship appearing off Cape Finisterre, Gow deemed her too heavy to attack, which enraged Williams, his lieutenant. The result was a violent quarrel in which Williams, after ordering Gow to attack, fired point blank at him with a pistol. The powder flashed and, before he could use a second weapon, he fell under a shot each from Winter and Peterson. He was little hurt and ran for the powder room in a raging fury to blow up the ship, but was grabbed, heavily ironed, and put with the other prisoners, who much objected to his society. It was resolved to send him away on the next capture, which proved to be the *Triumvirate* of

[253]

Bristol, Captain Davis, laden with salt fish. Her longboat and a few articles of silver were removed. The prisoners were now transferred to her, together with Williams, who before becoming one himself had urged that the ship be relieved of their company by the simple process of cutting throats. Gow pressed Thomas Courland and James Stammers from the *Triumvirate* and kept two Frenchmen, Philibert Le Leyer and Ervey Toul. Two of the old crew, Murphy the carpenter and Robert Read, begged to be allowed to depart, but were held. Davis took command of the liberated ship and men and brought her safe into Lisbon, where he found the *Argyle* man-of-war, who took over the refugees and the scoundrel Williams, shipping them to Sheerness.

It was certain that this delivery would bring the warships in search and much discussion followed on the pirate as to the next course. Some were for trying the coast of Guinea, but Gow thought the voyage too long, as their food supplies were short and ammunition too low and persuaded the company into going to the Orkneys, by pointing out that the government would never suspect them of such a move and that he knew of many gentlemen's houses that could be safely plundered before an alarm could spread. They therefore sailed for the north, reaching Stromness in mid-January, 1725, and anchoring just off a bit of land bought by William Gow, the pirate's father, in 1716 and known as Gow's Ness. Gow now caused the name *Revenge* to be erased and that of the *George* restored, though this would seem to have been anything but a disguise.

To explain their presence Gow concocted a story that they were bound from Cadiz for Stockholm, but being prevented by weather from passing the Sound had been driven far north and so put in to clean and procure water. He assumed an air of graciousness toward the people and put his own men under a severe code of rules. Supplies were obtained by bartering the goods on board. Money was spent liberally and there was always wine or brandy on tap for visitors from the shore. Gow was soon recalled as the son of a former merchant and this added to the good will with which he was received. The hospitality shown on the ship was reciprocated on shore and many pleasant parties resulted; but it was not long before rumors affecting the character of the ship came to hand. Before becoming the *George* the ship had been known as the *Caroline*.

Captain Watt, of the *Margaret*, coming into port, recalled having seen her in Amsterdam the previous June and reports had reached

Leith of her doings. These now filtered north. Gow, though calling himself "Smith," did not deny his true identity, as it had been spread about; it caused no great comment, because runaway lads before were known to change their names. Watt, however, who had sharp eyes, visited the ship and recognized Macauley and Henry Jamieson, of the old crew, as two boys who had been his apprentices and had run away in Holland. He demanded them of Gow, who refused to return them. The crew now began to be suspected of thefts that were occurring with uncommon frequency and Henry Jamieson, getting on shore, met Captain Watt and begged his help in freeing him from the life he was leading, and told the story of the massacre on leaving Santa Cruz. He said that eleven of the twenty-eight on board wished to get away and would try that night to persuade more to join. Nothing came of this. Watt left port on February 11th, after advising the authorities of his suspicions that Gow was a pirate and, reaching Edinburgh, posted the custom authorities.

Robert Read now managed to escape and borrowing a horse rode to Kirkwall to surrender himself to the magistrate. Archibald Sutor, the farmer to whom he appealed for the animal, heard his story and went himself to spread the alarm, Read having revealed Gow's plans to raid the homes of the gentry. Ten of the men now slipped away in the longboat, landing at Duncansby Head on the mainland, where they surrendered to a magistrate who, not believing their story and, with Scotch thrift, not caring to put so large a party in jail at public expense, sent them on their way. Four turned up in Aberdeen and were taken, the others falling into the hands of the law, five at Glasgow and one at Banff. Somerville and Cross now turned up with the vessel Gow had given them, and chancing to meet some of these men, Somerville's party were confronted with them and arrested.

Gow in the meantime recruited ten new hands at Stromness, and, though the ship was but half clean, he determined to sail on the night of February 10th, intending first to plunder Clestrain Hall, the seat of Mr. Robert Honeyman, before leaving. This was done with success, the landing party returning to the boat to the strains of a bagpipe, having found a piper among the laborers, whom they compelled to play, and then, enamored of his music, bore to the ship with the other spoil. As soon as the party reached the ship she made sail to the north among the minor islets. A new hand named Porringer, taken on at Stromness, acted as pilot and as they came near Eday at a point called

The Castles, the ship missing stays narrowly escaped grounding hard upon the Calf of Eday, a low island in the sound. As it was she touched, but was safely anchored, and so lightly held that had she boats and kedges she could readily have been worked off. Gow had neither and as the event showed was neatly trapped.

James Fea, of Carrick House, fearing Gow might use his guns on the mansion, which was within range, and to plunder which had been his plan, wrote him a friendly letter offering aid, as "an old school comrade," which indeed he had been, though perhaps not so warm as his note seemed to indicate. He sent the note by James Laing, a merchant of the Calf. He returned without a written reply, Gow only stating verbally that he would give a liberal reward for aid. This not coming, he sent an armed crew of five men ashore to enforce help. They were met by James Fea and beguiled into visiting the public house while he considered what was the best course to pursue. This was late on February 13th. When the men, well-fuddled, started for their boat in the darkness, they were seized and bound. Following the old custom, beacons were now lighted on the hills to summon the people to Carrick. Sunday, the 1st, passed without action, but at evening the wind rose right to move the ship. Murphy, the carpenter, bungled in cutting the cable, with the result that the ship swung about and drove ashore on the Calf at top-tide. She was now beyond release. That night the beacons were lit anew on the hills.

Monday morning Gow put up a white flag, to which Fea responded with a plea to him to give up under promise to do all he could for him. Gow replied offering a thousand pounds if helped to get off; otherwise he would fire the ship and perish with her. Fea again wrote inviting him ashore—to come unarmed. Gow agreed if Laing were sent as hostage. It was finally agreed between Fea and Gow to meet at a certain spot on the Calf, but he sent an emissary with a bottle of brandy instead and another letter bespeaking aid. A correspondence continued for several days without purpose. On the 17th, William Scollay went on board as hostage and Gow came to the appointed spot, where he conferred with some of the party sent over by Fea, though the latter had forbidden such a course. He followed on a boat and, all being on the island, Gow was seized with two of his men, Peterson and Winters. He called to the ship that he had been betrayed, but was carried along and imprisoned at Shapinshay, where the five were now confined. Fifty armed men that night went off and made the ship their own taking the crew to join their leader who had been so unfairly tricked. On February 20th, all were prisoners.

The *Greyhound*, man-of-war, came along in time to end a dispute over the possession of the ship and prisoners between the local authorities and the customs office and bore the pirates away to London, where they landed in the Old Bailey and were duly tried before the High Court of Admiralty. Williams, now brought from Lisbon, joined them in facing justice. In all thirty-two were captives. Five of the original crew were selected as state's witnesses. Gow himself stood mute, refusing to answer or plead until threatened with the torture of pressing, when he found voice, though silent during a preliminary test of whipcord twisted about his thumb and squeezed until it broke. Ten of the accused were found guilty of piracy and murder. The remainder showed themselves innocent, as were the men taken on at Stromness, and those pressed, including the boy Oliver whose pockets were to be filled with gold. Eight, headed by Gow, were hanged on June 11, 1725. The rope breaking that was attached to Gow, the audience had the double delight of seeing him twice ascend the ladder, the second time "with very little concern." Two, Robb and Moore, were reprieved for transportation, but Robb so misbehaved that his reprieve was canceled and he was hanged on the second of July in the presence of a large company. All swung at Execution Dock, this being opposite St. Mary's Church, Rotherhithe by Wapping Dock stairs.

XXXVI

OF WILLIAM FLY

IN April, 1726, Captain Green of Bristol shipped William Fly at Jamaica as boatswain for his snow, the *Elizabeth,* homeward bound. No sooner was the man well ensconced on board than he began to sound out other members of the crew with the object of inducing them to join him in seizing the vessel and turning pirate. He had, it would appear, seen some service under the black flag and longed for more, this time as a commander. A majority of the men were in a short time brought into accord and at one o'clock on the morning of May 27, 1726, Fly, being in charge of the watch, went up to Maurice Condon, who was taking his turn at the wheel, and warned him that if he stirred from the post or made a sound he would meet with instant death. The conspirators, who included beside Fly, Alexander Mitchel, Henry Hill, Samuel Cole, and others, took charge of the ship. Fly and Mitchel, each armed with a cutlass, then aroused the captain who had been asleep in his cabin and ordered him to turn out. On asking the reason therefor the captain was again told to turn out to save the trouble of scraping the cabin floor and rinsing it of his blood. He was further informed that Fly was now in command.

Green made no resistance, but pleaded his uniform good treatment of all as a reason for preserving his life, expressing a willingness to wear irons until he could be put on shore. "Ay, to live and hang us," replied Fly. At this he was dragged from his berth and forced to the deck, where he again made an earnest plea for his life, urging that he was not fit to die with his sins on his soul.

"Since he is so devilish godly," cried Fly, "we'll give him time to say his prayers. I'll be parson. Say after me, Lord have mercy on me. Short prayers are best, so no more words, and over with him, my lads."

The wretched skipper still cried for mercy, but was ruthlessly hurled over the side. In his fall he caught the main-sheet and there clung, at which Thomas Winthrop, taking the carpenter's broad-ax, cut off his hand, so that he dropped into the sea and disappeared from view. Thomas Jenkins, the mate, was brought to the deck and his prayers for his life fell equally upon deaf ears and he, too, was seized to be thrown into the sea. Making some resistance in his struggles, he was struck with the broad-ax. Aim at his head failing, his shoulder was deeply gashed and he was at once hurled overboard. The poor man swam about the ship, calling upon the surgeon to throw him a rope, but that personage lay snug in his cabin, well manacled by the mutineers. Some discussion followed as to the disposal of the medico, but his life was finally spared in the belief that there might be need for his professional services.

Fly was now proclaimed captain and put in possession of the great cabin. A bowl of punch was set upon the table and Maurice Condon, the helmsman brought down, a mutineer, John Fitzherbert, taking his place at the tiller. The carpenter and a seaman, Thomas Streaton, not in the conspiracy, were also taken below, where Fly told them they were all rascals who richly deserved to follow the captain and mate, but would be spared, at least to the extent of not being killed in cold blood. They were accordingly placed in irons. A ship coming within hail was found to be the *Pompey*, which had followed them from Jamaica, whose master inquired after Captain Green's health and was told he was very well. The wisdom of attacking the *Pompey* was debated and decided in the negative and the *Elizabeth*, now called *Fame's Revenge*, put about for the Carolinas.

Off Charleston bar they were discerned by Captain Fulker, of the sloop *John and Hannah*, lying within, who, thinking they might want a pilot, put out in a small boat with his mate, William Atkinson, and several other passengers, to bring her in. They were received on board very civilly by Fly, who invited them into the cabin to partake of some punch. Once in the cabin Fly told them he was no man to mince matters and that he and his companions were gentlemen of Fortune, who had decided the *John and Hannah* was a better craft than their own and he would save time and his life by bringing her out in exchange. To this end he sent Fulker with six hands in a boat to bring the sloop outside to the *Fame's Revenge* lying about a mile off shore. The wind proving contrary, the sloop could not be moved and the boat returned bringing Fulker. At this Fly flew into a violent passion and, after cursing Fulker for a lying dog, when he gave the wind as his reason, ordered him stripped and flogged, which was done with brutal thoroughness. Fly then said the vessel would either be brought off or burned. The boat went in again and worked the sloop as far as the bar, when she bilged and sank. The pirates set the wreck on fire but the flames ran out without doing their work.

Fulker and his friends begged to be put ashore and were told they would be transferred to the first vessel encountered. On the 5th of June they sailed from the coast and on the 6th chased the *John and Berry*, bound from Barbadoes to the Guinea coast. The Guineaman fled but was pursued through the night and overtaken the next morning, when, the wind coming to a calm, she was easily captured. They found nothing of value on board save some small arms, which were taken and six of the seamen impressed, while Fulker and his companions were set on board, except Atkinson and the mate, who were detained. Atkinson had, to the knowledge of the pirates, been master of the *Bonita*, a brigantine, and knew the New England coast. He demanded his liberty, which was refused with a volley of curses by Fly, which ended in the declaration that he would have to stay and perform his duty as pilot, like an honest man.

After they headed for New England a coaster sloop was taken off the Delaware capes. Fly put Atkinson on board of her with three of his own hands under orders to keep company. This he did for twenty-four hours, but when Fly found her of no use, she was released and Atkinson was taken again on board of the snow, with instructions to pilot her into Martha's Vineyard. Atkinson wilfully ran by, when Fly, finding their position to be beyond Nantucket, threatened his life as an obstinate villain. He called for a pistol and would have killed him on the spot, but Mitchel intervened and saved his life. Atkinson then changed his tactics and began to ingratiate himself with the crew, with such success that they offered him the command, as Fly was no better than a boatswain and not fit for the office. Atkinson, while keeping them in this humor evaded the responsibility, but did not serve to halt the hostility of Fly who several times wished him thrown overboard, but he was always protected by the crew and much less roughly used. A fishing schooner was stopped and seized, her captain and crew being dispossessed. To save himself the fisherman gave word of a better vessel that was near.

Fly put six pirates and George Tasker, a forced man, on board the smack and sent her in pursuit of the other, leaving with himself on the snow but three of his own men and fifteen of the forced seamen, thus

[260]

being outnumbered five to one. Atkinson, on perceiving this, took heart and resolved to capture the vessel and so free himself from the dangerous and detestable bondage he endured. Several fishing boats coming into sight, he called to Fly to come forward and observe them with his glass, which he did, leaving his arms behind on the quarter-deck. Two of the pressed men, Walker and Pembroke, quickly seized the weapons and so armed overpowered Fly. The three others were easily secured. This was all done by Atkinson and his two associates. The other pressed men stood inactive during the proceedings. Atkinson now took charge of the snow and sailed her into Brewster, in Barnstable County on Cape Cod, where they arrived June 28, 1729. On the fourth of July following, Fly and his three companions, viz: Samuel Cole, George Condick, and Henry Greenville were placed on trial in Boston, before a special court of the Admiralty, William Dummer, His Majesty's Lieutenant-Governor, presiding, assisted by eighteen gentlemen of the Council. All were found guilty of murder and piracy and were hanged on the 12th of July. Before going to the gallows the wretches were treated on July 10th to a sermon by the Rev. Benjamin Colman, pastor of the Manifesto Church and a brother-in-law of Sir William Pepperell. It was later printed under the title: "It is a fearful thing to fall into the hands of a living God. A sermon preached to some miserable pirates . . . on the Lord's Day before their execution."

Colman, in a footnote to his published sermon, observes: "Fly refused to come into public. I moved the others for his sake to let me preach to them in private, but they said it was the last Sabbath they had to live and they earnestly desired to be in an assembly of worshippers, that they might have the Prayers of many together over them, and that others might take the more warning by them."

After death Fly was hung in chains at Nix's Mate at the harbor entrance where his bones rattled a warning to reckless seamen for many a day thereafter. No record appears of the seven sent away in the schooner.

Organized piracy now disappeared for the balance of the century.

XXXVII

OF JEAN LAFITTE

T HE period of unrest and confusion that followed the French
Revolution and culminated in the Napoleonic wars brought in-
security into the New World as well as the Old. The taking
over by Napoleon of the dominions of Spain led to revolts in Spanish
America that continued beyond the return of the Austrian Bourbons
to Madrid, and ended in the breaking of all the shackles, save those
binding Cuba and Porto Rico. Miranda's move on Venezuela in
1806 was the first filibustering expedition out of the United States.
This, proving abortive, bred a real revolution in 1810, together with
one in Mexico under the priest Hidalgo. The French privateers,
driven out of Guadeloupe by the British, turned their attention to
the waters of the Gulf of Mexico and the Spanish commerce between
Cuba and her unruly states. These, taking on the habits of their bet-
ters, took to privateering as a means of crippling their former owner.
Not sea going people in themselves, they attracted adventurers from
Europe and North America, who soon lost their powers of discrimina-
tion and preyed alike on friend and foe. Many swift vessels were
equipped from Baltimore and laid the foundation of more than one
respectable fortune in this lawless way. The United States, buying
the vast region of Louisiana in 1804, knew very little about its new
possession. It installed a territorial government at New Orleans with
William C. C. Claiborne as governor and very little authority behind
him. The population was French and Spanish and hostile in habit
and desires. The bayous leading into the gulf and the many mouths of
the Mississippi afforded free entrance to contrabandists or smugglers,
who found eager purchasers among the planters who did not trouble
to ask questions about the paternity of the wares offered. These adventurers established a rude settlement on the Island of Grande Terre,
fronting the Bay of Barataria, from which the thieving, smuggling,
and trading expeditions set out. Here they prospered and grew in
numbers.

OF JEAN LAFITTE

This vagabond colony was soon to receive a place in history and romance through the connection with it of two brothers, Jean and Pierre Lafitte, whose birthplace is variously ascribed as being Bayonne and Bordeaux, but with a preference for the former. Both took to the ever-inviting sea. It is said that Jean began a sailor's life at thirteen and after various voyages to the African West Coast, and the Indies, became mate of a French East Indiaman, consigned to Madras. A storm damaging the ship off the Cape of Good Hope, she was compelled to put in for succor at Mauritius in the Isle of France, where Lafitte, having quarreled with his captain, left the vessel. Mauritius was a nesting place for privateers dating from the period of the American Revolution and the adventurer soon found his services in demand as captain of a letter of marque. British prey not being plentiful, he helped himself to the commerce of the Dutch and Portuguese in the Madagascar Channel, like the pirates of yore, and wound up his course by taking on board a cargo of slaves for Mauritius at the Seychelles. Chased by a British frigate, he was pushed northward toward the Bay of Bengal and, being short of provisions, boldly renewed operations as a privateer. The vessel under his command was of but two hundred tons burden, two guns, and carrying a crew of twenty-six men. With this petty force he took a well-armed British schooner, to which he transferred his crew, cruising along the Bengal shore. Off the mouth of the Ganges he took on the innocent guise of a pilot boat and as such beguiled the British East India Company's ship *Pagoda*, of twelve guns and one hundred and fifty men, into striking distance and boarding the unsuspecting craft took her with a rush, bringing the rich prize safely into Mauritius. Here he took command of *La Confiance*, a formidable privateer of twenty-six guns and two hundred and fifty hands, sailing again to the cruising grounds off Bengal.

Off Sands Head, in October, 1807, he waylaid the *Queen*, one of the largest East Indiamen afloat. She had for defense forty guns and a crew of about four hundred men. By swift manœuvering he laid *La Confiance* alongside the *Queen*, his men avoiding her broadside by lying flat on the deck and rising to shower the great ship with bombs and grenades. In the panic thus caused, a boarding party of forty men soon drove the defenders to the steerage where a semblance of defense was made. This broke down when a second party of boarders under Lafitte himself killed the captain and loading a carronade with grape brought the last of the defenders to terms with the threat of

[263]

instant extermination. The *Queen* was borne in triumph to the Isle of France, and the fame of *La Confiance's* exploit resounded across the seas. So strong had the privateers of Mauritius now become that heavy convoys began to escort the Indiamen from the Cape of Good Hope to their destinations. This interfered with the prosperity of privateering and made it a risky game. Lafitte therefore doubled the Cape and cruised off the Bight of Benin, picking up two prizes loaded with palm oil, ivory, and a modicum of gold dust which he brought safely in to St. Malo. The African and Indian waters being now unsafe, Lafitte fitted out a brigantine of twenty guns with one hundred and fifty men and made for the West Indies, using Guadeloupe as a base.

When Rodney's successes drove the French out of the West Indies, Lafitte and other privateers took refuge in Carthagena, from which point, there being no details extant, he came to New Orleans. It is a matter of record that, in 1809, Jean and Pierre Lafitte opened a blacksmith shop on the north side of St. Philip Street, between Bourbon and Dauphine, residing nearby, at the corner of Bourbon and St. Philip. They had slaves and other evidences of means, and were quickly in close touch with the life of the community. Perhaps the establishing of this workshop was part of their plan of operation, and intended as a means of acquiring acquaintance with the planters and traders dealing in New Orleans markets. At any rate they soon transferred their dwelling to Grande Terre and became masters of the smuggling and piratical center. It was not long before a fleet of sixteen sail were operating out of Barataria, against Spanish commerce ostensibly, but not particular about their pickings. Jean Lafitte became the commodore and with a stout schooner, the *General Bolivar*, as flagship, did about as he pleased. A great trade soon sprang up in captured and smuggled goods. Not infrequently cargoes of slaves were retrieved and brought in to be sold to Louisiana and Mississippi planters, despite the inhibition of United States laws. Thomas Billing Robertson, Secretary of the Territory, but for the moment acting as Governor in the absence at Baltimore of Claiborne, found it necessary on September 6, 1810, to issue this warning address to his citizens:

"You have no doubt heard of the late introduction of African slaves among us. Two cargoes have already been smuggled into this Territory by way of Barataria and La Fourche; and I am fully convinced, from a variety of circumstances which have come to my knowledge.

that an extensive and well-laid plan exists to evade or to defeat the operation of the laws of the United States on that subject. The open and daring course which is now pursued by a set of brigands who infest our coast and overrun our country is calculated to excite the strongest indignation in the breast of every one who feels the slightest respect for the wise and politic institutions under which we live. At this moment, upwards of one hundred slaves are held by some of our own citizens, in the very teeth of the most positive laws; and, notwithstanding every exertion which has been made, so general seems the disposition to aid in the concealment, that but faint hopes are entertained of detecting the parties and bringing them to punishment."

The "good people" of the Territory made not the slightest effort to respond to this appeal. Cotton and sugar fields called too loudly for help and the wines of Bordeaux and Xeres were sweet and cheap!

The National Government had in the meantime detailed the ketch *Vesuvius,* commanded by Lieutenant B. F. Reed, who undertook to curb the activities at Barataria. In February, 1810, he had taken two "privateers," the schooners *Duke of Montebello* and the *Diomede,* manned mainly by Frenchmen expelled from Cuba by the Spaniards. Next, later in the month, Midshipman F. H. Gregory, attached to the *Vesuvius,* cut out with boats the brig *Alexandria,* laden with slaves. The three captures were made off the mouth of the Mississippi while the vessels were seeking harbor at Barataria. All were sent to New Orleans and condemned. The *Alexandria* showed British colors. The *Vesuvius* was replaced by gunboat *No. 162,* one of President Jefferson's famous fleet, under command of Midshipman Gregory. On August 7th, 1811, he engaged and crippled during the night the schooner *La Franchise,* off Pensacola, and on the 10th near Mobile took the schooner *Santa Maria.* The navy record calls *La Franchise* "a former French privateer." The *Santa Maria* was evidently a plain smuggler and followed her sister to New Orleans. September 7th, Gregory captured the schooners *Sophia* and *La Vengeance* and the ship *La Divina Pastora,* west of Barataria. The schooners were set on fire by the "pirates," who escaped to the shore. The ship had a valuable cargo which was sent to New Orleans. British cruisers in the gulf also occasionally tried their hands at the "pirates" but the shallow waters of the bay protected Barataria, while the settlement was too numerous and well armed to be assailed by boat expeditions. March 15, 1812,

Governor Claiborne, exasperated by the continued lawlessness issued an appeal to the public reading:

"Whereas, I have received information that upon or near the shores of Lake Barataria, within the limits and the jurisdiction of this State, a considerable number of bandits, composed of individuals of different nations, have armed and equipped several vessels for the avowed purpose of cruising on the high seas, and committing depredations and piracies on the vessels of nations at peace with the United States, and carrying on an illicit trade in goods, wares and merchandise with the inhabitants of this State, in opposition to the laws of the United States, and to the great injury of the fair trade and of the public revenue; and whereas, there is reasonable ground to fear that the parties thus waging lawless war will cease to respect the laws and property of the good citizens of this State, I have thought proper to issue this my proclamation, hereby commanding the persons engaged as aforesaid in such unlawful acts to cease therefrom and forthwith to disperse and separate; and I do charge and require all officers, civil and military, in this State, and within their respective districts, to be vigilant and active in apprehending and securing every individual engaged as aforesaid in any violation of the laws; and I do caution the people of this State against holding any kind of intercourse, or being in any manner concerned with such high offenders; and I do earnestly exhort each and every good citizen to afford help, protection and support to the officers in suppressing a combination so destructive to the interests of the United States, and of this State in particular; and to rescue Louisiana from the foul reproach which would attach to her character should her shores afford any asylum, or her citizens any countenance, to an association of individuals whose practices are subversive of all laws, human and divine, and of whose ill-begotten treasure no man can partake without being forever dishonored and exposing himself to the severest punishment."

This document did not have the least effect. Indeed, the residents of Barataria came and went freely to New Orleans and were not molested, so popular were their operations with the public. Louisiana wanted free trade and the Lafittes provided it. That was enough. The revenue laws were regarded as oppressive and unjust, so that the officials received no support.

The War of 1812 was now well under way, and Barataria had a new and greater value as a means of evading the British blockade, which, keeping out honest goods, improved the market for the smugglers, sailing under neutral flags to the rendezvous on Grande Terre. Aware of this, on June 23, 1813, an English sloop of war attacked two schooners anchored off Cat Island. The "privateers" showed fight and beat off their assailants, who suffered some sensible damage.

November 24, 1813, Claiborne again attempted to curb the outlaws by proclamation, saying:

"Whereas, the nefarious practice of running in contraband goods, which has hitherto prevailed in different parts of this State, to the great injury of the fair trader and the diminution of the revenue of the United States, has of late much increased; and whereas, the violators of the law, emboldened by the impunity of past trespasses, no longer conceal themselves from the view of the honest part of the community, but, setting the Government at defiance, in broad daylight, carry on their infamous traffic; and, whereas, it has been officially known to me that, on the 14th of last month (October) a quantity of smuggled goods, seized by Walter Gilbert, an officer of the revenue of the United States, were forcibly taken from him in open day, at no great distance from the city of New Orleans, by a party of armed men under the orders of a certain John Lafitte, who fired upon and grievously wounded one of the assistants of the said Walter Gilbert; and although process has issued for the apprehension of him, the said John Lafitte, yet such is the countenance and protection afforded him, or the terror excited by the threats of himself and his associates, that the same remains unexecuted;

"And whereas, the apathy of the good people of this State in checking practices so opposed to morality and to the laws and interests of the United States, may impair the fair character which Louisiana maintains and ought to preserve as a member of the American Union;

"I have thought proper to issue this, my proclamation, hereby strictly charging and commanding all officers of this State, civil and military, in their respective departments, to be vigilant and active in preventing the violation of the laws in the premises, and in apprehending and securing all parties offending therein, and I do solemnly caution all and singular the citizens of this State against giving any kind of succor, support or countenance to the said John Lafitte and associates; but do call upon them to be aiding and abetting in arresting him and said associates, and all others in like manner offending; and I do furthermore, in the name of the State, offer a reward of five hundred dollars, which will be paid out of the treasury to any person delivering the said John Lafitte to the sheriff of the Parish of Orleans, or to any other sheriff in the State, so that the said John Lafitte may be brought to justice."

Instead of the people's upholding the Governor the traffic grew. As Major A. L. Latour says in his Historical Memoir: "At Grande Terre the privateers publicly made sale by auction of the cargoes of their prizes. From all parts of Louisiana people resorted to Barataria, without being at all solicitous to conceal the object of their journey. In the streets of New Orleans it was usual for traders to give and receive orders for purchasing goods at Barataria; with as little secrecy as similar orders were given for Philadelphia and New York. The most respectable citizens of the State, especially those living in the country, were in the habit of smuggling goods from Barataria. The frequent seizures made of these goods were but an ineffectual remedy for the evil as the great profit yielded by such parcels as escaped the vigilance of the Custom House officers indemnified the traders."

A crisis came January 24, 1814, when Collector Dubourg informed Governor Claiborne that a cargo of four hundred and fifteen slaves was about to be sold by public auction at Barataria, under assignment to Jean and Pierre Lafitte, and requested the aid of a sufficient force to "defeat the purposes of these law infractors." Four days later Custom Inspector Stout, with twelve men stationed at a place known as "The Temple" near Barataria for the purpose of preventing smuggling were attacked by Jean Lafitte, as a result of which Stout was slain and two of his men dangerously hurt. The Collector again hotly appealed to the Governor for sufficient aid to uphold the law and break up the contraband trade; the Governor in turn applied to the legislature which denied his request, and the "trade" went on more boldly than before. A daily argosy of smuggled goods was sent to Donaldsonville, at the junction of Bayou La Fourche and the Mississippi River for dispersal to customers, under a heavy guard, far too formidable for the revenue agents. The legislative excuse was the customary "lack of funds." On March 24th, the Governor again approached the legislature with this statement of the case:

"I lay before you a letter which was addressed to me on yesterday by Colonel Dubourg, Collector for the District of Louisiana, from which you will perceive the great and continued violations, within the State, of the Non-intercourse, the Embargo and other laws of the

United States, and the necessity of affording to the officers of the revenue the support of an armed force whilst in the discharge of their duty. General Flournoy, not deeming it prudent (on account of the fears of a British invasion) to withdraw for the present any of the regular troops under his command from the important and exposed posts they occupy, the Collector of the District conceives it a duty, in conformith with the instructions from the General Government, to apply once more to the Chief Magistrate of Louisiana for such aid as will enable the officers of the revenue to fulfill their obligations.

"I entreat you, therefore, to furnish me with the means of cooperating on this occasion with promptitude and effect. It is desirable to disperse those desperate men on Lake Barataria, whose piracies have rendered our shores a terror to neutral flags, and diverted from New Orleans that lucrative intercourse with Vera Cruz and other neutral ports which formerly filled our banks with the richest deposits. It is no less an object to put an end to that system of smuggling which exists, to the disgrace of the State, the injury of the fair trader, and the diminution, as I am advised, of the circulating medium of this city, in so great a degree as is likely to produce serious commercial embarrassments, than it is important, above all, to prevent breaches of the Embargo law, and to mar the projects of those traitors who wish to carry supplies to the enemy. To enable me to accomplish these ends, or at least some of them, I ask for authority to raise by voluntary enlistment a force of not less than one captain, one first lieutenant, one second lieutenant, one third lieutenant, one drummer, one fifer, and one hundred privates, to serve for six months, unless sooner discharged, and to be employed under the Government in dispersing any armed association of individuals within the State, having for object the violation of the laws of the United States, and to assist the officers of the revenue in enforcing the provisions of the Embargo, Non-intercourse, and other acts of Congress. The officers, non-commissioned officers and privates to be entitled to the same pay rations and emoluments as are allowed the troops of the United States, and to be subject to the rules and articles of war as prescribed by Congress.

"As this corps will be solely employed in enforcing the laws of the United States, I am persuaded the General Government will readily defray any expense which may attend the raising and maintaining of the same. But if in this reasonable expectation we should be disappointed, I would advise that the corps be immediately dispersed, for the present embarrassment of our treasury will not admit of its remaining in service at the expense of the State."

This was equally without effect, and Collector Dubourg turned for help to the United States Grand Jury at the July term of the district court, which made a "presentment" signed by Paul Lanusse, a prominent New Orleans merchant, but seems to have got no further. Indeed, John R. Grymes, the United States District Attorney, resigned to take a $20,000 retainer from the Lafittes and he in turn engaged Edward Livingston as an associate for an equal fee. Livingston was a New Yorker, and a direct descendant of that Robert Livingston who had been Captain Kidd's partner. He stood at the head of the Louisiana bar and was accounted the leading citizen of the State.

Dick, who succeeded as District Attorney, denounced Grymes for disgraceful conduct in the matter and was challenged to fight a duel in which the virtuous Dick came off with a wound in the hip which ever after made him lame. The "presentment" was stricken from the record and Grymes went openly to Barataria to collect the fee for himself and his colleague, Livingston. The latter, when invited to go along, remarked to Grymes: "As you are a well-known scape-grace, you have nothing to fear from congenial spirits. But as to me, they might hang me for being so different from you and them. Therefore, I propose to you to be my representative, and as a remuneration for your trouble, I will give you ten per cent of my fee if you bring it to me."

Grymes agreed and spent a week at Barataria. Finally, according to Charles Gayaré, the historian of Louisiana: "He was conducted by the Lafittes themselves to the banks of the Mississippi in a superb yawl, loaded with boxes of Spanish gold and silver. It was highly amusing to hear Grymes relate how gorgeously feasted he was at Barataria by these innocent and persecuted people, whom he represented as the most glorious fellows in the world. . . . 'What a cruel misnomer it is,' he would exclaim with mock solemnity, 'to call the most honest and polished gentlemen that the world ever produced, bandits and pirates.' "

Peace had been proclaimed between France and England and soldiers of the latter, justified by her alliance with Spain, made their headquarters at Pensacola in Florida, then a Spanish possession. The plan of taking New Orleans was being worked out. As a part of it, Capt. W. H. Percy, of H. B. M. frigate *Hermes,* sent a brig under a flag of truce, bearing Captains McWilliams and Lockyer, with a message from Lt. Col. Edward Nicholls, commanding His Majesty's forces in Florida, to Jean Lafitte, to induce him to join hands with the invaders. It read:

"I have arrived in the Floridas for the purpose of annoying the only enemy Great Britain has in the world, as France and England are now friends. I call on you, with your brave followers, to enter into the service of Great Britain, in which you shall have the grade of a captain; lands will be given to you all, in proportion to your respective ranks, on peace taking place, and I invite you on the following terms: your property shall be guaranteed to you, and your persons protected —in return for which I ask you to cease all hostilities against Spain or the allies of Great Britain—your ships and vessels to be placed under the orders of the commanding officer on this station, until the commander-in-chief's pleasure is known; but I guarantee their full value at all events. I herewith inclose you a copy of my proclamation to the inhabitants of Louisiana, which will, I trust, point out to you the honorable intentions of my government. You may be a useful instrument to me in forwarding them; therefore, if you determine, lose no time. The bearer of this, Captain McWilliams, will satisfy you on any other point you may be anxious to learn, as will Captain Lockyer, of the Sophia, who brings him to you. We have a powerful reinforcement on its way here, and I hope to cut out some other work for the Americans than oppressing the inhabitants of Louisiana. Be expeditious in your resolves and rely on the verity of your humble servant."

Captain Percy supplemented this document with the following bit of bait:

"Having understood that some British merchantmen have been detained, taken into and sold by the Inhabitants of Barataria, I have directed Captain Lockyer to proceed to that place and inquire into the circumstances, with positive orders to demand instant restitution, and in case of refusal, to destroy to his utmost every vessel there, as well as to carry destruction over the whole place, and, at the same time, I have assured him of the co-operation of all His Majesty's forces on this station. I trust, at the same time, that the Inhabitants of Barataria, consulting their own interest, will not make it necessary to proceed to such extremities. I hold out, at the same time, a war instantly destructively to them, and, on the other hand, should they be inclined

[271]

to assist Great Britain, in her just war against the United States, the security of their property, the blessings of the British constitution; and should they be inclined to settle on this continent, lands will, at the conclusion of the war, be allotted to them in His Majesty's colonies in America. In return for all these concessions on the part of Great Britain, I expect that the direction of their armed vessels will be put in my hands (for which they will be remunerated) also the instant cessation of hostilities against the Spanish government, and the restitution of any undisposed property of that nation.

"Should any inhabitants be inclined to volunteer their services into His Majesty's forces, either naval or military, for limited service, they will be received; and if any British subject, being at Barataria, wishes to return to his native country, he will, on joining His Majesty's service, receive a free pardon."

It has been asserted, also, that Lockyer offered Lafitte a post-captain's position in the British navy in return for his compliance, if he desired such a reward. It chanced at the moment that Pierre Lafitte was imprisoned in New Orleans on a smuggling charge and inferentially the right moment had been chosen for the negotiation. Instead, the two captains were received with such menace by the worthy "inhabitants" of Barataria, that Lafitte had to interpose his authority to preserve them from bodily harm. What followed is best told by Major Latour:

"When Mr. Lafitte had perused these papers, Captain Lockyer enlarged on the subject of them, and proposed to him to enter into the service of His Britannic Majesty, with all those who were under his command, or over whom he had sufficient influence; and likewise to lay at the disposal of the officers of His Britannic Majesty the armed vessels he had at Barataria, to aid in the intended attack of the port of Mobile. He insisted much on the great advantage that would thence result to himself and his crew; offered him the grade of captain in the British service, and the sum of thirty thousand dollars, payable at his option in Pensacola or New Orleans, and urged him not to let slip this opportunity of acquiring fortune and consideration. On Mr. Lafitte's requiring a few days to reflect upon these offers, Captain Lockyer observed to him that no reflection would be necessary respecting proposals that obviously precluded hesitation, as he was a Frenchman, and of course now a friend to Great Britain—proscribed by the American government—exposed to infamy—and had a brother at that very time loaded with irons in the jail of New Orleans. He added that, in the British service, he would have a fair prospect of promotion; that having such a knowledge of the country, his services would be of the greatest importance in carrying on the operations which the British government had planned against Lower Louisiana; that as soon as possession was obtained, the army would penetrate into the upper country, and act in concert with the forces in Canada; that everything was already prepared for carrying on the war against the American government in that quarter with unusual vigor; that they were nearly sure of success, expecting to find little or no opposition from the French and Spanish population of Louisiana, whose interest, manners and customs were more congenial with theirs than with those of the Americans; that, finally, the insurrection of the negroes, to whom they would offer freedom, was one of the chief means they intended to employ.

"To all these splendid promises and these ensnaring insinuations, Mr. Lafitte replied that in a few days he would give a final answer—his object in this procrastination being to gain time to inform the state officers of this nefarious project. Having occasion to go to some distance for a short time, the persons who had proposed to send the British officers prisoners to New Orleans went and seized them in his absence, and confined both them and the crew of their pinnace in a secure place, leaving a guard at the door. The British officers sent for Mr. Lafitte; but he, fearing an insurrection of the crews of the privateers, thought it advisable not to see them until he had persuaded his captains and other officers to desist from the measures on which they seemed bent, representing that besides the infamy that would attach to them if they treated as prisoners persons who came with a flag of truce, they would lose the opportunity of discovering the extent of the projects of the British against Louisiana, or the names of their agents in the country. While endeavoring to bring over his people to his sentiments, the British remained prisoners the whole night—the sloop of war continuing at anchor before the Pass, waiting for the return of the officers. Early the next morning Mr. Lafitte caused them to be released from their confinement, and saw them safe on board their pinnace, apologizing for the disagreeable treatment they had received, and which it had not been in his power to prevent."

In asking for the delay, Lafitte formally wrote Lockyer:

"Barataria, 4th Sept., 1814.

"Sir—The confusion which prevailed in our camp yesterday and

[273]

this morning, and of which you have a complete knowledge, has prevented me from answering in a precise manner to the object of your mission; nor even at this moment can I give you all the satisfaction that you desire; however, if you could grant me a fortnight, I would be entirely at your disposal at the end of that time. This delay is indispensable to enable me to put my affairs in order. You may communicate with me by sending a boat to the eastern point of the pass, where I will be found. You have inspired me with more confidence than the admiral, your superior officer, could have done himself; with you alone, I wish to deal, and from you also I will claim, in due time the reward of the services, which I may render to you."

Simultaneously he dispatched the following missive to Claiborne:

"Barataria, Sept. 4th, 1814.

"Sir—In the firm persuasion that the choice made of you to fill the office of first magistrate of this state, was dictated by the esteem of your fellow citizens, and was conferred on merit, I confidently address you on an affair on which may depend the safety of this country. I offer to you to restore to this state several citizens, who perhaps in your eyes have lost that sacred title. I offer you them, however, such as you could wish to find them, ready to exert their utmost efforts in defence of the country. This point of Louisiana, which I occupy, is of great importance in the present crisis. I tender my services to defend it; and the only reward I ask is that a stop be put to the proscription against me and my adherents, by an act of oblivion, for all that has been done hitherto. I am the stray sheep wishing to return to the fold. If you are thoroughly acquainted with the nature of my offences, I should appear to you much less guilty, and still worthy to discharge the duties of a good citizen. I have never sailed under any flag but that of the republic of Carthagena, and my vessels are perfectly regular in that respect. If I could have brought my lawful prizes into the ports of this state, I should not have employed the illicit means that have caused me to be proscribed. I decline saying more on the subject, until I have the honor of your excellency's answer, which I am persuaded can be dictated only by wisdom. Should your answer not be favorable, to my ardent desires, I declare to you that I will instantly leave the country, to avoid the imputation of having co-operated towards an invasion on this point, which cannot fail to take place, and to rest secure in the acquittal of my conscience."

Lafitte also sent the documents given him by Lockyer to John

[274]

Blanque, a member of the Louisiana legislature, as an earnest of his desire to serve the country. On the 7th he further advised Blanque: "You will always find me eager to evince my devotedness to the good of the country of which I endeavored to give some proof in my letter of the 4th, which I make no doubt you received. Amongst other papers that have fallen into my hands, I send you a scrap which appears of sufficient importance to meet your attention."

It was indeed of "sufficient importance to meet attention," conveying as it did information of the coming expedition formed of Wellington's veterans under Major-General Sir Edward Packenham, by an anonymous hand from Cuba. To this he added: "Since the departure (after vain waiting for a signal of acceptance) of the officers who came with the flag of truce, his ship, with two other ships of war, have remained on the coast within sight. Doubtless this point is considered as important. We have hitherto kept on a respectable defensive; if, however, the British attach to the possession of this place the importance they give us room to suspect they do, they may employ means beyond our strength. I know not whether, in that case, proposals of intelligence with the government would be out of season. It is always from my high opinion of your enlightened mind that I request you to advise me in this affair."

These letters were conveyed to Claiborne and Blanque by Pierre Lafitte, who had been released from jail by his powerful friends. They were at once laid before a council of army, navy, and state officers summoned to consider the situation, all of whom, with the exception of Gen. Villerè, were against accepting Lafitte as an ally. Claiborne was inclined to offer the amnesty, but yielded to the opinion of the majority and continued to treat the brothers and their followers as outlaws. The naval force at New Orleans, under Commodore David T. Patterson, consisting of the schooner *Carolina*, Captain Robert Henley; the schooner *Sea Horse*, under Lt. Louis Alexis; gunboat *No. 5*, Sailing Master J. D. Ferris; gunboat *No. 23*, Acting-Lieutenant Isaac McKeever, gunboat *No. 65*, Sailing Master William Johnson; gunboat *No. 156*, Lt. T. ap Catesby Jones; gunboat *No. 162*, Acting Lieutenant Robert Spedden; gunboat *No. 163*, Sailing Master George Ulrich and a one-gun launch commanded by Purser Thomas Shields, proceeded against the stronghold. Beside the seamen and marines, one hundred regular soldiers, under Colonel Ross, accompanied the expedition. The *Carolina* and *Sea Horse* arrived off Barataria on the 16th of September, but were beaten off in their first assault. The arrival of the gunboats enabled the force to get in close quarters, with the result that Lafitte's flagship, the *Simon Bolivar*, two schooners, and half a dozen smaller craft were taken and the "pirates" rendered helpless on the water. The settlement was broken up and destroyed, while, under charge of the gunboats, the prizes were taken to New Orleans, save one schooner which escaped on the night of September 23rd. All the rest arrived at New Orleans on October 1st. The escaping schooner carried the two Lafittes to the "German coast," as it was called, on the east part of the Delta. A large amount of spoil rewarded Patterson and his followers. General Andrew Jackson, who was on his way to succeed General Flounoy in charge of the defense of New Orleans, received news of the "victory" from Claiborne, who praised the destruction of the nest and acclaimed the amount of "ill-gotten treasures of the pirates." He also suggested to Jackson the expediency of directing immediate possession to be taken of Grande Terre and "The Temple." In a day or two he was able to inform Jackson that Lafitte was nursing his injuries on Last Island, or rather recovering from the surprise of having been assailed by Americans when he was expecting British.

Claiborne, who felt the injustice of the situation, wrote Benjamin Rush, Attorney General of the United States, on October 30, 1814:

"You no doubt have heard that the late expedition to Barataria had eventuated in the entire dispersion of the pirates and smugglers and capture of nearly all their vessels. It is greatly to be regretted that neither the general nor the state government had not sooner been enabled to put down those banditti. The length of time they were permitted to continue their evil practices added much to their strength, and led the people here to view their course as less vicious. Measures tending to the prevention of crimes can alone relieve us from the distress of punishing them. Had such measures, in relation to the offenders in question, been earlier taken, we should not have to lament the frequency of their commission. I have been at great pains to convince the people of the state that smuggling is a moral offense. But in this I have only partially succeeded. There are individuals here who, in every other respect, fulfill with exemplary integrity all the duties devolving upon them as fathers of families and as citizens. But, as regards smuggling, although they may not be personally concerned, they attach no censure to those who are. It is the influence of education, of habit, of bad example. Formerly, under the government of Spain, smuggling in Louisiana was universally practiced, from the highest to the lowest member of society. To show you the light in which it was then viewed, I will only observe that, occasionally in conversation with ladies, I have denounced smuggling as dishonest, and very generally a reply, in substance as follows, was returned: 'That is impossible; for my grandfather, or my father, or my husband, was, under the Spanish government, a great smuggler, and he was always esteemed an honest man.'

"Much has already been done to reconcile the Louisianians to the government, laws and usages of the United States, and more must yet be done to do away with all the traces of those improper feelings and sentiments which originated with, and were fostered under, the corrupt government of Spain. Prosecutions are now pending in the District Court against several of the Barataria offenders; and, in the course of the investigation, it is probable that the number implicated will be very considerable. Justice demands that the most culpable be punished with severity.

"But I see no good end to be obtained by making the penalties of the laws to fall extensively and heavily. The example is not the less imposing by circumscribing the number of its victims; and the mercy which should dictate it seldom fails to make a salutary and lasting impression. Should the president think proper to instruct the attorney for the district of Louisiana to select a few of the most hardened of the Baratarians for trial, and to forbear to prosecute all others concerned, I think such an act of clemency would be well received and be attended, at the present moment, with the best effects. A sympathy for these offenders is certainly more or less felt by many of the Louisianians. With some it arises from national attachment, but with most from their late trade and intercourse with them. Should the attorney for the district be instructed not to prosecute the case of minor offenders, it is desirable that such instructions be accompanied with the opinion of the executive as to the offense of smuggling, and that publicity be given to the same."

Jackson, who received a copy of the above, made haste to proclaim his purpose to have nothing to do with the "pirates," saying in a summons to the people of Louisiana, addressed to them from Mobile:

"I ask you, Louisianians, can we place any confidence in the honor of men who have courted an alliance with pirates and robbers? Have not these noble Britons—these honorable men, Colonel Nicholls and

Captain W. H. Percy, the true representatives of their royal master—done this? Have they not made offers to the pirates of Barataria to join them and their holy cause? And have they not dared to insult you by calling on you to associate, as brothers, with them and these hellish banditti? Confident that any attempt to invade our soil will be repelled, the undersigned calls not upon either pirates or robbers to join him in the glorious cause."

On reaching New Orleans, however, Jackson was jarred by the poverty of the means at hand or to come to resist the powerful English expedition and was soon in a state of mind agreeable to any aid. Jean Lafitte saw him in person and tendered the services of his men. The "hellish banditti" were promptly accepted. Some were sent to assist in defending fort St. Philip, Petites Coquilles, and Bayou St. John. Others who knew how to handle cannon were put with the artillery under two of Lafitte's lieutenants, Dominique You and Beluche. When the British, on December 30, 1814, began erecting earthworks to defend their right of line preparatory to the assault on Jackson's redoubt of cotton bales, one of You's field pieces came into play and destroyed it. When the famous battle of January 8, 1814—fought after peace had been signed, but without the knowledge of the combatants—it is related by Gayarre that Jackson, riding along the line, had this colloquy with You, whose guns were silent:

"What is the matter? You have ceased firing?"

"The powder is good for nothing—fit only to shoot blackbirds with and not redcoats."

"Tell the ordinance officer," said Jackson to his aide, "that I will have him shot in five minutes as a traitor if Dominique complains any more."

On his return in a short time, the guns were growling again.

"Ha! Ha! Friend Dominique," said Jackson, "I see you are hard at work."

"Pretty good work, too," was the reply. "I guess that the British have discovered by this time that there has been a change in powder in my battery."

In recounting his triumph on January 21, 1815, Jackson said:

"Captains Dominique and Beluche, lately commanding privateers at Barataria, with part of their former crews, and many brave citizens of New Orleans, were stationed at batteries Nos. 3 and 4. The general cannot avoid his warm approbation of the manner in which those gentlemen have uniformly conducted themselves while under his command, and of the gallantry with which they have redeemed the pledge they gave at the opening of the campaign, to defend the country. The brothers Lafitte have exhibited the same courage and fidelity, and the general promises that the government shall be duly apprised of their conduct."

To crown all, President Madison. gave a full and free pardon to the Baratarians. His proclamation, dated February 6, 1815, reads:

"Among the many evils produced by the wars, which, with little intermission, have afflicted Europe, and extended their ravages into other quarters of the globe, for a period exceeding twenty years, the dispersion of a considerable portion of the inhabitants of different countries, in sorrow and in want, has not been the least injurious to human happiness, nor the least severe in the trial of human virtue.

"It had been long ascertained that many foreigners, flying from the dangers of their own home, and that some citizens, forgetful of their duty, had co-operated in forming an establishment on the island of Barataria, near the mouth of the river Mississippi, for the purpose of a clandestine and lawless trade. The government of the United States caused the establishment to be broken up and destroyed; and, having obtained the means of designating the offenders of every description, it only remained to answer the demands of justice by inflicting an exemplary punishment.

"But it has since been represented that the offenders have manifested a sincere penitence; that they have abandoned the prosecution of the worst cause for the support of the best, and, particularly, that they have exhibited, in the defence of New Orleans, unequivocal traits of courage and fidelity. Offenders, who have refused to become the associates of the enemy in the war, upon the most seducing terms of invitation; and who have aided to repel his hostile invasion of the territory of the United States, can no longer be considered as objects of punishment, but as objects of a generous forgiveness.

"It has therefore been seen, with great satisfaction, that the General Assembly of the State of Louisiana earnestly recommend those offenders to the benefit of a full pardon; And in compliance with that recommendation, as well as in consideration of all the other extraordinary circumstances of the case, I, James Madison, President of the United States of America, do issue this proclamation, hereby granting, publishing and declaring, a free and full pardon of all offences committed

[279]

in violation of any act or acts of the Congress of the said United States, touching the revenue, trade and navigation thereof, or touching the intercourse and commerce of the United States with foreign nations, at any time before the eighth day of January, in the present year one thousand eight hundred and fifteen, by any person or persons whatsoever, being inhabitants of New Orleans and the adjacent country, or being inhabitants of the said island of Barataria, and the places adjacent; Provided, that every person, claiming the benefit of this full pardon, in order to entitle himself thereto, shall produce a certificate in writing from the governor of the State of Louisiana, stating that such person has aided in the defence of New Orleans and the adjacent country, during the invasion thereof as aforesaid.

"And I do hereby further authorize and direct all suits, indictments, and prosecutions, for fines, penalties, and forfeitures, against any person or persons, who shall be entitled to the benefit of this full pardon, forthwith to be stayed, discontinued and released: All civil officers are hereby required, according to the duties of their respective stations, to carry this proclamation into immediate and faithful execution.

"Done at the City of Washington, the sixth day of February, in the year one thousand eight hundred and fifteen, and of the independence of the United States the thirty-ninth."

So endeth the tale of the Baratarians. Their occupation gone, many settled into the life of honest citizens. Beluche went to South America and rose to high command with one of the new republics. You remained in New Orleans, where he died in such poverty that he was buried at public expense, but a fine monument reciting his patriotic services was raised over his tomb. Pierre Lafitte vanished from view after a residence in New Orleans where he and St. Gene, one of his lieutenants, acted as seconds in a duel between two leading citizens, indicating that both had established a social position.

Jean Lafitte heard the call of the old trade and with former Baratarians and new recruits set up a smuggling settlement on that sand bar where now rises the city of Galveston, Texas, in 1816. This grew and flourished on the same lines as that of Barataria. Mexico being in revolt against Spain, Texas was a sort of no-man's land, though beginning to receive settlers from the States and Galveston Island while more remote from New Orleans than Barataria, was still within reach of Lafitte's old customers in Louisiana and smuggling continued. He assumed the title of "governor" of Galveston Island,

OF JEAN LAFITTE

under a commission from General James Long, a Texan filibuster. Five vessels were kept at sea privateering and smuggling, carrying in all crews amounting to three hundred men.

These ventured so frequently beyond lawful bounds that the United States Government sent the armed schooner *Lynx*, under Lt. J. P. Madison to look into their operations. He captured two schooners and two open barges in the Sabine River on October 24, 1819, and one other small craft on November 5th. The two open boats, whose commander, one Brown, carried a commission from General Humbert, at Galveston, were charged with having plundered a plantation on the Marmento River, carrying away money and slaves. While Madison captured the boats the crews, led by Brown, escaped. Galveston being in a way blockaded by the *Lynx*, Lafitte sent Lt. Madison this message:

"I am convinced that you are a cruiser of the navy, ordered by your government. I have therefore deemed it proper to inquire into the cause of your lying before this port without communicating, your intention. I shall by this message inform you, that the port of Galveston belongs to and is in the possession of the republic of Texas, and was made a port of entry the 9th of October last. And whereas the supreme congress of said republic have thought proper to appoint me as governor of this place, in consequence of which, if you have any demands on said government, or persons belonging to or residing in the same, you will please to send an officer with such demands, whom you may be assured will be treated with the greatest politeness, and receive every satisfaction required. But if you are ordered, or should attempt to enter this port in a hostile manner, my oath and duty to the government compels me to rebut your intentions at the expense of my life.

"To prove to you my intentions towards the welfare and harmony of your government, I send inclosed the declaration of several prisoners, who were taken in custody yesterday, and by a court of inquiry appointed for that purpose, were found guilty of robbing the inhabitants of the United States of a number of slaves and specie. The gentlemen bearing this message will give you any reasonable information relating to this place, that may be required."

One of the results of this trial was the hanging of Brown by Lafitte. This act of justice did not, however, placate our government or purify the settlement. Soon after the revenue cutter *Alabama* captured a smuggling schooner of two guns and thirty men, commanded by one Lefage, a lieutenant of Lafitte's. The schooner resisted to the best of her ability. She was sent to Bayou St. John, where such of the crew as permitted themselves to be taken were tried and executed. Simultaneously with this ill-fortune a great Gulf gale swept Galveston and numbers of Lafitte's vessels were lost. One was wrecked on the Louisiana coast. This disaster and the warnings of our government impelled Lafitte to leave his rendezvous. Accordingly he sailed to the Island of Mugeres, off Yucatan, in a well-armed brig, the *Pride*, sixteen guns, 110 men.

At Mugeres he raised defenses and established a town. The brig, while cruising in the Yucatan Channel, fell in with a British warship and was destroyed. This was in 1821. The story spread that Lafitte perished in the fighting, but this is not substantiated. To the contrary, John L. Stephens, the explorer of Chiapas and Yucatan, and builder of the Panama Railroad, records in his "Incidents of Travel in Yucatan," published in 1843, that he visited the island in 1842, and there met a tall, thin man, about fifty-five years old, who had been one of Lafitte's captives. "We remarked," says Stephens, "that he was not fond of talking of his captivity; he said he did not know how long he was a prisoner nor where he was taken; and as the business of piracy was rather complicated in these parts, we conceived a suspicion that he had not been a prisoner entirely against his will. . . . He could not, however, help dropping a few words on behalf of Lafitte. . . . He did not know whether it was true what people said of him, but he never hurt the poor fishermen, and, led on by degrees he told us that Lafitte died in his arms, and that his widow, a Señora del Norte from Mobile, was then living in great distress at Silan, the port at which we intended to debark."

Once at Silan, Stephens could not find the unfortunate Señora del Norte, but did locate a negress who had been her servant, who, however, was so overloaded with mescal that she could not be seen. The prisoner of Mugeres had said that Lafitte died in Salin (in 1826, according to the best report) and was buried there. "The padre," whom Stephens consulted, "was not in the village at the time [of Lafitte's death] and did not know whether he was buried in the Campo Santo or the church, but supposed that, as Lafitte was a distinguished man, it was in the latter. We went thither and examined the graves in the floor and the padre threw out from some rubbish a cross, with a name on it, which he supposed to be that of Lafitte, but it was not. The sexton who officiated at the burial was dead; the padre sent for several inhabitants, but a cloud hung over the memory of the pirate; all knew of his death and burial, but none knew or cared to tell where he was laid."

Much romance has sprung up around Lafitte's memory and he seems destined to survive therein as "The Pirate of the Gulf."

XXXVIII

THE CUBAN PIRATES

A FTER almost a century of freedom from more than sporadic
ventures at lawlessness on the sea, another development occurred,
this time under the sheltering arms of Spain. Following the
indiscriminate pillagings of the "privateers" of the South American
republics and the liberation of those states, Cuba remained the only
considerable possession of all that Columbus had given Castile and
Leon in the Western world. The commerce of the island, as well as
that of the parent country, had suffered much from these aggressions,
and the islanders now began to retaliate. The islets southwest of
Santiago de Cuba and the commodious bay of Rio Medias afforded
concealment and harbors for the piratical vessels which soon became
numerous and active, American and English shipping being the principal sufferers.

Stirred by the growing boldness of the pirates, the United States
Government sent the *Hornet,* eighteen guns, Master-Commandant
Robert Henley; the *Enterprise,* now altered to a brig, twelve guns,
Lieutenant Lawrence Kearney; the *Porpoise,* twelve guns, Lieutenant
James Ramage; the *Grampus,* twelve guns, Lieutenant Francis H.
Gregory; the *Spark,* twelve guns, Master-Commandant J. H. Elton
and the *Shark,* twelve guns, Lieutenant M. C. Perry, to safeguard the
trade routes and hunt down the marauders. This proved to be a
difficult task, for the pirates were tacitly protected by the Cuban
authorities and their spoil was openly sold in Havana, while some of
the venturers operated directly from that port.

The industry in Cuba was not confined to vessels able to take to
the sea. There were frequent cases of offshore robberies, where the
pirates assailed becalmed vessels from open boats. One instance was
that of the schooner *Swan,* Captain Carter, from Havana to Mobile,
which was stopped near the Cuban coast, thirty miles from Havana, by
nine men in a longboat, armed with muskets, pistols, and cutlasses,
who overpowered the crew, stripped them of their clothes, shoes, and

[284]

valuables and even robbed a Spanish priest who was a passenger of $800 in cash which he possessed. The schooner was then released and ordered to steer east by northeast, keeping within three leagues of shore, it being their intent to return in the dark and take her. The captain had the courage to disregard threats and keep on to Mobile.

The Boston brig *Cobbossocontee*, Captain Jackson, was assailed four miles off Moro Castle, Havana, on October 8, 1821. The mate was beaten and strung up by the neck as a method of extorting money. The compass was broken, rigging cut, and considerable plunder removed, beside the captain's watch. In the effort to force knowledge of concealed specie from him, the captain was slashed with a knife and nearly bled to death from the wound. He had seen the pirate's sloop lying at Reglia in Havana harbor the day before he sailed.

During the same period the New Brunswick brig *Three Partners*, from Jamaica for St. John, was robbed by a Spanish pirate off Cape Antonio, her captain being strung up to the Yard-arm and so tortured until nearly dead. The brig *Sea Lion*, from Cape Hatyien to Belfast, Ireland, was another victim, while the *Harriet*, Captain Dimond, from St. Jago to Baltimore, with sugar, lost her cargo and three thousand dollars in coin off Cape Antonio, on October 12th. Two schooners were engaged in this enterprise and Captain Dimond was strung up by the neck until senseless. The Dutch brig *Mercury* was also relieved of $10,000 in goods by the thieves at Cape Antonio, reporting her loss at Havana on October 16.

The ship *Liverpool Packet*, of Portsmouth, N. H., Captain Ricker, was another victim. She was boarded off Cape Antonio by the crews of two barges, coming from as many schooners. They carried off everything movable, including a ship's boat that chanced to be in the water, taking along a boy who happened to be in it at the time. Captain Ricker was beaten black and blue and his mate strung up to the crosstrees until insensible. The day before the pirates had burned a brig and murdered all her men. Those on the *Liverpool Packet* were threatened but not harmed, the spite being wreaked on her officers.

On October 13th, the schooner *Combine*, a Catskill-on-Hudson, New York, Jacob Dunham, master, was working past Cape Antonio *en route* for Jerimie, when three small schooners, a sloop, and an open barge were noted at anchor about two miles off shore. What followed is best told in Captain Dunham's own words in his "Journal of Voyages," published some years after the event:

"In about the space of fifteen minutes the whole fleet got under weigh and bore down for us. One of the largest schooners ran down within musket-shot of us, fired a gun, and we have too, while the rest of the fleet surrounded us. The largest schooner immediately sent a boat alongside of us, containing eight or nine men, who boarded us with muskets and drawn cutlasses in their hands, each of them having a long knife and a dagger slung by his side. Immediately after getting on deck, one of them cried out, 'Forward,' two or three times in broken English, pointing at the same time toward the fore-castle. The mate, sailors, and two passengers who were on board, ran forward and jumped into the fore-castle. I being very weak, dragged along slowly, when the man who gave the order commenced beating me severely with the broad side of his cutlass. I remonstrated with him, saying I was sick and could not walk any faster; he answered me, 'No intende.' I then discovered he was a Portuguese, and not understanding that language, I excused myself as well as I could in the French language, hoping he understood me; but I found it did not relieve my back, as he continued to beat me all the way to the fore-scuttle, and there giving me a heavy blow on the head as I descended, closed it, where we remained about half an hour; they in the meantime appeared to be searching the vessel. After letting us up from the fore-castle they ordered the sailors to work the vessel in near the land and anchor her, which was soon accomplished. While beating the vessel toward the shore, they told me if I would give up my money they would let me go with my vessel. This I readily complied with, hoping to save the vessel and cargo. I then gave them all the money I had, consisting of four hundred and eighty dollars in gold and silver. After they had received it they broke open our trunks, seized all our clothes, taking the finest shirts and vests, and putting them on one over another.

"As soon as they had anchored my vessel they hauled their largest schooner alongside, while the rest of the fleet were lying within a few rods of us, and then all hoisted the bloody flag, a signal for death. I was ordered into the cabin, where one of the pirates, having found a bottle of cordial, took it up in one hand, and drawing his cutlass with the other, struck off the neck and handed it to me, flourishing his cutlass over my head, and making signs for me to taste it, which I found it difficult to do on account of the broken particles of glass. After I had tasted it he went to a case of liquor standing in the cabin, took out the bottles and compelled me to taste of them. After this ceremony was over one of the pirates drew a long knife from its sheath, and taking hold of the hair on the top of my head, drew the knife two or three times across my throat near the skin, saying, 'Me want to kill you.' Another pirate soon approached me with a dagger, with which he pricked me lightly in the body, two or three times, saying, 'Me kill you by and by.' I was then dismissed from the cabin and driven into the fore-castle with sailors and passengers. My cook was put on board the schooner lying alongside of us. Some of the pirates went aloft on board my vessel and cut loose her square-sail, top-sail, and top-gallant-sail, and afterwards took our fore-sail, boat, oars, loose rigging, one compass, one quadrant, all our beds and bedding, tea-kettle, all our crockery, knives and forks, buckets, &c. leaving us destitute of every kind of cooking utensil except the caboose. We remained some time in the fore-castle, when suddenly the fore-scuttle was opened and the mate called on deck, and the scuttle again closed, leaving us in the dark in a state of uncertainty. We soon heard them beating the mate; after that noise had ceased, we heard the word, 'Fire,' given with a loud voice, then after a moment's pause another voice was heard, saying, 'Heave him overboard.' I had a desperate sailor, called Bill, who flew to his chest for his razor to cut his own throat, saying he would be damned before he would be murdered by them rascals. The pirates had previously robbed the sailors' chests of all the articles they contained, and among them Bill's razor. After a little while the scuttle was again opened, when they called for a sailor. There were four in the fore-castle, who looked earnestly at each other, when Brown, a favourite old sailor, arose and addressed me, saying, 'Captain, I suppose I might as well die first as last,' then taking me by the hand gave it a hearty shake, saying, 'Good bye.' I told Brown to plead with them in the French language, as I thought I had seen some Frenchmen among them, and knew that he spoke French fluently. When he had got upon deck I heard him speak a few words in that language, but soon after we heard them beating him severely. As soon as they had finished beating him we again heard the word fire, and soon after, heave him overboard. Shortly after, the scuttle was again opened and the captain was loudly called. I crawled up the scuttle, being very feeble; they then told me if I did not tell them where the money was they would serve me as they had the mate and sailor, shoot and then throw me overboard. I still persisted that there was no money on board, and entreated them to search the vessel. An old Spaniard was pointed out

[287]

to me who they said was the commodore. I asked him what he wanted of me, looking him earnestly in the face. He replied, he wanted my money. I told him I had no money, but if I had I would give it to him; that the property belonged to him, but he had no right to take my life, as I had a family depending on me for support. Previous to this, the man who had flogged me before had made a chalk ring on the deck, saying, 'Stand there,' beating me with the flat side of a heavy cutlass until the blood ran through my shirt. During my conversation with the commodore, finding all my entreaties unsuccessful, and my strength much exhausted, I took a firm stand in the ring marked out for me, hoping to receive a ball through the heart, fearing if I was wounded I should be tortured to death, to make sport for the demons. Two of the pirates with loaded muskets took their stand and fired them toward me, when I cast my eyes down toward my feet looking for blood, thinking that I might have been wounded without feeling the pain. During this time the man who had beat me before commenced beating me again, pointing aft toward the cabin door, where I proceeded, followed by him, beating me all the time: he forced me into the cabin, at the same time giving me a severe blow over the head with his cutlass. When I entered I found both the mate and sailor there whom I supposed had been murdered and thrown overboard. The next person called out of the fore-castle was Mr. Peck, a passenger, who was immediately asked where the money was; he told them he knew of no more money on board. One man stood before him with a musket and another with a cutlass, they knocked him down and beat him for some time, took him by the hair and said they would kill him. He was then ordered to set upon the bit of the windlass to be shot and thrown overboard, as the captain and others had been. He took his station by the windlass, when a musket was fired at him; he was then driven into the cabin. They then called up the remainder of the men from the fore-castle, one after the other, and beat and drove them into the cabin also, except a Mr. Chollet, a young man, passenger, who escaped beating. We were kept in the cabin some time, and after repeated threats that they would kill us, were all driven into the fore-castle again. They took all our cargo, consisting of coffee, cocoa, tortoise-shell, eight kedge anchors, all our provisions, except part of a barrel of beef and about thirty pounds of bread. After they had taken all the cargo, spare rigging, &c. of any value, they shifted all the ballast in the hold of the vessel in search of money, and calling us on

deck, we were told to be off. After getting under weigh we proceeded
but slowly, having no other sails left but the two jibs and the mainsail. We looked back with a great deal of anxiety, and saw the pirates
seated on the deck of the largest schooner, drinking liquor and making
themselves merry, while we feared that they might change their minds,
pursue us and take our lives. Night beginning to approach, I thought
best to go down into the cabin and see what we had left to eat or drink.
As soon as I had reached the cabin, it being dark, I stumbled against
something on the floor, which I found to be our cook, whom we supposed we had left behind, having seen the pirates put him on board
the schooner which was lying alongside of us, but knew nothing of his
return. I spoke to him, but received no answer, I hustled him about
the cabin, but could not make him speak. I at last got a light and
looked about for some provisions, cooking utensils, &c. and found
about thirty pounds of bread, a little broken coffee, and most of a
barrel of beef, but no cooking utensils except the caboose, with one
or two pots set in it. The next morning I called all hands into the
cabin, showed all the bread we had left, and told them it was necessary
to go on allowance of one biscuit a day per man, which was agreed
to, until we could get further supplies. I then questioned the cook,
(knowing that he was driven into the hold of the pirate schooner,) as
to what kind of a cargo she had. He said there were calicoes and all
kinds of dry goods scattered about, and more than a hundred demi-
johns; and 'O captain, it was the best old Jamaica rum that you ever
tasted.' I told him if the pirates had caught him drinking their rum
they would have killed him. He said it looked so tempting he
thought he would try it. I suppose that after having drank a large
quantity he made his escape on board of the *Combine* before he felt
the effects of it, as he was not aware of our release."

The day after being released, Dunham hailed a Spanish war vessel,
requesting her commander to pursue the pirates. This she refused to
do on the ground that they were outside his cruising limits. He also
declined to give the *Combine* any food. Dunham soon reached Havana,
and there found friends and relief.

Retribution was, however, very near. On the 15th of October, the
British brig *Aristides*, Captain Couthony, was halted off Cape Antonio
in the early evening by the same vessels that had robbed Dunham.
Nine men came on board from the open boat, knocked the captain
down and, taking the helm, headed the brig for the shore. Perceiving

their purpose to ground the ship, Couthony remonstrated and was again felled to the deck, but permitted the crew to lower an anchor when in shoal water. All personal articles of value were taken and notice given that all hands could prepare for death, as their captors were pirates and intended to leave no living witnesses. During the night the vessel pounded heavily on the shoal and the pirates compelled the raising of the anchor, at which the brig drifted ashore, and, the light vessels coming alongside, removal of the cargo began. The captain and mate were repeatedly beaten to compel the revelation of hidden coin and the cabin boy nearly strangled for the same purpose.

By sunrise one schooner was well laden with spoil and the plundering was proceeding rapidly when at seven o'clock a sail appeared in the offing, whose rig plainly showed her to be a warship. The cutthroats debated killing their captives, but, having little time, concluded to flee without slaying them, and made haste to get away. The cruiser proved to be the *Enterprise*, under Lieutenant Lawrence Kearney, who at once sent a boat in and Couthony told his story. The American ship *Lucier* and the British brig *Larch* were also being held and, recruiting from their crews, Kearney made sail after the pirates, who worked their vessels inside the cape, ran them all ashore, and took to the woods. A boat party under Lieutenant McIntosh captured the vessels, but the barge got away. One of the five was set on fire by the fugitives and destroyed. The others were hauled off and became prizes. Kearney loaded all the vessels with spoils. The *Aristides* was badly bilged and so was set on fire and abandoned. One of the pirate captains thus discomfitted was Charles Gibbs, of whom more will be heard later.

The *Hornet*, cruising among the West India Islands, took a schooner called the *Moscow*, on October 29th, and sent her into Norfolk as a prize, and the *Porpoise* seized a boat laden with plunder off Cape Antonio, on November 8th. The crew escaped.

Though zealous, the United States force was too small to accomplish much and the territory covered was too wide and too full of retreats and protection to make its task easy. So the freebooters continued to prosper. A piracy of peculiar picturesqueness was that committed upon the schooner *Experiment*, Boston for Trinidad, Barnabas Lincoln, master, December 15, 1821. The *Experiment* was of 107 tons burden, the property of Messrs. Joseph Ballister and Henry Farnam, of Boston, which port she had left on the 13th of November, with a cargo valued at $8,000, consisting mainly of provisions. Her crew, beside the captain, included Joshua Bracket, mate, of Bristol, Rhode Island; David Warren, cook, of Saco, Maine, and four seamen, Thomas Goodall, George Reed, Thomas Young, and Francis de Suze.

The *Experiment*, had reached the keys off Cape Cruz on the date noted, which chanced to be Monday, when at three o'clock in the afternoon a schooner was sighted coming out from the keys into a channel, charted as the Boca de Cavalone. The wind being light, she worked toward the *Experiment* with sweeps, flying the flag of the revolting Republic of Mexico and was soon near enough to reveal the presence on her decks of some forty armed men. She hailed and ordered Lincoln to come on board with his papers. He lowered his boat for the purpose, but she filled before the captain could get into her. The *Experiment* was then ordered to lay by until a boat could come aboard. Soon a lieutenant called Bolidar, with a gang of heavily armed ruffians, reached the schooner and drove Lincoln into it, when two rowed him to the *Mexican,* which was the name of the vessel. The rest kept possession of the *Experiment*. The captain whom Lincoln names "Jonnia" instructed Bolidar to follow the *Mexican* into an anchorage at Key Largo, a shelter some thirty or thirty-five leagues from Trinidad. By six A. M. she was anchored in eleven feet of water under the guns of the pirate, which she soon proved herself to be.

Early the next morning the pirate captain visited the *Experiment* and made a survey of her cargo and fittings, after which the pillaging began again. Such spirits as were on board, together with some bottled cider, gave the material for a general carouse. The third day the pirate moved his anchorage to Brigantine Key, but the robbing of the schooner continued. The navigator and interpreter was a Scotchman named Jamison, called Nichola by his comrades, who explained that he had joined the company as a legitimate privateer and had no heart for her piratical proceedings. It seems the ship he had come to in the first place was properly commissioned, but was soon exchanged for a more commodious prize, the *Mexican.* The captain had also been deposed when piracy became the open occupation, to give way to the present incumbent. Each day the cargo of the *Experiment* yielded up its stores until all were exhausted. Then the chests and trunks were rifled, all the clothing being taken.

On New Year's Day, 1822, Lincoln with his crew and four prisoners captured from a Spanish brig were marooned on a desolate key where there was no water, or any means of sustenance. They had only a meager supply of food and two or three kegs of brackish fluid, an old sail and a cooking pot. This was a mile or so from the *Experiment*, which lay in sight. The supplies were renewed from day to day, until January 5th, when two more captives were added to the party. In this wise matters went until the 19th, when all of the *Experiment's* people were taken to her and hope rose that she was to be restored. Instead, they were borne to a desolate key two miles distant, eleven prisoners in all, and once more marooned, with even less to sustain them than before. The next day the pirate sailed and was never seen again. On the 20th, David Warren, the Saco cook, died suddenly and was buried in the sand. The survivors had found a few old planks and nails and managed with great patience to construct a boat in which, though frail and leaky, Bracket and four others departed in search of aid. They never returned, though rescued, for the boat came drifting by empty and added to the despair of the company, who could only believe their companions lost.

On the 6th of February, just as water and food were about exhausted, they were rescued by Jamison, who had left the pirate and whose first thought was their succor. He came in a sloop and landed from a boat with two Frenchmen. With him on his vessel was Thomas Young, one of Lincoln's men who had been imprisoned but escaped with Jamison. The sloop belonged in Jamaica and had been captured by the Mexicans a few days before. Jamison and some others took advantage of being made a prize crew to elope. They were now taken off and at Lincoln's desire visited the *Experiment*. She was found useless, masts and rigging having been cut away, and so was abandoned. The friendly Jamison sailed with the party for Trinidad. Five miles off the harbor they were overhauled by another republican privateer, the brig *Prudence*, of eighteen guns. Jamison and his men were held as possible recruits, but Lincoln and his crew were landed at Trinidad, whence they were taken to Boston by Captain Matthew Rice, of the schooner *Galaxy*, having had a rare enough adventure.

Recurring to the naval operations: On December 21, 1821, the *Enterprise* took a thirty-five-ton schooner off Cape Antonio, but her crew evaded capture. On January 7, 1822, the *Porpoise* rounded up six small sailing vessels off Cuba, but succeeded in taking but three members of their crews. On the same day the *Spark* took, near St. Thomas, a sloop armed with two guns, and carrying "a crew of twenty gallows-looking scoundrels," and sent her to Charleston as a prize. On January 16, 1822, the brig *Dover*, Captain Sabine, bound from Matanzas to Charleston, was stopped by an armed boat off the peak called the Pan. The crew were beaten and robbed of all valuables. A small drogher, putting out from Matanzas, was then brought near and the *Dover's* crew compelled to shift the plunder, which included some of the cargo, spare rigging, stores, etc. They were then ordered to stand to the north, only to be overhauled later by another boat, which released them on the evident assurance that they had already been despoiled. January 24th the Boston schooner *Jane* was taken by a schooner, and carried into a port where there were three other pirate craft and plundered. She was then allowed to depart.

The Government had now sent more vessels into tropic waters, including the frigates *Macedonian* and *Congress*, the corvette, *John Adams*, the sloop of war *Peacock*, the twelve-gun schooner *Alligator* and the *Revenge*, gunboat. Captain James Biddle acted as commodore for the fleet. On the 18th of March, Lieutenant G. W. Hammersly in the *Revenge* destroyed an open barge whose crew escaped. The *Enterprise* destroyed on March 8th four barges and three launches off Cape Antonio, their crews escaping. On April 30th, the *Alligator* caught the Colombian privateer *Cienaqa* among the Windwards. Her officers had been overpowered by the crew and their intent was obvious. She was sent to the States with her thirty-five mutineers. On the 1st of May, Lieutenant R. F. Stockton, in the chartered schooner *Jane*, with a crew of sixty men picked from the *Alligator* and the *Grampus*, cleaned out a nest at Sugar Key. Two schooners were boarded and burned by Acting Sailoring-Master Barney; a third was chased ashore, her crew escaping and a fourth was taken filled with plunder from the British brig *Cherub*, which also recaptured and released. In June the *Sharp* and *Grampus* captured the pirate schooner *Bandana d' Sangaree* and another schooner not named in the record. Only three men were taken. The vessels were sent to the United States as prizes.

One of the rare adventures to be recorded at this period was that of Aaron Smith, first mate of the merchant brig *Zephyr*, Lumsden, master, from Kingston, Jamaica, for London. The brig sailed from Kingston on the 29th of June, 1822, having beside a cargo of sugar and coffee, Captain Cowper and his children as passengers. Lumsden was an obstinate and rather ignorant man with whom his mate was soon on ill terms. In deciding upon the homeward course, Smith advised taking the Windward passage in the interest of safety, as that of the Leeward was known to be infested by the Cuban rovers. Lumsden disregarded this suggestion, with the result that the brig was headed for Grand Cayman as the first leg of the voyage. As she was a heavy sailor, it was the fifth day before they were off Cape Antonio on the southwest point of Cuba, rounding which, with a fair breeze, they noted about two o'clock in the afternoon a sail standing out from the land, which by her actions at once aroused suspicion. Smith urged Lumsden to alter the *Zephyr's* course, the brig being then about six leagues from Cape Roman. The master declined to believe that anything could happen to a ship under the English flag and obstinately refused to be guided by what soon proved to have been superior wisdom.

In half an hour the sail, which developed into a sharp-nosed schooner of rakish rig, came near and her deck was seen to be full of men. Drawing close to the brig she began to hoist out her boats, at which hostile manifestation Lumsden ordered the course altered two points. It was then too late. The schooner was now in gunshot and hailed the *Zephyr* in English with an order to lower the boat astern and send the captain on board. Lumsden, pretending not to understand, did not respond and the pirate, for such she was, treated him to a round of musket fire. The frightened captain then laid the sails aback and was almost immediately boarded by a boatload of heavily armed ruffians who took over the brig and sent Lumsden, Captain Cowper, and Smith, to the schooner. They were hastened in departing by cutlass blows and much Spanish profanity. Once on board the schooner, they were confronted by the captain, a thick-set, swarthy villain, who was a half-breed Yucatanian.

He could speak some English and in this broken tongue wished to know the identity of two other vessels with which the *Zephyr* had been in company. He was told they were French and ordered a pursuit. He then asked for and was given an account of the brig's cargo. The captain demanded dollars and Lumsden, denying the presence of any specie, was threatened with the destruction of his ship if any were found concealed. They were then regaled with a supper, consisting of garlic and onions chopped fine and mixed with bread in a bowl from which the officers and prisoners all partook, using fingers for table utensils. Both vessels had now proceeded inshore and were set at anchor. The pillaging of the *Zephyr* began at once. The three were

[294]

THE CUBAN PIRATES

taken to the brig and measures used to extract any hidden money. Captain Cowper and Lumsden were told that they must produce the cash or the vessel would be burned and they with it. Persisting in denial both were chained to the pumps and a ring of combustibles laid around each. Lumsden then revealed the hiding place of a small box of doubloons. Cowper gave up nine, which he said were the property of a poor woman who might even then be starving. "Do not speak to me of poor people," screamed the captain. "I am poor and your countrymen and the Americans have made me so. I know there is more money and I will have it or burn you and the vessel."

The fire was now started but the victims, feeling it scorch, could only implore that fiend to put them in a boat and keep the *Zephyr*, where if there was any money he would find it. At this the flames were extinguished and the two put in the roundhouse, while Smith and Cowper's children, who were on the schooner, were returned to the brig where the pirates exulting in their spoil left him alone for the moment. The pillaging completed, the pirates ordered Smith to go to the schooner and on his refusal forced him with knives at his throat. He went, but was soon taken back. The son of the brig's owner, who was along studying navigation, now said his quadrant had been taken and he wanted it back. His request was refused and the motive for retaining Smith appeared. He was asked if he had all the instruments he needed for purpose of navigating; if not, to get them or they would kill him. Smith said he had enough.

The *Zephyr* was then cast off and allowed to depart, her boats being first cut loose and set adrift. The schooner then proceeded to the harbor of Rio Medias, which was entered at nine the next morning. The people in the village on shore gave the schooner a rousing welcome, in which their priest took a share. Smith was regarded as one of the company, though kept in mild surveillance, and treated sociably by the people. After a few days of feasting the schooner again put to sea. The cruise was unproductive and on her return it was learned that Lumsden and the *Zephyr* had reached Havana, with their tale of robbery and torture. The captain was enraged at them and renewed his brutality at Smith, which had been pronounced during the trip. He sent a man to the Cuban capital with orders to find and kill Lumsden while the schooner resumed her search for plunder.

A Dutch ship was taken, the tactics used on the *Zephyr* being repeated to extort concealed cash. The ship was run ashore, her cargo

[295]

of gin and merchandise confiscated, and her crew impressed. The *Industry*, English brig, Captain Cooke, rum-laden, was next taken. Smith knew the skipper and, by claiming him as a cousin, persuaded the pirate chief to let him off lightly. While she was being held the *Victoria*, Captain Hearin, another English vessel, came into sight and was pursued and taken. The *Industry* was allowed to go, after being stripped of her cargo, the clothes even being taken from the crew, and Captain Hearin and his men went with her. The *Victoria* was worked into port. She had a cargo of coffee and was a valuable prize. Two Havana lighters came the next day and carried it off to market. The complaints at Havana of their operations had now become loud and word came that a party of police were *en route* to investigate. The Dutch ship was accordingly burned and her crew liberated on shore, following a hint from Havana, while the pirate kept the offing.

The police in the meantime arrived and searched the village, but the schooner coming into port and firing her guns, all ran away. The *Victoria* was beached. Continuing to cruise, the schooner took an American. The captain quickly giving up his cash, she was robbed tenderly and released, and the crew of a French ship, also a victim, was taken on. An American schooner was next on the list, the usual formula being followed.

Putting in again with a great store of spoil at Rio Medias, the corsairs heard that one hundred soldiers were being sent from Havana to do the work abandoned by the cowardly police, at which they took to the sea, cruising off Cape Antonio awaiting events. The local magistrate at Rio Medias thoughtfully burned the *Victoria;* the plunder, had of course been carefully removed. The pirate lounged off Cape Antonio until his agent had posted him on an expected move by the authorities which consisted in a few armed boats pulling out towards his anchorage. They were slow and, the wind rising, were easily evaded. The pirates then returned to Rio Medias, where the obliging magistrate reported the departure of the troops without any evidence.

A few weeks later Smith managed to get hold of a canoe, in which he succeeded in getting to Havana, where he went on board an American schooner, whose captain, one William, he knew. The latter welcomed him and promised to find him a berth. Foolishly going ashore, he was arrested as a "pirate." After being held for weeks in prison, with all the horrors that such confinement then meant in Cuba, he was delivered to Admiral Sir Charles Rowley of H. M. S. *Sybille*, on which ship he was confined in double irons, though sick and suffering from a wound. He was kept in this severe duress until the ship reached Deptford, where he was transferred by the *Aske*, tender to the guardship *Genoa*, at Sheerness, being very badly treated by Lieutenant Bennett, the officer in charge, on the way. After six days on the guardship, where he was decently regarded he was sent to London and after examinations before a magistrate, committed to Newgate for trial. This took place on December 19, 1823, on complaint of the owners of the *Industry* and *Victoria*. Twenty witnesses testified as to his character and his own graphic story stood him in good stead. He was acquitted and his little book detailing "The Atrocities of the Pirates," which he published in 1824, remains one of the most interesting of human documents.

On August 8, 1822, the U. S. S. *Grampus* captured the Spanish privateer brig *Palmyra*, of Porto Rico, better known as the *Panchita* and little better than a pirate, which had previously fired into the *Porpoise*. She resisted for four minutes, during which the fire of the *Grampus* killed one man, wounded six, and brought the brig to a sinking condition. Her leaks were stopped and she was held a prize. The *Peacock* on September 28th gathered in a fleet of five schooners in Honda Bay, one a capture which was restored to her owners. The crews of the other four escaped. Two were burned and two were sent to New Orleans as prizes. The *Peacock* put a landing party ashore and destroyed the settlement. One schooner at anchor was burned previous to the shore attack. Later the *Alligator* seized a suspicious Portuguese ship, the *Mariano Faliero*, and sent her to Boston.

Early in November, 1822, two captains of American vessels came to Matanzas seeking money to ransom their ships, which had been taken near key Romain and were being held in the Bay of Leguapo fifteen leagues east of the city. The *Alligator*, Lieutenant Commandant William Howard Allen, coming in at the moment (November 9th) and learning of the facts, without dropping anchor, proceeded at once in search of the freebooters. Arriving in the bay Allen found five vessels under restraint. The water being too shallow for the *Alligator* he headed a boat expedition against the *Sangarina*, an eighty-ton pirate schooner carrying a long eighteen-pounder and defended by many men, commanded by Domingo, a notorious cutthroat. The lieutenant went well ahead of the rest of his flotilla in a boat manned by twelve hands and accompanied by Captain Freeman of the marines. He succeeded in boarding the schooner, but fell pierced by two bullets, the wounds proving fatal in four hours. The pirates, with one exception, escaped by taking to their boats, and also worked two other schooners into safety by the use of sweeps. Lieutenant J. M. Dale succeeded in the command and captured three other schooners of forty, fifty and sixty tons respectively. The Americans lost three men killed, besides Lieutenant Allen and three wounded. Fourteen of the pirates were slain and several drowned in their efforts to escape. The five vessels rescued were all American, viz: ship *William and Henry* of New York; brig *Iris*, Boston; brig *Sarah Marœl*, New York; schooner *Sarah*, Boston; schooner *Mary Ann*, Salem. Captain Freeman took the captured schooners to Charleston. Ill fortune followed the *Alligator*, as she was lost on Carysford Reef, the night of November 20th, eleven days after beating the rovers.

Lieutenant Allen was greatly esteemed in the navy for his courage and character. When the British frigate *Leopard* fired into the *Chesapeake* off the Capes, June 22, 1807, James Barron, the captain of the *Chesapeake*, begged on the deck of his shattered ship that at least one gun be fired in defense. Allen, picking a live coal from the galley fire with his fingers, discharged a shot that hulled the *Leopard* just as the *Chesapeake's* flag came down. In the War of 1812, Lieutenant Allen won high fame in the desperate action, August 14, 1812, in St. George's Channel, off the Irish coast, between the *Argus* and the *Pelican*, taking command of the former when his superiors were shot down and, though beaten, winning the high respect of his opponents. His body was borne to Matanzas and there buried the next day, November 10th, with military honors, in which the Spanish soldiers of the garrison joined. Lieutenant Allen's parents came from Nantucket, with a considerable number of other whaling families, to Hudson, N. Y., where he was born, and to which town his remains were borne and interred by Act of Congress in 1833. His sister, Harriet, became the mother of William Allen Butler, named after his heroic uncle, famous both as an eminent New York lawyer, and as the author of "Nothing to Wear."

The death of Lieutenant Allen aroused deep feeling in the United States. Widespread comment followed in the press and the public pulse was further stirred by a poem written by Fitz Greene Halleck in his memory which was printed in the *Evening Post* December 4, 1822. The situation was brought home with emphasis to Congress, where an act was passed authorizing the creation of an additional force for the suppression of piracy in the West Indies, which became a law on December 20, 1822. Under the terms of this enactment $160,000 was appropriated for the purchase and construction of the needful vessels and to provide proper equipment. Commodore David Porter, the famous captain of the *Essex* in the War of 1812, took an active hand in the preparation of the squadron.

President Monroe's signature was scarcely dry on the document before Porter had matters under way. On December 21st he advised the Navy Deparment from Baltimore that he had purchased eight light schooners, viz: *Ferret; Weazle, Terrier, Wild Cat, Greyhound, Beagle, Fox* and *Jackall* all of about 50 tons, paying therefor $10,190, or about $1,273 each. All were in good repair and were forwarded within the week to Norfolk for equipment. Porter next purchased in Philadelphia a small steam galley, the *Sea Gull*, for $16,500, which thus became the first vessel to go forth on a warlike errand under mechanical power, though not the first so designed, for Robert Fulton had launched in 1815 his *Demologus*, which was moved five miles an hour with the tide. He died before she was put to trial and Porter, fresh from the Pacific, took charge of the novel craft. Peace coming, her mechanical imperfections were never remedied, and she became receiving ship at the Brooklyn yard, remaining there until destroyed by an explosion in 1829.

On February 23, 1823, Porter, from Hampton Roads, notified Secretary of the Navy Smith Thompson that he was about to sail. His fleet was made up and officered as follows: *Peacock*, Master-Commandant, Stephen Cassin; *Shark*, Lieutenant-Commandant, Matthew C. Perry; *Greyhound*, Master-Commandant, John Porter; *Jackall*, Lieutenant-Commandant, Thomas H. Stephens; steamer *Sea Gull*, Lieutenant-Commandant, William H. Watson; *Fox*, Lieutenant-Commandant, William H. Cooke; *Wild Cat*, Lieutenant-Commandant, Charles W. Skinner; *Beagle*, Lieutenant-Commandant, John T. Newton; *Ferret*, Lieutenant-Commandant, Samuel Henley; *Terrier*, Lieutenant-Commandant Robert M. Rose; *Weazle*, Lieutenant-Commandant, Beverley Kennon; supply ship *Decoy*, Lieutenant-Commandant, Lawrence Kearney. These were supplemented by five barges of twenty oars each, appropriately named *Mosquito, Gnat, Midge, Sandfly* and *Gallinipper* and which were ordered direct to Thompson's Island, the Key West of our day, which had been selected as a rendezvous. The vessels already in the West Indies were also placed under Porter's command.

The fleet reached St. Thomas in the Virgin Islands on March 3d, with the exception of the *Greyhound*, which had been separated in a gale. From this point Porter dispatched Lieutenant M. C. Perry, with the *Shark* and three of the small schooners to scour the south side of Porto Rico, while the Commodore forwarded a letter to the Spanish governor, announcing the purpose of his coming and requesting co-operation. Getting no response he sent the *Fox*, Lieutenant W. H. Cocke commanding, to San Juan to secure a reply from the Governor. As she entered the harbor, a shot was fired over her from the fort, and as she did not halt at once another struck the vessel, killing her commander. Four more rounds were fired as she rounded to. Porter protested, but was informed that the Governor was absent and had left strict orders that no suspicious vessel should be allowed to enter, hence the attack. The assault was duly laid before the American Government, but no action followed. In the fleet it bred the belief that it was a wanton revenge for the taking of the *Palmyra* and led to lasting ill-feeling against Porto Rico that was to have a further echo.

On March 28th, Porter reached Matanzas, after "giving the north coast of St. Domingo and Cuba as thorough an examination as practicable" without having "in this long route been able to detect a single pirate," despite which "since my arrival here I have heard of the most horrible atrocities committed by them. They spare no one; whole ship's crews are burnt with their vessels and there has been an instance recently of the murder of a crew under the wall of the Morro." He was also "surprised and mortified" to find the United States warships had left the coast, while many American vessels lay in the harbor, not daring to depart without a convoy. He also learned that the Spanish captain-general had sent out a circular to the local authorities forbidding the entrance of any of his ships into harbors, or the landing of any men in pursuit of pirates.

After taking all possible steps to ensure the safety of commerce, the commodore proceeded to Thompson's Island, on reaching which point early in April he at once began vigorous operations. Shore works were set up and shelters erected, the small town thus created being named "Allenton" after the lamented Lieutenant whom he had come to avenge. The Spanish authorities at Havana were advised of his coming and of his purpose. They affected a welcome, though the piratical operations were carried on openly before their eyes and the mercantile backers of the thieves were perfectly well known. Bribes

THE CUBAN PIRATES

had stilled the official conscience, but no open opposition was made to Porter's program.

During the period of his preparations the British had been somewhat active under Sir Thomas Cochrane and Sir Edward W. C. R. Owen, making some notable captures and executing ten pirates at Port Royal on February 7, 1823. Early in March following, the British cutter *Grecian* encountered a famous pirate, La Cata, off the Isle of Pines, having a crew of 100 men and eight guns. The *Grecian* had but fifty in her crew. She killed thirty of forty of the pirates, all but three of the rest reaching shore. The prisoners were taken to Jamaica, where in the curt comment of the day there was "more law to reach cases of piracy than in these United States."

Porter at once established an entente with the English commanders, by which they co-operated with a code of signals in common and this relationship continued throughout the operations. His task was very difficult, as the coast line of Cuba alone covered nearly two thousand miles, while the Yucatan shore was also infested. The south side of Cuba, near Trinidad, was a center of piratical activity. An early complaint from there, written January 25th, by Robert R. Stewart, reported numerous seizures of American vessels, the earliest being that on January 20, 1823, of the brig *Mechanic* of New York, whose captain, second mate, and carpenter were being held as hostages for the ransom of the ship at $3,000. Twelve men waylaid her in an open boat. Shipping masters then in port at Trinidad sent the commodore an earnest appeal for protection, which he had anticipated by sending two schooners and two barges to patrol that neighborhood. No word remains of the fate of the hostages.

Having learned at Matanzas that the American schooner *Pilot*, of Norfolk, had been taken by pirates led by Domingo, who had commanded the schooner *Sangarina*, in the cutting out of which Lieutenant Allen fell, steps were taken for her recapture. Two barges were fitted out, the *Gallinipper*, under Lieutenant A. K. Stribbling and the *Mosquito*, Midshipman J. Kelley acting as Lieutenant, and these, escorted by the *Wild Cat* and *Beagle*, located the pirate off Havana and pursued her under a running fire all day on April 8th. The pirate's people got out their sweeps when the wind fell at nightfall and worked to the land, where the barges pursued and after a ten-minute fight captured her. Domingo and two of his men escaped. One was taken, the rest killed. There was no loss among the Americans. The

[301]

shooner had been in possession of the Cubans for eight days, having been cut out by a boat party and turned into a cruiser with a long Tom amidships.

A wide patrol was maintained, ranging from the Virgin Islands to Tampico, with some minor results. On April 16, 1823, the *Peacock* chased a launch and barge ashore at Coloradas, their crews escaping after some resistance. In mid-April, the *Grampus*, Lieutenant F. H. Gregory, was at New Orleans and there learned of the capture in the Bay of Campeche of the American brig *Belisarius*, by pirates who murdered her captain and cook under circumstances of the greatest atrocity. He went in pursuit of the scoundrels, none of whom appear to have been taken. On April 24th, the *Jackall*, Lieutenant-Commandant John H. Lee and the *Wild Cat*, Lieutenant Legare, were sent to Mugeres Island, Lafitte's last haunt, on a rumor that it harbored a piratical colony. No trace of such was found. On the 11th of May H. M. S. *Bustard*, Captain R. Maclean, found the brig *Two Brothers* in Cumberland Harbor on the southeast end of Cuba. She had been plundered by pirates and abandoned.

During May and June 1823, Lieutenant-Commandant Gregory, in the *Grampus*, convoyed and cruised in Yucatan waters, where, as he reported, there were "several gangs of pirates, who had been guilty of every atrocity imaginable." On May 22d, he chased a suspicious schooner to windward off Sisal. On May 24th, the *Grampus* forced two piratical craft ashore near Campeche, the crews, however, getting away. June 11th, Gregory seized a schooner in the harbor of Campeche and turned her over to the authorities. She hailed from New Malaga, near Cape Calouche, where pirates were known to have an establishment, backed by a fort armed with two twenty-four-pounders. Fourteen members of this community had on the second of June captured the American schooner *Shibboleth*, Captain Perry, of New York, from an open boat, murdering the watch. Eight others of the crew were locked in the hold, the vessel was set on fire and sent adrift. The men broke out in time to save their lives, but not the vessel, from which they were rescued by the *Grampus*. Two days after the same crowd took the schooner *Augustus and John*, burnt her, and putting the crew in an open boat left them to their fate.

These doings aroused the authorities, who broke up the settlement with a party of dragoons, whose captain and several men were killed in the attack, while the pirates escaped in their boats. The scoundrels had earlier in the year taken the *Flyer*, a Bahama schooner and butchered all hands but one. This survivor picked up by Lieutenant Gregory said that shortly before the pirates held as prizes a Guineaman with two hundred slaves and much ivory and two small Yankee schooners. They were in close communication with traders in Havana and Merida, who bought their pelf.

June 14th, the *Ferret*, Lieutenant-Commandant Newell, and the *Beagle*, Lieutenant Newton, began a cruise to Trinidad, on the south side of Cuba. At Bacuna Yeagua, June 28th, an armed barge of sixteen oars was discovered. Lieutenant Downing, who went to reconnoitre, was fired upon and his boat so damaged as to be useless. Newell thereupon commandeered a small coaster and manned her with fifteen men, intending to stand in and take the barge, but was frustrated by a heavy sea, which drove him out of the harbor. The next day when he went in, he found two boats sunk, which he raised, but the barge had been pushed too far up the lagoon to be followed with the means at hand. The boats were seized and held as prizes.

July 21st and 22d the *Greyhound*, Lieutenant Lawrence Kearney, and the *Beagle*, Lieutenant J. T. Newton, operating near Cape Cruz, uncovered a piratical nest, guarded by a battery of one 4–pounder and two swivels. The village was burned, the guns taken and eight boats destroyed. One of the junior officers was Lieutenant David Glasgow Farragut, afterwards the great admiral, who has left this account of the affair in his journal:

"Cruising all through the Jardines and around the Isle of Pines we kept a watchful eye on the coast, but nothing occurred until one day when we were anchored off Cape Cruz in company with the Beagle. Kearney and Newton went on shore in one of the boats to see if there was any game in the neighborhood. The boat's crew was armed as usual, and had been on shore but a short time when a man suddenly crossed the path. From his suspicious appearance one of the sailors, named McCabe, leveled his gun at the stranger and was about to pull the trigger, when his arm was arrested by Kearney, who asked what he was aiming at. 'A d—d pirate, sir,' was the response. 'How do you know?' 'By his rig,' said the man promptly. By this time the fellow had disappeared; but our men had scarcely taken their seats in the boat in readiness to shove off, when they received a full volley of musketry from the dense woods or chaparral. The fire was returned as soon as possible, but with no effect as far as could be

[303]

ascertained, the pirates being well concealed behind the bushes. On board the Greyhound we could hear the firing, but could render no assistance, as Lieutenant Kearney had the only available boat belonging to the vessel. Kearney reached us at dark, related his adventure, and ordered me to be in readiness to land with a party at three o'clock the next morning.

"The schooner was to warp up inside the rocks to cover the attacking party. I landed, accompanied by Mr. Harrison, of the Beagle, the marines of both vessels, numbering twelve men, and the stewards and boys, making in all a force of seventeen. We had orders to keep back from the beach, that we might not be mistaken for pirates and receive the fire of the vessels. We were all ignorant of the topography of the coast, and when we landed found ourselves on a narrow strip of land covered with a thick and almost impassable chaparral, separated from the mainland by a lagoon. With great difficulty we made our way through marsh and bramble, clearing a passage with cutlasses, till we reached the mouth of the lagoon. We were compelled to show ourselves on the beach at this point, and narrowly escaped being fired upon from the Greyhound, but luckily, covered with mud as I was, Lieutenant Kearney with his glass made out my epaulet and immediately sent boats to transport us across to the eastern shore. We found the country there very rocky, and the rock was honeycombed and had the appearance of iron, with sharp edges. The men from the Beagle joined us, which increased my force to about thirty men. The captain, in the meantime, wishing to be certain as to the character of the men who had fired on him the previous evening, pulled boldly up again in his boat with a flag flying. Scarcely was he within musket range when from under the bluffs of the cape he received a volley of musketry and a discharge from a 4-pound swivel. There was no longer any doubt in the matter, and, considering that the enemy had too large a force to imperil his whole command on shore, Kearney decided to re-embark all but my original detachment, and I was ordered to attack the pirates in the rear while the schooners attacked them in front. The pirates had no idea that our schooners could get near enough to reach them, but in this they were mistaken, for, by pulling along among the rocks, our people were soon able to bring their guns to bear on the bluffs, which caused a scattering among the miscreants. My party all this time were struggling through the thicket that covered the rocks, the long, sharp thorns of the cactus giving us a great deal of trouble.

THE CUBAN PIRATES

Then there was a scrubby thorn bush, so thick as almost to shut out the air, rendering it next to impossible to get along any faster than we could hew our way with the cutlasses. The heat had become so intense that Lieutenant Somerville, who had accompanied us, fainted. Our progress was so slow that by the time the beach was reached the pirates were out of sight. Now and then a fellow would be seen in full run, and apparently fall down and disappear from view. We caught one old man in this difficult chase.

"Our surprise was very great, on returning to make an examination of the place lately vacated by the pirates, to find that they had several houses, from fifty to one hundred feet long, concealed from view, and a dozen boats and all the necessary apparatus for turtling and fishing as well as for pirating. An immense cave was discovered, filled with plunder of various kinds, including many articles marked with English labels, with saddles and costumes worn by the higher classes of Spanish peasants. In the vicinity were found several of these caves, in which a thousand men might have concealed themselves and held the strong position against a largely superior force. We contented ourselves with burning their houses and carrying off the plunder, cannon etc., and returned to the vessel. The only man we captured, who had every appearance of being a leper, was allowed to go.

"My only prize on this occasion was a large black monkey, which I took in single combat. He bit me through the arm, but had to surrender at discretion. In our first march through the swamp our shoes became much softened, and in the last many were completely cut from the feet of the men. Fortunately for myself, I had put on a pair of pegged negro brogans and got along pretty well, while some of my comrades suffered severely. One of the officers lost his shoe in the swamp, and one of the men, in endeavoring to recover it, was mired in a most ludicrous manner—one arm and one leg in the mud and one arm and one leg in the air. Nothing could exceed the ridiculous appearance we made when we got to the shore. My pantaloons were glued to my legs, my jacket was torn to shreds, and I was loaded with mud. The men under Somerville saluted me as their commander, but the sight was too much for all hands and there was a general burst of laughter. Another ridiculous incident of the expedition may as well be mentioned. When we had advanced about half a mile into the thicket I ordered a halt, to await the preconcerted signal gun from the schooner to push forward as rapidly as possible. At this moment I heard a great noise in our rear, and it occurred to me that the pirates might be behind us in force. In forming my men to receive the attack from that direction, I made a most animated speech, encouraging them to fight bravely, but had scarcely concluded my harangue when, to my great relief, it was discovered that the noise proceeded from about ten thousand land crabs making their way through the briers."

Late in July Lieutenant Newell, searching the banks of the Artigos River, found five cannon and a new gun carriage hidden in the mangroves. In the same month, the *Gallinipper*, Lieutenant W. H. Watson, and the *Mosquito*, Lieutenant William Inman, encountered the pirate schooner *Catalina* and a launch in Sigaunupa Bay near Port Hicacos. She was commanded by a famous rogue called Diaboleto and was taken after a running fight.

In the terse language of Lieutenant Watson's report this is what happened:

"They engaged us without colors of any description, having hauled down the Spanish flag after firing the first gun; and on approaching to board (our men giving three cheers and discharging their muskets) the pirates fled precipitately, some to their launch (lying in shore, from whence a firing was still kept up) whilst others endeavored to escape by swimming to the land. A volley of musketry directed at the launch, completed their disorder, and drove them into the sea; but the boats, going rapidly through the water, cut off their retreat, with the exception of fifteen, eleven of whom were killed or desperately wounded and taken prisoners by our men, who landed in pursuit; and the remaining four apprehended by the local authorities and sent to Matanzas." A thorough job indeed! Of the eleven, five only survived to be turned over to Spanish justice.

Lieutenant Beverly Kennon, in the *Weasel*, on August 3d, took the schooner *Gallego secunda* at Colorados, but she proved herself to be a Spanish trader and was released.

Porter had in preparation an expedition against a piratical headquarters at New Malaga, but in this he was anticipated by the British and called it off. The service now became very trying. Intense heat, and annoying sand flies made life a burden for the shore detachment at Allenton. At sea the patrols worked in open barges in bays, inlets, and mangrove swamps, exposed to great discomfort and the deadly stings of the fever-carrying mosquitoes. On August 31st, Porter reported that the yellow plague had broken out in his fleet with several fatalities. It continued to rage with alarming results. Poorly supplied with physicians as they were, and ignorant of ways of prevention and cure, which had to wait three quarters of a century for discovery, deaths were numerous among both officers and men. Twenty-three of the former who were stricken died. Porter himself was taken seriously ill. It seems also that no one knew of the unhealthful character of the season from August to November at Key West, and, as Porter observed in his official report, "it took us by surprise and the malignity of the disease was unparalleled." Conditions reached the limit of danger in September and on the 13th, Porter ordered the *Peacock* and *John Adams* to return to Hampton Roads for medical aid, instructing them to keep together for mutual assistance in case of need, so crippled were their crews. He came home himself on the *John Adams*, weak and worn with fever. Numbers of other vessels were in bad repair, used up by the hard service, and these also had to be recalled.

On July 19th, Lieutenant Thomas W. Freelson began an arduous and dangerous cruise in the Barge *Gnat*. Without shelter from the rain or heat, he worked in and out of the keys and creeks hunting pirates. In mid-August, out of provisions, he landed Midshipman Hunter and an interpreter to seek supplies. Thinking to allay alarm, Hunter left his arms and those of his companions on the beach. Approaching some houses he was seized by a dozen men. The interpreter fled, followed by a volley. Freelson landed some sailors, but Hunter's assailants, fled, taking him along. About midnight Hunter returned, reporting that he had been released on condition that he would ask the Lieutenant not to destroy their boats. Freelson began a pursuit at two A. M. with twenty officers and men, but could not catch up with the fugitives. He accordingly seized their boats and remained awaiting their return. At the end of six days, out of food and with many of his men ill, he destroyed the boats and abandoned the effort.

For the rest of the summer and fall there appears no incidents of record indicating piratical activity. Commodore Porter returned to his station on the *John Adams* in December and at once caused a general resumption of surveillance, taking cognizance of the slave trade and extending his supervision to the African coast.

During January, 1824, report came of the recent carrying off of two armed vessels by their crews bent on piracy. One was the Colombian

[307]

cruiser *Oronoke* and the other the brig *Scipio*, of Porto Rico. Several vessels in the Mona passage suffered at their hands. Two small piratical sloops, armed with swivel guns, also plundered the brig *William Henry*, Captain Lester, at the Island of Mona. The American brig *Harriet and Lucy*, of Hallowell, Captain Farnswart, was taken at the mouth of the Tabasco River on the Yucatan coast by sixteen men in an open boat carrying a four-pound gun. Their rendezvous was given as the island of Mugeres and the company was reported to number twenty in all.

Commodore Porter wrote to Secretary Southard, from Havana on April 8, 1824, announcing his arrival there after a long cruise through the West Indies, during which he discovered piratical evidence but made no captures. April 24th, he was at headquarters on Thompson's Island. There were no prizes or adventures in the month that followed, but an outbreak of the dreaded fever occurred in May and on the 28th of that month Porter notified the department of his purpose to remove a good part of his force north in June. This letter was sent by Lieutenant Legare on the *Wild Cat*, who sailed May 29th. Porter, following on June 15th, in the steam galliot *Sea Gull*, arrived at Washington on June 24th, passing the *Wild Cat* in the river on the way up, thus beating his message several hours. Legare had been nearly a month on the way, while the *Sea Gull* took but nine for the passage.

Porter's arrival, being thus unheralded, was taken as a breach of naval procedure in that he had returned from his station without authority from the department. That the exigencies of the case were plain and that he was quite warranted in his course could hardly be disputed, but it was seized upon by the bureaucrats as an instance of insubordination. Porter's prestige was so great that he was not openly reproved, but President Monroe caused Commodore Chauncey to intimate to him that he should return to his post. The hint was not heeded, if understood, though in August we find the Commodore writing the department to have a fitting ship provided for him and suggesting the *John Adams* as best suited to his taste.

During the summer his squadron was further depleted by the loss of several vessels, the sale of others as unseaworthy after their hard service, and the return of more to refit and avoid the fever. This led to a revival of rascality.

Thomas Randall, United States commercial agent at Havana, writing to John Quincy Adams, then Secretary of State, on July 5, 1824, cited further outrages, mainly off Matanzas. The brig *Castor*, Captain Hood, of Portland, Maine, was taken by an armed boat's crew of seven men and carried into Escondido, an obscure harbor, and there plundered, by a large party from shore, coming with boats and horses. The captain and the crew were severely beaten and then allowed to proceed to Havana. The same day, date not given, the brig *Betsey*, Captain Doane, of Newport, Rhode Island, was robbed in like fashion, her boats cast adrift and the vessel set on fire, leaving the crew to their fate. They succeeded by great effort in extinguishing the flames. A brig named *John*, from a New England port, a ship, and the schooner *Mercator*, Captain Henry Allen, with dry goods from New York, were also reported as taken and despoiled.

Mr. Randall laid these operations to the absence of the warships from the vicinity. The *Mercator* had been pillaged by a "sharp-built, fore-topsail schooner, with about forty armed men." The captain of the British cutter *Thracian*, then in port at Matanzas, promised the United States Vice-Consul to pursue the pirate, but there is no record of his success. The brig *Industry*, of Baltimore, while lying in harbor two miles from Matanzas was attacked, but beat off her assailants. On August 8th, Lieutenant Paine, in the *Terrier*, took a piratical launch with eight or ten men off Matanzas.

Baya Honda, near Cape Antonio, now developed new activity. The American fleet being too depleted to give the point attention, Captain Graham, of the British sloop-of-war *Icarus*, was called upon to act. This he did on August 21st, capturing two vessels and killing several of their crews. About forty escaped to the bush. The captain and crew of the brig *Henry*, of Hartford, Conn., were found confined on one of the vessels, having been captured five days before. She had been dismasted and stripped, while her men had been cruelly treated and told they were to die. The wrecks of twelve vessels, some large, were found in the bay, all recent captures, representing at least 120 men, no trace of whom could be found. The men of the *Henry* who asked their captors what had become of these, were answered with significant shrugs of the shoulders. Captain Graham also destroyed a pirate settlement at the Isle of Pines, killing "Pepe," the leader of the gang.

Commodore Porter remained in Washington, despite the intimation of President Monroe that he should resume his station. The administration still hesitated to deal with an officer of such standing, until Mr. Randall's report of the above incidents came to hand, coupled with urgent requests for action on the part of our government. Peremptory orders were issued on October 14, 1822, for Porter's immediate return to Cuban waters on the *John Adams,* and he took his departure at once. The vessels on the ground had been as active as their numbers permitted. Lieutenant C. W. Skinner, of the *Porpoise,* who had done much convoying between Matanzas and Havana, on October 19th sent a boat expedition under Lieutenant Hunter and Acting Lieutenant Johnson to search the region about Point Yeaco, Sewappa Bay, and Camarico. They returned to Matanzas on the evening of the 22d, with a one-gun schooner, a new American cutter and two boats, one of the latter having three men on board, which he had taken in Sewappa Bay. The crews of the others had fled to the shore. Bloody clothes, an American flag, and sundry nautical instruments indicated the recent piracy of the brig *Morning Star.* Lieutenant Paine, in the *Terrier,* caught a launch off Havana, on October 20th.

On the night of October 23, 1824, the store of Messrs. Cabot, Bailey & Company, American citizens in the city of St. Thomas, on the island of that name, was entered and robbed of a large amount of goods. Suspicion pointing to a raid by water from the town of Foxardo, a near point on Porto Rico, then a Spanish possession, the firm appealed to Lieutenant Charles T. Platt, of the United States schooner *Beagle,* one of Commodore Porter's pirate hunters, to proceed in pursuit. The *Beagle* at once sailed for Foxardo, reaching port on October 26th.

The next morning in citizen's clothes, Lieutenant Platt went ashore and informed the captain of the port of the nature of his errand. After breakfast, at a public house, he was summoned before the Alcalde and asked by the captain of the port to produce his register. He explained that a vessel of war carried no such document, and was informed that unless it was produced he would be imprisoned. Lieutenant Platt then requested that an officer accompany him to the *Beagle,* where he would afford proper evidence of his character. This not being agreed to, he attempted to depart for the vessel, when he was collared by soldiers taken back to the Alcalde's residence, and put in durance under charge of an armed sentry. Two companions, Lieutenant Ritchie and the pilot, were also detained for an hour when they were allowed to go to the *Beagle* to fetch Platt's commission and his uniform. Donning the latter and producing the former failed to convince his captors, for the commission was called a forgery and he was denounced as "a damned pirate." Orders were then given to carry him to the *calaboʒo*

[310]

or jail. When he came near enough to the jail to recognize it, he declared he would not enter unless forced. At this he was again taken back to the Alcalde's, and after being threatened with detention until the authorities at San Juan, forty miles distant could be consulted, he was told that he had not shown his orders. These were sent for and produced. Finally at sunset he was ordered to depart, and did so, insulted by the rabble *en route* to the beach.

Lieutenant Platt reported the affair to Commodore Porter, who, without lodging complaint with the Spanish governor at San Juan and demanding apologies from the authorities proceeded directly to Foxardo on the *John Adams*. At midnight on November 13th, in company with the *Beagle* and the *Grampus*, the *Adams* being then at anchor near Passage Island, an expedition was sent out against the town. The two schooners, towing a number of boats with a landing party of 200 men, were delayed by light winds and did not reach the shore until between eight and nine A. M. on the 14th, instead of at daybreak as planned.

The Spanish were aroused and manned a two-gun battery near the beach, beside giving other signs of resistance. The launch from the *Grampus*, Lieutenant G. J. Pendergast commanding, first took fourteen marines ashore under Lieutenant Thomas B. Barton, with orders to spike the guns. The landing was made in such fashion as to take the battery in the rear and its defenders fled without firing. One gun was loaded, the other partly, and lighted matches with ammunition were at hand. The guns spiked and the ammunition destroyed, the party joined the others who by this time had landed on the beach. They were left to guard the boats, while two other parties under Lieutenants Crabbe and C. K. Stribling proceeded to the town, a mile and a half distant. On approaching it, the entrance was seen to be guarded by sixty or seventy men, some cavalry, and two small cannon. A white flag being shown, Lieutenant Stribling met the bearer and as a result of the parley halted Lieutenant Crabbe. Commodore Porter now joined with the main force, having spiked two nine-pounders on the way, so placed as to command the road. The Alcalde then appeared and admitted that he had acted blamefully in the matter, but had been compelled to do so by others. He was given a few minutes to write an apology or to have his town seized by force. This he did and the incident ended—so far as Foxardo was concerned.

Following this episode came one of the darkest tragedies in the annals of the Antilles, in the murder of five members of the crew of the brig *Betsey*, of Wiscasset, Maine, wrecked on the Cuban coast. She sailed from Wiscasset for Matanzas on the 28th of November, 1824, laden with lumber. Ellis Hilton of Wiscasset was captain, Joshua Merry of Edgecomb first mate, and Daniel Collins, of Wiscasset, second mate. Charles Manuel, a Portuguese, Seth Russel, and Benjamin Bridge were seamen and Delrey Jeome, cook. The passage was uneventful until they reached the vicinity of Double Shot Keys, within a day's sail of port. Hilton had been sick most of the trip, and when the weather fell foul refused to accept a suggestion from Collins that sail be shortened as he was anxious to make Matanzas the next day. It was then the 14th of December. The breeze blew strong from the north and the *Betsey* bounded along in the dark that evening at a nine-knot gait, when she struck a rock and came up all a-standing. Bow and stern gave way and with the latter went the yawl. By hard work the longboat, carried amidships, was made available but, the ship collapsing under them, the men followed the boat into the sea. A plank in her bottom was damaged, but she floated and all succeeded in climbing in. The crew stood near during the night with wreckage drifting by from which they were able to salvage only a blanket, which was hoisted for a sail and the boat headed for Matanzas. No food or water had been secured.

All the next day and night they rowed, coming at dawn in sight of a small island some fifteen miles ahead. By hard pulling they reached the shore and found themselves on a small key about three acres in extent, called Cruz del Padre—Cross of Our Father—lying some twenty-seven leagues east by north from Matanzas. The boat grounded about one hundred yards out. Fortunately, they were then in view of five Cuban fishermen who lived in two huts on the key, the chief of whom, who chanced to know Captain Hilton, came off in a canoe and carried them to the shore where they were given food, water, and shelter. It was agreed that the fishermen would carry the party to Matanzas for forty dollars and the longboat.

After several days' rest a small schooner was warped out of the creek in which she lay and with four of the fishermen as crew, preparations were made for a start to Matanzas. Just as they were ready to make sail a smart sailing cutter came in, which at once began firing blunderbuss balls at the schooner, whose crew ran below. She was soon near enough to order a boat sent aboard and three of the crew went off to the cutter, which was a large open boat about thirty-five feet long, manned by ten armed men, all villainous-looking scoundrels. After examining the *Betsey's* papers, which Captain Hilton had preserved, the pirates began operations by binding him with cords, having first passed a couple of doubloons to the chief of the fishermen. They announced that they were going to carry the *Betsey's* people to Matanzas as "prisoners of war," and proceeded to tie the others as they had the captain. Then they threw them like so much baggage into the canoes and paddled out to the cutter, where knives and machetes were passed out to the seven pirates and four fishermen who now had them in charge, while significant gestures and remarks indicated only too well their purpose, which was to murder the Americans.

They were now paddled along the beach and to a cove a mile distant from the huts, where in walking about the day before Daniel Collins had noted a number of skeletons without heads, lying in the sand, and here landed. The gang sang and laughed on the way observing that "Americans were very good beef on their knives." The canoes were kept abreast near the shore and the bloody work at once began. Captain Hilton was the first victim. His shoulders were forced to the gunwale and his head hacked off so that it fell into the water. His poor dog, which had followed him into the canoe, made an effort to aid him and then crept to the body, whining dolefully. Merry was next stabbed with a cutlass and his throat cut from ear to ear. Bridge and Jeome, the cook, were then stabbed and their heads split with cutlass blows. A single stroke of heavy blade cut deep into Russel's skull, and he fell dead in the canoe. Manuel, the Portuguese, had somehow loosed his bonds and leaped into the water, which was only knee deep, and he fled to the shore. A pirate struck at Collins's head, but it was covered with a stiff tarpaulin hat which caused the blow to glance and by a strange fortune to cut the cord that held his hands behind him. He was half stunned and, losing his balance, rolled over the side into the shallow sea. As he rose in the water a pirate threw his knife at him, which struck but did no injury. He now staggered toward the beach. Two of the men followed him, the rest being engaged in chasing Manuel. Fear lent wings to both fugitives. Collins succeeded in getting into a mangrove swamp about ten feet ahead of his pursuers. Luckily he was barefooted and so less encumbered in the mud than the shod pirates, who were also entangled by their arms. Miraculous as it seems, Collins succeeded in working deep into the swamp, where he hid among the mangroves, lying the rest of the day and all of the following night. At sunrise, finding himself near the sea, he stripped himself to all save his shirt, of which he tore off the sleeves, and keeping on his tarpaulin, and bundling his jacket on his back, plunged in and swam two miles to the next key. Resting here, he swam again two miles to another, where he passed the night hiding again in the mangroves. On the morning of the third day, having had no water or food except a few mangrove leaves, he again began wading and swimming from key to key he crossed a half mile passage, which brought him to what he later found was the mainland of Cuba. Here he came upon a large yawl stranded, with her foremast standing. Two crawfish found under her stern sheets gave him his first morsel of food, which proved nauseating and made him ill. As he proceeded, a small spring trickled across the path, giving him the first refreshment he had since the morning of the murders. Large herds of cattle now appeared and a grove of lime trees gave him a bountiful repast of fruit. He had left his bloody shirt on one of the keys, thinking it might lead to suspicion, and was clad only in his jacket. In this fashion he staggered along, his body covered with sores and his stomach aching. On the sixth day he had not yet encountered a human habitation, but following a path he saw some bean pods and husks of corn.

At sunset as he was about to give up in despair a colored man on horseback, followed by a pack of hounds, came into view and was soon in speaking distance. He restrained the dogs and putting the exhausted sailor on his horse conveyed him three miles to a plantation, the owner of which, a venerable Spaniard, received him with the utmost kindness, especially as on Collins's arm he saw the tattooed outline of a crucifix. A colored slave who knew some English enabled Collins to make his story known and after a few days' rest he secured a pass from the Alcalde, which allowed him to go to Matanzas. An English carpenter who met him at the Alcalde's house where he had been working gave him clothes and money and escorted him some distance on his way. After leaving him the luckless Collins was held up and beaten by some ruffians, who took his small store of money and all his clothes, except shirt and trousers. They were frightened off by an approaching mule caravan, but Collins, fearing it might produce more thieves, hid by the wayside until it passed and then traveled off the road until nightfall, when he came to a house where he was refused refreshment and so passed the night hungry and in the woods. The next afternoon he reached a village where he found food and a kind soul gave him a meal. The second night he was refused shelter and again slept in the woods. The next morning he came to a large house where he was decently treated and given breakfast. He took to the road again and a horseman who could speak English heard his tale, gave him four dollars, and directed him to the house of the Alcalde's sister, where he was made welcome. He was now near Matanzas and in another day came to the Caminar River, where he found a number of American and English coopers at work. They kept him over night and sent him to the city in a barge the next morning. A heavy wind made traveling slow and he did not arrive until eight o'clock in the evening and slept, or tried to, on the barge. The following morning he reported to Mr. Adams, the United States agent, who sent him to Mr. Lattin, consignee of the brig. The United States schooner *Ferret* was in port and Collins went on board of her and sailed at once in search of the murderers, who, after twenty-one days of seeking, were not found. Manuel also turned up in Matanzas having, as he claimed, got away in one of the canoes. The Wiscasset brig *Shamrock*, Captain Holmes, restored Collins to his home on April 2, 1825.

Further outrages may be cited in the case of the American brig *Edward*, whose captain and part of the crew were murdered; the brig *Laura Anne*, Captain Shaw, from Buenos Ayres to Havana, all hands murdered, but one who hid in the hold. The vessel was fired and the survivors made land on a bit of wreckage. It sometimes happened that the same cargo of coffee would be several times sold in Havana, being stolen and restolen from its several purchasers who essayed to carry it north.

It now came to pass that Commodore Porter was to reach an ignoble end to his great exertions. The affair at Foxardo, reaching the ears of the administration, stirred up a commotion in Washington over what was deemed a high-handed action, America being too remote to acquire the feeling rampant in the squadron against the cruelty and rascality of the Spanish half-castes against whom the ships were employed. At President Monroe's instance, orders were issued for Commodore Porter's recall on December 27, 1824, Captain Lewis Warrington being sent to command in his stead. His return coming at the close of Monroe's term, the case was left open to the administration of John Quincy Adams.

More or less piratical activity followed the commodore's departure for the States in December, but no captures were made until March, 1825, when Lieutenant J. D. Sloat, cruising near Boca del Inferno discovered that a pirate sloop had been operating in the vicinity. Securing a trading sloop, he armed her and putting Lieutenant G. J. Pendergast in charge sent her in pursuit. On the fourth of the month Pendergast encountered the rover and running alongside without exciting suspicion opened fire, which was smartly returned. The sloop fled after a forty-minute action and was run ashore by her crew, of whom two were killed and ten captured and hanged by the Porto Rico authorities, among them Colpecinas, their leader.

There now followed an atrocity equal in villainy to that perpetrated on the hapless crew of the *Betsey.* This was the case of the *Eliza Ann,* Charles Smith, captain, from St. Johns, New Brunswick to Antigua taken by Cuban pirates on March 12, 1825. The sloop sailed from St. John on the 28th of February, having one female passenger on board, Miss Lucretia Parker, who was bound to join her brother in Antigua and who alone was spared to tell the bloody tale. When eleven days out the *Eliza Ann* was overhauled by a small schooner, carrying a large and well-armed crew, who overflowed the sloop's deck and with yells and imprecations began their dreadful work. Miss Parker fell upon her knees and prayed for mercy. This was granted. One of the pirates led her to the companion-way and told her to descend to the cabin, where she would be safe. "Although pirates," he said, "we do not destroy the lives of innocent females." Here she remained, horrified by the sound of groans and shrieks of suffering from the deck above, which died down in an hour or so, and was caused by the torture inflicted on members of the crew to make them divulge the presence of treasure. At the end of this period a gang carrying blood-stained swords broke into the cabin and began to search its belongings for valuables and cash. They found only a few dollars in the captain's chest and, after ransacking the lockers, returned to deck and made sail for a key near the Cuban coast.

It was nothing but a barren bar, on reaching which the hatches were taken off and the crew ordered up. The men were bloody with cuts and black with bruises. They were all tightly bound and forced into a small, leaky boat and rowed to the shore. Here, after being stripped of their clothing, the unfortunates were butchered in cold blood. The captain pleaded for his life, telling them of wife and children to be left in need. He was stabbed to the heart, with Miss Parker standing by his side. The mate was on his knees offering submission of any sort, when killed with a club. The lady kept on her knees in prayer and after the massacre was taken by the same man who had sent her to the cabin, to a small hut, where he said she could rest and be assured of her personal safety.

The next morning the sighting of several sail caused all the pirates but four to set out in rowboats in an effort to waylay them. They were successful in overtaking the first, but the second was a British war sloop, which ran up and opened fire. The scoundrels endeavored to flee, some leaping overboard from their boats and endeavoring to swim ashore. These were shot in the water. Those who stuck to their boats were soon overtaken by the cutters from the cruisers. Miss Parker witnessed this diversion with emotion that can well be imagined. The four who remained on the island with their fair prisoner took good care promptly to escape view from the sea. One of these, who exercised some authority over the others, treated the woman with consideration, indeed, expressing abhorrence at the conduct of his associates and claiming to have in the beginning been forced into their company. The hut was razed and the goods buried, save some bags of dollars, and on the eleventh night after the capture of the *Eliza Ann* the four and Miss Parker embarked at midnight for what proved to be the Cuban mainland.

Landing at dawn, Miss Parker was given a few ship biscuits and told to walk three quarters of a mile in a north-easterly direction when she would come to a house where she would be cared for. This proved correct, a humble Spanish family giving her food and shelter and guiding her to Matanzas, whence she was forwarded by the British Consul to Jamaica, on the road to Antigua. Before leaving she visited the prison in Matanzas and there had the pleasure of recognizing the chief of the murderous band, who, with six others, had been brought in by the cruiser and delivered to the Spanish authorities for punishment. Her testimony was taken and sufficed to convict them all. They were duly hanged, the chief expressing deep regret that he had been so soft-hearted as to save the lady's life. It would seem probable that these were some of the same wretches who murdered the *Betsey's* men, place and method of procedure being much the same.

On the 24th of March, Lieutenant Isaac McKeever, in the steam galley *Seagull*, in company with the barge *Gallinipper*, co-operated with a British squadron formed of the frigate *Dartmouth* and several armed schooners in surprising a piratical company. A schooner with a crew of thirty-five was taken after a fight. Eight pirates were killed and nineteen taken prisoners. She carried two six-pounders and four swivels, sailing under a false Spanish clearance. A considerable quantity of American goods was found on board and in the bushes. On the 25th, McKeever chased a schooner-rigged boat ashore, her crew escaping. This was the last action of record in the American naval campaign.

The Adams Administration early took cognizance of Commodore Porter's case. Samuel L. Southard continued as Secretary of the Navy and one of his first acts was to institute a Court of Inquiry to look into Porter's action at Foxardo, to which was added a further charge that, instead of hunting pirates, his squadron had spent much of its time transporting specie for merchants from Mexico at a fee of two and a half per cent., of which the Commodore received a third. The court convened in Washington on the 2d of May, 1825. It was headed by Commodore Isaac Chauncey, with Captains William M. Crane and George C. Read as fellow members and Richard S. Coxe, Judge Advocate. Porter objected to the two captains as being his juniors, and to the Judge Advocate as a partisan against him, and declined to appear. The specie charge was dismissed as unfounded, the officers having followed long-established custom and really performed a public service. As to Foxardo, the court decided the episode was not properly before them, Porter having refused to put in a defense. He did, however, prepare and issue one in pamphlet form and had already had recourse to the columns of the *National Intelligencer* to uphold his cause.

This result not being satisfactory to Porter's prosecutors in the Navy Department, he was haled before a court martial on July 7, 1825, presided over by Captain James Barron, who had himself been off the navy list under a five-year sentence as punishment for the affair on the *Chesapeake*, when he was fired upon by the British frigate *Leopard* and being unprepared, surrendered, and had in its membership Captain Jesse D. Elliott, whose controversy with Oliver Hazard Perry over his conduct at the Battle of Lake Erie was long a cause of bitter disturbance in and out of the Navy. Two charges were made, the first covering the Commodore's action at Foxardo as being "Disobedience of orders and conduct unbecoming an officer" and the second re-

THE CUBAN PIRATES

lating to his letters and the defensive pamphlet as "Insubordinate conduct and conduct unbecoming an officer." On August 10th, the court found Porter guilty on both charges, ascribing his fault under the first, however, "to an anxious disposition on his part to maintain the honor and advance the interests of the country and the service." He was sentenced to suspension from the duty for six months from date.

Indignant at such treatment, obviously unfair, in the face of his great labors, Porter resigned in 1826 and became commander-in-chief of the Mexican Navy, holding the place until 1829, when Andrew Jackson, coming into power, made him Consul at Algiers. Subsequently he was promoted to Charge d' Affairs at Constantinople and later, in 1831, became Minister to Turkey. He died at his post March 3, 1843.

The task of cleaning up the Cuban coast and the West Indies was now left to the British, who, having Jamaica as the base of operations, proceeded with characteristic energy and firmness to clear the tropical waters. They wasted little ceremony in dealing with Spanish authorities, but took their captives into Port Royal and hanged them as fast as gathered.

In 1827, the Mediterranean was infested with pirates from the Greek Islands, who attacked all commerce. Lieutenant L. M. Goldsborough, on October 27th, boarded the British brig *Comet*, then in the hands of the robbers, and recaptured her, off the Island of Andros.

Lieutenant John A. Carr killed the Greek captain in a hand-to-hand conflict. This was the last of our naval actions against pirates of Caucasian blood.

Note: Incredible as it may appear, the editor of the *United States Gazette*, published in Philadelphia, claimed to have kept a record of the piracies committed from the close of the War of 1812 to 1823, in West Indian, Gulf, and Central American waters, and that they amounted to a total number of three thousand and seven.

XXXIX

OF CHARLES GIBBS

BUT one of the Cuban pirates came to justice in the United States and this not as the result of crimes committed there, but for an act of murder at sea. We had in the first chapter on these desperadoes an account of the destruction by Lieutenant Lawrence Kearney in the *Enterprise* of the settlement at Cape Antonio, with its mention of Charles Gibbs. There is no reliable record extant of his beginnings. In a "confession" made by him before his execution he claimed to have been the son of a petty officer in the American Navy and to have served as "James D. Jeffers" under the gallant James Lawrence on the *Hornet* and *Chesapeake*, being captured when the latter struck to the *Shannon*, of Boston Harbor, in 1814. The records of the Navy Department at Washington prove this to be entirely untrue; nor is there any trace in the archives of the name of Jeffers, which his father bore, according to his claim.

There is, curiously enough, a "Charles Gibbs" in the record, and he was a gunner on the British sloop-of-war *Pelican*, taken by the U. S. S. *Hornet* off Tristan d'Acuhna, March 23, 1815. The *Hornet* was then under command of Captain Nicholas Biddle. This Gibbs was taken with other captives to St. Salvador and freed on April 27, 1815. It would have been an easy step from St. Salvador to Cuba and the free-booters. Yet he could hardly have been the same man if only thirty-four years of age when hanged in 1831, as stated at the time.

His further story was that following his naval service he returned to Rhode Island, of which state he claimed to be a native, where he entered on a ship bound for New Orleans and thence to Stockholm. Returning from the latter port they put in at Bristol, England, where the vessel was found unseaworthy, condemned, and sold. Gibbs said he then journeyed to Liverpool and found a berth on the ship *Amity*, Captain Maxwell, on which he returned to the United States. Here the death of an uncle gave him a legacy of $2,000. With this capital he set up a small grocery business in Boston, which proved unprofitable because of neglect and dissipation on the part of the proprietor, and he again took to the sea in the ship *John*, Captain Brown, for the Island of Margarita. On arriving at that port Gibbs left the vessel and enlisted on board a Colombian privateer, the *Sans Souci*, in 1816, later joining the *Maria*, Captain Bell. A two months' cruise in Cuban waters ended in a mutiny growing out of dissatisfaction over the distribution of prize money and the men, seizing the schooner, set the officers ashore near Pensacola, Florida.

After a few days of uncertainty over their future course the crew decided to operate independently, in short, to become pirates. A few ships were stopped and searched, but yielding no specie were allowed to go. It was then suggested by one of their number, named Antonio, that they could make arrangements for the sale of goods to a merchant in Havana. Sail was therefore made for that port to complete an arrangement, Gibbs becoming navigator. Lying two miles off the Morro, they landed Antonio at Havana to make the deal, which he did, appointing Cape Antonio as the place of rendezvous. The *Maria* now began her career with a crew of some fifty Spaniards and outcast Americans. Her first capture was the British ship *Indispensable*, which was carried to Cape Antonio and there rifled. Her officers and crew were killed; those who resisted were cut to pieces; the others shot in cold blood. A French brig laden with silks and wine shared a like fate, her men being also murdered. Gibbs now became captain, acquiescing in the policy that "dead men tell no tales," justifying himself on the ground that as death was the punishment for piracy the safest plan was to leave no living accusers.

Cruising now to the Bahama banks, Gibbs took the brig *William* from New York bound for Mexico. Her crew was slain and the cargo of furniture taken to Cape Antonio and thence transferred to Havana for sale. During this cruise the *Maria* was chased by the American frigate *John Adams*. She flew the Colombian colors and got away. Early in the summer of 1817 the *Earl of Morla*, an English ship laden with dry goods, was taken, the crew murdered, and the vessel burned. Her cargo was disposed of by the Havana agent and the profits divided. On the proceeds of this robbery Gibbs lived for a time in Havana, posing as a merchant, enlarging his acquaintance among officials and picking up considerable knowledge of the moves of the American ships in the West Indies, which were very ineffectually looking out for pirates, being all large cruisers and unfitted to hunt down the

[321]

off-shore operators. Returning to Cape Antonio he found his associates in turmoil, many quarrels having broken out and numbers of murders having been committed. Taking charge of the situation, he restored a kind of order among them and enforced obedience to his rule.

There now occurred a tragedy of the cruelest sort. As they were cruising at the end of 1817, or at the beginning of 1818, a Dutch ship from Curaçao was taken and her passengers and crew to the number of thirty were butchered. One survivor, a charming girl of seventeen, Gibbs kept for his own pleasure and took her to Cape Antonio. Here her presence was so resented as imperiling the "dead tell no tales" that he at last agreed to accomplish her death by poison and the poor victim was thus disposed of under a sentence from a council of war.

The *Maria* was driven ashore in a storm while anchored at Cape Antonio, and so damaged that she had to be destroyed. The Havana agent speedily provided another, the *Picciana*, Baltimore built, on true piratical lines, long and low and rakish, in which the "trade" was continued and other vessels acquired for the same purpose. Slipping out of Havana in 1819, Gibbs came to New York with $30,000 in his pockets, and went thence to Boston. Here he spent much of his money and then sailed to Liverpool on the ship *Emerald*. After some months of dissipated life in England, Gibbs returned to Boston on the ship *Topaz*, Captain Lewis, and being out of funds found his way back to Cuba and rejoined the pirates, eventually commanding a schooner called the *Margarita*, one of the Cape Antonio fleet. The pirates ventured successfully, making many captures and invariably killing the captives. How this was permitted remains one of the mysteries of the day. The gang had one narrow escape from the hands of the the British frigate *Coronation*, but this seems to have been their only hazard for four years of active operations, during which they took and despoiled many vessels and murdered their crews. The list included the brig *Jane*, from Liverpool; the brig *Belvidere*, of Boston; three French brigs; the ship *Providence*, of Providence, R. I., with $10,000 in specie; the ship *Wallace*, of Salem; the bark *Dido*, of Bremen; a Genoese brig whose principal cargo was made up of pianofortes, which soon graced Cuban mansions. Matters went thus profitably until October 16, 1821, when the robbers were surprised in their lair by the U. S. Brig *Enterprise*, Lieutenant Lawrence Kearney, commanding, the full story of which encounter has already been told.

After this disaster Gibbs and his followers took refuge in the hills until the coast was clear and resumed operations, continuing until the activities of the American and British fleets made the business impossible. He then got back to New York and appears to have kept himself well submerged until 1826, when he sailed for Buenos Aires from Boston, on the brig *Hetty*, of Portsmouth, and there joined the navy of the New Republic then at war with Brazil. He soon became fifth lieutenant on a warship called the *Twenty-fifth of May*, from which after four months' service he was transferred to the command of a privateer on which he made several cruises. He then bought a half interest in the *Spitfire*, a privateer schooner, fitted out from Baltimore, and again went to sea, only to be captured when a week out and taken to Rio de Janeiro. Here he remained until peace came and returned to New York by way of Buenos Aires.

The French movement against Algiers now being under way, Gibbs decided to offer his services to the Bey of that piratical province. He accordingly sailed for Barcelona, in the *Sally Ann*, of Bath, reached Port Mahon and sought to get from there to Algiers. The French blockade preventing this, he crossed to Tunis, thinking to reach his destination by the desert route. When this proved too difficult, he took passage for Marseilles and thence to Boston. From this port he shipped to New Orleans on the ship *Lexington*. There, with a nose for specie, in company with Aaron Church, an Indian, and John Brownrigg, fellow seaman on the *Lexington*, he joined the crew of the Boston brig *Vineyard*, Captain William Thornby, bound for Philadelphia with a cargo of cotton, sugar, and $50,000 in silver on board belonging to the famous "merchant and mariner," Stephen Girard. On the voyage north the crew conspired to take the vessel and her treasure under the leadership of Gibbs. The other members of the vessel's company were Thomas J. Wansley, colored, steward; James Talbot, Henry Atwell and Robert Dawes.

One man alone, James Talbot, refused to join and Robert Dawes, appears to have kept out of the first moves, which were made by Gibbs and Thomas J. Wansley, the mulatto steward, who on the night of November 23, 1830, while the brig was in a heavy seaway, killed the captain during his watch on deck. Wansley struck the captain down with a pump handle and as he cried "murder" Gibbs seized him and with the aid of the steward threw him into the sea. William Roberts, the mate, who was asleep below, roused by the noise, came on deck where he was assaulted by Henry Atwell and Aaron Church. He fled to his cabin, where he was followed by Gibbs, who, unable to locate him in the dark took the binnacle lantern and making Dawes, the helmsman, carry it, went below, followed by Atwell and Church. Roberts being found, he was beaten, dragged to the deck, and thrown into the sea, whence his cries followed the brigantine as she lurched on through the darkness.

During this time the terrified Talbot was in the forecastle praying. Neither he nor Dawes were harmed, but the latter was restored to the tiller and ordered to steer for Long Island. The money and Captain Thornby's valuables were divided and when they sighted Long Island in the neighborhood of Mattituck, the brig was scuttled and a fire set in her cabin, while the crew, including the unwilling members, took the two boats for shore. They had first divided the specie, which was contained in ten kegs holding $5,000 each and making a heavy load. Some of it was sewed up in bags to be carried on the person. Gibbs, Dawes, Wansley, and Brownrigg were in the longboat and Atwell, Church and Talbot in the jolly boat. The latter carried $35,000 of the silver and the longboat $15,000. During the night they pulled along the coast toward New York. A heavy sea rose and so imperiled the longboat that two thirds of the silver was thrown into the sea. About eight o'clock in the morning the jolly boat was seen to capsize and it disappeared with its crew and treasure.

The longboat, lightened, kept afloat and in the late afternoon reached the entrance of Jamaica Bay, where Gibbs and his companions landed on Barren Island, long the ill-smelling place where the offal of New York is converted into fertilizer. It then held but a single house—a fisher's hut occupied by John Johnson and his young brother William. To this the pirates were directed by a hunter who was seeking snipe on the beach at sunset. They asked the loan of a horse and cart to remove some property they had in a boat on the beach. Each carried a pair of pistols and an ugly knife. The animal and vehicle were loaned to them and they came back several hours later, their hands covered with mud, bringing Dawes and the boy Brownrigg with them and requesting shelter for the night. This was granted.

The next morning, March 30th, Gibbs handed the Johnsons a bag of Mexican dollars, with the remark: "For that you can, maybe, keep a close tongue in your heads," and all departed with William for the

[324]

mainland where they were left at Samuel Leonard's hotel and arranged for a team to take them to Brooklyn. Here several of them drank liquor and a quarrel broke out, as the result of which the boy Brownrigg said he would go no further in their company as they were "pirates and murderers." Steps were at once taken to seize the four. Wansley broke away and made for the woods, where he was soon captured by Robert Greenwood. The prisoners were taken to the Flatbush jail and on December 1st were examined before Magistrates Elias Hubbard and John Terhune. Brownrigg told the story in detail and revealed the place where the money brought on shore had been buried. Two inspectors from the Ocean Insurance Company went at once to the spot on Barren Island, but found the cache rifled. The Johnsons were suspected and had some quarrel over the money, according to the younger brother, who left his relative as the result. Johnson, however, gave up a few dollars, the captain's watch, a spy-glass, and a sword cane as all that had been given him for his hospitality. None of the money was ever recovered. The prisoners were taken to New York by Thomas Morris, the U. S. Marshal, and lodged in Bellevue Prison. Brownrigg, who was a lad of eighteen, and Dawes turned state's evidence. Wansley was tried first in the United States Court on March 7th, and convicted of the murder of Captain Thornby. Gibbs was found guilty the next day of killing mate Roberts. The pair were sentenced by Judge Betts to be hanged on April 22d. James A. Hamilton, the United States District Attorney, was prosecutor, while H. E. Davis and N. B. Blunt appeared for the defense.

During the period in prison before his execution Gibbs made a series of "confessions," telling more or less truth concerning his past life to Thomas Morris, the United States Marshal, and Justice James Hopson. He alleged that he had $150,000 in specie hidden in Cuba and $50,000 in trustworthy hands in Buenos Aires—statements undoubtedly made as feelers for aid in securing salvation from the gallows. He reckoned the spoils of the operations at Cape Antonio as amounting to $1,500,000, of which the pirates received little better than a third, the rest going to enrich their rascally partner, the Havana merchant.

Of futher interest in this excerpt from the New York *Evening Post* of April 7, 1831:

"To correct the impression which some of our public prints have thrown out that Gibbs, like other criminals, is disposed to magnify and exaggerate his crimes, it may be well to state that few days since a chart of the West Indies (Jocelyn's) was handed to him containing the names of about ninety vessels which were boarded and plundered by pirates from 1817 to 1825, with a request that he would mark those of whose robbery he had any recollection. The chart was returned with but one mark and that upon the ship Lucies of Charleston. When questioned afterwards in regard to that vessel he gave such an account of her and of her subsequent recapture by the Enterprise as left no doubt respecting the truth of his statement. Had he been desirous of increasing the black catalogue here was so fine an opportunity that he would undoubtedly have availed himself of it. He has repeatedly stated that he was concerned in the robbery of more than forty vessels and in the destruction of more than twenty with their entire crews. Many of those destroyed had passengers on board which makes it probable that he has been an agent in the murder of nearly four hundred human beings! Gibbs was married in Buenos Ayres where he now has a child living. His wife is dead. By a singular concurrence of circumstances a woman with whom he became acquainted in Liverpool and who is said at that time to have borne a decent character, is now lodged in the same prison with himself. He has written her two letters since his confinement, both of which are before us. They indicate a good deal of native talent but very little education."

In further corroboration of Gibbs's crimes, he was visited in prison by Captain Kearney, who commanded the U. S. brig *Enterprise* when she recaptured the ship *Lucies* and other vessels at Cape Antonio. Gibbs immediately recognized him and in the course of the conversation referred to numerous incidents that occurred there, which none but a person present could have known. He inquired of Captain K. if he found some warm coffee on board of the ship when he took possession of her, and on being answered in the affirmative he added, with a half smile, "You didn't drink any of it," intending to convey the idea that it was prepared and poisoned for their destruction. Captain Kearney was fully satisfied that he had been a pirate and one of the Cape Antonio freebooters.

In the course of his conversation with Captain Kearney, Gibbs remarked: "I suppose, Captain, you think it quite a difficult matter to make a pirate, but I can assure you it is not so; on the contrary, I

[326]

can make an excellent pirate in a few weeks, even of a pious young man." Being questioned as to the method of transformation, he continued: "In one of our cruises we took a vessel with some eight or ten men. Among them were two stout young fellows, who we thought would be useful to us and therefore agreed among ourselves to make them join us. Accordingly all the crew were killed in their presence. After this we put a rope around each of their necks, with a block to the main yard to hang them. They were then blindfolded. When everything was thus prepared, we asked them whether to save their lives they would join us and become pirates? They gladly assented to the terms, which were not only to unite with us, but also to do all the killing required of them. Accordingly, the next vessel we captured they performed all the butchery, and, in a few weeks became first-rate pirates."

It was further proven that Gibbs had once ventured as far north as the Delaware Capes, when he robbed the ship *Providence* and was probably rightly suspected of sinking the *Rebecca Sims*, bound for East India with all on board on the same cruise.

On the morning of April 22d, Gibbs and Wansley were taken from Bellevue prison under a guard of marines and conveyed on the steamer *Bellona* to Ellis Island, where the immigrant station now stands. The time had been set between ten and three o'clock. At the request of the men their departure from earth was delayed until noon, during which time they were confined in one of the casemates of the fort. The occasion was like a gala day in the harbor. The island was crowded with people and the bay with vessels loaded with spectators. Both made addresses full of penitence and Wansley led the singing of a hymn. When the drop fell the mulatto died almost instantly, but Gibbs struggled for some minutes. He met his fate firmly.

When the bodies were cut down Ball Hughes, a local sculptor, made a plaster cast of Gibb's bust, the face preserving what the *Evening Post* called "a really fine expression." Both bodies were then turned over to the surgeons for dissection. They were taken for this purpose to the medical college in Barclay Street, and exhibited for a short time. That of Wansley was found to be a perfect specimen of anatomy. Gibbs was abnormally constructed. A peculiarly confidential portion of his person, preserved by petrification, was long used in class demonstrations by no less a personage than Dr. Oliver Wendell Holmes.

UNDER THE BLACK FLAG

William Johnson died at Canarsie, L. I., February 23, 1907. He was born November 27, 1809 and had almost bridged a century despite the hard life of a bayman, culling his living from the sea.

Note: Gibbs and Wansley were not the last persons to be executed for piracy in New York. That distinction fell to Albert W. Hicks, who murdered the captain of a Baltimore oyster sloop and went a-cruising by himself. He was sent to the gallows July 13, 1860, Isaiah Rynders, the United States Marshal of the day, officiating in a swallow-tail coat of blue broadcloth, adorned with brass buttons. Nathaniel Gordon, of Portland, Maine, captain of the ship *Erie*, was hanged for the crime of transporting slaves from Africa to Cuba, having had the audacity to carry a cargo to that island in 1861, in the midst of an anti-slavery war waging in his own country. He was captured by the U. S. S. *Michigan*, fifty miles off the Cuban coast, having landed his cargo, and was executed in the Tombs Prison, New York, February 7, 1862—the only person to be so punished in the forty years in which slave trading had been a capital crime.

LX

OF BENITO DE SOTO

ORGANIZED piracy on the high seas had its last representative
in Benito de Soto, a native of a small village near Corunna,
in Spain. De Soto became a sailor and so reached South
America, where, in November, 1827, he joined, at Rio de Janeiro, a
Brazilian slaver, the brig *Defensor de Pedro,* equipping for a voyage
to the Guinea coast, the Portuguese then being exempt from the inter-
national prohibition against slave trading.

The *Pedro* was commanded by a lieutenant of the Royal Navy, Don
Pedro de Maria de Souza Sarmento, with a crew of forty, among whom
he had the ill luck to sign eleven hands who had been engaged in piracy
along the Cuban shores, and who when that industry had been broken
up, had sought new fields for roguery and so reached Rio and found
the slaver inviting.

Not content to be mere seamen on a slave ship, when once at sea
they plotted to take the vessel and resume their old trade. They found
the mate a willing listener to the plan and de Soto also fell in with it.
When they reached Miña on the Guinea coast the crew, on being
sounded by the conspirators, did not show sufficient eagerness to assure
the mate of the success of the undertaking and he abandoned the plan,
but de Soto and the former pirates persisted in carrying it out and only
awaited a favorable opportunity. This came on January 26, 1828,
when, the captain and all the officers but the hesitating mate and a
number of the men not in the conspiracy being on shore, the ship was
seized. Such of the crew as refused to join were put into a boat, which
was lost with all hands in a rising gale. The local pilot Manuel Antonio Rodriguez was detained on board with a promise of release when
the brig was once safely south of the line—a promise that was never
kept. The mutineers numbered sixteen and elected the mate captain.
No sooner was the ship at sea than rum and riot ruled. The new captain, under the spell of drink, soon revealed himself as a brutal tyrant
and de Soto, seeing the early ruin of their enterprise under his control,

[329]

shot him in a drunken sleep and took command himself. The real business now began. De Soto steered his course toward the Island of Ascension, across the path of the rich East Indiamen, homeward bound, who were in the habit of calling at the rock for refreshment.

The brig mounted one long gun amidships and her crew were amply armed with muskets, pistols, and cutlasses, as well as the inevitable knives. According to the confession of one of their number, several vessels were overtaken early in the undertaking, but their chief exploit came on February 13, 1828, when off Ascension they chased and overtook the English ship *Morning Star*, Captain Gibbs, from Colombo, Ceylon, to London. A blank shot was fired to bring her to, while at the same time the pirate put out the British colors. The *Morning Star* not heeding, a round of solid shot followed, but fell short. The ship continued on her course but the brig, a fast sailor, drew up, until de Soto sent a shower of canister aboard, one of which wounded a man, hauled down the English ensign, and displayed that of the new republic of Colombia. He was now within hail and ordered the *Morning Star* to send a boat.

There was much confusion on the Indiaman, which carried besides a cargo of coffee and cinnamon between forty and fifty souls, seventeen of whom were invalided soldiers in charge of Major Logie, from whom some resistance might have been expected. There were also a number of women and children in the company, as well as several male passengers, one of whom volunteered to go aboard the pirate. The second mate, three of the soldiers, and a sailor went with him. They were roughly received by de Soto, who stood with drawn cutlass at the gangway and ordered the seamen to attend him at the mainmast, while the mate was told to go to the forecastle. Both obeyed and both were instantly killed. The others were detained while de Soto sent five men under St. Cyr Barbazan, a ferocious Frenchman, to seize the ship. This was soon accomplished, no resistance being made by passengers or crew, coerced as they were by the long gun of the *Pedro*, beside which, fifty yards away, stood de Soto with a lighted match. The invalid soldiers were beaten and driven to the hold with some of the crew, others of whom were forced to assist in the pillaging that now took place. The women were locked in the roundhouse on deck. One of the mates, Mr. Gibson, who was ill in his berth, was dragged out on deck and so savagely treated that he died later. The passengers were stripped of their clothing. Wine flowed freely and a general carouse followed, during which the women were treated to such outrage that cannot be repeated here. Major Logie, whose wife was one of the victims, was thrown, bruised and bleeding into the hold, despite his entreaties and pleadings for the safety of the lady. The orgy was ended by orders from de Soto to return to the pirate. This was coupled with instructions to kill all the people on board. Instead of doing so Barbazan cut the rigging, bored holes in the bottom of the craft, and left her to her fate. The *Pedro* then sailed away. De Soto was not informed until later that the ship had been scuttled with her people left alive and was greatly enraged. He put about in search of her, but she had vanished. She sank, but not before a passing ship had rescued her unfortunate people.

The men held on the *Pedro* were ruthlessly murdered and she proceeded on her cruise, next overhauling the American ship *Topaz* of Boston, homebound from Calcutta. She was plundered and set on fire, after all of her crew had been killed, but the captain and three hands were taken in the pirate and butchered after a day or two.

De Soto now turned toward the Azores, with the intent of reaching Spain and scattering his company. On the way they boarded and plundered the *Cassnak,* Captain Thompson; *New Prescott,* Captain Cleland; the Portuguese ship *Malinda,* the crew of which ship recognized them from having laid near them in Rio de Janeiro and the *Simbury.* De Soto put in at Pontevedra and sailed thence for Corunna. Quarrels broke out in the company, as a result of which Miguel Terreira and one Caravallo and the cook were slain. During the voyage a small Spanish brig was taken and all her crew killed save one who knew the course to Corunna, to which port de Soto decided to steer.

The forced pilot did his duty until Corunna came in sight, when, having served his purpose he was shot by de Soto himself, who, as the harbor appeared, remarked:

"My friend, is that the harbor of Corunna?"

"Yes," answered the pilot.

"Then," replied de Soto, "you have done your duty well. I am obliged to you for your services."

With this remark he coolly shot the man and, throwing his body into the sea, took the helm himself and ran the brig into port.

Here he sold some of his cargo and departed for Cadiz, where he expected to dispose of the remainder, but was caught off shore in a severe gale and wrecked. De Soto and his men reached the land in safety and the brig piled up on the beach. Posing as honest seamen, the gang presented themselves to the authorities and sought help, which was given them. The wreck was put up on sale and an offer of $1,700 was about to be accepted when by some chance their true character was revealed. De Soto, with Jose de los Santos, one of the crew, made his escape, but the others were arrested and put on trial, where the court speedily convicted them. In default de Soto and Santos were condemned to be hanged and quartered. Of those at the bar Nicholas Fernandez, Antonia de Logoa, Saint Cyr Barbazan, Maria Guillermo Teto, Frederica Larenda, and Nuna Pereyra were sentenced to be hung, quartered, and their heads to be placed on hooks on the sea shore; Francisco Goubin, Pedro Antonio, Domingo Antonio, and Joaquin Francisco to be hung; the pilot Manuel Antonio Rodriguez to ten years in the House of Correction and to be present at the execution; Cayetano Ferreira to eight years in the House of Correction and to be present at the execution; Manuel Jose de Freitea to be six years in the House of Correction from the time he had been in prison and to be present at the execution; the negro slave Joaquin Palabro to be present at the execution and to be given up to the Portuguese consul to be sent to his owner. The sentence was executed in the fort of La Puerta de Tierra at Cadiz, in the front of the bay, on the second and third of December, 1829.

De Soto and Santos took refuge in a village on the neutral ground between Spain and the British reservation at Gibraltar, from which the former made his way to that stronghold, where he took up his residence at an obscure tavern. Santos disappeared and was never taken, but de Soto was identified after a few weeks' stay at the Rock, arrested and held in confinement in the old Moorish castle. After many months' duress he was tried, convicted of piracy, and executed, the chief evidence of his crimes being found in his trunk, which held among other items, clothes that had belonged to the unfortunate Gibson and the pocket book of the *Morning Star's* captain. The negro slave held at Cadiz was also a witness against him.

Nicholas Fernandez, one of the crew hanged at Cadiz, made a confession in which he laid his evil course to strong drink. It was published in Spanish by Ferdinand Bayer and afterwards issued in an English translation in London as "a solemn warning to youth (and others) to beware of the baneful habit of intemperance."

LXI

THE PIRACY OF THE BRIG *MEXICAN*

PIRACY died hard. The Guinea slavers running to Cuba and Brazil were not above a turn at the game, when safe and convenient, and even the Mediterranean was not wholly free, despite the crushing of the Barbary corsairs. On October 16, 1827, the *Porpoise*, Lieutenant B. Cooper, overhauled a group of piratically manned boats off Andros Isle, in possession of a newly captured brig. In the fight that followed ten of the pirates were killed, the rest driven ashore, and the brig retaken.

Of the slaver ventures the last to occur in American waters was that of the brig *Mexican*, of Salem, Mass., Captain John Groves Butman, which sailed from her home port for Rio de Janeiro on the 29th of August, 1832. In addition to a good trading cargo she carried $20,000 in silver, stored in the run. The voyage proceeded without event until four o'clock on the morning of September 20th, in latitude 33, longitude 34.30, when a schooner of the Baltimore clipper type, "long, low and rakish" crossed the Mexican's bow. She stood off until day had well broken and then fired a gun to bring the *Mexican* to.

As she was within easy gunshot, Captain Butman obeyed the summons. The schooner came to within thirty or forty yards of the *Mexican* and ordered the captain on board. He saw two guns and a large crew, so deemed it prudent to obey. Taking four men in a boat he rowed to the schooner, but reaching the gangway was told to go to the fore-chains. Here five of her crew leaped into the boat and made the captain row them back to his ship, none of his men going on the schooner. When once on the *Mexican* the strangers shoved Butman into the cabin and, drawing long knives, threatened him with throat-cutting, at which he called to his men to get the dollars out of the runway. John Lewis, colored, the steward, and another lifted out the money. They were clubbed by the pirates to make them hasten.

As the boxes were lifted up the rascals called joyously to their companions on the schooner that there were plenty of dollars on board, and sent the boat for reinforcements. A dozen swarthy ruffians responded, each armed with long, cruel knives, carried in the sleeve. These at once began an eager search for valuables, abusing and beating members of the crew. Benjamin Brown Reed, the first mate, was driven forward by the Spanish boatswain and then kicked into the forecastle, where he was left under a guard who asked him for the time and then snatched his watch. Reed had hidden his money in the wood pile on deck near the galley, but yielding to threats revealed its hiding place. The chronometer was taken and the seamen robbed of their clothes, the pirates making exchange on deck. Captain Butman was again threatened with death if he had concealed anything more, but being at last convinced that all the treasure was in hand, the pirates confined the crew in the hold, while they busied themselves in slashing sails and rigging to render the *Mexican* helpless in the wind.

Not satisfied with this, they filled a tub with rope yarn and tar and set it on fire in the caboose. Then the gang departed with the dollars. The acrid smoke crept into the hold from the caboose and threatened to suffocate the prisoners. By lucky chance, in their haste the pirates had neglected to lock the cabin skylight and through this Reed, the mate, reached the deck and released his fellows in the hold. The fire was already licking the slashed mainsail, but luckily the flames had made but slight progress and were easily stamped out. The schooner had piled on all sail and was fast vanishing.

Yet the pirates were not to escape justice. Chance was all the while working against them. Mr. Gould, a Salem merchant located at Port Antonio on the Portuguese Isle of Princes, was in the habit of receiving newspapers from home. In February, 1833, a copy of the Salem *Commercial Advertiser* arrived containing an account of the assault on the *Mexican* and a good description of the vessel carrying her assailants, which seemed to cover that of a Spanish schooner, the *Panda*, which had been in harbor after supplies. She had come over from the mainland, and departed in such haste that part of her purchases were left behind. The crew were well supplied with dollars and during their brief stay had been lavish in distributing them. He communicated his suspicion to the Portuguese authorities, who took no interest in them, but quite probably warned the people of the *Panda*, which possibly accounts for her sudden departure.

Late in May following, H. M. S. gun-brig *Curlew*, Commander Henry Dundas Trotter, one of the British cruisers employed against

THE PIRACY OF THE BRIG *MEXICAN*

the slave trade, dropped into Port Antonio, where she seldom called. She was a vessel of note, stoutly built at Wivenhoe and served in all forty years on the station. Mr. Gould at once communicated his story to Commander Trotter, together with the information that the *Panda* was believed to be then lying in the Nazareth River, near Cape Lopez, just below the line. The *Curlew* lost no time in seeking her out, sailing from Port Antonio on the night of May 31st. She reached the mouth of the Nazareth after dark on June 3d and anchored about nine miles off shore. At 2 A. M. three armed boats under Commander Trotter left the *Curlew* for the schooner, crossing the bar at daylight. Three miles up the river the *Panda* was seen lying in the stream. The current being of great strength, the boats made slow work of it and were plainly in view for a long time, during which the *Panda's* people were seen to go ashore in the boats, with the exception of one man, who followed later in a canoe.

Captain Trotter endeavored to head off the fugitives, but could not come up with them. When he boarded the schooner a train of cotton and sulphur leading to the magazine was found burning, which was extinguished by the prompt action of John Trumbull, a seaman. A keg of gunpowder, with its head open, was also placed near the galley fire. No papers were found relating to the vessel, but letters addressed to the carpenter and boatswain, in which the name "Panda" appeared, signed by Pedro Gibert, captain, sufficiently identified her as the visitor at Port Antonio, while the conduct of the crew in fleeing seemed to favor Mr. Gould's suspicions.

Commander Trotter now took over the vessel and made preparations to secure the slavers, who had taken refuge in the village of Nazareth. Five Portuguese surrendered, saying they were new hands taken on at Port Antonio, but asserting they had heard the others talk of piracy. Trotter called upon Passall, King of Urungu, the native ruler, to give up the men. This he declared he was unable to do, as they had taken to the bush. Trotter now determined to burn the town. The *Curlew* drawing too much water to get within range, the *Panda* was employed for the purpose, a long twelve-pounder mounted amidship being put into action.

Just as the firing was well under way a Kroo boy sweeping up loose powder on the deck brushed some of it near the gun, a spark falling ignited the explosive, and leading the flame through a hole in the deck to the magazine, which had been kept in the disordered state in

[335]

which it was found. A terrible explosion followed in which the stern of the *Panda* was blown away. Thomas Johnson, the purser, Robert Lewis, the gunner and John Pilling, a private marine, were fatally injured, while no trace was ever found of the Kroo boy. Captain Trotter was badly bruised and several of the crew severely injured.

The *Curlew* came in to the rescue, but the explosion halted effort for the moment as a good share of the small arms and ammunition were lost with the *Panda*. Salvaging what she could from the wreck, the *Curlew* proceeded along the coast, calling at the several ports in the hope of picking up some of the refugees. Reaching Fernando Po on August 17th, Captain Trotter was taken with fever, which held the ship in port, during which time Captain Beecroft, a trading officer, came from the island of Bimbia with five Spanish sailors who had told him a story of shipwreck. They were speedily identified by the Portuguese on the *Curlew* as members of the *Panda's* crew. Joseph Perez, a boy of eighteen, turning King's evidence, completely revealed the story of the piracy. The *Panda* had been out thirteen months in all and had robbed an English ship a few days before she held up the *Mexican*. One of the crew, Manuel Delgardo, had been left at Bimbia. He was sent for and secured. One Juan Lopez, the boatswain, died at Fernando Po. The surviving five, Delgado, the boy Perez, Gusto Baldez, Juan Montenegro, and Antonio Garcia, were sent to Ascension on the transport *William Harris*, while the *Curlew* remained to continue her hunt for the others.

The barque *Princess Elizabeth*, Captain Fatio, coming in to Fernando Po, and being better fitted for river work than the *Curlew*, Captain Fatio volunteered her for the service. Thirteen of Trotter's men under H. J. Matson, mate, went on the *Princess Elizabeth* for Nazareth, while the *Curlew* searched along the coast. Matson, landing at Nazareth in the guise of a trader, soon located a gentlemanly Spaniard, armed with a sword, who was no other than Don Pedro Gibert, owner of the *Panda*. The *Curlew* now coming in, Matson communicated his luck to Trotter after dark, and the warship kept out of sight of shore until daylight, when she came in under the Brazilian flag. King Passall, who was visiting a Portuguese vessel in port, sent two messengers in a canoe to greet the newcomer, one of whom was his son, Prince Narshin. They were held while a boat went to catch Papa on the Portuguese, but he reached shore before it arrived. Narshin admitted that Gibert and several men were on shore, the remainder having gone

THE PIRACY OF THE BRIG *MEXICAN*

to Cape Lopez on a slaver called the *Esperanza*. Word was sent to Passall that his son and head men would be held until he gave up the Spaniards. He hesitated under Gibert's threats and persuasions, but after a day sent word that he would surrender them. Trotter went on shore himself the next morning and, walking along the beach toward the bush, came face to face with Gibert, whom he at once grappled. They struggled until others came to aid Trotter and the slave captain was secured. He was taken on board with his papers and later three other Spaniards were sent off by the King.

Narshin and his fellows were put on shore and the *Curlew*, with the *Princess Elizabeth*, sailed for St. Thome in search of the *Esperanza* and her passengers. The *Esperanza* was gone and the Portuguese governor denied all knowledge of the *Panda's* men. Mr. Holmes, an American trader soon found means to advise him that the *Esperanza* was hiding behind the island. She had brought over the pirates from the coast and they were still on St. Thome, having bought a small vessel in which to depart. The *Esperanza* was found and seized. At this the Portuguese governor who had denied all knowledge of the pirates, then owned to their presence and delivered the five; viz. Bernardo de Soto, mate of the *Panda;* Francisco Ruiz, carpenter; Manuel Boyga, Domingo de Guzman, and Juan Antonio Portana, sailors. Thus fifteen of the *Panda's* men had been secured. This was a pretty good bag, but Trotter, was an indefatigable man of purpose, hearing that one of the men was lurking at Cape Lopez, determined to seek him out.

In company with the *Esperanza*, which was held as a prize, the *Curlew* reached Cape Lopez on January 19, 1844. Mr. Matson, who was well known, went ashore to demand the pirate from the African king. He was locked up along with his boat's crew. King Passall was drunk and ugly, which may explain the unexpected aggression. Lieutenant Pyke, who had gone in the *Curlew's* gig to examine the papers of a Portuguese schooner lying near the beach, was suddenly surprised by the outpouring of three hundred blacks in canoes from ambush. His crew of six Kroomen were at once disposed of and Pyke was dragged ashore, stripped, and left naked in his wounds to lie all day in the open. No news reaching the *Curlew*, which was out of view of the transaction, Lieutenant McNeale took six seamen in the galley boat, without advising Captain Trotter, who was down with fever, and made the shore, with Mr. Chapman the purser in his company. The

[337]

party was at once taken. Matson, who had been released and allowed to go where he pleased, going toward the shore fell in with the excitement and learned of the seizure of his associates. He was led to a small hut where he found McNeale, naked and in irons. Just then another white man, naked and covered with mud and blood, was brought in and proved to be the unfortunate Pyke. The King drunkenly talked of out-trotting Trotter and would not let Matson do more for Pyke than give him a kerchief. He did consent to taking the irons off McNeale. Prince Narshin, who had been well treated by Matson when held hostage on the *Curlew*, used him kindly and his night was made wretched only by the mosquitoes and the fear that the *Curlew* might have been surprised in the darkness.

In the morning all of the *Curlew's* men, quite naked except Matson, were brought before the King, who demanded $5,000 ransom and allowed Pyke to be taken off to bear the message to the ship and have his wounds cared for. Trotter offered $500 in goods and this was accepted. These were sent ashore. The King, however, did not stand on his bargain, saying it was not one quarter enough. They were thus held in tantalizing durance for three days, when the warship *Fair Rosamund*, coming in, alarmed the King and he sent his captives off the fourth day. Trotter now demanded the return of the ransom and when Passall refused he sent Matson in the *Esperanza* to Cape Lopez after H. M. S. *Trinuculo*, which returned with him and aided in an attack on the town by armed boats from both vessels. A twelve-pounder on the *Trinuculo's* pinnace shelled the village and musket fire and rockets added to the African dismay, the populace taking refuge in the bush where it was not safe to follow them. The attack, therefore, went no further and no record of the damage done appears.

Both the *Curlew* and the *Esperanza* then went to Ascension, where after recuperating for a month they proceeded to Plymouth. Trotter now found he had much of his labor for his pains. Lord Palmerston's government decided the *Esperanza* was not a proper prize and had her refitted at her captor's expense and sent to the Portuguese Government at Lisbon. She subsequently became a cruiser in its navy. The prisoners of the *Panda* on being brought to England proved to be a problem, as no witnesses were to be had against them either for piracy or slave dealing. The Government, therefore, determined to send them to Salem, whither they were borne in H. M. S. *Savage*, which was the first British vessel to appear in that patriotic port for fifty years and caused exciting interest. The delivery of the pirates was considered a highly delicate compliment on the part of the British Government, which was none too well loved in that vicinage. The *Savage* arrived on August 24, 1834 and after a preliminary examination in the town hall before John Davis, the United States District Judge, the prisoners were taken to Boston to be held for trial. This began on the 11th of November, Judge Joseph Story, the distinguished jurist, sitting. Mr. D. L. Child acted as counsel for the defense and Mr. Andrew Dunlap prosecuted as United States District Attorney.

At the trial Captain Butman of the *Mexican* was unable to identify any of the prisoners, but recalled seeing on the arrival of the men at Salem one of the men who had placed a knife at his throat in the cabin of the *Mexican*. This was shown to be Manuel Delgado, who had committed suicide in prison at Boston. Much testimony was introduced showing the general good standing in Cuba of Gibert and de Soto. Reed, the mate, recognized Francisco Ruiz as the man who had stood guard over him in the forecastle and Manuel Boyga, a seaman. Benjamin Larkum, one of the *Mexican's* crew also identified Ruiz and Boyga, as did John Battis, another. Thomas Fuller also one of the men, picked out Ruiz as one he had seen on the brig and in doing so stepped up to the prisoner and struck him a heavy blow, for which infraction he was "reproved" by the judge. Benjamin Daniells, another *Mexican* man, also identified Ruiz and Lewis, the steward recalled him as one of those who had beaten him to hurry uncovering the silver. Joseph Perez, who turned state's evidence, clinched the case. The defense was a general denial and claim of mistaken identity as to the *Panda*. It was shown, beside the identification of the several seamen, that her signal had been altered in unmistakable effort at disguise and there was no doubt about the dollars so lavishly used at Port Antonio. On November 26th, the jury, composed of Charles Lawrence, Jeremiah Washburn, Charles Hudson, Leavitt Covett, Joseph Kelley, Anthony Kelly, Isaac K. Wise, Thatcher R. Raymond, William Knight, Peter Brigham, Jacob H. Bates and John Beal, found Don Pedro Gibert, captain; Bernardo de Soto, mate; Francisco Ruiz, carpenter; Manuel Boyga, Manuel Castillo, Juan Montenegro, and Angel Garcia guilty. Antonio Ferrer, the cook who was elaborately tattooed, Nicola Costa, cabin boy, Juan Antonia Portana, and Domingo de Guzman were acquitted.

The seven were sentenced on December 16th, but, owing to legal processes taken to save them, execution was stayed until June 11, 1835 when all went to the gallows save de Soto and Ruiz, who received reprieves. Manuel Boyga attempted suicide by cutting a vein with a piece of tin shortly before the hour of execution and was hanged sitting in a chair, being too weak from loss of blood to stand. Captain Gibert, having been found with a piece of glass in his pocket, was kept manacled for some hours before execution. He went calmly to his doom. All signed a protestation of innocence and continued to acclaim their guiltlessness up to the last moment on the scaffold. Ruiz was finally hanged on Sept. 12, 1835.

De Soto was pardoned by President Andrew Jackson as the result of a petition signed by merchants and shipping men, reciting his conduct in the rescue of the passengers and crew of the American ship *Minerva*, stranded on the Bahama bank out of sight of land and in great peril from a cargo of lime, the slacking of which in contact with the sea water promised to set the ship on fire. An American vessel, the *Chariot*, had passed them by, not heeding their signals, when toward evening de Soto came along in the Spanish brig *Leon*, of which he was master. This was on October 19, 1831. Seeing her signals of distress de Soto steered toward the wreck and a boat coming off informed him of her condition. He therefore stood by for the night. The transfer took all the next day and until about nine in the evening, when just after the captain, crew and two passengers who were the last to leave had been taken into boat, the *Minerva* burst into flame. De Soto, though crowded by the coming of sixty-eight passengers and having but three barrels of beef in store, made for Havana and reached there safely on October 25th. For this action de Soto received a piece of plate from the merchants of New Orleans, a medal from President Jackson, together with a letter of thanks. During the period of reprieve Donna Petrona Percyra, wife of de Soto, came from Spain where she was living and brought the petition to President Jackson who acted accordingly. Returning to Havana de Soto was for many years captain of a steamer plying between that city and Matanzas. Perez, the witness, also returned to Havana only to be assassinated on the very day of his arrival. A tale of wonder and strange consequences this of the pirates of the *Panda*, the last of their kind on the high seas.

Two survivors of this final piracy, John Battis and Thomas Fuller, he who struck the pirate in court, lived into the twentieth century.

Both ended their days as they had begun them, in Salem. Battis died, February 18, 1903 aged 87, and Fuller on February 1, 1909 in his ninety-fourth year. John R. Nichols and Benjamin Larcom, were two other long-lived survivors, close matching the others in touching the new century.